Child Abuse

Quick Reference

THIRD EDITION

For Health Care, Social Service, and Law Enforcement Professionals

STM **Learning,** Inc.

Leading Publisher of Scientific, Technical, and Medical Educational Resources

Saint Louis

www.stmlearning.com

Our Mission

To become the world leader in publishing and information services on child abuse, maltreatment, diseases, and domestic violence. We seek to heighten awareness of these issues, and provide relevant information to professionals and consumers.

A portion of our profits is contributed to nonprofit organizations dedicated to the prevention of child abuse and the care of victims of abuse and other children and family charities.

Child Abuse

Quick Reference

Third Edition

For Health Care, Social Service, and Law Enforcement Professionals

Randell Alexander, MD, PhD
Professor and Chief
Division of Child Protection and Forensic Pediatrics
Department of Pediatrics
Program Director
Pediatric Child Abuse Fellowship
University of Florida College of Medicine—Jacksonville
Director, Institute for Child Abuse Prevention
Wolfson Children's Hospital
Jacksonville, Florida

Diana K. Faugno, MSN, RN, CPN, SANE-A, SANE-P, FAAFS, DF-IAFN
Forensic Nurse Examiner
Board Director: End Violence Against Women International
Eisenhower Medical Center
Barbara Sinatra Children's Center
Rancho Mirage, California

Patricia M. Speck, DNSc, ARNP, APN, FNP-BC, DF-IAFN, FAAFS, FAAN
Professor and Coordinator of Advanced Forensic Nursing
Department of Family, Community and Health Systems
University of Alabama at Birmingham (UAB) School of Nursing
Birmingham, Alabama

Publishers: Glenn E. Whaley and Marianne V. Whaley
Graphic Design Director: Glenn E. Whaley
Managing Editor: Paul K. Goode, III
Print/Production Coordinator: Jennifer M. Jones and G.W. Graphics
Cover Design: Jennifer M. Jones and G.W. Graphics
Acquisitions Editor: Glenn E. Whaley
Developmental Editor: Paul K. Goode, III
Copy Editor: Paul K. Goode, III
Proofreader: Emily A. Ploch

Printed in the United States of America

Publisher:
STM Learning, Inc.
Saint Louis, MO
www.stmlearning.com

Library of Congress Cataloging-in-Publication Data

Names: Alexander, Randell, 1950- editor. | Faugno, Diana K., 1950- editor. | Speck, Patricia M., 1948- editor.
Title: Child Abuse Quick Reference : For Health Care, Social Service, and Law Enforcement Professionals / [edited by] Randell Alexander, Diana K. Faugno, Patricia M. Speck.
Other titles: Child abuse (Monteleone) | Based on (work): Chadwick's child maltreatment. 2014.
Description: Third edition. | Saint Louis, MO : STM Learning, Inc., [2017] | Preceded by: Child abuse / [edited by] Angelo P. Giardino, Randell Alexander. 2nd ed. c2006. | Based on: Chadwick's child maltreatment / [edited by] David L. Chadwick, Randell Alexander, Angelo P. Giardino, Debra Esernio-Jenssen, Jonathan D. Thackeray. 4th edition. Saint Louis : STM Learning, Inc., [2014]. | Includes bibliographical references and index.
Identifiers: LCCN 2017013947 (print) | LCCN 2017014709 (ebook) | ISBN 9781936590766 (e-book) | ISBN 9781936590346 (pbk. : alk. paper)
Subjects: | MESH: Child Abuse | Wounds and Injuries--diagnosis | Child | Adolescent | Handbooks
Classification: LCC RC569.5.C55 (ebook) | LCC RC569.5.C55 (print) | NLM WA 39 | DDC 616.85/8223--dc23
LC record available at https://lccn.loc.gov/2017013947

Contributors to the Third Edition

Cathy Baldwin-Johnson, MD, FAAFP
Medical Director
Alaska CARES
Department of The Children's Hospital at Providence
Anchorage, Alaska
Medical Director
The Children's Place
Wasilla, Alaska

Jack Ballantyne, PhD
Professor
Department of Chemistry
University of Central Florida
Orlando, Florida

Kathy L. Bell, MS, RN
Forensic Nursing Administrator
Tulsa Police Department
Tulsa, Oklahoma

Sylvia E. Britt, PhD, RN
Assistant Professor
Department of Family, Community and Health Systems
University of Alabama at Birmingham (UAB) School of Nursing
Birmingham, Alabama

Karen M. Coles, DNP, RN
Instructor
Department of Family, Community and Health Systems
University of Alabama at Birmingham (UAB) School of Nursing
Birmingham, Alabama

Lisa Creamer, MSHS, BSN, RN
Assistant Director
Child Abuse Pediatrics Department
Section of Public Health Pediatrics
Texas Children's Hospital
Houston, Texas

Melissa L. Currie, MD
Professor of Pediatrics
Medical Director and Chief
Kosair Charities Division of Pediatric Forensic Medicine
University of Louisville School of Medicine
Louisville, Kentucky

Cynthia J. Curtsinger, BSN, RN, CCM, CFN, SANE
Nurse Manager
Department of Pediatrics, Division of Forensic Medicine
University of Louisville School of Medicine
Louisville, Kentucky

Donna Dunn, PhD, CNM, FNP-BC
Associate Professor
Jacksonville State University
School of Health Professions and Wellness
Jacksonville, Alabama

Mary Katherine Dunne, MSN, AGPCNP-C, WHNP-BC
Nurse Practitioner
Department of Neurology
University of Alabama at Birmingham (UAB) Epilepsy Center
Birmingham, Alabama

Diana K. Faugno, MSN, RN, CPN, SANE-A, SANE-P, FAAFS, DF-IAFN
Forensic Nurse Examiner
Board Director: End Violence Against Women International
Eisenhower Medical Center
Barbara Sinatra Children's Center
Rancho Mirage, California

Christopher Spencer Greeley, MD, FAAP
Associate Professor of Pediatrics
University of Texas Health Science Center at Houston
Houston, Texas

Richard Gunderman, MD, PhD
Vice Chair, Radiology
Professor
Indiana University
Indianapolis, Indiana

Melanie Gibbons Hallman, DNP, CRNP, CEN, TCRN, FNP-BC, ACNP-BC
Instructor and Emergency Nurse Practitioner Subspecialty Track Coordinator
University of Alabama at Birmingham (UAB) School of Nursing
Birmingham, Alabama

John Hankins, EdD, MBA, MSN, RN
State Nursing Director
Alabama Department of Public Health
Montgomery, Alabama

Aimee Chism Holland, DNP, WHNP-BC, FNP-C, RD
Assistant Professor
Department of Family, Community and Health Systems
University of Alabama at Birmingham (UAB) School of Nursing
Birmingham, Alabama

Karmie Johnson, DNP, RN, PMHNP-BC
Instructor
Department of Family, Community and Health Systems
University of Alabama at Birmingham (UAB) School of Nursing
Birmingham, Alabama

Brooke E. Jones, MD, MSc, FAAP
Child Abuse Pediatrics Fellow
Department of Pediatrics, Kosair Charities Division of Pediatric Forensic Medicine
University of Louisville
Louisville, Kentucky

Megan B. Marine, MD
Assistant Professor of Radiology
Pediatric Radiology Department
Riley Hospital for Children
Indiana University School of Medicine
Indianapolis, Indiana

Annie McCartney, MSN, CRNP, WHNP
Nurse Practitioner, Maternal Fetal Medicine
Sacred Heart Medical Group
Pensacola, Florida

Steadman McPeters, DNP, CRNP, CPNP-AC, RNFA
Assistant Professor and Dual Option Pediatric Nurse Practitioner Special Track Coordinator
Department of Family, Community and Health Systems
University of Alabama at Birmingham (UAB) School of Nursing
Birmingham, Alabama

Patricia A. Melton, PhD
Senior Research Forensic Scientist
Center for Forensic Sciences
RTI International
Research Triangle Park, North Carolina

Janetta Michaels, BSW, MPA
Child/Adolescent Forensic Interviewer
Federal Bureau of Investigation
Dallas, Texas

Stacey A. Mitchell, DNP, MBA, RN, SANE-A, SANE-P
Clinical Associate Professor
College of Nursing
Texas A&M University
Bryan, Texas

Susan B. Patton, DNSc, PPCNP-BC, AFN-BC, FAANP, FAAN
Professor
University of Alabama at Birmingham (UAB) School of Nursing
Birmingham, Alabama

Shannon Polson, MSN, MSW, RN, LCSW, CNL, CWCN, PIP
Instructor
Department of Family,
Community and Health Systems
University of Alabama at Birmingham (UAB) School of Nursing
Birmingham, Alabama

Vinod B. Rao, MD, FAAP
Assistant Professor of Pediatrics
Board-Certified Child Abuse Pediatrician
Pediatrics Department, Kosair Charities
Division of Pediatric Forensic Medicine
University of Louisville
Louisville, Kentucky

Jeff Rich
Police Detective
Criminal Investigation
Plano, Texas Police Department
Plano, Texas

Rosario V. Sanchez, MSN, RN, CCRN, CFN, SANE-A, D-ABFN
Doctoral Scholar, Graduate Assistant,
Jonas Nurse Leader Scholar
School of Nursing
Rutgers University
Newark, New Jersey

Sallie Shipman, EdD, MSN, RN, CNL
Assistant Professor
Department of Family, Community and Health Systems
University of Alabama at Birmingham (UAB) School of Nursing
Birmingham, Alabama

Patricia M. Speck, DNSc, ARNP, APN, FNP-BC, DF-IAFN, FAAFS, FAAN
Professor and Coordinator of
Advanced Forensic Nursing
Department of Family,
Community and Health Systems
University of Alabama at Birmingham (UAB) School of Nursing
Birmingham, Alabama

Mary J. Spencer, BA, MD, FAAP
Medical Director,
Sexual Assault Response Team (SART)
Forensic Health Services
Palomar Health
Escondido, California

Ashton Tureaud Strachan, DNP, RN, CRNP, FNP-C
Nurse Practitioner
Student Health and Wellness Center
University of Alabama at Birmingham (UAB)
Birmingham, Alabama

Samuel Strachan, MD, FAAP
Pediatric Emergency Medicine Fellow
Department of Pediatrics
University of Alabama at Birmingham (UAB) School of Medicine
Birmingham, Alabama

Tracey Wiese, DNP, APRN
Nurse Practitioner
Anchorage, Alaska

David A. Williams, DDS, MS, MPH
Manager, Oral Health Programs
Carroll County (MD) Health Department
Westminster, Maryland

Joyce P. Williams, DNP, AFN-BC, FAAFS, FAAN
Associate Professor
Graduate and Professional Studies
Stevenson University
Owings Mill, Maryland

Contributors to the Second Edition

Sergeant Joanne Archambault (Retired SDPD)
President
SATI, Inc. (Sexual Assault Training & Investigations)
Executive Director
End Violence Against Women International
Addy, Washington

Kirsten Bechtel, MD
Assistant Professor of Pediatrics
Yale University School of Medicine
Attending Physician—Pediatric Emergency Department
Yale-New Haven Children's Hospital
New Haven, Connecticut

Kathy L. Bell, MS, RN
Forensic Nursing Administrator
Tulsa Police Department
Tulsa, Oklahoma

Terry Chianello, MA, MSW, LCSW
Psychotherapist
Behavioral Health Clinic
St. Charles Medical Center
Bend, Oregon

Tracey S. Corey, MD
Clinical Professor & Division Director
Division of Forensic Pathology
Department of Pathology
Clinical Associate Professor of Pediatrics
Department of Pediatrics
University of Louisville School of Medicine
Chief Medical Examiner
Office of the Medical Examiner
Kentucky Cabinet of Justice & Public Safety
Louisville, Kentucky

Martin A. Finkel, DO, FACOP, FAAP
Professor of Pediatrics
Co-Director
NJ Child Abuse Research Education & Service Institute
School of Osteopathic Medicine
University of Medicine & Dentistry of New Jersey
Stanford, New Jersey

Deborah A. Frank, MD
Professor of Pediatrics
Boston University School of Medicine
Assistant Professor of Social & Behavioral Sciences
Boston University School of Public Health
Director, Grow Clinic for Children
Boston Medical Center
Boston, Massachusetts

Lori D. Frasier, MD, FAAP
Associate Professor of Pediatrics
University of Utah School of Medicine
Medical Director,
Medical Assessment Team
Center for Safe & Healthy Families
Primary Children's Medical Center
Salt Lake City, Utah

Gina M. French, MD
Ambulatory Pediatrics
Children's Hospital
Associate Professor of Clinical Pediatrics
The Ohio State University
Columbus, Ohio

Joseph Giangiacomo, MD
Professor of Ophthalmology and Child Health
University of Missouri—Columbia
Columbia, Missouri

Angelo P. Giardino, MD, PhD
Professor and Section Chief
Academic General Pediatrics
Baylor College of Medicine
Senior Vice President/Chief Quality Officer
Texas Children's Hospital
Houston, Texas

Michael Graham, MD
Professor of Pathology
Saint Louis University School of Medicine
Chief Medical Examiner
Saint Louis, Missouri

Mark D. Joffe, MD
Director, Community Pediatric Medicine
Associate Professor of Pediatrics
The Children's Hospital of Philadelphia
University of Pennsylvania School of Medicine
Philadelphia, Pennsylvania

Charles E. Johnson, MD, FAAP
Professor of Pediatrics
The Ohio State University College of Medicine & Public Health
Staff Physician,
Child & Family Advocacy Program
Children's Hospital
Columbus, Ohio

Lakshmi Kolagotla, MD
Fellow, Division of General Pediatrics
Department of Pediatrics
Boston Medical Center
Boston, Massachusetts

Gus H. Kolilis, BS Ed
Missouri Department of Social Services
Deputy Director
Division of Legal Services
Chief, State Technical Assistance Team (STAT)
Jefferson City, Missouri

Jane M. Lavelle, MD
Associate Professor of Pediatrics
Associate Director of Pediatric Emergency Medicine
The Children's Hospital of Philadelphia
Philadelphia, Pennsylvania

Patrick O'Donnell, PhD
Supervising Criminalist and Technical Manager
DNA Laboratory
Forensic Science Section
San Diego Police Department
San Diego, California

Ann L. O'Sullivan, PhD, FAAN, CPNP, CRNP
Professor of Primary Care Nursing
School of Medicine and School of Nursing
University of Pennsylvania
Nurse Practitioner
University City Primary Care Center
The Children's Hospital of Philadelphia
Philadelphia, Pennsylvania

Robert T. Paschall, MD
Assistant Professor of Pediatrics
Washington University School of Medicine
Saint Louis, Missouri

Susan K. Reichert, MD, FAAP
Pediatrician
Child Abuse Specialist and Consultant
Bend, Oregon

Lawrence R. Ricci, MD
Director
The Spurwink Child Abuse Program
Portland, Maine

Mary T. Rourke, PhD
Psychologist
Director of Psychosocial Services,
Division of Oncology
The Children's Hospital of Philadelphia
Philadelphia, Pennsylvania

Megan Sandel, MD
Assistant Professor of Pediatrics
Boston University School of Medicine
Boston, Massachusetts

Andrew Sirotnak, MD, FAAP
Associate Professor of Pediatrics
University of Colorado
School of Medicine
Director
Kempe Child Protection Team
The Children's Hospital & Kempe
Children's Center
Denver, Colorado

Suzanne P. Starling, MD, FAAP
Medical Director
Child Abuse Program
Children's Hospital of The King's
Daughters
Associate Professor of Pediatrics
Eastern Virginia Medical School
Norfolk, Virginia

Joyce Wientzen, LCSW
Associate Program Director
Spurwink Child Abuse Program
Portland, Maine

Foreword to the Third Edition

Child abuse and neglect is a public health crisis affecting children, families, and communities. More than 1500 children die yearly from child maltreatment, a rate that exceeds deaths from childhood cancer. Physical abuse disproportionately affects our most vulnerable children, with rates of serious injury and abusive head trauma in infants being more than twice the rate in children between the ages of 1 and 3 years. Because injuries may be occult, diagnostic testing for additional serious injury is an important component of the trauma evaluation of children. However, multiple studies have highlighted disparities in both screening and referral to child protective services that persist despite a wealth of literature. Evaluating a child or adolescent for concerns of child abuse is challenging and requires additional medical expertise as well as a comprehensive multidisciplinary approach.

Child Abuse Quick Reference provides essential tools for the child abuse professional, with detailed, yet practical, approaches to the identification and documentation of injury, the developmental approach to understanding children and language, evidence collection, biomechanics of injury, and recommended medical evaluations and management. An essential element of the text is the multidisciplinary approach modeled by the diversity of professionals who have collaborated on this invaluable resource.

As we improve the identification, medical evaluation, and investigation of child abuse and neglect, our multidisciplinary teams must become increasingly trauma-focused and provide education on the need for prevention of child maltreatment as well as effective services for children and families. Child abuse is considered a toxic stress in early brain development, associated with changes in behavior and risk for permanent changes in brain function. These adverse childhood experiences, known as ACEs, have been the subject of large studies into the associations between child maltreatment and subsequent adult medical and psychological health. *Child Abuse Quick Reference* encourages child abuse professionals and medical providers to partner with caregivers in identifying risk factors for violence and child maltreatment and to incorporate prevention into practice.

Nancy S. Harper, MD, FAAP
Medical Director, Otto Bremer Trust Center for Safe and Healthy Families
Associate Professor of Pediatrics, Department of Pediatrics
University of Minnesota Masonic Children's Hospital
University of Minnesota
Minneapolis, Minnesota

FOREWORD TO THE THIRD EDITION

Despite a multitude of ongoing prevention initiatives, child maltreatment remains a public health problem. The Adverse Childhood Experiences Study clearly demonstrated the long-term, adverse outcomes associated with each form of child maltreatment and the significant impact these experiences have on overall morbidity and mortality across the lifespan. Over the past two decades, great strides have been made in the prevention and treatment of child abuse, but continued progress is essential to the health and well-being of our most vulnerable population.

Professionals working in health care, social services, and law enforcement play an instrumental role in protecting children and preventing abuse, and an evidence-based, multidisciplinary team approach is essential to the proper investigation of any child maltreatment case. A clear understanding of pathophysiology and mechanisms of injury is vital when determining potential causes for physical findings that may be consistent with abuse. The health care professional's ability to make those determinations and child protection and law enforcement personnel's ability to understand the significance of such findings are imperative to proper execution of justice and protection of all children. Accurate identification also plays an important role in secondary and tertiary prevention efforts by disrupting the cycle of violence and preventing future generations of victims through proper case management, child placement, caregiver education, and ongoing surveillance.

The intersection of medical and forensic science is constantly and rapidly evolving, and an evidence-based approach is absolutely essential to justice and child protection. Featuring an easy-to-understand bullet point format, the third edition of *Child Abuse Quick Reference* is a true evidence-based quick reference written and edited by experienced members of multidisciplinary teams for busy professionals charged with investigating reports of child maltreatment. Covering a wide range of topics related to prevention, identification, and treatment, this quick reference clearly outlines current, evidence-based practices to facilitate high-quality child maltreatment investigations with a focus on promoting the best possible outcomes for all children and their families.

Trinity L. Ingram-Jones, DNP, CPNP, PCNS, AFN-BC, SANE-A, SANE-P
Pediatric Medical-Forensic Examiner and Consultant to
Helen's Haven Children's Advocacy Center
Owner, Expert, and Consultant
Ingram-Jones & Associates, LLC
Richmond Hill, Georgia

Foreword to the Second Edition

In countries where child maltreatment is manifestly illegal and where sanctions exist against the abuser, the challenge of recognition is one of detection and identification. Instances of maltreatment can be hidden or caregivers may claim that injuries are caused by accidental events or organic illness. The veracity of children who disclose abuse and the expertise of professionals who testify to the features of maltreatment may be called into question. The lack of rigorous experimental studies may be cited as evidence of the unreliability of child witnesses or the ingenuousness of forensic professionals. When lies, misunderstandings, or lack of sufficient knowledge or evidence prevents a clear distinction between abuse and a more benign explanation, it is the task of the responsible professional to make this distinction clear. However, when presented with signs of maltreatment, or a strong possibility of maltreatment, professionals must make that case and advocate for measures to ensure the child's safety. To increase the likelihood of reaching accurate conclusions, professionals must clearly understand the harm attributable to maltreatment, the mechanisms that cause injury, and the signs that identify the lesions produced.

Use of this quick reference will contribute to the accurate identification of abuse and, in so doing, the wider recognition of maltreatment as a violation of children's rights, safety, and well-being. One of the benefits of globalization is that this knowledge and attitude may be disseminated in order to make the world a safer place for children everywhere.

Marcellina Mian, MDCM, FRCPC, FAAP
Pediatrician, Suspected Child Abuse & Neglect (SCAN) Program
Director, Undergraduate Medical Education
Hospital for Sick Children
Professor, Faculty of Medicine
University of Toronto
Toronto, Ontario

Foreword to the Second Edition

Safeguarding the health and well-being of all children has been an increasing focus of modern society. We have come far from the days when parents considered their children "property." Along the way, we have instituted many measures to improve the health of children: immunizations, car seats, lead detection and abatement, the "Back to Sleep" campaign, and the "Reach Out and Read" campaign, to name a few.

The battle against child abuse and neglect has also made significant strides, although the war is far from over. The challenges that face those who seek to protect children from maltreatment include moving forward, preventing abuse before it starts, and reducing the rate of recidivism in those who have been abused. Professional education and early identification are critical to secondary prevention. Appropriate judicial decisions are also essential to ensure that children are not returned to parents who lack the necessary skills to care for their offspring. Interventional programs must be created to make reunification a safe and satisfactory experience for children and their parents. Primary prevention is perhaps even more complicated. Although epidemiological studies have identified high-risk factors for abuse, providing anticipatory interventional services is costly and only partially validated. The societal issues of poverty, violence, and substance abuse are clearly contributing factors.

As professionals committed to helping children reach their potential, we must take steps to ensure that all children are cared for in a safe, nurturing environment. Up-to-date, evidence-based literature plays a vital role in the educational process. *Child Abuse Quick Reference*, with its wealth of information compiled by multiple child care professionals who work individually and collectively to prevent, identify, evaluate, and treat children and families facing the many challenges associated with a high risk of child maltreatment, is part of this process. The more we learn, the stronger our ability to effectively keep children safe. Our resolve to work tirelessly to reduce and eventually remove the threat posed to the well-being of all children by child maltreatment remains strong. With education, sound information, research, and advocacy, we can work individually and collectively to influence the future of the most vulnerable members of our society.

Carol Berkowitz, MD, FAAP
Executive Vice Chair
Department of Pediatrics
Harbor-UCLA Medical Center
Professor of Clinical Pediatrics
David Geffen School of Medicine at UCLA
Torrance, California

Foreword to the First Edition

Each and every day, frontline professionals in hospitals, medical offices, child protective service agencies, law enforcement agencies, mental health agencies, and prosecutors' offices confront allegations of child abuse. In these situations, the stakes are enormous and there is little margin for error. For many medical professionals who do not see severely abused children daily, the complexities of identification and diagnosis can be daunting. For non-medical professionals, the meaning of the medical terminology and diagnoses they encounter can be overwhelming. Even if exposed to periodic training in these issues, many are challenged to retain, in immediate recall, the details and terminology of another discipline or area of specialty. Errors and misinterpretations can, and have, cost the lives of young children.

Knowledge and education are our best weapons to fight child abuse. Any action we take that elevates the understanding of those on the frontline of practice makes accurate diagnosis, assessment, and intervention more likely. With accurate information and interpretation, we can better protect and treat children and hold those who abuse them accountable. Without accurate information, children are endangered.

Most professionals are exposed to great quantities of information. So much, in fact, that a good deal of important information is not retained. What many professionals need is an easy way to access information when and where it is needed. *Child Abuse Quick Reference* is a timely and user-friendly reference that allows professionals to access needed information about the medical aspects of child abuse in a rapid and mobile form. It will allow professionals to quickly find summaries of all the major medical dimensions of child abuse. In the everyday world of protecting children, a resource such as this will allow professionals to rapidly refresh their understanding of important subtleties of maltreatment. It is portable enough to be carried in the field as a working reference and detailed enough to be useful in academic settings. With this reference, many child abuse professionals will be better equipped to confront the challenges they face daily.

Charles Wilson, MSSW
Executive Director
National Children's Advocacy Center
Huntsville, Alabama

Preface to the Third Edition

Every day, children across the globe are at risk for the deleterious impact of child abuse and neglect. Children of every ethnic and economic background may suffer abuse at the hands of trusted friends or family members, out among their communities or, tragically, in their own homes. For the recovery of survivors and, ideally, the prevention of abusive acts before they occur, multidisciplinary professionals who work with children must be prepared to identify and intervene on behalf of the abused and those at risk for abuse.

Now in its third edition, *Child Abuse Quick Reference: For Health Care, Social Service, and Law Enforcement Professionals* still strives for the best in contemporary, updated guidelines and recommendations for a more effective response to child maltreatment. The editors and authors—a team of physicians, nurses, and law enforcement personnel—intend this book to support their colleagues across disciplines in the investigation, diagnosis, and treatment of child abuse in all its forms. It is our sincere hope this concise reference will augment and enhance established frontline protocols and foster better outcomes for children and their families.

Children depend on adult caregivers for their continued health and well-being. In that sense, the abuse of a child is not only a physical violation, it is a violation of the trust foundational to a healthy childhood and thriving adulthood. It is incumbent upon those professionally tasked with the care and protection of children to safeguard against those most egregious disruptions in caretaking lest abused children be left to an entirely uncertain future and the potential for lifelong instability. In that spirit, we present this book in hopes of a safer world for children everywhere.

Randell Alexander, MD, PhD

Preface to the Second Edition

Child maltreatment in its various forms remains a significant problem confronting children and their families worldwide. The incidence and prevalence statistics surrounding child maltreatment continue to be staggering when compared to the reduction in pediatric morbidity and mortality associated with infectious disease over the past 100 years. This reference is put forth to help health care professionals, social service providers, and law enforcement personnel meet the challenges that arise in dealing with this preventable problem. We have emphasized the multidisciplinary team approach to caring for children who are maltreated. Specialists in each area offer insights regarding approaches to identifying and managing specific forms of child maltreatment, including procedures for evaluation and practical guidelines for handling cases.

It is hoped that this quick reference will help the professional who deals with any area of child maltreatment to be more fully equipped to assess situations appropriately and determine the best course of action. Information is a vital ally in recognizing the signs of maltreatment. A thorough clinical examination, interviews with the child and family, and depending on the situation, properly conducted site investigations are critical. Ultimately, all professionals have the shared goal of preventing child maltreatment. By more accurately identifying child maltreatment, both the victim and other children may be spared further harm. Because time is sometimes of the essence in cases of maltreatment, this quick reference provides a portable means to access important information. The focus of all our work is the health and well-being of children and their families, and we offer this reference as a powerful tool for creating a better future for them.

Angelo P. Giardino, MD, PhD, FAAP
Randell Alexander, MD, PhD

Preface to the First Edition

Almost daily, we see reports of unbelievable maltreatment of children. Child abuse is a phenomenon that crosses all social, ethnic, religious, cultural, and professional lines. As children are brought for treatment to emergency rooms, the need is for a quick review of pertinent physical and emotional signs indicating abuse so that cases can be handled effectively. This book was written to meet that need, to give medical and allied health practitioners, social services personnel, law enforcement, and safety offices faced with possibly abused children ready access to the facts required to handle these cases.

Child Abuse Quick Reference provides information to help readers recognize child maltreatment, identify those children who are at high risk for abuse and neglect, and realize strategies for preventing and intervening in abuse situations. This material is organized in an easy-to-retrieve format, with simple lists organized under major topical headings. The chapters emphasize what to look for and what steps are to be taken. This step-by-step outline of pertinent procedures helps the health care professional handle communications properly and effectively in potentially sensitive situations.

Included in this book are chapters that address the most common types of child abuse, as well as chapters on uncommon but possible causes. Each offers clear descriptions of what is and what is not abuse. Thus, this book provides valuable information to help the practitioners discern abuse situations versus cultural or religious practices, helping to avoid mistakes in reporting.

This handy pocket guide represents the experiences of acknowledged experts in the various fields that deal with abuse. For easy access to the chapters, both a brief and detailed tables of contents are included. In addition, this book contains an extensive index. Everything is geared to making this quick reference an invaluable resource in the handling of child abuse cases.

James A. Monteleone, MD

Reviews

Child abuse and neglect are complex issues and may be difficult to distinguish from typical childhood injuries. In the third edition of Child Abuse Quick Reference, *leading researchers and clinicians provide up-to-date, comprehensive information for easy identification and reporting of child abuse and neglect. It is particularly exciting to see a section on prevention included in a text of this type, because many families come into contact with various service sectors before child abuse and neglect occur, and professionals equipped to assess factors that put families at risk may have the opportunity to prevent abuse and neglect. Health care, social service, and law enforcement professionals will find this text an important resource in preventing, identifying, and responding to child abuse and neglect.*

Beverly L. Fortson, PhD
Behavioral Scientist
Division of Violence Prevention
Centers for Disease Control and Prevention
Atlanta, Georgia

Child Abuse Quick Reference, Third Edition *is an invaluable resource that offers detailed guidance for the assessment and care of suspected or confirmed victims of child abuse and includes useful information for providing expert witness testimony in court. I applaud the authors for devising a text intended to assist a variety of multidisciplinary team members in the assessment and interpretation of medical findings in cases of suspected abuse. This text will allow health care providers, social workers, law enforcement personnel, and their colleagues in related fields to answer questions that may arise in the course of their work without having to search through several sources.*

Qiana A. Johnson, DNP, FNP-C
Nurse Practitioner
Atlanta, Georgia

Child Abuse Quick Reference: For Health Care, Social Service, and Law Enforcement Professionals *provides readers a comprehensive overview of child maltreatment in a quick reference format. The extensive definitions of terms provided throughout the book are very useful for quick review. While every chapter is very informative, the chapters "Neglect, Abandonment, and Failure to Thrive," "The Chemically Abused Child (Poisoning)," and "Prevention" were particularly instructive. Written by leading experts in the field, this field guide is highly recommended for professionals from a broad array of disciplines who are committed to identification, treatment, and prevention of various forms of child maltreatment.*

Susan J. Kelley, RN, PhD, FAAN
Professor
Associate Dean and Chief Academic Officer for Nursing
Byrdine F. Lewis School of Nursing and Health Professions
Georgia State University
Atlanta, Georgia

The new third edition of Child Abuse Quick Reference: For Health Care, Social Service, and Law Enforcement Professionals *is an easy-to-use guide to the assessment and care of the child abuse victim. The book covers a comprehensive list of topics that must be considered when confronted with child abuse cases. It focuses on methods for assessment, evaluation, treatment, and prevention that can be utilized across professions. Key images in radiology provide a quick guide to injuries in abused children, stressing differences across age groups. An in-depth discussion of the sexual abuse interview for children is a major strength, from which any clinician can glean important techniques for trauma-informed care in the process of interviewing a child. This is a handy guide for all child care professionals.*

L. Kathleen Sekula,
PhD, PMHCNS, FAAN
Professor, Director:
Graduate Forensic Nursing Programs
School of Nursing
Duquesne University
Pittsburgh, Pennsylvania

Contents in Brief

Contents in Detail

Child Abuse

Quick Reference

THIRD EDITION

For Health Care, Social Service, and Law Enforcement Professionals

STM **Learning,** Inc.

Leading Publisher of Scientific, Technical, and Medical Educational Resources
Saint Louis
www.stmlearning.com

Chapter 1

INTRODUCTION TO CHILD MALTREATMENT

Sallie Shipman, EdD, MSN, RN, CNL
John Hankins, EdD, MBA, MSN, RN
Rosario V. Sanchez, MSN, RN, CCRN, CFN, SANE-A, D-ABFN
Patricia M. Speck, DNSc, ARNP, APN, FNP-BC, DF-IAFN, FAAFS, FAAN

DEFINITIONS

— *Child maltreatment*: Any act or series of acts of commission[1] or omission by a parent[2] or other caregiver that results in harm, potential for harm, or threat of harm to a child.[3]

— *Acts of commission (child abuse)*[4]:

— Words or overt actions that cause harm, potential harm, or threat of harm to a child.

— Acts of commission are deliberate and intentional; however, harm to a child may or may not be the intended consequence.

— Intentionality only applies to the caregivers' acts, not the consequences of those acts. For example, a caregiver may intend to hit a child as punishment (ie, nonaccidental hitting, intentional) but not intend to give the child a concussion.

— The following types of maltreatment involve acts of commission: physical abuse, sexual abuse, psychological abuse.

— *Acts of omission (child neglect)*:

— Failure to provide for a child's basic physical, emotional, or educational needs or to protect a child from harm or potential harm.[5]

  - Like acts of commission, harm to a child may or may not be the intended consequence.
  - The following types of maltreatment involve acts of omission: failure to provide, physical neglect, emotional neglect, medical/dental neglect, educational neglect, failure to supervise, inadequate supervision, exposure to violent environments.[6]

- ***Human trafficking***: Recruitment, transportation, transfer, harboring, or receipt of persons by means of threat, force, or other forms of coercion (eg, abduction, fraud, deception, abuse of power/vulnerability, bribery of caretakers) for the purpose of exploitation.[7]
- ***Human sex trafficking (HST)***: Recruitment, harboring, transportation, provision, or obtaining of a person for the purpose of a commercial sex act.
- ***Debt bondage***: Forced labor/prostitution by means of unlawful "debt" for trafficking victims' transportation, recruitment, or sale. Exploiters insist the debt must be paid before a trafficked person can go free.[8,9]
- ***Commercial sexual exploitation of children (CSEC)***: Exploitation of persons under the age of 18 for the purposes of commercial sex acts induced by force, fraud, or coercion. Consequences include physical/psychological trauma, disease (including HIV/AIDS), addiction, unwanted pregnancy, malnutrition, social ostracism, death.[9]
- ***Trauma bonding***: Bond of exploited person to pimp/exploiter based in perception of sharing an intense or strong relationship, rather than an exploitative realationship.[10]

Introduction

Child abuse is declining, due in part to statewide primary and secondary prevention efforts, including early intervention for at-risk children.[11] While not all states report a decrease in child abuse, those that do have implemented innovative systematic changes to advance early recognition of at-risk children.

- From 2009 to 2013, overall rates of victimization declined from 9.3 to 9.1 per 1000 children (702 000 victims in 2009, 679 000 victims in 2013 [est.]).[11]

— Since 2009, overall rates of children who received a CPS response increased from 40.3 to 42.9 per 1000 children (3 043 000 children in 2009, 3 188 000 children in 2013 [est.]).[11]

— Nationally, 79.5% of victims were neglected, 18% were physically abused, 9% percent were sexually abused, and 8.7% percent were psychologically maltreated.[11]

— In 2013, 1520 children died of abuse and neglect, at a rate of 2.04 children per 100 000 (est.).[11]

Statistics are accurate for reported child abuse cases; however, there is a developing awareness of human trafficking, which is not easily identified by current health care provider statistical systems. This chapter will familiarize the health care provider with unique presentations of trafficked children and introduce the consequences of toxic stress on childhood development (ie, adverse childhood experiences [ACEs]).

Human Trafficking

— Human trafficking cases may involve both documented and undocumented migrants, men, women, and children, as well as developmentally delayed adults.

— Despite the seriousness of this crime, there are no reliable estimates for the prevalence of human trafficking in children nor reliable methods to identify victims.[12]

— Currently, there is no ICD10 code for human trafficking; however, the federal government supports the development of intervention strategies in health care settings, where health outcomes of trafficking are uniquely identified through existing ICD10 codes, making it difficult to determine incidence and prevalence of child trafficking.[13]

— Commercial sexual exploitation of children (CSEC) goes underreported due to traffickers' astute evasions, inadvertently aided by inappropriate identification of victims, lack of awareness among providers, and lack of training for multiagency professionals.[12]

— Developmental gaps in life experience and desire for independence leave adolescents particularly vulnerable to CSEC. Prior history of abuse/neglect, foster care placement, runaway status, and homelessness present risk for targeting by traffickers, who lure vulnerable adolescents by satisfying basic needs.

Estimated Statistics

— Twenty-six percent of global trafficking victims are children.[14]

— In 2014, 1 in 6 US runaways were likely victims of child sex trafficking.[10]

— In 2014, 978 allegations of human trafficking were filed with Florida's child welfare system.[15]

Adverse Childhood Experiences (ACEs): Outcomes

— Adverse childhood experiences include verbal/physical/sexual abuse and family dysfunction (eg, incarcerated/mentally ill/substance-abusing family members, domestic violence, absent parent[s]).[16]

— Routine screening for developmental signs indicating toxic stress (eg, unexplained injuries, school failures, sexually transmitted infections (STIs), early pregnancy, poor speech, developmental delays) mitigates long-term effects, including:

  — Substance abuse

  — Depression

  — Cardiovascular disease

  — Diabetes

  — Cancer

  — Premature mortality (as much as 20 years earlier)[16,17]

— Childhood trauma related to sex trafficking is likely to cause premature mortality (at a rate 40% higher than the national average).[18]

— Traumatic outcomes of sex trafficking include:

  — Posttraumatic stress disorder (PTSD)

  — Depression

  — Anxiety

- — Suicide
- — Inability to participate in community
- — Lack of self-esteem
- — Infertility
- — STIs
- — Genitourinary dysfunction

Guidelines for Assessment

— Note poor physical health: Children may appear malnourished or show signs of poor growth/development, physical/sexual abuse, physical restraint/confinement, or torture.[8,9]

— Note poor mental health/abnormal behavior: Children may be fearful, anxious, depressed, submissive, or avoid eye contact.[8,9]

— Note lack of school ID and/or the inability to identify school.[8,9]

— Take note if child is not allowed to speak for himself/herself or if guardian/trafficker insists on being present throughout examination.[8,9]

— Note any characteristics of the parent-child relationship that may contribute to possible abuse or neglect.[4]

— Note inconsistencies in presentation of injury, medical history, personal history, evidence of branding, recurrent patterns of injury over time, patterned injury, unexplained injury, or inconsistent explanation for injury.[8,9,19]

Reporting

— Mandated reporters are individuals mandated by law to report any reasonable suspicion of child abuse/neglect.

— Mandated reporters may include:

- — Health care professionals
- — Child protection/social workers
- — Law enforcement officers

    — School personnel
    — Mental health professionals
    — Child care workers
    — Medical examiners
- — Eighteen states and Puerto Rico require all citizens to report suspected child abuse/neglect.[20]
- — Collaborative efforts among designated agencies, including development of multidisciplinary teams (MDTs), may be mandated by law.
- — State statutes protect mandated reporters from lawsuits for reporting in good faith.[21]
- — Mandated reporters should follow established guidelines for interviewing children about suspected sexual abuse.

Legislation

Child Abuse Prevention and Treatment Act

- — The Child Abuse Prevention and Treatment Act (CAPTA)[22] was originally enacted in 1974 and has been amended many times since. Most recently, CAPTA was reauthorized and amended by the CAPTA Reauthorization Act of 2010.
- — CAPTA allows the government to protect children by intervening when adults fail to provide proper care, supported by preexisting child protection programs with funds funneled through the US Children's Bureau.
- — CAPTA funds infrastructure and education to enhance goals in legislation (ie, building prevention and intervention capacities in individuals, families, communities, systems).

Trafficking Victims Protection Act

- — The Trafficking Victims Protection Act[23] establishes human trafficking and related offenses as federal crimes and attaches severe penalties to offenders. TVPA provides for:
    - — Mandated restitution to victims of human trafficking.

— T-visas, granting victims and their families temporary resident status and eligibility for permanent resident status after 3 years.

— Emergency response protocols within the State Department for quick response to disaster areas and crises where people are particularly susceptible to trafficking.

— TVPA 2013 reauthorization[24] strengthened collaborations between state and local law enforcement agencies to ease charging and prosecuting traffickers and established programs to ensure US citizens do not purchase products made by victims of human trafficking.

Safe Harbor Laws

Safe harbor laws were developed to address inconsistencies in treatment of CSEC.[25] Their two main components are:

1. Legal protection: Immunity from prosecution for child victims forced or compelled to commit certain illegal acts.
2. Provision of service: Medical/psychological treatment, emergency and long-term housing, education assistance, job training, language assistance, and legal services.

References

1. Kempe CH. Sexual abuse, another hidden pediatric problem: the 1977 C. Anderson Aldrich Lecture. *Pediatrics*. 1978;62(3):382-389.
2. Kairys SW, Johnson CF; Committee on Child Abuse and Neglect. The psychological maltreatment of children: technical report. *Pediatrics*. 2002;109(4):e68.
3. Bavolek SJ. *The Nurturing Parenting Programs*. Washington, DC: Office of Juvenile Justice and Delinquency Prevention, US Dept of Justice; 2000.
4. Bernet W. Practice parameters for the forensic evaluation of children and adolescents who may have been physically or sexually abused. American Academy of Child and Adolescent Psychiatry. *J Am Acad Child Adolesc Psychiatry*. 1997;36(10 suppl):37S-56S.
5. Jones DPH. *Communicating With Vulnerable Children: A Guide for Practitioners*. London, England: Royal College of Psychiatrists; 2003.

6. Leeb RT, Paulozzi LJ, Melanson C, Simon TR, Arias I. *Child Maltreatment Surveillance: Uniform Definitions for Public Health and Recommended Data Elements, Version 1.0.* Atlanta, GA: Centers for Disease Control and Prevention, National Center for Injury Prevention and Control; 2008.

7. United Nations. *Protocol to Prevent, Suppress and Punish Trafficking in Persons, Especially Women and Children, Supplementing the United Nations Convention Against Transnational Organized Crime.* New York, NY: United Nations; 2000.

8. Polaris Project. Human trafficking: recognize the signs. Polaris Project Web site. https://polarisproject.org/recognize-signs. Accessed August 22, 2016.

9. US Department of State. Definitions and methodology. *Trafficking in Persons Report 2013.* Washington, DC: US Department of State. US Department of State Web site. http://www.state.gov/j/tip/rls/tiprpt/2013/210543.htm#. Accessed August 22, 2016.

10. National Center for Missing & Exploited Children. Child sex trafficking. National Center for Missing & Exploited Children Web site. http://www.missingkids.com/1in6. Accessed August 22, 2016.

11. US Department of Health and Human Services, Administration for Children and Families, Administration on Children, Youth and Families, Children's Bureau. *Child Maltreatment 2013.* Washington, DC: US Department of Health and Human Services, Administration for Children and Families, Administration on Children, Youth and Families, Children's Bureau; 2015. Administration for Children & Families Web site. https://www.acf.hhs.gov/sites/default/files/cb/cm2013.pdf. Accessed August 22, 2016.

12. Farrell A, McDevitt J. Hidden in plain sight: challenges to identifying, investigating, and prosecuting human trafficking. *JRSA Forum.* 2014;32(3):1-15. Justice Research and Statistics Association Web site. http://www.jrsa.org/pubs/forum/forum_issues/for32_3.pdf. Accessed August 22, 2016.

13. Children's Healthcare of Atlanta. *Clinical Practice Guideline for Assessment and Treatment of Potential Victims of Child Sex Trafficking and Commercial Sexual Exploitation (CSEC) ≥ 11yrs old.* Atlanta, GA: Children's Healthcare of Atlanta; 2015.

14. International Labour Organization. New ILO global estimate of force labour: 20.9 million victims. International Labour Organization Web site. http://www.ilo.org/global/about-the-ilo/newsroom/news/WCMS_182109/lang--en/index.htm. Accessed August 22, 2016.

15. Florida Department of Children and Families. *Florida Department of Children and Families Annual Human Trafficking Report: 2013-14 Federal Fiscal Year.* Ocala, FL: Florida Department of Children and Families; 2014. Florida Department of Children and Families Web site. http://www.dcf.state.fl.us/programs/childwelfare/docs/2014LMRs/2013-14HumanTraffickingAnnualReport.pdf. Accessed August 22, 2016.

16. Centers for Disease Control and Prevention. Adverse childhood experiences reported by adults --- five states, 2009. *MMWR.* 2010;59(49):1609-1613.

17. Brown DW, Anda RF, Tiemeier H, et al. Adverse childhood experiences and the risk of premature mortality. *Am J Prev Med.* 2009;37(5):389-396.

18. Cecchet SJ, Thoburn J. The psychological experience of child and adolescent sex trafficking in the United States: trauma and resilience in survivors. *Psychol Trauma.* 2014;6(5):482-493.

19. Epstein R, Edelman P. *Blueprint: A Multidisciplinary Approach to the Domestic Sex Trafficking of Girls.* Washington, DC: Georgetown Law; 2013.

20. US Department of Health and Human Services, Administration for Children and Families, Administration on Children, Youth and Families, Children's Bureau. *Mandatory Reporters of Child Abuse and Neglect.* Washington, DC: US Department of Health and Human Services, Administration for Children and Families, Administration on Children, Youth and Families, Children's Bureau; 2015. Children's Welfare Information Gateway Web site. https://www.childwelfare.gov/pubPDFs/manda.pdf. Accessed August 22, 2016.

21. US Department of Health and Human Services, Administration for Children and Families, Administration on Children, Youth and Families, Children's Bureau. *Immunity for Reporters of Child Abuse and Neglect.* Washington, DC: US Department of Health and Human Services, Administration for Children and Families, Administration on Children, Youth and Families, Children's Bureau; 2015. Children's Information Gateway Web site. https://www.childwelfare.gov/pubPDFs/immunity.pdf. Accessed August 22, 2016.

22. Child Abuse Prevention and Treatment Act of 2003, Pub L No. 93-247, 88 Stat 4.

23. Victims of Trafficking and Violence Protection Act of 2000, Pub L No. 106-386, 114 Stat 1464.

24. Trafficking Victims Protection Reauthorization Act of 2013, HR 898, 113th Cong, 1st Sess (2013-2014).

25. Polaris Project. Human trafficking issue brief: safe harbor. Polaris Project Web site. https://polarisproject.org/sites/default/files/2015%20Safe%20Harbor%20Issue%20Brief.pdf. Accessed August 2016.

Chapter 2

Radiology

Megan B. Marine, MD
Richard Gunderman, MD, PhD

Imaging of Child Abuse
(**Table 2-1**)

Table 2-1. American College of Radiology (ACR) Guidelines for Imaging in Physically Abused Children[1]
— Younger than 24 months: X-ray skeletal survey and head computed tomography (CT) without contrast are usually appropriate radiologic procedures.
— Older than 24 months: The value of the skeletal survey is less and radiographs should be tailored to the suspected area of injury.

— Radiographic skeletal survey should be obtained using high-detail imaging and honed down to the area of interest for each body part (**Table 2-2**).

Table 2-2. Components of the Radiographic Skeletal Survey[1]
— Frontal and lateral views of skull
— Lateral views of cervical and thoracolumbosacral spine
— Single frontal views of chest and abdomen
— Oblique views of ribs
— Frontal views of long bones

— Tc-99m whole body bone scan may be appropriate if skeletal survey is negative and high clinical suspicion remains.[1]

— Head MRI may be appropriate if further evaluation is indicated from head CT or neurologic signs and symptoms are present.[1]

— In suspected thoracic and/or abdomen/pelvis injuries, CT of chest and/or abdomen/pelvis with intravenous contrast is recommended.[1]

— When a child is identified as a suspected victim of abuse, siblings and other child contacts of the suspected abuser should also be assessed for injuries.[2]

Manifestations of Child Abuse

Musculoskeletal Findings

— No single fracture is characteristic of child abuse; however, particular fractures strongly suggest it (**Table 2-3**).

Table 2-3. Fractures Characteristic of Child Abuse (by Specificity)[3]

High Specificity	Moderate Specificity	Low Specificity
— Classic metaphyseal lesions — Posterior rib fractures — Scapula fractures — Spinous process fractures — Sternal fractures	— Multiple fractures — Fractures of different ages — Epiphyseal separations — Vertebral body fractures — Digital fractures — Complex skull fractures	— Subperiosteal new bone formation — Fractures of the clavicle and long bone shaft — Simple skull fractures

— Posterior and lateral rib fractures are considered to be caused by squeezing or compressive forces and are not uncommonly multiple.[4]

— When faced with multiple fractures, it is important to determine their ages, as fractures of differing ages increase concern for child abuse.

— The timetable of radiographic changes include:

1. Soft tissue swelling
2. Subperiosteal new bone formation as early as 4 days and always by 2 weeks
3. Loss of fracture line and soft callus, hard bony callus, and bony remodeling peaking at 8 weeks

— Bear in mind that considerable overlap renders dating of fractures an inexact science, reliant on the radiologist's clinical experience (**Figures 2-1-a** and **b**).[5]

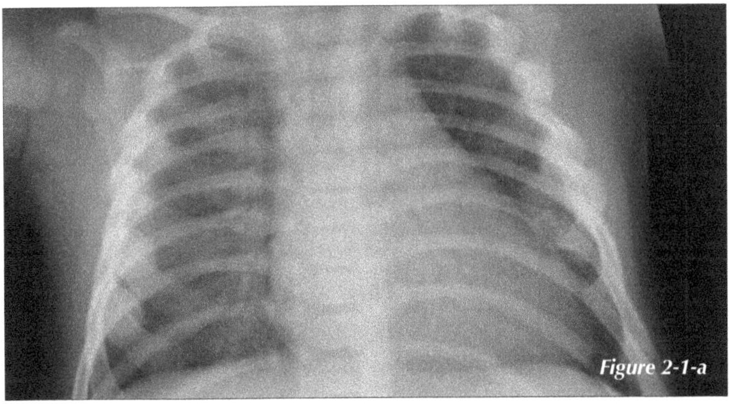
Figure 2-1-a

Figure 2-1-a. *Girl, 3 months old, with multiple bilateral posterior and lateral healing rib fractures with hard bony callus formation.*

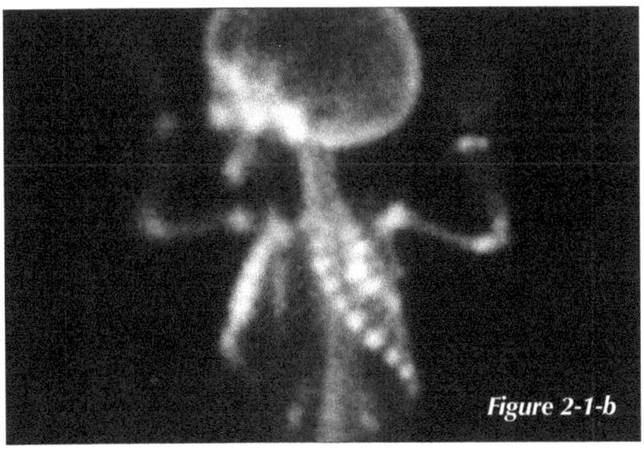
Figure 2-1-b

Figure 2-1-b. *Same patient as in* ***2-1-a****, 2 days later. Technetium 99m MDP bone scan demonstrates multiple bilateral rib fractures.*

— Repeat radiographs or skeletal survey performed 2 weeks after initial examination can provide additional information on presence and age of abusive fractures.[6] Should be performed when abnormal or equivocal findings are found on initial study and abuse is suspected on clinical grounds (**Figures 2-1-c** and **2-2-a** and **b**).[7]

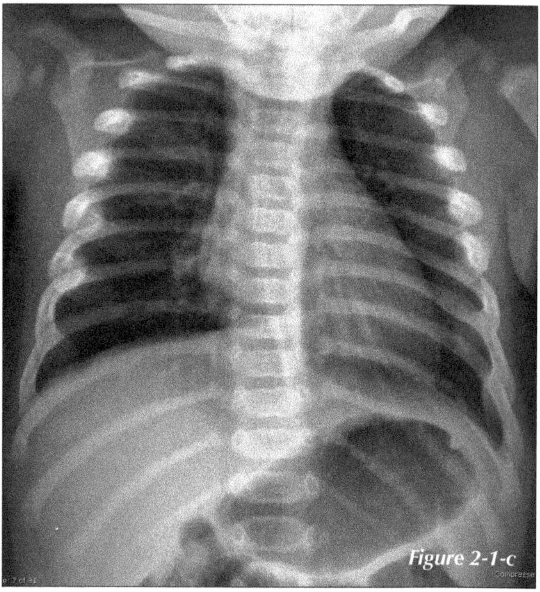

Figure 2-1-c. *Nineteen days later. Note the change in the appearance of the healing rib fractures. The proximal left humeral metaphyseal fracture now also noted.*

***Figures 2-2-a** and **b.** Boy, 22 days old, with bilateral acute posterior rib fractures. On the right, 14 days later, the fractures now show bony callus formation.*

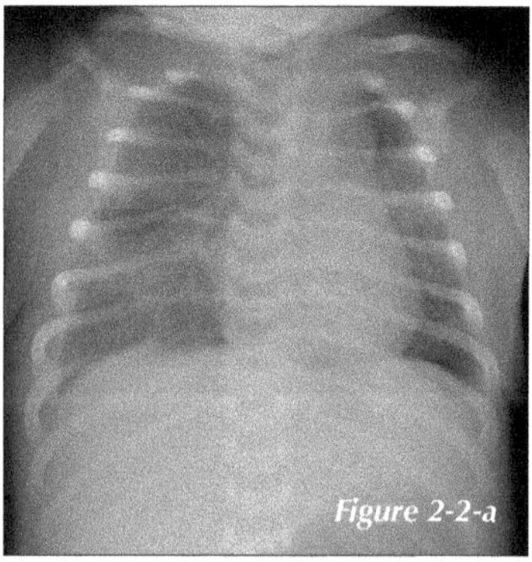

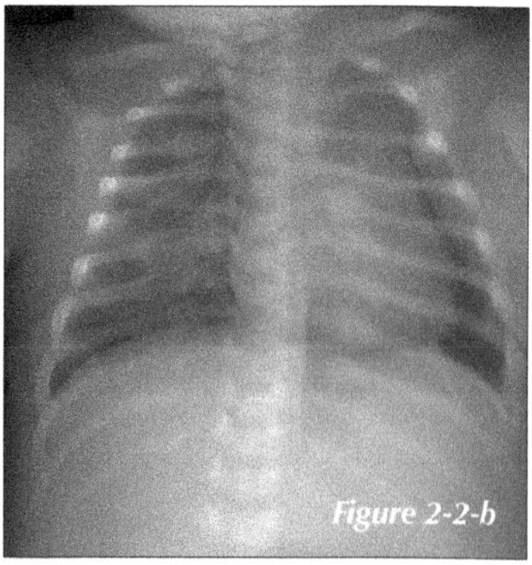

— Classic metaphyseal lesion occurs when acceleration-deceleration and/or torsional force is applied to immature primary spongiosa adjacent to cartilaginous growth plate (**Figures 2-3-a** through **d**, **2-4**, and **2-5-a** through **c**).[8]

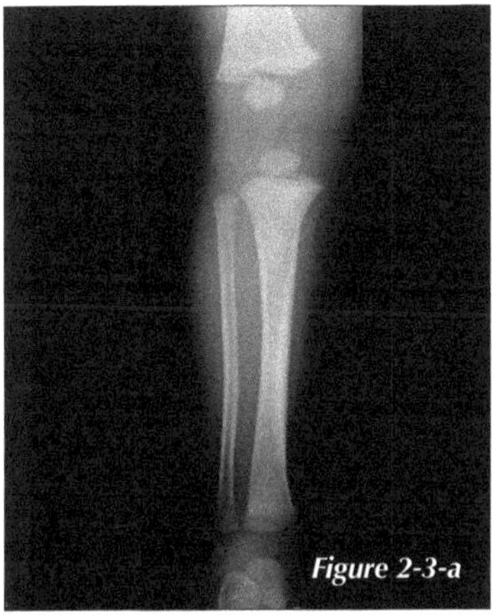

Figure 2-3-a

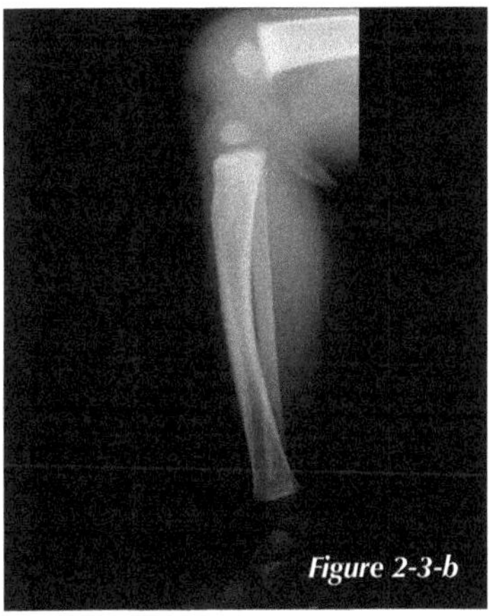

Figure 2-3-b

***Figures 2-3-a** and **b**. Girl, 5 months old, with slight irregularity of the proximal tibia metaphysis.*

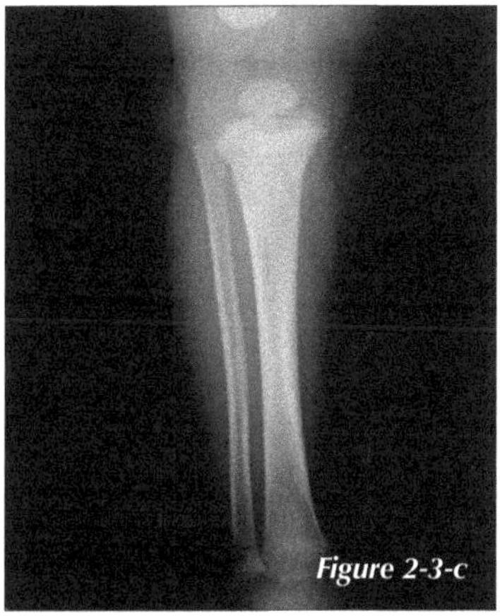

Figure 2-3-c

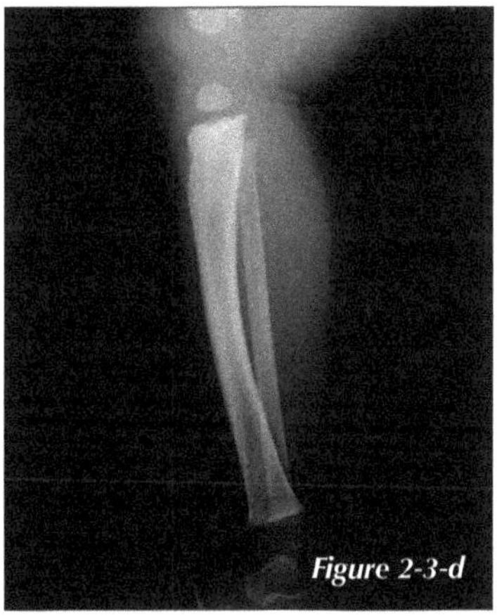

Figure 2-3-d

***Figures 2-3-c** and **d**. Follow-up radiographs 16 days later better demonstrate the healing proximal tibia classic metaphyseal lesion or "bucket handle" fracture.*

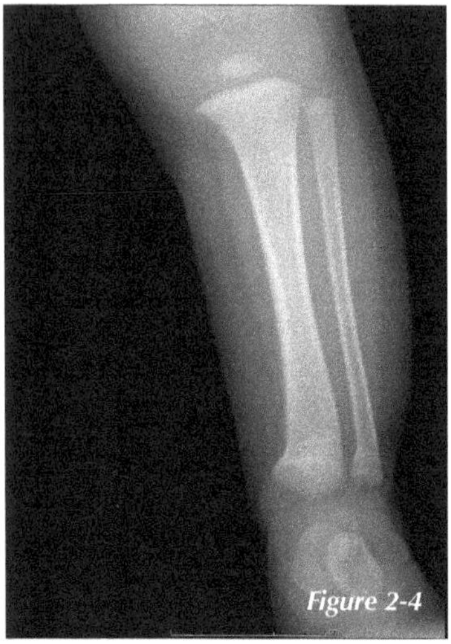

Figure 2-4. *Girl, 3 months old, with healing distal tibia and fibula metaphyseal fractures.*

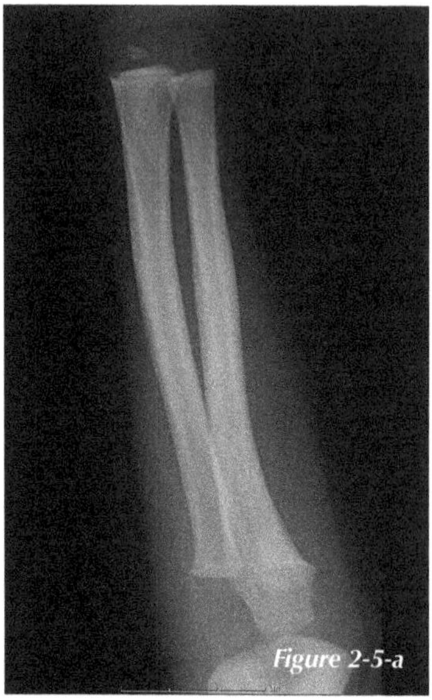

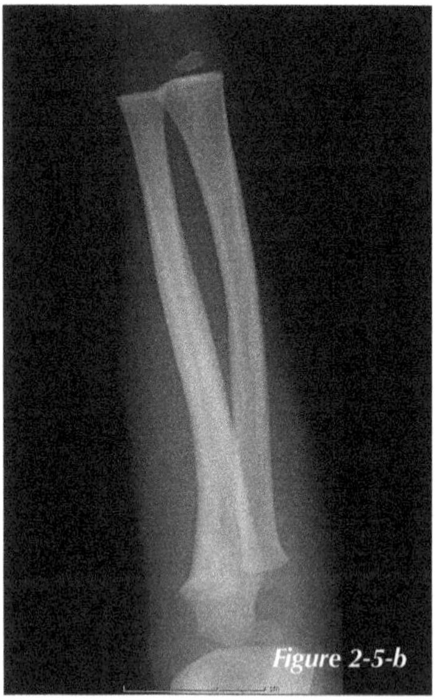

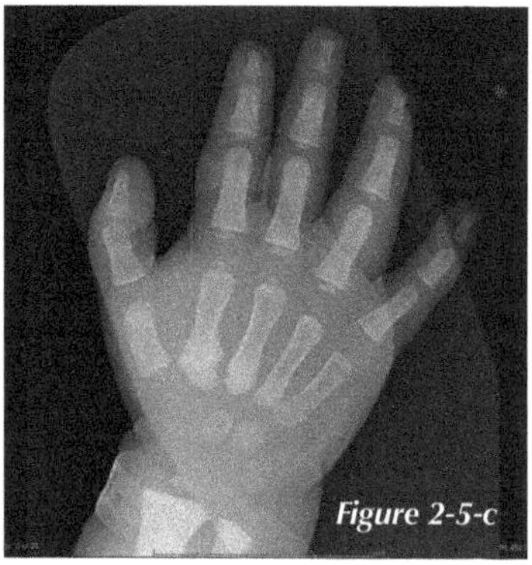

Figures 2-5-a *and* **b.** *Boy, 20 months old, with acute distal radius CML. Normal left side is shown for comparison.*

Figure 2-5-c. *Same patient as in* **2-5-a** *and* **b**, *with less commonly seen healing metacarpal fractures, moderately specific for child abuse.*

— Sternal fractures have a higher specificity for child abuse but are uncommon. Mechanism of fracture is likely a direct blow or forceful compression of chest.[9,10]

— Scapular fractures are also rare, and the mechanism is typically severe, high-energetic trauma. Acromion is the most common location for a fracture, which can result from indirect trauma (**Figures 2-6-a** and **b**).[10]

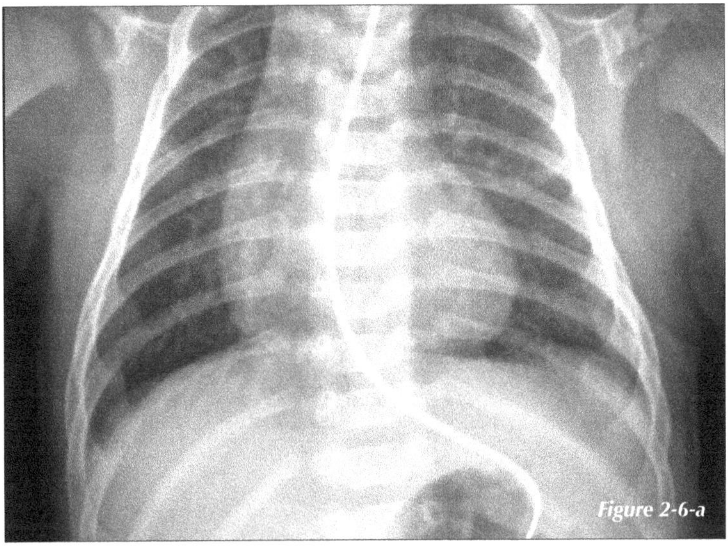

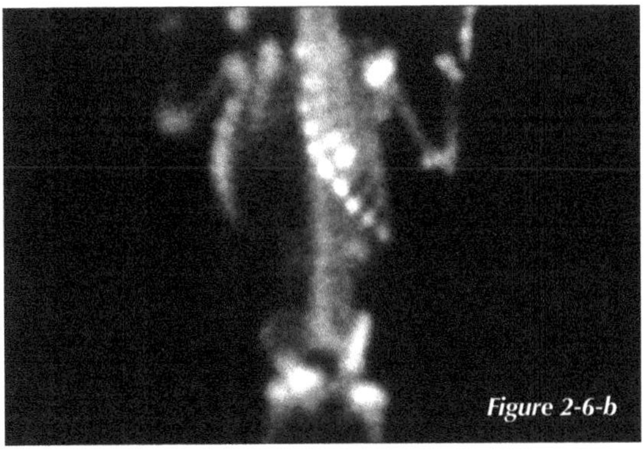

Figure 2-6-a. *Child, 2 months old, with left acromion fracture.*

Figure 2-6-b. *Three days later, bone scan demonstrates left acromion fracture and better shows left lateral rib fractures.*

— Spinous process fractures, while more specific for child abuse, are less common than vertebral body fractures, which are only moderately specific. In a child with a thin abdominal wall, the fulcrum of a flexion injury would be at the body of the spine.[11] Compression fractures also result from direct impact as well as shaking with hyperextension/hyperflexion (**Figure 2-7-a** and **b**).[10]

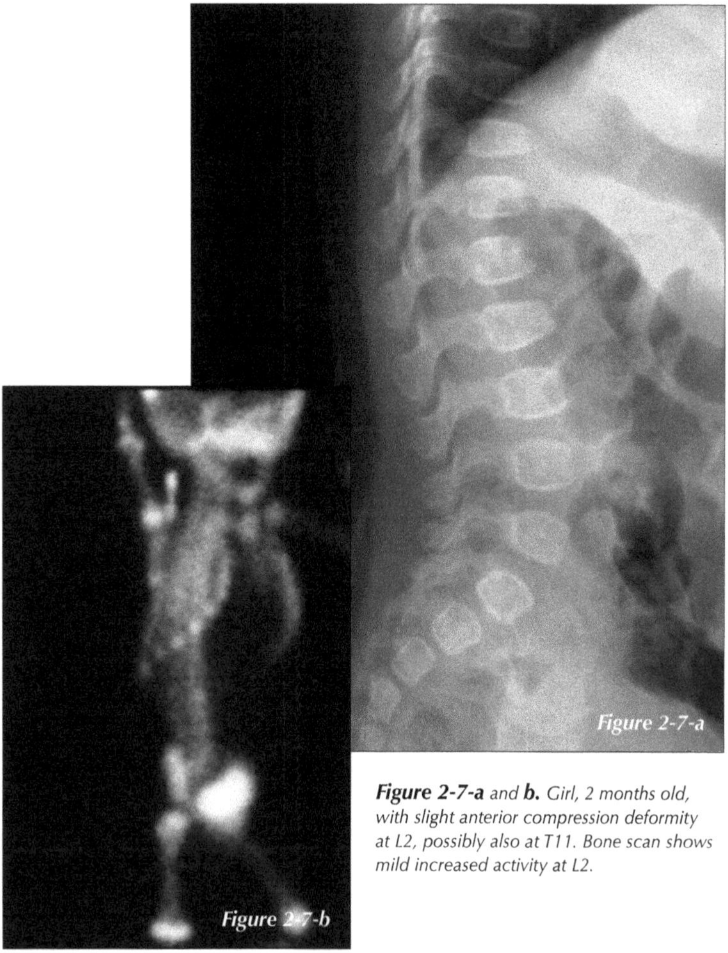

***Figure 2-7-a** and **b.** Girl, 2 months old, with slight anterior compression deformity at L2, possibly also at T11. Bone scan shows mild increased activity at L2.*

Musculoskeletal Child Abuse Mimics

- Skeletal dysplasias and disorders resulting in decreased bone mineralization may mimic musculoskeletal findings in child abuse.
- Normal skeletal variants may mimic abusive fractures, particularly classic metaphyseal lesions.
- Osteogenesis imperfecta (OI): Common heritable disorder of collagen synthesis resulting in weak bones, multiple fractures, and progressive bony deformity. May present with bowing of the long bones, spinal abnormalities, hearing loss, blue sclerae, dentinogenesis imperfecta, and/or hyperlaxity of ligaments and skin (**Figures 2-8-a** through **c** and **2-9-a** through **c**).[12,13]

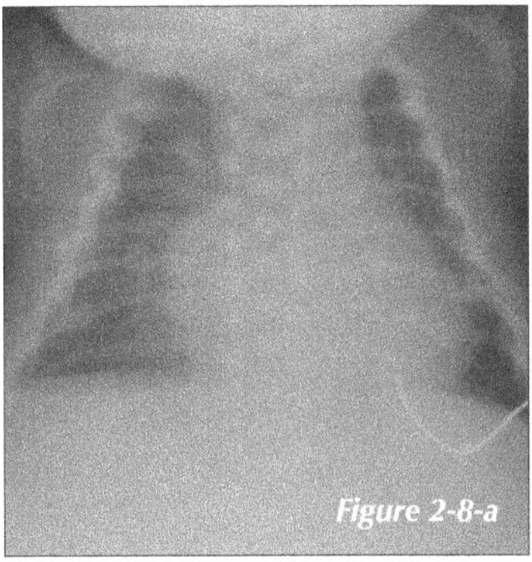

Figure 2-8-a. *Child, 17 days old, with multiple bilateral bony callus formations of the ribs, consistent with healing fractures. Underlying ribs are gracile with decreased bony mineralization.*

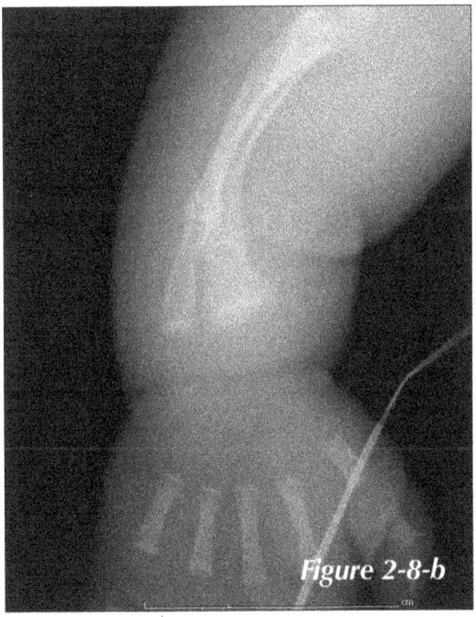

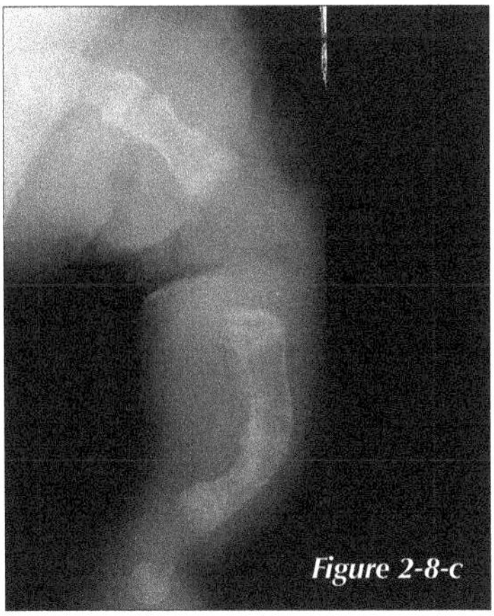

Figures 2-8-b *and* ***c.*** *Same patient as in* ***2-8-a****. Note multiple fractures with variant healing stage. Osteopenia and shortened, bowed extremities support known diagnosis of osteogenesis imperfecta.*

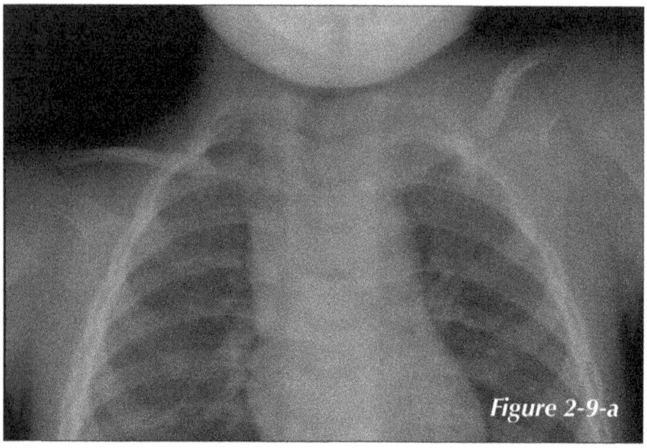

Figure 2-9-a. *Boy, 18 months old, with acute left clavicle fracture.*

Figures 2-9-b and **c.** *Follow-up skeletal survey demonstrates wormian bones of the skull in this same patient with a family history of osteogenesis imperfecta.*

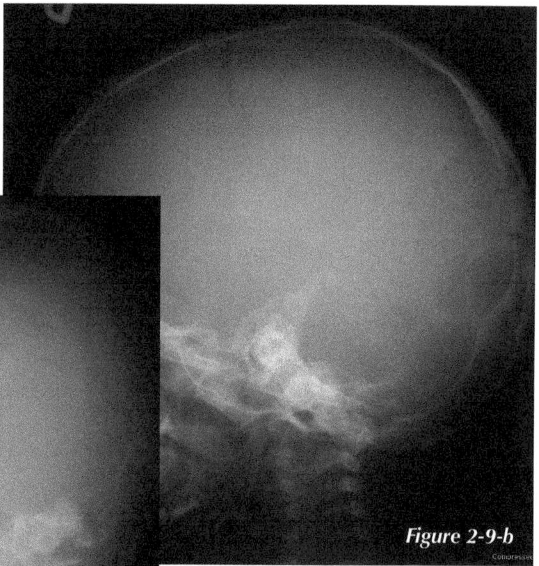

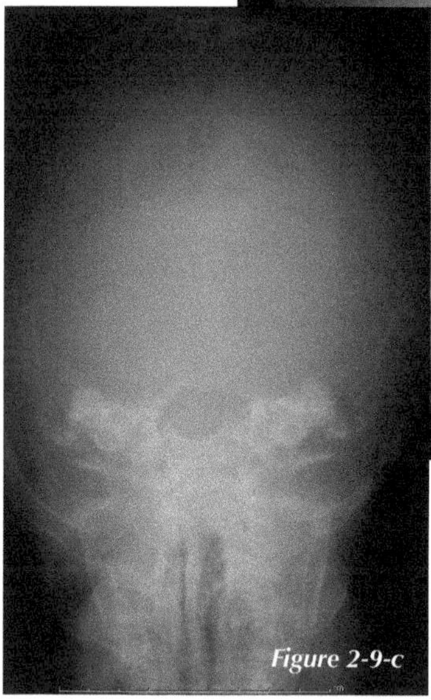

— Normal metaphyseal variants mimicking classic metaphyseal lesions are differentiated from actual injuries by absence of separate fracture fragment.

— Step-off: A near-90-degree angulation in the metaphysis adjacent to the physis, most commonly seen in the distal femur, proximal tibia and fibula, and distal radius and ulna.

— Beak: Medial projection of the metaphysis, most commonly seen in proximal humerus or proximal tibia.

— Spur: Longitudinal bone projection beyond metaphysis, most commonly seen in lateral distal femur, lateral distal radius, medial distal ulna, and lateral metacarpals and metacarpals (**Figure 2-10-a** through **f**).[14]

Figures 2-10-a, b, *and* **c.** *Boy, 5 months old, with skull fracture reportedly dropped onto concrete floor by sibling. Frontal, lateral, and magnified images demonstrate distal medial femoral metaphyseal irregularity with longitudinal bony projection.*

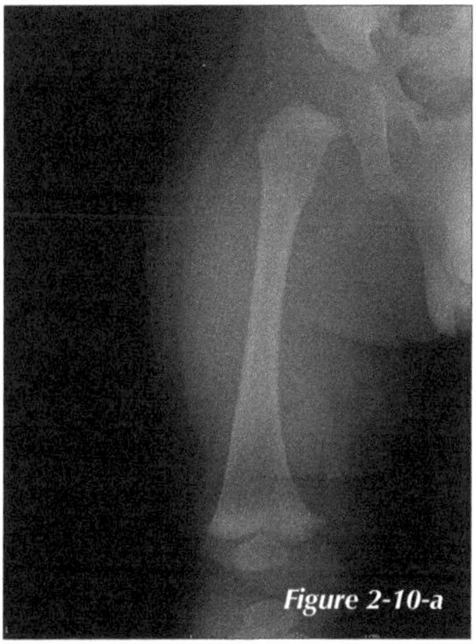

Figure 2-10-a

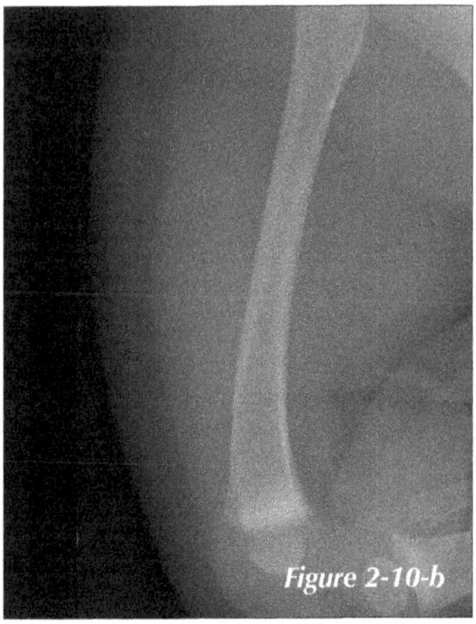

Figure 2-10-b

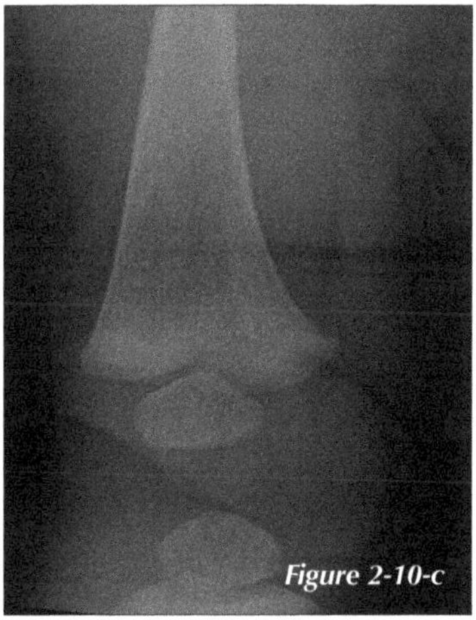

Figure 2-10-c

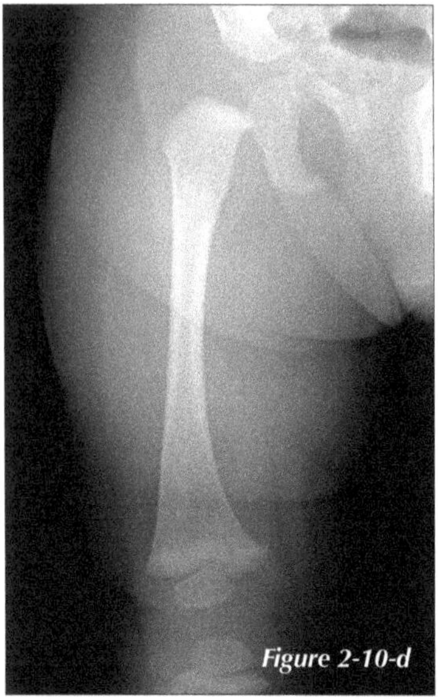

Figure 2-10-d

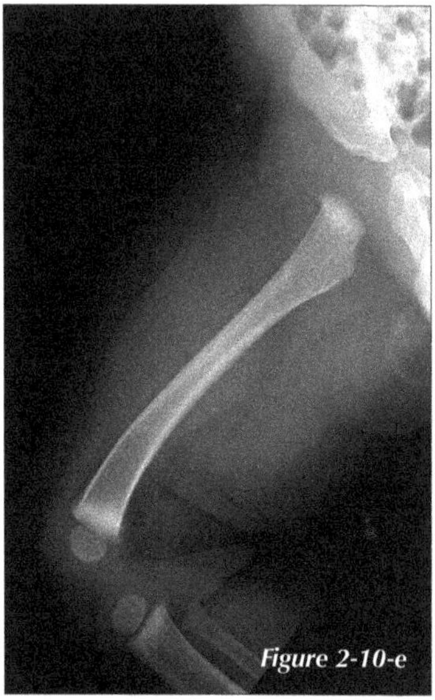

Figure 2-10-e

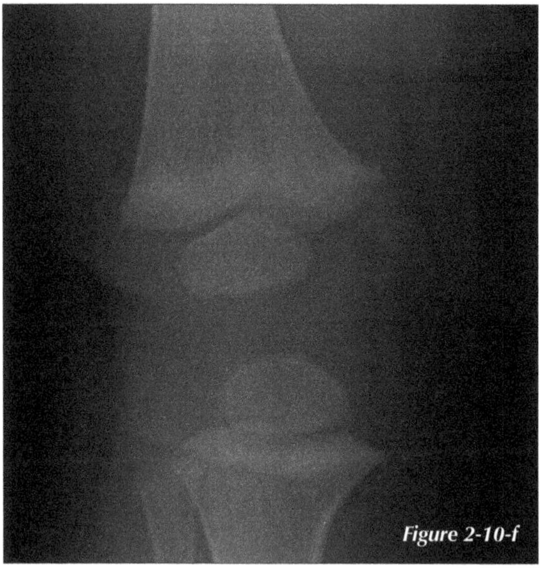

Figure 2-10-f

Figures 2-10-d, e, *and* ***f.*** *Follow-up skeletal survey 14 days later demonstrates no interval change, consistent with spur metaphyseal variant.*

Neurological Findings

— Typically, the mechanism of brain injury is significant differential movement of the brain relative to the skull during violent shaking, ie, shaken baby syndrome/abusive head trauma (SBS/AHT).

— Subdural hemorrhage is a characteristic finding of SBS/AHT (**Figures 2-11-a** and **b**).[15]

— Hematomas of differing ages are more specific for child abuse, indicating multiple abusive episodes. Age is estimated via CT, based on its density (**Table 2-4**).

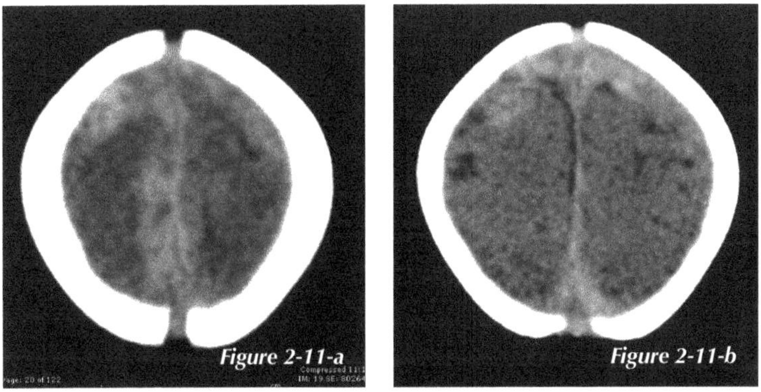

Figures 2-11-a *and* ***b.*** *Boy, 2 months old, with interhemispheric and bilateral crescenteric hyperdense acute subdural hematomas.*

Table 2-4. Aging Hematomas Via CT
— Hyperacute blood is isodense (< 3 hours)
— Acute blood is hyperdense (between 3 hours and 7 to 10 days)
— Subacute blood is isodense (2 to 3 weeks)
— Chronic blood is hypodense (> 3 weeks)

— MRI detects smaller subdural hematomas and may estimate hematoma age with greater accuracy, depending on the T1 and T2 features, as depicted in **Table 2-5** (**Figures 2-12-a** through **c** and **2-13**).[16]

— Some dispute the accuracy with which subdural hematomas can be dated by CT and MRI. Careful confirmation with an experienced pediatric neuroradiologist is ideal.

— Retinal hemorrhage and cerebral edema are commonly found in victims of child abuse.[15] Acceleration-deceleration trauma results in numerous and multilayered hemorrhages in the retina. Appropriate evaluation requires a 3-dimensional view of retina with an indirect ophthalmoscope through dilated pupils.[17]

Table 2-5. T1 and T2 Signals in Differing Ages of Subdural Hematomas

Age	Hemoglobin	Timing	T1	T2
Hyper-acute	Oxyhemoglobin	Up to 24 hours	Hypointense or isointense	Hyperin-tense
Acute	Deoxyhemo-globin	1-3 days	Hypointense or isointense	Hypoin-tense
Early subacute	Intracellular methemoglobin	2-3 days to 1-2 weeks	Hyperintense	Hypoin-tense
Late subacute	Extracellular methemoglobin	1-2 weeks to 1-2 months	Hyperintense	Hyper-intesnse
Chronic	Hemosiderin in the subdural membrane	3 weeks to months or years	Isointense	Hypoin-tense
Chronic	Nonparamagnetic hemichromes in subdural content	3 weeks to months or years	Hypoin-tense > CSF	Hyperin-tense

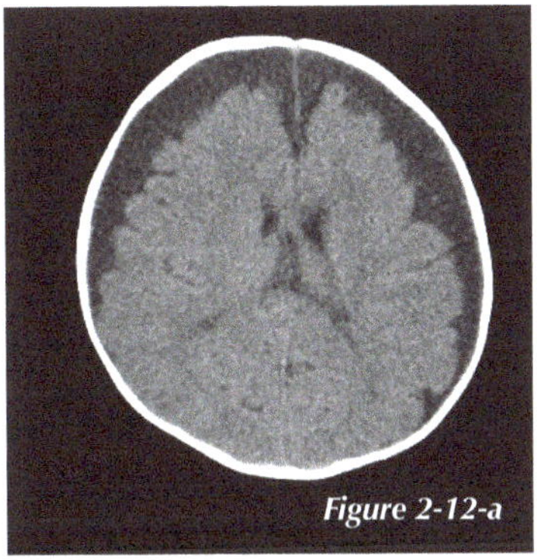

Figure 2-12-a

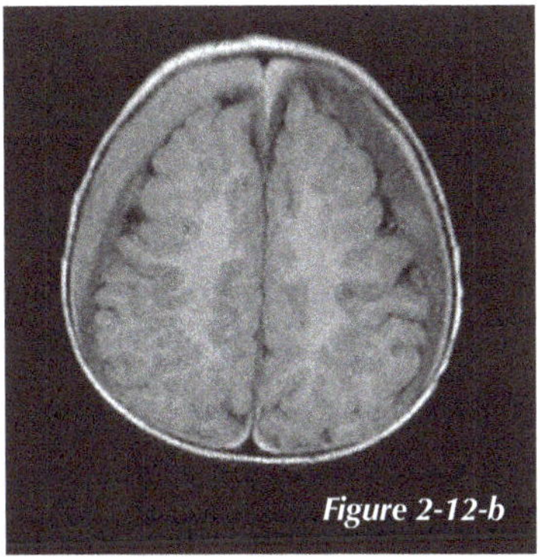

Figure 2-12-b

Figures 2-12-a, b, and **c.** *Child, 85 days old, with questionable presence of subdural hygromas or hematomas on CT. T2 FLAIR and T1 weighted MRI images demonstrate subdural hematomas of differing signal intensities, consistent with differing ages.*

Figure 2-13. *Girl, 3 months old, with bilateral chronic subdural hematomas demonstrated by head ultrasound.*

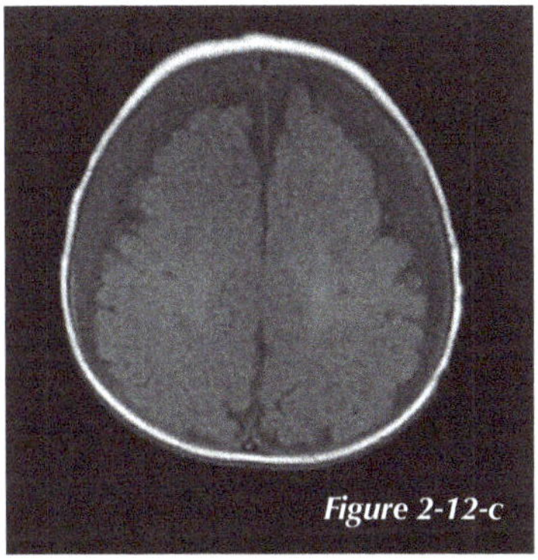

Figure 2-12-c

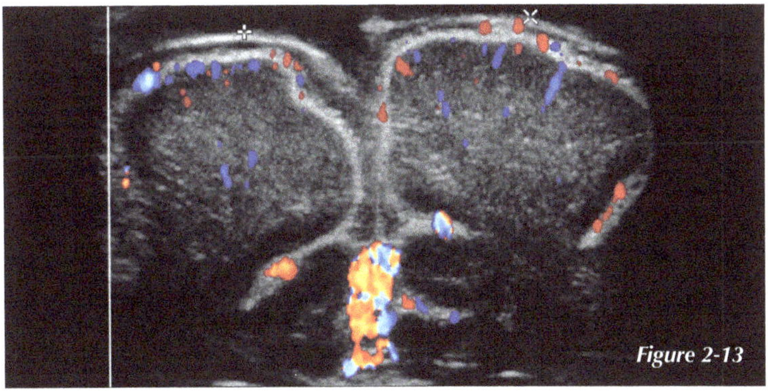

Figure 2-13

— Diffuse cerebral edema can be seen in cases of secondary brain injury from diffuse hypoxic injury, whether from prolonged apnea, asphyxiation, or vascular injury. Findings include loss of gray-white matter differentiation with sparing of the basal ganglia, cerebellum, thalami, and brainstem, ie, CT reversal sign (**Figures 2-14-a** through **f**).[18]

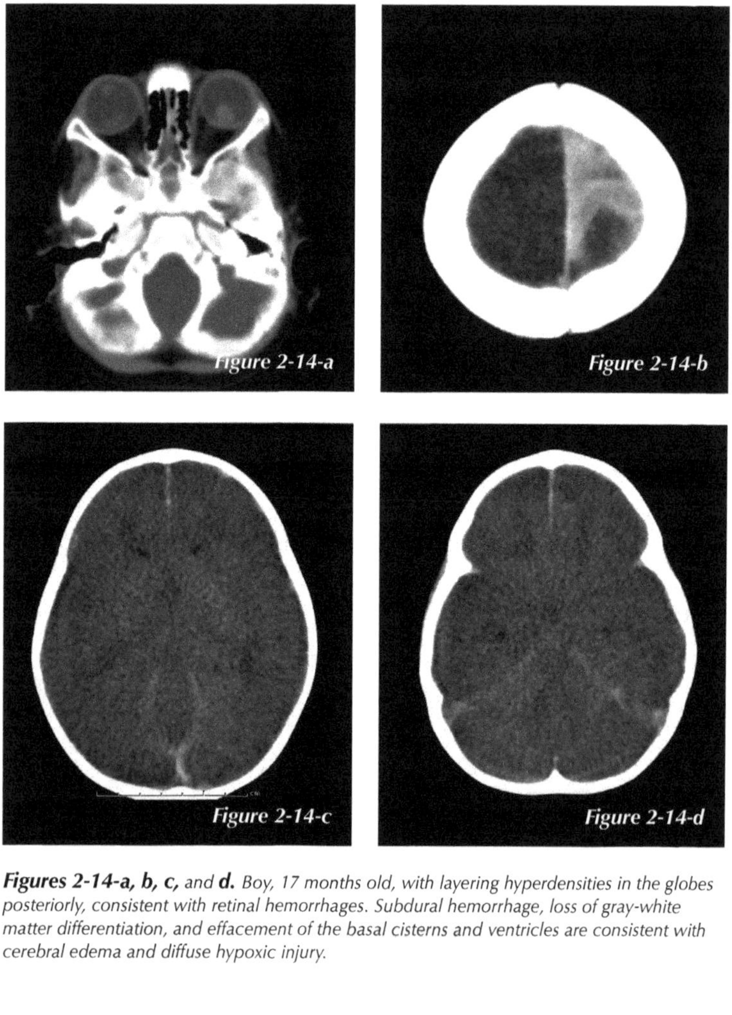

***Figures 2-14-a, b, c,** and **d.** Boy, 17 months old, with layering hyperdensities in the globes posteriorly, consistent with retinal hemorrhages. Subdural hemorrhage, loss of gray-white matter differentiation, and effacement of the basal cisterns and ventricles are consistent with cerebral edema and diffuse hypoxic injury.*

Figure 2-14-e

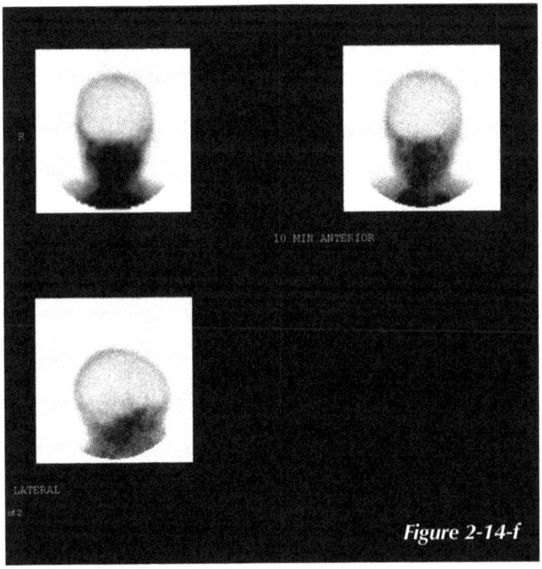

Figure 2-14-f

Figures 2-14-e *and* **f.** *Same patient as in Figures 2-14-a through 2-14-d the following day. Tc-99m HMPAO brain death study demonstrates no intracranial blood flow, compatible with brain death.*

— Complex skull fractures are considered moderately specific for abuse. The infant skull is extremely thin and pliable; however, the unfused cranial sutures make the skull resistant to complex fractures, except in the case of severe direct impact trauma. This can magnify additional intracranial injuries, including parenchymal hemorrhage and focal and/or diffuse parenchymal injury (**Figure 2-15-a** and **b**).[8]

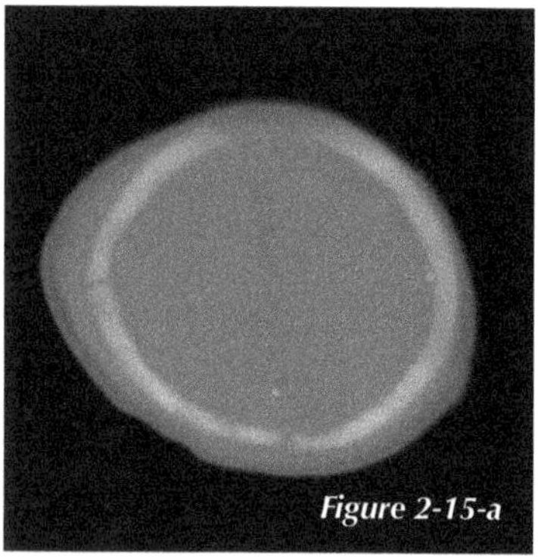

Figure 2-15-a

Figures 2-15-a and b. Girl, 50 days old, with right parietal bone fracture and associated soft tissue swelling on CT. Follow up x-ray 17 days later clearly shows fracture line.

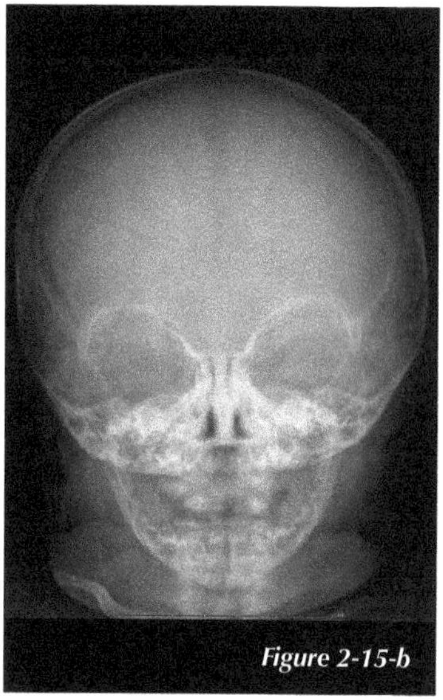

Figure 2-15-b

Abdominopelvic Findings

— While no abdominal injury pattern is specific for abuse, hollow viscous, pancreatic, and other solid organ injuries should promote a high index of suspicion. CT with intravenous contrast is the recommended imaging modality.[19]

— Solid organs are the most commonly seen abdominal injuries in child abuse. The liver, hollow viscous structures, and the pancreas are the most commonly injured organs.[20,21]

— Liver injuries include lacerations, contusions, and subcapsular hematomas (**Figures 2-16-a** and **b**).[19]

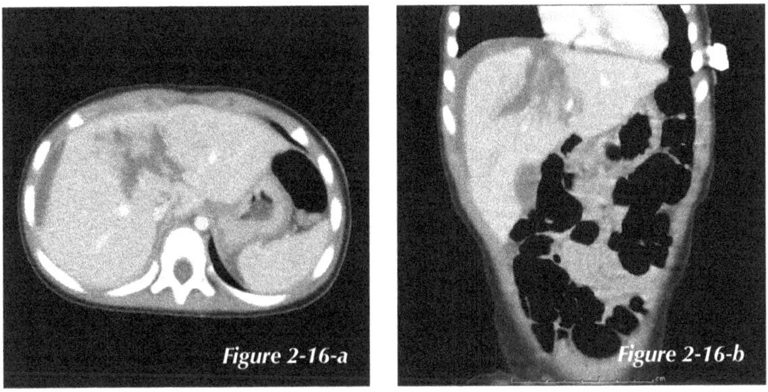

Figures 2-16-a *and* **b.** *Girl, 17 months old, with a history of non-accidental trauma (NAT) and elevated liver enzymes demonstrating grade 3 liver laceration and subcapsular hematoma.*

— Hollow viscous injuries, including duodenal and jejunal hematomas and small bowel contusions and perforations, are commonly described in child abuse.[22] Intramural hematomas of second and/or third portions of duodenum are seen most frequently. Upper GI fluoroscopic study classically shows intramural mass with "stacked coin" appearance of thickened folds (**Figures 2-17-a** through **d**).[23]

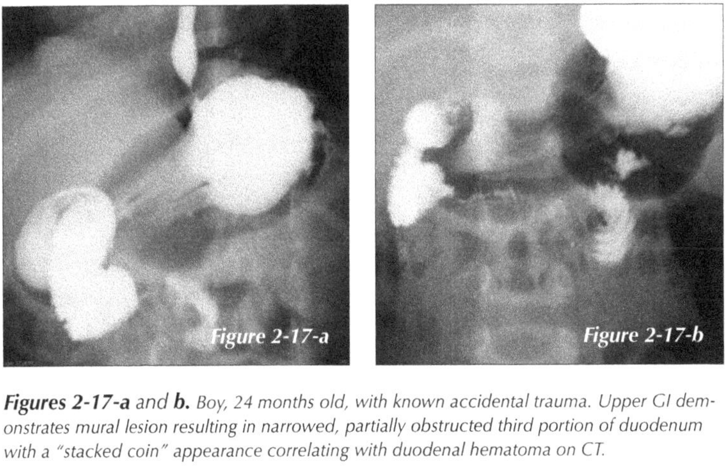

Figures 2-17-a and **b.** *Boy, 24 months old, with known accidental trauma. Upper GI demonstrates mural lesion resulting in narrowed, partially obstructed third portion of duodenum with a "stacked coin" appearance correlating with duodenal hematoma on CT.*

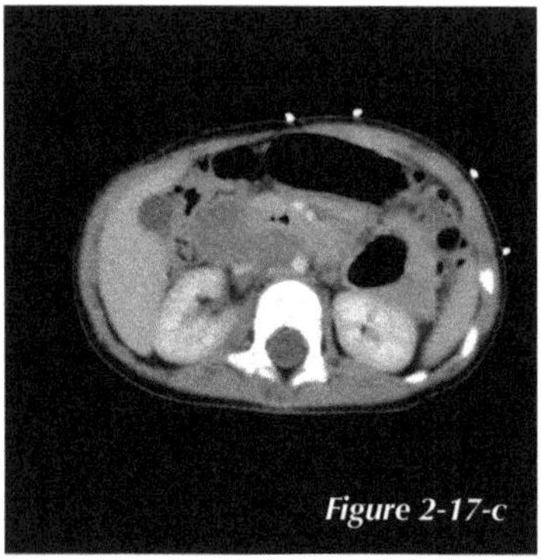

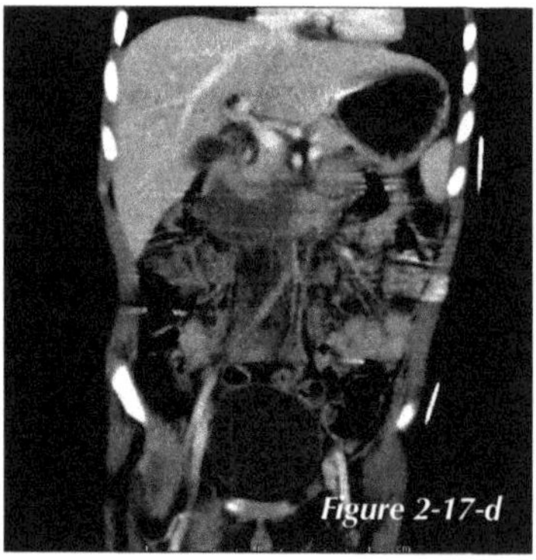

Figures 2-17-c** and **d. *Boy, 24 months old, with known accidental trauma. Upper GI demonstrates mural lesion resulting in narrowed, partially obstructed third portion of duodenum with a "stacked coin" appearance correlating with duodenal hematoma on CT.*

— Pancreatic injuries account for 8.6% of abusive abdominal injuries, including laceration, transaction, and pancreatitis. Peripancreatic fluid is the most common finding; linear hypoattenuating laceration and/or enlarged, edematous gland are less common (**Figures 2-18-a** through **f**).[24]

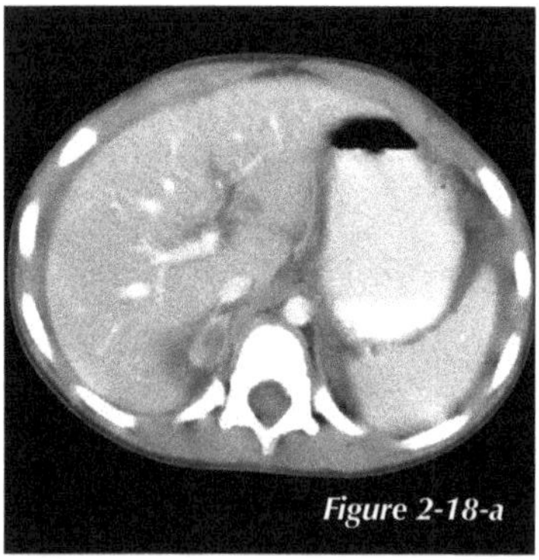

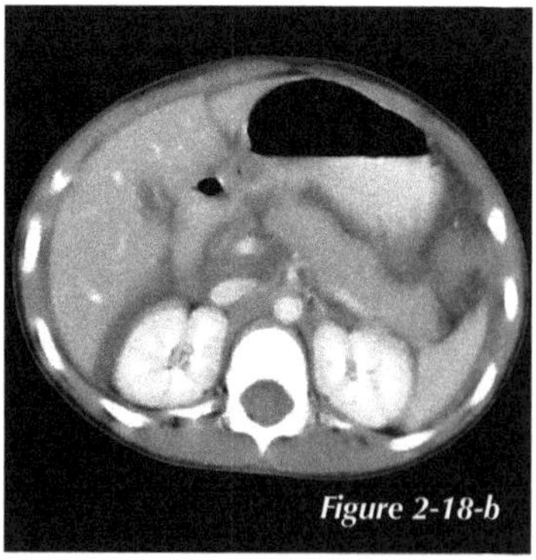

Figures 2-18-a** and **b. *Boy, 3 years old, with peripancreatic fluid, edematous gland, and linear transection of the pancreatic neck. Right adrenal hemorrhage is also present. The patient was also found to have rib fractures and liver contusions.*

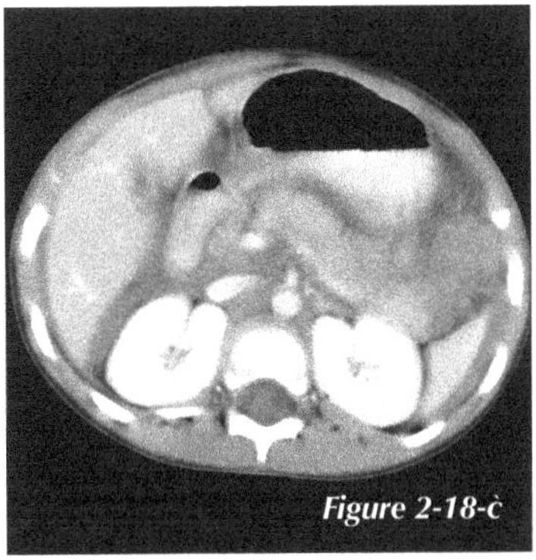

Figure 2-18-c

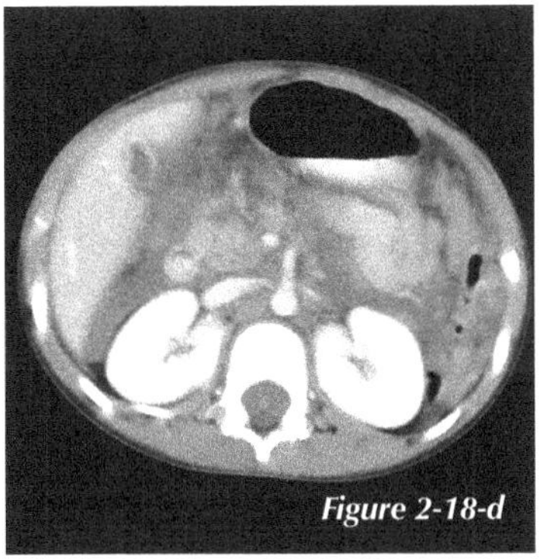

Figure 2-18-d

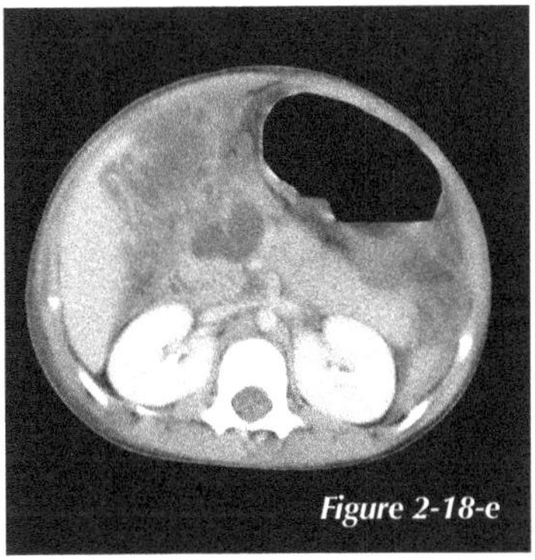

Figure 2-18-e

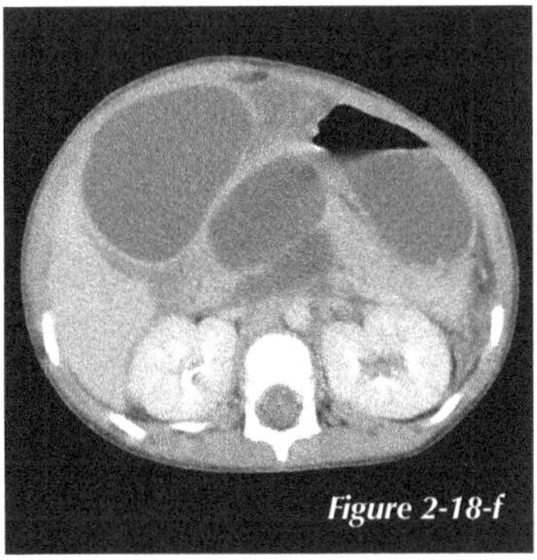

Figure 2-18-f

***Figures 2-18-c** and **d.** Boy, 3 years old, with peripancreatic fluid, edematous gland, and linear transection of the pancreatic neck. Right adrenal hemorrhage is also present. The patient was also found to have rib fractures and liver contusions.*

***Figure 2-18-e** and **f.** Same patient as in **2-18-a** through **2-18-d**, 5 and 11 days later, demonstrates enlarging pancreatic pseudocysts at the level of transection.*

— Spleen, kidneys, mesentery, stomach, colon, adrenals, genitalia, and bladder are less commonly involved in child abuse.[19]

— In young children, the intestine is not fully attached within the peritoneal cavity, making it potentially more vulnerable to injury due to sudden deceleration and/or abdominal compression.

— The bladder extends to the level of the umbilicus at birth and is, therefore, more exposed in a direct impact to the lower abdomen.[25]

— Lower fat content and more elastic attachments are typical of intra-abdominal organs in children, reducing energy absorption and potentially resulting in increased vulnerability (**Figures 2-19-a** and **b** and **2-20-a** and **b**).[25]

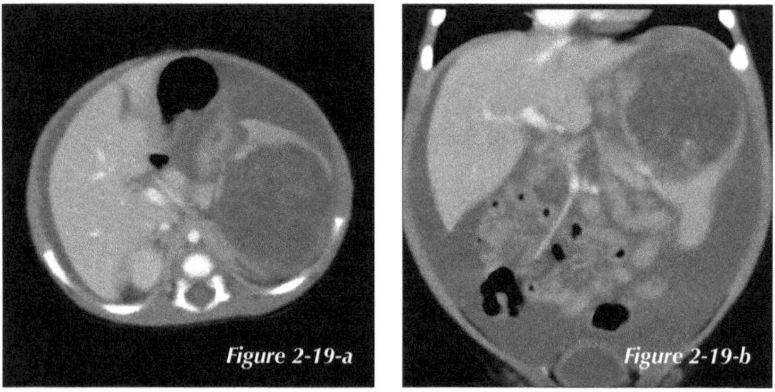

***Figures 2-19-a** and **b.** Boy, 55 days old, with large splenic laceration, intraparenchymal splenic hematoma, and hemoperitoneum.*

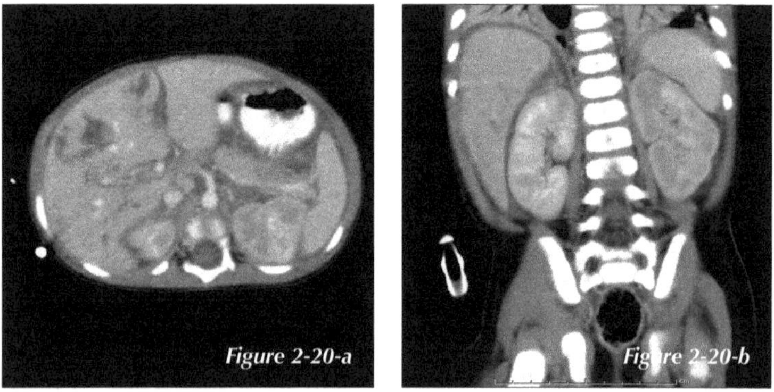

***Figures 2-20-a** and **b.** Boy, 9 months old, with grade 4 liver laceration and enlarged, hypoattenuating left kidney, possibly the result of vascular and/or torsional injury compromise.*

Chest Findings

— Intrathoracic trauma is most commonly seen with blunt trauma and is uncommon in child abuse.

— Soft chest wall offers less protection to underlying lung parenchyma and allows for direct transfer of energy to the lung.

— Greater cartilage content and nonossified ribs of the pediatric thorax allow for greater mobility of chest wall and mediastinum, which may result in significant intrathoracic injury in absence of external signs of trauma.[26] Examples include pneumothorax, hemothorax, pulmonary contusion, myocardial contusion, and aortic transection (**Figures 2-21-a** and **b**).

— Noncardiogenic pulmonary edema, particularly neurogenic pulmonary edema after head injury or acute airway obstruction, has been associated with abuse. This could be important when other causes, such as suffocation, are under consideration.[27]

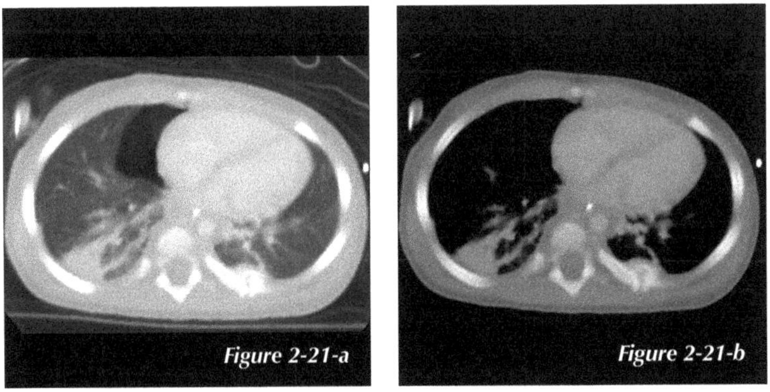

Figure 2-21-a *and* **b.** *Girl, 13 months old, with right pneumothorax; airspace opacities, possibly representing contusions or atelectasis; and evidence of healing left posterior rib fracture.*

References

1. Meyer JS, Gunderman R, Coley BD, et al. ACR Appropriateness Criteria® on suspected physical abuse-child. *J Am Coll Radiol.* 2011;8(2):87-94.

2. Kellogg N; American Academy of Pediatrics Committee on Child Abuse and Neglect. Evaluation of Suspected child physical abuse. *Pediatrics.* 2007;119(6):1232-1241.

3. Kleinman PK, ed. *Diagnostic Imaging of Child Abuse.* Saint Louis, MO: Mosby; 1998.

4. Ng CS, Hall CM. Costochondral junction fractures and intra-abdominal trauma in non-accidental injury (child abuse). *Pediatr Radiol.* 1998;28(9):671-676.

5. Prosser I, Maguire S, Harrison SK, et al. How old is this fracture? Radiologic dating of fractures in children: a systematic review. *AJR.* 2005;184:1282-1286.

6. Kleinman PK, Nimkin K, Spevak MR, et al. Follow-up skeletal surveys in suspected child abuse. *AJR.* 1996;167:893-896.

7. Hudson M, Kaplan R. Clinical response to child abuse. *Pediatr Clin North Am.* 2006;53(1):27-39, v.

8. Lancon JA, Haines DE, Parent AD. Anatomy of the Shaken Baby Syndrome. *Anat Rec.*1998;253(1):13-18.

9. Wada A, Fujii T, Takamura K, et al. Sternal segment dislocation in children. *J Pediatr Orthop.* 2002;22:729-31.

10. Bilo RAC, Robben SGF, van Rijn RR. *Forensic Aspects of Pediatric Fractures: Differentiating Accidental Trauma from Child Abuse.* New York, NY: Springer; 2010.

11. Clark P, Letts M. Trauma to the thoracic and lumbar spine in the adolescent. *Can J Surg.* 2001;44(5):337-345.

12. Burnei G, Vlad C, Georgescu I, Gavriliu TS, Dan D. Osteogenesis imperfecta: diagnosis and treatment. *J Am Acad Orthop Surg.* 2008;16(6):356-366.

13. Petruzzellis M, De Blasi R, Lucivero V, et al. Cerebral aneurysms in a patient with osteogenesis imperfecta and Exan 28 polymorphism of COL1A2. *Am J Neuroradiol.* 2007;28:397-398.

14. Kleinman PK, Belange PL, Karellasa A, Spevak MR. Normal metaphyseal radiologic variants not to be confused with the findings of infant abuse. *Am J Roengenol.* 1991;156(4):781-783.

15. Dubowitz H, Bennett S. Physical abuse and neglect of children. *Lancet.* 2007;369(9576):1891-1899.

16. Vezina G. Assessment of the nature and age of subdural collections in nonaccidental head injury with CT and MRI. *Pediatr Radiol.* 2009;39(6):586-590.

17. Levin AV. Retinal hemorrhage in abusive head trauma. *Pediatrics.* 2010;126(5):961-970.

18. Chiesa A, Duhamie A. Abusive head trauma. *Pediatr Clin North Am.* 2009;56:317-331.

19. Raissaki M, Veyrac C, Blondiaux E, Hadjigeorgi C. Abdominal imaging in child abuse. *Pediatr Radiol.* 2011;41:4-16.

20. Sivit CJ, Taylor GA, Eichelberger MR. Visceral injury in battered children: a changing perspective. *Radiology.* 1989;173(3):659-661.

21. Trokel M, Discala C, Terrin NC, et al. Patient and injury characteristics in abusive abdominal injuries. *Pediatr Emerg Care.* 2006;22:700-704.

22. Lonergan GJ, Baker AM, Morey MK, Boos SC. From the archives of the AFIP. child abuse: radiologic-pathologic correlation. *Radiographics.* 2003;23(4):811-845.

23. Sivit CJ, Taylor GA, Bulas DI, Kushner DC, Potter BM, Eichelberger MR. Posttraumatic shock in children: CT findings associated with hemodynamic instability. *Radiology.* 1992;182(3):723-726.

24. Benya EC, Bulas DI, Eichelberger MR, et al. Splenic injury from blunt abdominal trauma in children: follow-up evaluation with CT. *Radiology.* 1995;195:685-688.

25. Saxena AK. Pediatric abdominal trauma. Medscape Web site. http://emedicine.medscape.com/article/1984811-overview. Accessed April 29, 2016.

26. Bryan AC, Gaultier C, Hodson WA. Chest wall mechanics in the newborn. *Development of the Lung*. 1977;6:871-888.

27. Rubin DM, McMillan CO, Helfaer MA, Christian CW. Pulmonary edema associated with child abuse: case reports and review of the literature. *Pediatrics*. 2001;108(3):769-775.

Chapter 3

Head Trauma

Melissa L. Currie, MD
Cynthia J. Curtsinger, BSN, RN, CCM, CFN, SANE
Brooke E. Jones, MD, MSc, FAAP
Vinod B. Rao, MD, FAAP
Suzanne P. Starling, MD, FAAP

Head injury is the leading cause of death and disability in physically abused children, especially in children younger than 4 years.[1] Infants rarely suffer serious injuries as a result of accidental head trauma. In the absence of a history of a severe accidental traumatic event, abusive injury should be strongly suspected. Historically, various terms have been used to describe abusive head trauma (AHT), including abusive head injury, shaken infant syndrome, shaken baby syndrome, shaken impact syndrome, and nonaccidental brain trauma. Although these diagnostic terms have all been used in the past, the terminology "abusive head trauma" was adopted in 2009 to encompass the full spectrum of clinical findings.[2] Forces generated during AHT can cause serious and permanent brain damage.

Mechanisms of Injury (Table 3-1)

— Contact force

1. Occurs from blunt trauma such as falls or abusive impact.
2. Can produce bruising, fractures, and/or intracranial injuries.

— Acceleration/deceleration/rotational forces

1. Occur during shaking or rare, serious accidental injuries such as a high-speed motor vehicle collisions and falls from significant heights (multiple stories).
2. Can cause serious intracranial injury, but there may be no external evidence of injury.

Table 3-1. Mechanisms of Head Injuries in Abusive Head Trauma
PRIMARY CONTACT INJURIES
Example: Direct impact — Soft tissue injury — Subgaleal hemorrhage (although more common from tractional force) — Subperiosteal hemorrhage — Skull fracture — Focal intracranial hemorrhage underlying skull fracture or impact site — Focal parenchymal injury underlying skull fracture or impact site — Focal parenchymal injury distant from contact site (ie, contrecoup)
PRIMARY ROTATIONAL INJURIES
Example: Shaking — Subdural hemorrhage not associated with skull fracture — Concussion without prolonged traumatic coma — Immediate loss of consciousness with prolonged traumatic coma
HYPOXIA/ISCHEMIA INJURIES
Example: Apnea, occuring in response to the primary injury — Focal cerebral edema — Diffuse cerebral edema

BLUNT IMPACT HEAD INJURY

EXTERNAL CRANIOFACIAL INJURY

— Minor blunt head trauma may occur after either accidental or abusive incidents.

— Head impact can be single or multiple and produce various types of injuries.

— When external injuries to the head, such as lacerations, abrasions, or contusions of the face, ears,[3,4] scalp, or mouth, are identified, screening for suspected abusive trauma is warranted.

— Discriminating bruising characteristics between abusive and accidental injury have been described using the acronym TEN-4 (**Table 3-2**).[5]

Table 3-2. TEN-4 Bruising Rule for Suspected Child Abuse

Infant < 4 months of age	Child < 4 years of age
— Any bruising, anywhere	— Bruising to the **T**orso, **E**ar, or **N**eck

— Children who are cruising (walking along furniture while holding onto it) or walking may sustain accidental bruises to the forehead and other bony prominences.[6] Bilateral "black eyes" can result from a single blunt impact to the forehead or anterior scalp with blood migrating (tracking) under the skin, which may be delayed from the initial injury.

— Absence of visible scalp injury does not preclude impact head trauma.[7]

1. If the head strikes a broad surface, the underlying scalp injury may be more diffuse and not externally visible.
2. Scalp hemorrhage not visible externally may appear on computed tomography (CT) scans, magnetic resonance imaging (MRI), or at autopsy (**Figures 3-1-a** and **b**).

Figure 3-1-a. *CT showing significant subgaleal hemorrhage overlying a skull fracture.*

Figure 3-1-b. *Right frontal subgaleal hemorrhage found during autopsy. This corresponds to the area of bruising noted on the forehead. However, it is possible to have either external bruising or subgaleal hemorrhage without the other being present.*

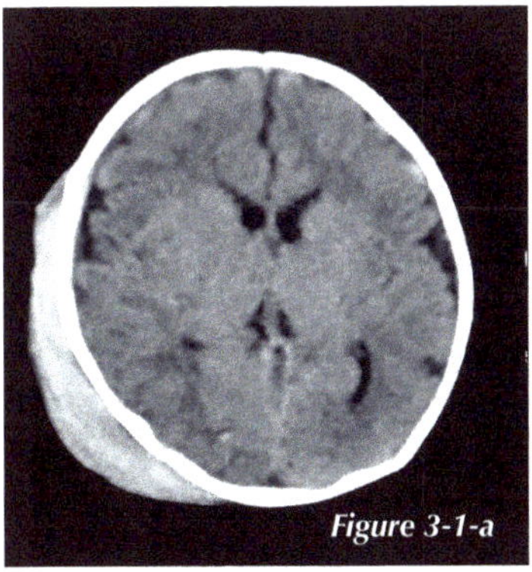

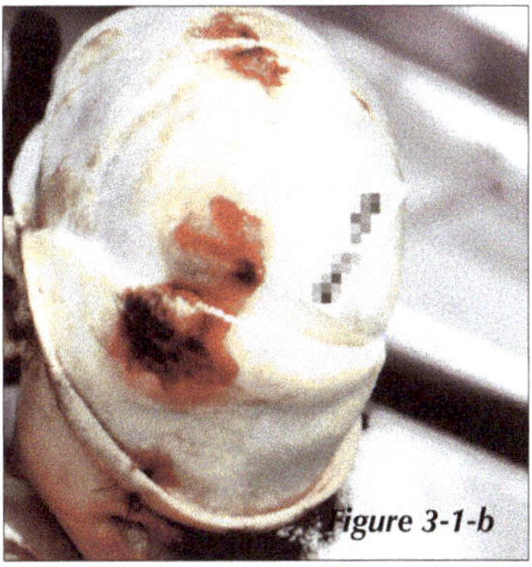

3. Scalp impact may appear as a soft fluctuant mass with or without bruising.
4. Simple subcutaneous scalp bleeding may occur with minor impact trauma and is seen as a hematoma or "goose egg" of subcutaneous tissue.
5. Mechanisms can include impact on soft surfaces that can cause intracranial injury without external cranial injury.

— Caput succedaneum, or subcutaneous bleeding, can occur in childbirth, and hemorrhage can cross suture lines.

— Cephalohematoma:

1. Cephalohematoma is a deeper hemorrhage that occurs under the fibrous periosteum of the skull.
2. It may occur during childbirth.
3. Bleeding does not cross suture lines.

— Subgaleal hemorrhage:

1. Subgaleal refers to potential space under galea aponeurotica. The aponeurosis is a dense sheet of connective tissue covering the cranial vault, over a loose layer of areolar tissue.
2. Subgaleal hemorrhage poses more adverse outcomes than previous discussed external craniofacial injuries.
3. Scalp traction (such as violent pulling of the hair) with significant shearing force can separate scalp and skull along the axis of the aponeurotic membrane, rupture veins, and produce traumatic hemorrhage into the potential space.
4. Injury can occur with impact trauma or traction injuries (although traction is more common); forcefully pulled hair should be considered, particularly in the presence of alopecia.
5. Signs may develop several days after injury, when the blood accumulated in the space becomes visible or palpable to a caregiver.
6. A significant amount of blood can accumulate with minimal increase in head circumference.[8,9] For this reason, hemoglobin and hematocrit should be monitored carefully.

Skull Fractures

— Skull fractures can be simple linear fractures or more complicated branched, stellate, or depressed fractures.

1. Linear fractures are common in both accidents and abuse.[10]
2. Nondisplaced linear fractures can occur in falls of less than 4 feet.[11-13]

— Cephalohematoma may occur early.

— Scalp swelling over the fracture line may occur.

— Scalp swelling from cephalohematoma may not be noticed for several days, if at all, due to gradual increase in size or the area being obscured by hair.

— Minor falls in ambulatory children are common, and simple skull fractures in children this age are not specific for child abuse; however, risk factors, additional history, and/or absence of history should be considered when interpreting these findings.

— Consider skull fractures in nonambulatory infants as concerning for abusive injury even in the presence of an appropriate mechanism of injury.

— More complicated fractures require more force; basilar, bilateral, and depressed fractures are rarely seen with falls less than 4 feet.[13]

— Complex, multiple, nonlinear, bilateral, displaced, depressed, and diastatic fractures are more common in abusive events than in accidental events (**Figures 3-2-a, b,** and **c**).[14,15,16]

— Complex fractures can occur in accidents including, but not limited to:

1. Falls onto contoured objects, which can produce depressed fractures even from relatively low heights.[17] Ping-pong skull deformities result when the skull is indented from a blunt impact (**Figure 3-3**).
2. Bilateral skull fracture can result from a single impact.

— Fractures sustained during impact may have small subdural hematomas under the point of contact caused by direct contact forces that disrupt bridging veins. With a corroborated history of accidental injury, such hemorrhages are not diagnostic of abuse.

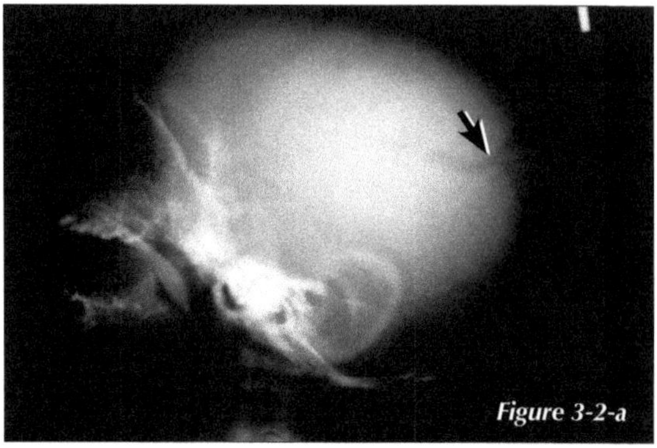

Figure 3-2-a. *Lateral skull film. Note the complex branched diastatic fracture (arrow).*

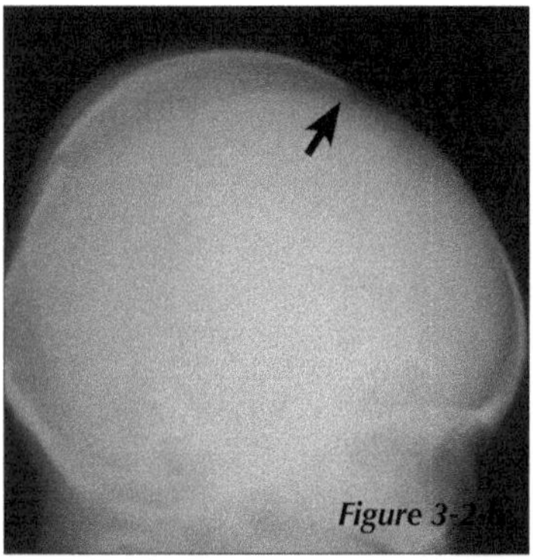

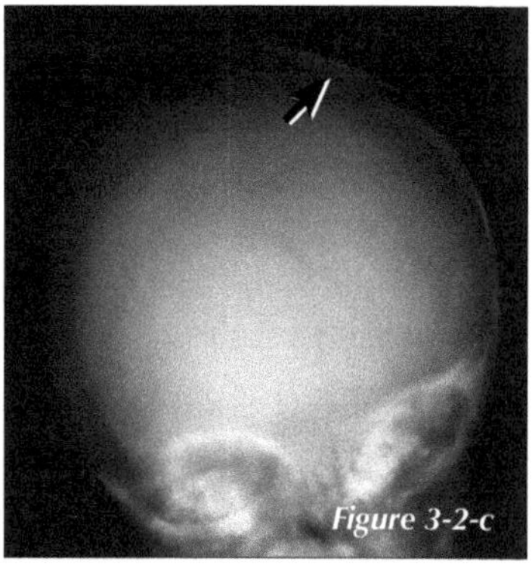

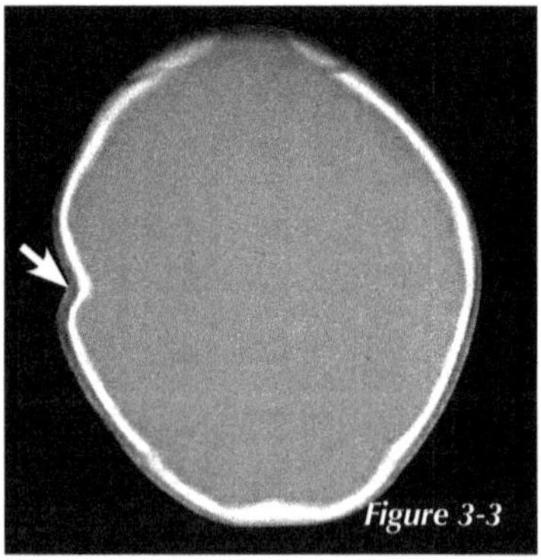

Figure 3-2-b and **c.** *The infant has a diastatic fracture of the right parietal bone (arrows). Note that the fracture margins are widely separated, indicating a high-velocity impact injury or a severe force applied to the skull. Accidental (short fall) injuries are usually linear, short in length, and pencil-line thin. Short falls to flat surfaces should not be fatal.*

Figure 3-3. *CT revealing ping-pong fracture of the skull (arrow).*

— Periorbital ecchymosis, Battle's sign (postauricular ecchymosis), hemotympanum, and/or CSF otorrhea or rhinorrhea may indicate a basilar skull fracture.[18]

Epidural Hemorrhage

— Epidural hemorrhage (EDH) is relatively uncommon in children, but it can occur with seemingly minor trauma (**Figure 3-4**).

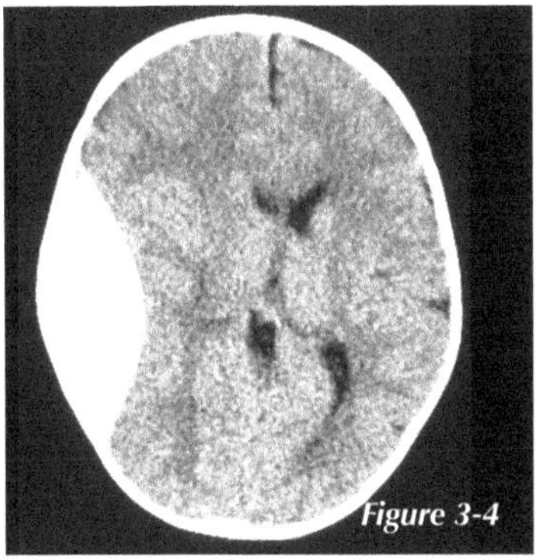

Figure 3-4. *A CT scan illustrating a large hyperdense acute epidural hematoma in the right parietal region with convex margins. There is effacement of adjacent sulci and the right lateral ventricle with shift of the midline structures. There is a parietal bone fracture on the bone window setting. Epidural hemorrhages are often the result of accidents but can occur with an abusive impact as well.*

— The majority of EDH are associated with skull fractures; however, they can rarely occur without.

  — The infant's immature skull cannot resist compression and deforms easily.[19]

  — Arteries and veins adhere tightly beneath the skull, so impact and deformation can rupture vessels and produce EDH.

— About 45% of EDHs in children occur in falls less than 5 to 6 feet.[20,21]

— Most children with EDH (with or without skull fracture) have no other injuries, and isolated cases with a clear history rarely suggest abusive trauma.[21,22]

— Children with epidural bleeding can have no or minor direct brain injury, producing no or limited symptoms initially.

— After initial symptoms resolve, children may behave relatively normally (lucid period) until the pressure of the expanding hematoma impairs consciousness.

Rotational Head Injury and Abusive Head Trauma

Mechanisms of Injury

— Findings associated with AHT may include but are not limited to parenchymal injury, intracranial hemorrhage, retinal hemorrhage, fractures, and bruising.

— Hemorrhage and contusion of the brain can occur with rotational displacement of the head, with or without impact.[23-25]

— The shearing force associated with rapid acceleration causes tension on the bridging veins' attachments to the sagittal sinus, producing subdural hemorrhage.[26]

— Any mechanism with significant repetitive whiplash rotation of the head creates rotational acceleration, potentially causing the findings seen in AHT.

Clinical Presentation

— AHT can occur at any age but is most common in infants averaging 4 months of age.[6,27,28]

— The stimulus for abuse is usually inconsolable crying.[28,29] The age-specific incidence curve for normal infant crying and for hospitalized AHT cases has a similar starting point and shape; however, the peak for AHT occurs about 4-6 weeks later.[30]

— Sign and symptoms may be dramatic or subtle enough to be missed by a clinician.

— Signs and symptoms may include vomiting, irritability, bulging fontanel, and sleepiness. These mimic those of infection and result in missed diagnoses in more than 30% of cases.[31]

1. The most common mistaken diagnoses in cases of AHT are gastroenteritis, accidents, sepsis, increased head circumference, otitis media, and seizures.
2. If a lumbar puncture is done to diagnose infection and returns bloody cerebrospinal fluid (CSF), it may be misinterpreted as a traumatic tap, overlooking the presence of subarachnoid hemorrhage (SAH).[32,33] SAH can be distinguished by finding xanthrochromia on a spun CSF sample, indicating the breakdown

of blood products in the subarachnoid space. Steps should be taken to rule out increased intracranial pressure prior to lumbar puncture to prevent brainstem herniation.

— Head trauma is more likely to be considered when children are brought to medical attention with facial bruising, compromised breathing, seizures, or in a comatose state.[31]

— Steps in evaluation include:

1. Elicit a specific history and timeline of the injury. The usual history is a minor accidental blunt head trauma, which delays the diagnosis, especially when no external injuries are visible. Caregivers with knowledge of abusive acts may minimize or not provide any history of trauma.
2. Explore and document details of the reported mechanism of injury, eg, height of the fall, type of flooring/surface present, position of the child upon impact.
3. Note if the history varies over time or between caregivers, the reported child behavior is not developmentally appropriate, or the described events do not explain the injuries.
4. Investigators should obtain history from all verbal children in the environment.

Retinal Hemorrhages

— Retinal hemorrhage occurs in 70% to 90% of abusive head trauma cases.[7,34-37]

— Retinal hemorrhages are described according to the layer in which they occur, their location on the retina, and their number or severity.

1. ***Preretinal hemorrhages*:** Occur in front of the retina and lie directly under the vitreous layer, obscuring the vessels under them. They are also called subhyaloid hemorrhages.
2. ***Subretinal hemorrhages*:** Are beneath the retina and are characterized by seeing retinal vessels over them.
3. ***Intraretinal hemorrhages*:** Are in retinal layers and are typically described as flame, dot, or blot, based on size and appearance.

— If the blood of the hemorrhage mixes with the vitreous, it is called a vitreous hemorrhage.

— Hemorrhages in multiple layers of the retina, vitreous, and/or reaching to the retina's edge are more specific for abusive head trauma.[38]

— Because visual loss is related more to cortical brain injury than retinal damage, more severe brain injury correlates with worse visual prognosis.[36,39]

— The hemorrhage may be secondary to severe angular acceleration with or without impact and without direct ocular injury.[40]

Differential Diagnosis

— The normal birth process by vaginal delivery causes retinal hemorrhages in 25.6% of cases, with an increased incidence with assisted delivery.[41]

1. These hemorrhages are typically posterior, intraretinal, and range in severity.[41]
2. Birth-related hemorrhages typically fully resolve by 1 month of age.[42]

— Childhood sources include sepsis, leukemia, meningococcal meningitis, coagulopathy, and vasculitis.[43]

1. Hemorrhages are usually minor and limited to posterior retina.
2. Seizures do not cause retinal hemorrhages.[44,45]

— Serious accidental trauma can produce retinal hemorrhages.[22,46-50] In rare cases, cardiopulmonary resuscitation in children after such trauma can produce small posterior hemorrhages.

— Adults can develop retinal hemorrhages in Terson syndrome and Purtscher disease.[37] These entities are extremely rare in children, and when they have been reported, the type and distribution has been different than the type and distribution of retinal hemorrhages seen in AHT.[51,52]

Diagnosis of Brain Injury

— A dilated ophthalmologic examination by a trained pediatric ophthalmologist is warranted. Hemorrhage is missed in 29% of cases when non-ophthalmologists perform the examination.[36]

— Dilated examination is ideal; however, if the patient is too unstable for dilation, a nondilated examination may be a reasonable first step. A dilated examination should occur when stable and medically cleared in coordination with neurosurgery.

— Direct ophthalmoscopy yields a limited view of the posterior retina and does not diagnose more extensive hemorrhage.

— Indirect ophthalmoscopy allows a more complete examination and possibly photographic documentation.

Diagnostic Imaging

Skull films, ultrasound, CT, and magnetic resonance imaging (MRI) are the modalities that may be used during the course of evaluation of head injury (**Table 3-3**). (See also Chapter 2, "Radiology.")

— It is important to remember that head ultrasound has limited utility in the evaluation of AHT.

Table 3-3. Diagnostic Imaging of Head Injuries in Child Abuse

	Skull Film	Head U/S*	CT	MRI
Fracture	+++	+++	++	–
SAH	–	‡	+++	+
Acute SDH†/EDH	–	‡	+++	++
Chronic SDH	–	+/–	+	+++
Parenchymal Contusion/ Shear Injury	–	+(frontal)	+	+++
Parenchymal Atrophy Encephalomalacia	–	–	++	+++

* *Head U/S should be used only if accompanied by CT or MRI.*

† *SDH, subdural hemorrhage*

‡ *Reliably differentiates convexity SDH from SAH.*

Key: +++ Very useful; ++ moderately useful; + occasionally useful; – not usually helpful.

— A brain MRI should be strongly considered when there are findings on head CT. This includes the finding of enlarged subarachnoid spaces, as this can be an indication of subdural hemorrhage.

Associated Injuries in Abusive Head Trauma

— AHT may be brought to medical attention with or without extracranial markers of abuse: (ie, bruising, fractures, spinal injury, and/or abdominal trauma).[53]

— Any fracture can be seen with AHT. The most common are metaphyseal injuries, rib fractures (both posterior and lateral), and skull fractures.[54]

— Burns or abdominal trauma may be noted.

— Infants with normal respirations, no seizures, no facial bruising or other bodily trauma, or living in 2-parent homes are more likely to be missed.[31]

— Even with no risk factors suggesting abuse, infants with unexplained subdural hematomas may need to be reported to child protective agencies.[55]

Intracranial Injury

— Infants are more prone to abusive traumatic brain injury because:

1. Their heads are large in proportion to their bodies.
2. They have underdeveloped neck musculature.
3. Their brains are less myelinated and have higher water content, permitting greater compression and excessive stretching of the bridging vessels and the parenchyma.
4. Their skull bases are shallow, permitting greater rotation of the brain in response to external forces.

Subdural Hemorrhage

— Subdural hemorrhage (SDH) is the intracranial finding most often associated with AHT; others include interhemispheric falx hemorrhage, excess nonacute extra-axial fluid, subarachnoid hemorrhage, axonal injury, and basal ganglia edema.[56]

— Bilateral convexity SDH correlates significantly with abuse, although unilateral SDH can be seen.[57] The specific site most related to abuse is the interhemispheric region, found in 61% to 89% of abusive cases.[57,58]

— The small amount of blood tracking between the brain hemispheres can be mistaken for the normal falx[59,60] and vice versa.

— Intracranial hemorrhages in abuse can be nonsurgical and may or may not constitute a surgical emergency.

— Initial imaging can be normal, with follow-up imaging showing an evolving hemorrhage. Follow-up CT scans are recommended and can lead to significant changes in clinical management.[61,62]

— Hyperacute subdural hemorrhages may involve mixed densities and the appearance of layering,[63] causing the potential for inaccurate interpretation of multiple ages of blood.

Axonal Injury

— Axonal injury resulting from abuse can be focal or diffuse.

— Diffuse axonal injury (DAI) is a form of widespread brain injury that occurs when the mechanical forces of trauma cause direct damage to the brain's axons. Immature brains have less myelination and are more prone to axonal injuries.

— In severe DAI, children suffer immediate loss of consciousness.[23,56,64]

— With less severe DAI, the level of consciousness is immediately diminished, as in concussion.[23,56,64]

— Shear injury, visible on CT or MRI, can accompany severe DAI and may appear as cleftlike tears at the cortex–white matter junction (gliding contusion) (**Figure 3-5**).

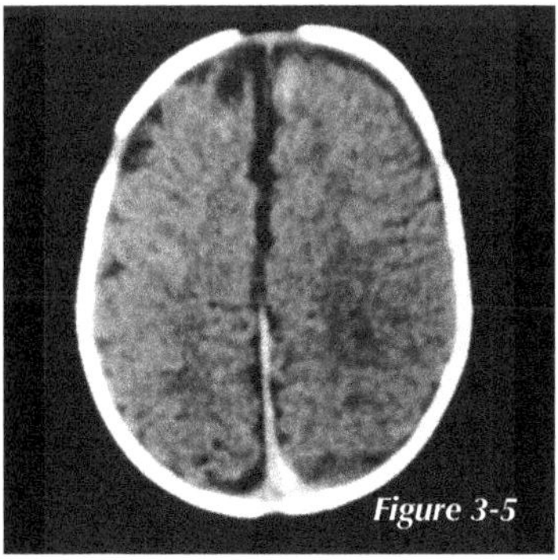

Figure 3-5. *Interhemispheric subdural hemorrhage. Note also intraparenchymal bleeding and shearing injury.*

1. Shear injuries are subtle and vary in radiologic interpretation.[56]
2. MRI is more sensitive in diagnosing shear injuries than CT.[65]

— DAI can be undetectable on CT or MRI, but at autopsy, gross hemorrhagic lesions of white matter may be seen in the corpus callosum and brainstem.

— Microscopically, DAI is visible using special staining that reveal accumulation bulbs (axonal retraction balls).

1. When axons are injured, materials being transported down the axon accumulate at the area of cellular damage.
2. The injury may take hours to days to develop sufficiently for visualization of DAI on microscopy, depending on the stain used.
3. If the injury is rapidly fatal, no axonal material accumulates and bulbs are not seen at autopsy. Lack of pathologic evidence of DAI does not prove that it did not occur. Pathologic evidence may be lacking even when other signs are found.[66]

Primary Versus Secondary Injuries

— Primary injuries[67,68]:

- — Primary parenchymal injuries occur at the moment of trauma due to deformational trauma of the brain tissue itself.
- — Primary injuries can be either contact or inertial injuries and include intracranial bleeding, contusions, DAI, and fractures. Severe DAI may be irreversible.
- — Severity of injury depends on direction of forces, amount of force applied, and when present, the repetitive nature of the trauma.[22,23,69,70]

— Secondary injuries:

- — Secondary injuries occur when brain cells die in response to the primary injuries.
- — They can include intracranial hypertension from space-occupying lesions, acquired coagulopathy from brain injury, molecular responses to primary injury,[71,72] and cerebral infarction from shock, apnea, or cerebral edema.

— Trauma-induced apnea is a significant secondary cause of injury. Primary traumatic axonal injury of the medullary centers of respiration can cause apnea and respiratory difficulty in infants, which then cause hypoxia and/or ischemia that affect the brain globally, leading to cellular destruction.[73] In theory, hypoxia from any cause should affect both halves of the brain symmetrically, producing bilateral damage.

— Cerebral edema evolves with traumatic brain injury, but it is often evident on CT images taken 1 to 3 hours after injury.[61,74] MRI evidence of restricted diffusion of focal areas of edema may take up to 3 days to appear.[75]

— Cerebral edema may be found with regional loss of cerebrovascular autoregulation or vascular occlusion from herniation, but can also occur as a result of local molecular responses to injury.[71,72]

— Severe edema can manifest as a "reversal sign" on CT (**Figure 3-6**). The deep cerebral nuclei and cerebellum appear denser (brighter) than the cerebral hemispheres.[76]

— Finding a reversal sign and SDH, especially falcine hemorrhage, is highly suggestive of AHT[56,57] and is a very poor prognostic sign.[77]

— Cerebral infarction, brain atrophy, and encephalomalacia are common sequelae of AHT (**Figure 3-7**). Dead cells are resorbed, producing volume loss and generalized atrophy. The onset of atrophy can be rapid, occurring as early as 7 days after injury.[61]

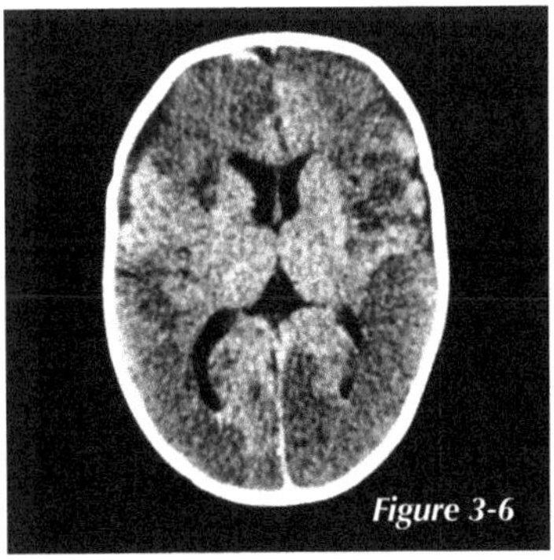

Figure 3-6. *Reversal sign. Note the paradoxically bright-appearing central structures with the lower attentuation of the cortex.*

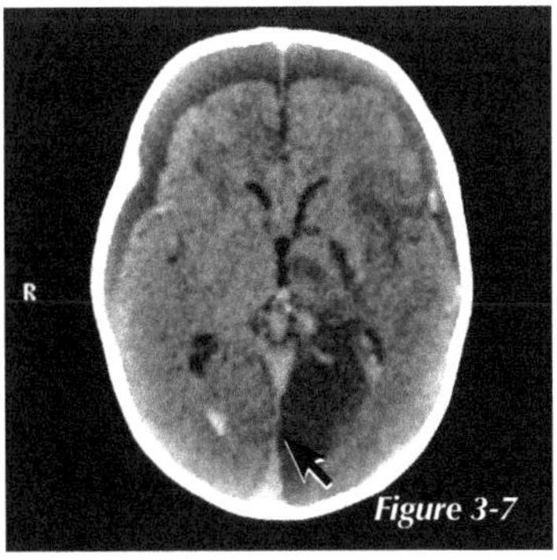

Figure 3-7. *Cystic encephalomalacia (arrow) subsequent to abusive head trauma. Note also the chronic bilateral subdural hemorrhages.*

Spinal Injury

— Spinal injury has accompanied AHT,[78,79,80] but it is not required to support the diagnosis.

— Spinal injury is often occult, particularly in the setting of coma or altered mental status.

— MRI of the entire spine occurs more often in clinical settings to detect spinal cord, vascular, and ligamentous injury.[80,81] While vertebral fracture is uncommon, ligamentous injury can be detected, as well as spinal subdural bleeding and epidural bleeding.

— The approach to clinical management of these injuries is not yet clear.

— The increased awareness of and screening for spinal injury confirms the need for cervical collar prior to complete evaluation.

Timing of Injury

— All aspects related to determining the timing of injury should be done in consultation with a child abuse specialist.

— Determining when an abusive event took place may help investigators identify the perpetrator, but critical histories are often falsified or minimized.

— **Table 3-4** lists important historical information in developing a timeline of events[82]:

Table 3-4. Important Historical Questions/Components

Timeline of symptoms	Detailed History of Trauma (When Applicable)

— What were the events before and after symptoms development?
— When was the child last "normal?"
— What did the caretaker do after the child developed symptoms?
— How long did it take to seek care?
— Who was caring for the child?
	— What happened?
	— Was it witnessed?
	— How was the child found?
	— How did the child act after the trauma?
	— If there is a history of a fall:
	  — How did the child land?
	  — Where did the child fall from?
	  — Height of the fall?
	  — What did the child land on (ie, flooring material)?

— A comprehensive medical evaluation, including imaging studies, laboratory studies, physical findings, and clinical history/ presentation is essential when determining timing of injuries.

1. ***Imaging studies***: Dating intracranial hemorrhages using CT and MRI should be approached with caution. Unless clear signs of acute injury correlate with clinical status, the ability to date head injury is limited.

2. ***Physical findings***: Head injuries with mild symptoms, chronic head injuries, retinal hemorrhages, and bruises are difficult to date.[37,83-85]

3. ***Combined history and clinical presentation***: Child accident victims and abused children differ in mechanism of injury, but the symptoms of traumatic parenchymal brain injury are always immediate, whether mild or severe. Children who appear well, eat, and are playful did not suffer a devastating parenchymal injury earlier in the day.[74,86] Symptoms secondary to intracranial hemorrhage may have more variability in timing of onset.

Differential Diagnosis

— No medical condition completely mimics all the signs and symptoms of AHT. Most disorders in the differential are readily excluded with history, physical examination, and preliminary testing.

— Several illnesses can produce retinal hemorrhages or intracranial bleeding, but none encompass both to the same extent as seen in AHT.

— The presence of an underlying medical condition (with some features of AHT) does not preclude the possibility of AHT.

— The most common differential diagnosis for AHT is accidental injury.

— **Table 3-5** lists clinical conditions to consider in the differential diagnosis.[87]

— **Table 3-6** compares the findings in accidents with those of AHT.

Bleeding Disorders

— Platelet dysfunction, as seen in Von Willebrand disease and idiopathic thrombocytopenic purpura, usually causes superficial bleeding into soft tissue and is not generally seen with intracranial hemorrhage.

Table 3-5. Differential Diagnosis of Abusive Head Trauma

Accidents — Falls — Other household injury — Motor vehicle collision **Infection** — Meningitis — Encephalitis — Sepsis **Birth/prenatal** — Birth trauma — Prenatal abdominal assaults (from intimate partner violence) — Maternal pre-eclampsia associated subdural hemorrhages **Metabolic and genetic diseases/ nutritional deficiencies** — Glutaricaciduria type 1 (GA-1) — Menkes kinky hair syndrome — Scurvy — Osler-Weber-Rendu syndrome	**Hematologic/oncologic diseases** — Platelet or factor disorders — Idiopathic Thrombocytopenic Purpura — Liver disease — Vitamin K deficiency — Disseminated intravascular coagulation — Leukemia — Lymphoma **Autoimmune/vasculitis conditions** — Moyamoya disease — Systemic lupus erythematosus **Intracranial pathology** — Subarachnoid cysts — Sinus thrombosis — Ruptured arteriovenous malformation — Tumors — Ruptured cerebral aneurysm — Encephalocele

— Infants with hemophilia can initially have intracranial hemorrhage,[88] but the clinical history, family history, and laboratory results usually differentiate it from abuse. A study evaluating head trauma in patients with Hemophilia A, Hemophilia B, and Von Willebrand disease showed that out of 43 patients with a reported 109 episodes of head injury, only 5 had intracranial injury.[89]

— Infants who did not receive vitamin K at birth may have hemorrhagic disease of the newborn caused by vitamin K deficiency. This disorder occurs in 1 of 200 to 400 births[90] and responds to treatment with vitamin K, confirming the diagnosis.

— Bleeding disorders do not explain retinal hemorrhages or brain injury.

Table 3-6. Comparison of Accidental and Abusive Head Trauma	
ACCIDENTAL	ABUSIVE
— Low incidence of intracranial hemorrhage and parenchymal injury	— High incidence of intracranial hemorrhage and parenchymal injury
— SDH found in 10% of cases[10,91]	— SDH found in 50% of cases[10,91]
— SDH and more severe parenchymal injury are more common with motor vehicle collision, which are usually witnessed events	— Injuries occur, but event is claimed not to have been witnessed
— Severe cases cause intracranial hemorrhage, cerebral edema, and posterior retinal hemorrhage	— Magnitude of injury is much greater than would be found with minor reported event
— Extensive retinal hemorrhage and diffuse brain injury do not result from minor falls and household accidents	— Histories of minor falls are often provided as an explanation for extensive retinal hemorrhage and diffuse brain injury
— Victims are significantly older[91]	— Victims are usually nonambulatory infants

— Prolonged clotting times occur in children hospitalized with severe traumatic head injury, but the prolonged clotting studies are of lesser magnitude than in overt bleeding disorders.

— When coagulopathy is found with traumatic brain injury and evidence of parenchymal injury, coagulopathy occurs as a result of the injury.[92]

Metabolic Disorders

— Glutaric aciduria type 1 (GA-1) is a rare autosomal recessive metabolic disorder. It usually manifests after 6 to 18 months of normal development. Features consist of hypotonia, loss of head control, seizures, dystonia, macrocephaly at birth, encephalopathy, and motor delay. CT scans can show dilated lateral ventricles, widened cortical sulci, and frontotemporal brain atrophy.[93] Children with GA-1 are susceptible to subdural hematomas, due to cerebral atrophy and stretching of the cortical veins. When subdural hematomas are detected, CT imaging will also demonstrate other brain abnormalities seen with GA-1.[94]

— Retinal hemorrhages are not part of GA-1, and a careful history and examination rules out the disorder.

Birth Injury

— Asymptomatic intracranial hemorrrhage can occur in newborns, most often following vaginal birth, assisted vaginal birth, or a trial of labor followed by cesarean section.

— The deformity of the skull during delivery may result in strain and disruption of the dura, resulting in subdural hemorrhage.

— These hemorrhages are generally small and resolve within a month.[95]

— Due to their unique characteristics, birth-related hemorrhages are not generally confused with AHT.[96]

Intracranial Pathology

— Ruptured subarachnoid cysts, venous sinus thrombosis, arteriovenous malformations, and intracranial tumors may cause intracranial hemorrhage.[87]

— Usually the bleeding distribution does not resemble that of abusive trauma, and retinal hemorrhages are not seen in most cases.

Outcomes

— AHT has a very high mortality rate, estimated to be between 11% and 33%.[82]

— Survivors of AHT are likely to have significant morbidity associated with their injury, including long-term developmental, cognitive, and behavioral delays.[82]

— The most common disabilities that may occur as a result of AHT range from mild learning disorders to devastating neurological sequelae, such as paralysis, blindness, hearing impairment, and vegetative states.[97]

— At least 40% will have severe deficits requiring long-term care.[98]

— Deficits in younger children are frequently underestimated and only become apparent as the child fails to achieve developmental milestones or experiences cognitive and behavioral difficulties in school.[98]

References

1. Michaud LJ. Inflicted childhood neurotrauma: outcomes and rehabilitation. In: Reece RM, Nicholson CE, eds. *Inflicted Childhood Neurotrauma*. Evansville, IL: American Academy of Pediatrics; 2003:255-264.
2. Christian CW, Block R. Abusive head trauma in infants and children. *Pediatrics*. 2009;123(5):1409-1411.
3. Hanigan WC, Peterson RA, Njus G. Tin ear syndrome: rotational acceleration in pediatric head injuries. *Pediatrics*. 1987;80(5):618-622.
4. Feldman KW. Patterned abusive bruises of the buttocks and the pinnae. *Pediatrics*. 1992;90(4):633-636.
5. Pierce MC, Kaczor K, Aldridge S, O'Flynn J, Lorenz DJ. Bruising characteristics discriminating physical child abuse from accidental trauma. *Pediatrics*. 2010;125(1):67-74.
6. Sugar NF, Taylor JA, Feldman KW. Bruises in infants and toddlers: those who don't cruise rarely bruise. *Arch Pediatr Adolesc Med*. 1999;153(4):399-403.
7. Duhaime AC, Gennarelli TA, Thibault LE, Bruce DA, Margulies SS, Wiser R. The shaken baby syndrome: a clinical, pathological and biomechanical study. *J Neurosurg*. 1987;66(3):409-415.
8. Levkoff AH, Macpherson RI, Wood BP. Radiological case of the month: unrecognized subaponeurotic hemorrhage. *Am J Dis Child*. 1992;146(7):833-834.
9. Kuban K, Winston K, Breanan M. Childhood subgaleal hematoma following minor head trauma. *Am J Dis Child*. 1983;137:637-640.
10. Reece RM, Sege R. Childhood head injuries: accidental or inflicted? *Arch Pediatr Adolesc Med*. 2000;154(1):11-15.
11. Helfer RE, Slovis TL, Black M. Injuries resulting when small children fall out of bed. *Pediatrics*. 1977;60(4):533-535.
12. Lyons TJ, Oates RK. Falling out of bed: a relatively benign occurrence. *Pediatrics*. 1993;92(1):125-127.
13. Nimityongskul P, Anderson LD. The likelihood of injuries when children fall out of bed. *J Pediatr Orthop*. 1987;7(2):184-186.

14. Hobbs CJ. Skull fracture and the diagnosis of abuse. *Arch Dis Child.* 1984;59(3):246-252.
15. Meservy CJ, Towbin R, McLaurin RL, Myers PA, Ball W. Radiographic characteristics of skull fractures resulting from child abuse. *AJR Am J Roentgenol.* 1987;149:173-175.
16. Kelly P, John S, Vincent AL, Reed P. Abusive head trauma and accidental head injury: a 20-year comparative study of referrals to a hospital child protection team. *Arch Dis Child.* 2015;100(12):1123-1130.
17. Williams RA. Injuries in infants and small children resulting from witnessed and corroborated free falls. *J Trauma.* 1991;31(10):1350-1352.
18. Baugnon KL, Hudgins PA. Skull base fractures and their complications. *Neuroimaging Clin N Am.* 2014;24(3):439-465.
19. Margulies SS, Thibault KL. Infant skull and suture properties: measurement and implications for mechanisms of pediatric brain injury. *J Biomech Eng.* 2000;122(4):364-371.
20. Schutzman SA, Barnes PD, Mantello M, Scott RM. Epidural hematomas in children. *Ann Emerg Med.* 1993;22(3):535-541.
21. Shugerman RP, Paez A, Grossman DC, Feldman KW, Grady MS. Epidural hemorrhage: is it abuse? *Pediatrics.* 1996;97(5):664-668.
22. Duhaime AC, Alario AJ, Lewander WJ, et al. Head injury in very young children: mechanisms, injury types, and ophthalmologic findings in 100 hospitalized patients younger than 2 years of age. *Pediatrics.* 1992;90 (2 pt 1):179-185.
23. Ommaya AK, Faas F, Yarnell P. Whiplash injury and brain damage: an experimental study. *JAMA.* 1968;204(4):285-289.
24. Gennarelli TA, Thibault LE. Biomechanics of acute subdural hematoma. *J Trauma.* 1982;22(8):680-686.
25. Case ME, Graham MA, Handy TC, Jentzen JM, Monteleone JA; National Association of Medical Examiners As Hoc Committee on Shaken Baby Syndrome. Position paper on fatal abusive head injuries in infants and young children. *Am J Forensic Med Pathol.* 2001;22(2):112-122.
26. Case ME. Inflicted traumatic brain injury in infants and young children. *Brain Pathol.* 2008;18(4):571-582.

27. Keenan HT, Runyan DK, Marshall SW, Nocera MA, Merten DF, Sinal SH. A population-based study of inflicted traumatic brain injury in young children. *JAMA*. 2003;290(5):621-626.
28. Adamsbaum C, Grabar S, Mejean N, Rey-Salmon C. Abusive head trauma: judicial admissions highlight violent and repetitive shaking. *Pediatrics*. 2010;126(3):546-555.
29. Barr M, Barr RG, Taylor T, Wicks A, Williams D, Coleman K. Prevention and education. In: Frasier L, Rauth-Farley K, Alexander R. *Abusive Head Trauma in Infants and Children: A Medical, Legal & Forensic Reference*. Saint Louis, MO: GW Medical Publishing, Inc; 2006:485-503.
30. Barr RG, Trent RB, Cross J. Age-related incidence curve of hospitalized shaken baby syndrome cases: convergent evidence for crying as a trigger to shaking. *Child Abuse Negl*. 2006;30(1):7-16.
31. Jenny C, Hymel KP, Ritzen A, Reinert SE, Hay TC. Analysis of missed cases of abusive head trauma. *JAMA*. 1999;281(7):621-626.
32. Apolo JO. Bloody cerebrospinal fluid: traumatic tap or child abuse? *Pediatr Emerg Care*. 1987;3(2):93-95.
33. Spear RM, Chadwick D, Peterson BM. Fatalities associated with misinterpretation of bloody cerebrospinal fluid in the shaken baby syndrome. *Am J Dis Child*. 1992;146(12):1415-1417.
34. Ludwig S, Warman M. Shaken baby syndrome: a review of 20 cases. *Ann Emerg Med*. 1984;13(2):104-107.
35. Billmire ME, Myers PA. Serious head injury in infants: accident or abuse? *Pediatrics*. 1985;75(2):340-342.
36. Kivlin JD, Simons KB, Lazoritz S, Ruttum MS. Shaken baby syndrome. *Ophthalmology*. 2000;107(7):1246-1254.
37. Levin A. Retinal haemorrhage and child abuse. In: David TJ, ed. *Recent Advances in Paediatric*. No. 18. London, England: Churchill Livingstone; 2000:151-219.
38. Betz P, Puschel K, Miltner E, Lignitz E, Eisenmenger W. Morphometrical analysis of retinal hemorrhages in the shaken baby syndrome. *Forensic Sci Int*. 1996;78(1):71-80.

39. McCabe CF, Donahue SP. Prognostic indicators for vision and mortality in shaken baby syndrome. *Arch Ophthalmol.* 2000;118(3):373-377.

40. Ophthalmology Working Party of the Royal College of Ophthalmologists. Child abuse and the eye. *Eye.* 1999;13:3-10.

41. Watts P, Maguire S, Kwok T, et al. Newborn retinal hemorrhages: a systematic review. *J AAPOS.* 2013;17(1):70-78.

42. Hughes LA, May K, Talbot JF, Parsons MA. Incidence, distribution, and duration of birth-related retinal hemorrhages: a prospective study. *J AAPOS.* 2006;10(2):102-106.

43. Levin AV. Retinal hemorrhage in abusive head trauma. *Pediatrics.* 2010;126(5):961-970.

44. Sandramouli S, Robinson R, Tsaloumas M, Willshaw HE. Retinal hemorrhage and convulsions. *Arch Dis Child.* 1997;76(5):449-451.

45. Tyagi AK, Scotcher S, Koxeis N, Willshaw HE. Can convulsions alone cause retinal hemorrhages in infants? *Br J Ophthalmol.* 1998;82:659-660.

46. Elder JE, Taylor RG, Klug GL. Retinal hemorrhage in accidental head trauma in childhood. *J Paediatr Child Health.* 1991;27(5):286-289.

47. Buys YM, Levin AV, Enzenauer RW, et al. Retinal findings after head trauma in infants and young children. *Ophthalmology.* 1992;99(11):1718-1723.

48. Johnson DL, Braun D, Friendly D. Accidental head trauma and retinal hemorrhage. *Neurosurgery.* 1993;33(2):231-235.

49. Gilliland MG, Luckenbach MW, Chenier TC. Systemic and ocular findings in 169 prospectively studied child deaths: retinal hemorrhages usually mean child abuse. *Forensic Sci Int.* 1994;68(2):117-132.

50. Kivlin JD, Currie ML, Greenbaum VJ, Simons KB, Jentzen J. Retinal hemorrhages in children following fatal motor vehicle crashes: a case series. *Arch Ophthalmol.* 2008;126(6):800-804.

51. Pham H, Enzenauer RW, Elder JE, Levin AV. Retinal hemorrhage after cardiopulmonary resuscitation with chest compressions. *Am J Forensic Med Pathol.* 2013;34(2):122-124.

52. Binenbaum G, Rogers DL, Forbes BJ, et al. Patterns of retinal hemorrhage associated with increased intracranial pressure in children. *Pediatrics*. 2013;132(2):e430-e434.
53. Parks SE, Kegler SR, Annest JL, Mercy JA. Characteristics of fatal abusive head trauma among children in the USA: 2003–2007: an application of the CDC operational case definition to national vital statistics data. *Inj Prev*. 2012;18(3):193-199.
54. Merten DF, Osbourne DRS, Radkowski MA, Leonidas JC. Craniocerebral trauma in the child abuse syndrome: radiological observations. *Pediatr Radiol*. 1984;14(5):272-277.
55. Morris MW, Smith S, Cressman J, Ancheta J. Evaluation of infants with subdural hematoma who lack external evidence of abuse. *Pediatrics*. 2000;105(3 pt 1):549-553.
56. Hymel KP, Rumack CM, Hay TC, Strain JD, Jenny C. Comparison of intracranial computed tomographic (CT) findings in pediatric abusive and accidental head trauma. *Pediatr Radiol*. 1997;27(9):743-747.
57. Rao P, Carty H, Pierce A. The acute reversal sign: comparison of medical and nonaccidental injury patients. *Clin Radiol*. 1999;54(8):495-501.
58. Zimmerman RA, Bilaniuk LT, Bruce D, Schut L, Uzzell B, Goldberg HI. Computed tomography of craniocerebral injury in the abused child. *Radiology*. 1979;130(3):687-690.
59. Zimmerman RD, Russell EJ, Yurberg E, Leeds NE. Falx and interhemispheric fissure on axial CT: II. recognition and differentiation of interhemispheric subarachnoid and subdural hemorrhage. *AJNR Am J Neuroradiol*. 1982;3(6):635-642.
60. Cohen RA, Kaufman RA, Myers PA, Towbin RB. Cranial tomography in the abused child with head injury. *AJR Am J Roentgenol*. 1986;146(1):97-102.
61. Dias MS, Backstrom J, Falk M, Li V. Serial radiography in the infant shaken impact syndrome. *Pediatr Neurosurg*. 1998;29(2):77-85.
62. Feldman KW, Brewer DK, Shaw DW. Evolution of the cranial computed tomography scan in child abuse. *Child Abuse Negl*. 1995;19(3):307-314.

63. Fernando S, Obaldo RE, Walsh IR, Lowe LH. Neuroimaging of nonaccidental head trauma: pitfalls and controversies. *Pediatr Radiol.* 2008;38(8):827-838.

64. Parker JR, Parker JC Jr, Overman JC. Intracranial diffuse axonal injury at autopsy. *Ann Clin Lab Sci.* 1990;20(3):220-224.

65. Sato Y, Yuh WT, Smith WL, Alexander RC, Kao SC, Ellerbroek CJ. Head injury in child abuse: evaluation with MR imaging. *Radiology.* 1989;173(3):653-657.

66. Alexander RC, Levitt CJ, Smith WL. Abusive head trauma. In: Reece RM, Ludwig S, eds. *Child Abuse: Medical Diagnosis and Management.* 2nd ed. Philadelphia, PA: Lippincott; 2001:47-80.

67. Zuckerman GB, Conway EE Jr. Accidental head injury. *Pediatr Ann.* 1997;26(10):621-632.

68. Hymel KP, Bandak FA, Partington MD, Winston KR. Abusive head trauma: a biomechanics-based approach. *Child Maltreat.* 1998;3:116-128.

69. Bonnier C, Mesples B, Carpentier S, Henin D, Gressens P. Delayed white matter injury in a murine model of shaken baby syndrome. *Brain Pathol.* 2002;12(3):320-328.

70. Anderson RWG, Sandoz B, Dutschke JK, et al. Biomechanical studies in an ovine model of non-accidental head injury. *J Biomech.* 2014;47(11):2578-2583.

71. Berger RP, Kochanek PM, Pierce MC. Biochemical markers of brain injury: could they be used as diagnostic adjuncts in cases of inflicted traumatic brain injury? *Child Abuse Negl.* 2004;28(7):739-754.

72. Papa L, Ramia MM, Kelly JM, Burks SS, Pawlowicz A, Berger RP. Systematic review of clinical research on biomarkers for pediatric traumatic brain injury. *J Neurotrauma.* 2013;30(5):324-338.

73. Johnson DL, Boal D, Baule R. Role of apnea in nonaccidental head injury. *Pediatr Neurosurg.* 1995;23(6):305-310.

74. Willman KY, Bank DE, Senac M, Chadwick DL. Restricting the time of injury in fatal inflicted head injuries. *Child Abuse Negl.* 1997;21(10):929-940.

75. Buttram SD, Garcia-Filion P, Miller J, et al. Computed tomography vs magnetic resonance imaging for identifying acute lesions in pediatric traumatic brain injury. *Hosp Pediatr.* 2015;5(2):79-84.

76. Han BK, Towbin RB, de Courten-Myers G, McLaurin RL, Ball WS Jr. Reversal sign on CT: effect of anoxic/ischemic cerebral injury in children. *AJR Am J Roentgenol.* 1990;154:361-368.

77. Duhaime AC, Christian CW, Moss E, Seidl T. Long-term outcome in infants with shaking-impact syndrome. *Pediatr Neurosurg.* 1996;24:292-298.

78. Hadley MN, Sonntag VK, Rekate HL, Murphy A. The infant whiplash-shake injury syndrome: a clinical and pathological study. *Neurosurgery.* 1989;24(4):536-540.

79. Kemp A, Cowley L, Maguire S. Spinal injuries in abusive head trauma: patterns and recommendations. *Pediatr Radiol.* 2014;44(4):604-612.

80. Choudhary AK, Bradford RK, Dias MS, Moore GJ, Boal DK. Spinal subdural hemorrhage in abusive head trauma: a retrospective study. *Radiology.* 2012;262(1):216-223.

81. Kadom N, Khademian Z, Vezina G, Shalaby-Rana E, Rice A, Hinds T. Usefulness of MRI detection of cervical spine and brain injuries in the evaluation of abusive head trauma. *Pediatr Radiol.* 2014;44(7):839-848.

82. Chiesa A, Duhaime AC. Abusive head trauma. *Pediatr Clin North Am.* 2009;56(2):317-331.

83. Langlois NE, Gresham GA. The ageing of bruises: a review and study of the colour changes with time. *Forensic Sci Int.* 1991;50(2):227-238.

84. Swartz AJ, Ricci LR. How accurately can bruises be aged in abused children? literature review and synthesis. *Pediatrics.* 1996;97(2):254-257.

85. Maguire S, Mann MK, Sibert J, Kemp A. Can you age bruises accurately in children? a systematic review. *Arch Dis Child.* 2005;90(2):187-189.

86. Duhaime AC, Christian CW, Rorke LB, Zimmerman RA. Nonaccidental head injury in infants—the "shaken-baby syndrome". *N Engl J Med.* 1998;338(25):1822-1829.

87. Sirotnak AP. Medical disorders that mimic abusive head trauma. In: Frasier L, Rauth-Farley K, Alexander R. *Abusive Head Trauma in Infants and Children: A Medical, Legal, and Forensic Reference*. Saint Louis, MO: GW Medical Publishing; 2006:191-226.

88. Yoffe G, Buchanan GR. Intracranial hemorrhage in newborn and young infants with hemophilia. *J Pediatr*. 1988;113(2):333-336.

89. Dietrich AM, James CD, King DR, Ginn-Pease ME, Cecalupo AJ. Head trauma in children with congenital coagulation disorders. *J Pediatr Surg*. 1994;29(1):28-32.

90. Lane PA, Hathaway WE. Vitamin K in infancy. *J Pediatr*. 1985;106(3): 351-359.

91. DiScala C, Sege R, Li G, Reece RM. Child abuse and unintentional injuries: a 10-year retrospective. *Arch Pediatr Adolesc Med*. 2000;154(1):16-22.

92. Hymel KP, Abshire TC, Luckey DW, Jenny C. Coagulopathy in pediatric head trauma. *Pediatrics*. 1997;99(3):371-375.

93. Baric I, Zschocke J, Christensen E, et al. Diagnosis and management of glutaric aciduria type I. *J Inherit Metab Dis*. 1998;21(4):326-340.

94. Vester ME, Bilo RA, Karst WA, Daams JG, Duijst WL, van Rijn RR. Subdural hematomas: glutaric aciduria type 1 or abusive head trauma? a systematic review. *Forensic Sci Med Pathol*. 2015;11(3):405-415.

95. Rooks VJ, Eaton JP, Ruess L, Petermann GW, Keck-Wherley J, Pedersen RC. Prevalence and evolution of intracranial hemorrhage in asymptomatic term infants. *AJNR Am J Neuroradiol*. 2008;29(6):1082-1089.

96. Hedlund GL, Frasier LD. Neuroimaging of abusive head trauma. *Forensic Sci Med Pathol*. 2009;5(4):280-290.

97. King WJ, MacKay M, Sirnick A, Group CSBS. Shaken baby syndrome in Canada: clinical characteristics and outcomes of hospital cases. *Can Med Assoc J*. 2003;168(2):155-159.

98. Barlow KM, Thomson E, Johnson D, Minns RA. Late neurologic and cognitive sequelae of inflicted traumatic brain injury in infancy. *Pediatrics*. 2005;116(2):e174-e185.

Chapter 4

Nonfatal Strangulation in Children

Cathy Baldwin-Johnson, MD, FAAFP
Tracey Wiese, DNP, APRN

Introduction

Strangulation is a potentially lethal form of assault. Investigation and medical care for patients who have experienced strangulation can be complicated by the fact that there are often little to no physical signs that strangulation occurred. These same difficulties are encountered when pediatric patients are victims of strangulation. Furthermore, strangulation also occurs in very young children and in children who are developmentally unable to provide histories for their assaults. These situations present even more challenges for law enforcement and health care professionals when working with this unique population.

Challenges in Evaluating Pediatric Strangulation Cases

- Typically, children under the age of 3 will be unable to participate in a forensic interview. Brain development prohibits ability to create an accurate timeline for either a legal investigation or medical history.
- Expressive/receptive speech delays
- Cognitive, behavioral, or physical disabilities
- High rates of abuse among children with disabilities
- Children are most often abused by people that they know and trust and as a result:
  - May hesitate to disclose details of assault if they feel disclosure might cause trouble for a caregiver/loved one

- The perpetrating caregiver may have told the child to lie about the assault
- The perpetrator may have threatened the child with emotional or physical harm should they disclose

— Chronic domestic violence in the home:

- The child may be afraid to report to law enforcement or medical professionals.
- Physical assaults are a "normed" behavior.

Pediatric Anatomy of the Head and Neck

Differences between pediatric and adult anatomy of the head and neck have significant implications when considering potential findings and sequelae after a strangulation assault. While there is an absence of literature specifically concerned with these implications, health care providers can glean educated inferences supported by literature from other disciplines (eg, anesthesiology, biomechanics, child car seat safety studies).

Airway (**Figure 4-1**)

Figure 4-1. *Structural differences between the pediatric and adult airways become less marked with age. Figure courtesy of Jessica Nichols.*

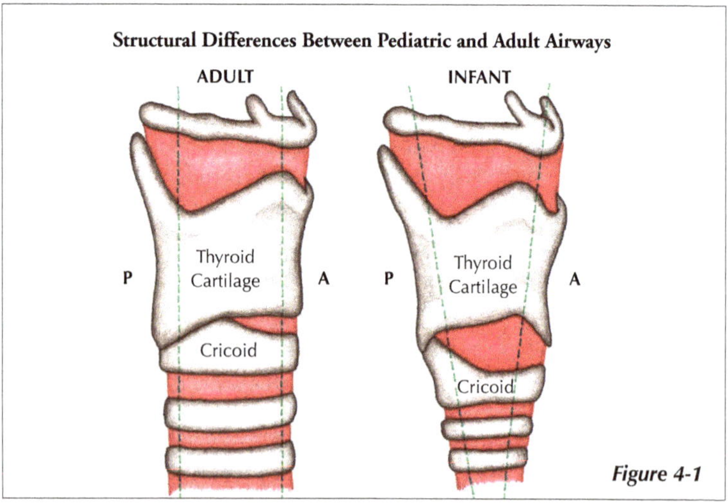

— The infant and pediatric airways are higher in the neck when compared to that of an adult.

— Rather than being a linear structure, the airway in infant and young pediatric patients is funnel shaped, with the cricoid cartilage as the most narrow component.

  — At birth, the lower border of the cricoid cartilage lies opposite the lower border of the fourth cervical vertebra.

  — At 6 years of age, the cricoid cartilage is at the level of the fifth cervical vertebra.

  — In the adult, the cricoid cartilage lies at the level of the sixth cervical vertebra.

— Because the cricoid cartilage is smaller and forms a complete ring around the trachea during pediatric development, mucosal edema at this site will severely compromise the airway.[1]

— Shape of the epiglottis:

  — Broad and leaf-shaped in the adult, its axis lies parallel to that of the trachea.

  — In the infant patient, the epiglottis is narrower, softer, and more horizontally positioned than in the adult.

  — By the age of 4 or 5 years, the epiglottis is more consistent with the adult form.[1]

— Other anatomical differences that increase vulnerability in the pediatric patient for an obstructed or compromised airway:

  — Proportionally larger head and occiput relative to body size increases susceptibility to flexion of the neck, potentially obstructing the airway when lying in a supine position.

  — Smaller nasal apertures that can become easily obstructed by secretions, edema, or blood.[1,2] It is known that infants are obligate nasal breathers and the above differences can create a situation in which the infant will need to work much harder to breathe.

— With relatively large tongue size and decreased muscle tone of the pediatric patient, there is a decrease in the size of the oral cavity allowing obstruction to occur more easily.[1,3]

— The position and softer form of the epiglottis in the younger pediatric patient may increase risk of aspiration.

Head and Neck

— In an infant and also in the pediatric patient, there is a compliant nature to the skull. It is made up of curved plates of bone that are loosely associated.

— The skull becomes more rigid as the child ages.

— Clinical data collected from impact injury studies shows that the unique properties of infant skulls result in a lower level of injury threshold for the infant brain.

— The adult skull's resistance to fracture is 11 times greater than a neonate's and over 2 times greater than a young child's.

— Given the relative proportional differences of pediatric head size, differential motion of the brain and skull is amplified due to the weak neck in infants and young children.[2,3]

— The vascular system in infants is thought to be more fragile and much more susceptible to abrupt pressure changes when compared to adults.[2]

Clinical Presentation

— It is common for strangulation injuries to be missed or underestimated in children, where the clinical spectrum may range from mild, self-limiting symptoms to severe neurologic sequelae or death.

— Some symptoms in adults may not be as helpful in assessing young children, such as incontinence.

— Up to 50% of children will not have clinically apparent signs of strangulation.

— Typical symptoms reported by children include:

  — Voice changes, sore throat or neck pain, difficulty breathing, and problems swallowing

— Older children may report urinary and/or fecal incontinence

— Dizziness or a loss or near-loss of consciousness

— First responders and health care providers should be alert that a child may describe his/her symptoms in developmentally appropriate ways that are very different than an adult, such as "I talked like a duck," "I saw sparkles in my eyes," or "I fell asleep." Some children may be able to articulate that they thought they were going to die.

— Children may present due to physical findings reported to child protection or law enforcement by neighbors, teachers, daycare providers, or family members. Findings may include:

— Petechiae of neck, face, conjunctivae

— Bruising of neck, potentially patterned from fingers/thumbs, ligatures, or clothing

— Swelling in the neck and face

— Defensive scratch marks on neck

— Abrasions or patterned injury from jewelry worn by child or assailant

— Bruising and injuries elsewhere on the child's body

— Children may also present initially with:

— Seizures or altered level of consciousness due to hypoxic brain injury

— Altered mental status including agitation or confusion, likely due to hypoxic brain injury

— Respiratory distress due to acute lung injury, aspiration, or hypoxic brain injury

— Some case reviews that included imaging studies have found fractures of the bony and cartilaginous structures of the neck in up to 25% of pediatric strangulation deaths, including the thyroid cartilage and the hyoid bone.[4] Others have found these injuries to occur much less frequently in children than adults, while sequelae from soft tissue edema in the neck were more common in children.

— Severe delayed effects of strangulation reported in children include[5-8]:
  - — Vocal cord paralysis
  - — Hypoxic-ischemic encephalopathy
  - — Cerebral edema
  - — Cerebral infarction
  - — Aspiration pneumonia
  - — Fractures of the hyoid bone or thyroid cartilage
  - — Behavioral changes
  - — Cognitive deficits
  - — Injury to the carotid artery (carotid dissection has been reported in adults and may be under-recognized in children)
  - — Death

— Most reported deaths in strangled children have been due to cerebral asphyxia from obstruction of carotid artery flow to the brain and jugular venous return. Early and delayed deaths due to carotid hematomas and cerebral infarction have been reported. It is possible that cardiac dysrhythmias play a role.

— Thyroid storm induced by strangulation has been reported as an uncommon but potentially life-threatening complication in adults.[9]

— Poor prognostic signs include prolonged coma, seizures, need for ventilatory support, elevated intracranial pressure, diabetes insipidus, or blood sugar > 300 on admission.[10]

— Consideration should always be given to concurrent additional types of child abuse including sexual abuse/assault, abusive head trauma, and other forms of physical abuse.

Differential Diagnosis

Choking Game

An activity in which persons strangulate themselves or others to achieve euphoria through brief hypoxia. Known by a number of different names, including choke out, pass out game, rush, and flat lining.

— Higher rates of participation in rural populations, Hispanic, and American Indian/Alaska Native youth

— Participants are more likely to report substance use and mental health problems.[11]

— The majority of deaths (86.6%) have been in boys, with a mean age of 13.3 years and the youngest being 6.

— The age distribution for choking game deaths in children and teens differed from suicides by hanging or suffocation: choking game deaths tend to occur in younger children, peaking at age 13, whereas suicides by hanging or suffocation became more prevalent with age.[12]

— A survey conducted in Oregon found that 36.2% of eighth grade respondents had heard of the choking game, 30.4% had heard of someone participating, and 5.7% had participated themselves.

— Primary care and emergency medical providers should be alert to symptoms, including bloodshot eyes, marks on the neck, altered mental status, severe headache, vision loss, seizures, and syncopal episodes.

— A thorough medical history should include questions about the choking game as part of routine assessment of other risk-taking behaviors.[13,14]

Accidental

— Infants and young children are especially vulnerable to accidental strangulation injuries from cribs, other furniture, ropes and cords, and entanglement in clothing, high chairs, and playground equipment.[15]

— A careful history that includes child's developmental status along with a scene investigation and reenactment by law enforcement partners in the multidisciplinary team will help distinguish accidental from inflicted strangulation.

Suicide

— It may be challenging to distinguish strangulation suicide from the choking game or autoerotic asphyxiation.

— Studies have indicated teenaged males are at higher risk for suicide by strangulation and that the age distribution is somewhat different for suicide attempts/completions versus injuries related to the choking game or accidental strangulation.

— A careful history that includes prior behavioral health concerns as well as scene investigation from law enforcement will help determine the cause of the injuries found.

Medical Mimics

— Facial and conjunctival petechiae from prolonged vomiting, coughing, or other significant Valsalva maneuvers, even in the absence of a bleeding diathesis, are considered medical mimics.

— A thorough medical history and exam should usually distinguish medical causes of petechiae from strangulation injuries.

Recommendations for Health Care Providers and First Responders

History

It is critical to remember that a lack of visible external neck injuries does not mean that strangulation did not occur and that strangulation victims may die with or without visible external injuries.[16] A medical history should include:

— The situation in which the strangulation occurred

— The method of strangulation

— Symptoms the child may have experienced during and after the strangulation episode as well as current symptoms at the time of presentation to medical care, remembering that children may describe their symptoms differently than adults

  — Ask specifically about loss of urine or stool during the incident, as this information may not be spontaneously volunteered

— Time elapsed between the strangulation episode and presentation to medical care

— Presence or absence of witnesses

— Presence of any medical conditions that might predispose the child to facial and conjunctival petechiae

— Child's developmental level

— History of prior or concurrent additional forms of child abuse

Physical Exam

A child presenting with a potential strangulation injury should have a thorough medical evaluation that includes[17]:

— Vital signs including pulse oximetry

— Complete survey of all skin surfaces, particularly looking for petechiae, bruising, bites, redness, tenderness, patterned marks (eg, from ligatures, fingers), and tender areas

— Assessment for intraoral injury, including frenular tears, petechiae, bruising, and tongue injuries

— Serial measurements of the neck circumference every 10 to 12 hours (in the same marked spot each time) if admitted for observation; the admitting physician should be notified promptly if neck swelling increases

— Assessment for respiratory distress, stridor, difficulty swallowing or speaking, voice changes, cough, hemoptysis, voice changes

— Eye exam for petechiae and redness with consideration of a dilated retinal exam by an ophthalmologist

— Otoscopic exam for ear complaints

— External examination of anogenital area

— Neurologic exam including age-appropriate mental status assessment, presence of irritability, somnolence, behavioral changes, seizures, or localizing findings

Forensic Evaluation

Depending on how long ago the strangulation incident occurred and interim hygiene activities, it may be possible to find forensic evidence on the child's body. If applicable:

— Collect debris or foreign material. Label, seal, and maintain chain of evidence until transferred to law enforcement.

— Swab the child's neck for possible assailant epithelial cells left on the skin. Follow local crime laboratory directions for the technique to use for swabbing.

— Additional forensic evidence collection may be indicated, such as situations where strangulation occurs during sexual abuse or sexual assault.

Diagnostic Testing

Depending on the clinical presentation of the child and time elapsed since strangulation incident, consideration should be given to:

— Admission for minimum 12 to 24 hours of observation for history of loss of consciousness and/or other neurologic signs and symptoms, facial/conjunctival petechiae, soft tissue injury to neck, incontinence (if age-appropriate concern), voice changes, respiratory distress, concern for safety of child

— Imaging studies of the neck, including:

- — CT angio of carotid/vertebral arteries for evaluation of vascular, bony, and cartilaginous structures, especially if lateralizing neurologic symptoms OR
- — Neck CT to identify injuries to bony, cartilaginous, and soft tissues in the neck OR
- — MRA of neck (less sensitive than CT angio for vascular injury)
- — For history of loss of consciousness, evidence of soft tissue injury to neck, consider neck MRI to identify intramuscular hemorrhage, hematomas, and swelling in other soft tissues and hemorrhage into lymph nodes (all associated with more severe, life-threatening strangulation).[18,19]

— Pharyngoscopy or laryngoscopy for stridor, voice changes, dyspnea

— Chest x-ray for any respiratory symptoms

— EEG for concerns for hypoxic-ischemic encephalopathy

— Head CT/MRI for concerns for intracranial injury or hypoxic-ischemic encephalopathy

- Skeletal survey for occult fractures in children < 2 to 3 years of age, with consideration for children up to 5

Diagnostic testing may not be indicated in children presenting days after the strangulation incident with no current symptoms. Consideration should still be given to obtaining a skeletal survey in very young children, as studies have indicated a significant yield of occult fractures in young children with other physical abuse findings.

Documentation

Comprehensive documentation improves patient care and increases the likelihood of achieving both justice and future safety for child victims. Documentation should include:

- Child or adolescent's verbatim description of the strangulation incident(s), demeanor, and mental and emotional status
- Any disclosure of prior or concurrent other abuse
- History provided by caregiver accompanying the child (if present)
- Any subjective complaints such as pain, sore throat, difficulty swallowing, loss of memory (using the child's own words)
- Shape, size, color, and location of any observed injuries (described with words, drawn on traumagrams)
- Photographs to demonstrate presence or absence of visible injuries (Some injuries may not be readily apparent immediately after the event.)
  - Photos of each injury should include a distance orientation image, a close-up, a close-up with scale, and 360-degree photos of the neck area.
  - Photos of the eyes should include all 4 quadrants of gaze (up, down, left, right).
  - Photos should also be taken of areas where pain or tenderness are present even if no current visible injury, as bruises may surface later.
  - Follow-up photos should be obtained until near or complete resolution of visible injuries.

Follow-up

Discharge instructions should include specific warning signs that would indicate a child should be brought back for urgent reevaluation. These include:

— Difficulty breathing or shortness of breath

— Loss of consciousness

— Changes in voice or difficulty speaking

— Difficulty swallowing, lump in throat, muscle spasms in throat/neck

— Swelling of tongue, neck, throat

— Prolonged nose bleed

— Persistent cough or coughing up blood

— Persistent vomiting or vomiting up blood

— Left- or right-sided weakness, numbness, tingling

— Headache not relieved by over-the-counter pain medication taken as directed on bottle

— Seizures

— Behavior changes or memory loss

— Thoughts of harming self or others

A scheduled follow-up exam should occur within 1 to 2 weeks. Long-term neurologic sequelae have been reported in some children who have sustained either inflicted or accidental strangulation injuries, ranging from mild learning problems to severe cognitive and motor impairment.[20] It is, therefore, important that these children have appropriate long-term medical follow-up for monitoring and treatment of any identified adverse outcomes.

Reporting

All 50 states have laws that require mandatory reporters to make a report to their designated child protection agency if there is reasonable cause to suspect that child abuse or neglect has occurred. Since strangulation is a criminal act, a concurrent report to the appropriate local law enforcement agency is also indicated.

Conclusion

The significance and potential lethality of strangulation injuries in children is often underestimated due to delayed presentation and children's barriers to communicating details about strangulation events as well as their symptoms. Recognition, a thorough medical evaluation, detailed documentation, and prompt involvement of child protection workers and law enforcement officers will help provide current and future safety for the affected child. Medical providers with specialized child abuse and forensic training can provide invaluable assistance with forensic evidence collection and photo-documentation as well as recommendations and referrals.

References

1. Adewale L. Anatomy and assessment of the pediatric airway. *Pediatr Anesth.* 2009;19(suppl 1):1-8.
2. Ommaya AK, Goldsmith W, Thibault L. Biomechanics and neuropathology of adult and paediatric head injury. *Br J Neurosurg.* 2002;16(2):220-242.
3. Burdi AR, Huelke DF, Snyder RG, Lowrey GH. Infants and children in the adult world of automobile safety design: Pediatric and anatomical considerations for design of child restraints. *J Biomech.* 1969;2(3):267-280.
4. Verma SK. Pediatric and adolescent strangulation deaths. *J Forensic Leg Med.* 2007;14(2):61-64.
5. Bird CR, McMahan JR, Gilles FH, Senac MO, Apthorp JS. Strangulation in child abuse: CT Diagnosis. *Radiology.* 1987;163(2):373-375.
6. Jain V, Ray M, Singhi S. Strangulation injury, a fatal form of child abuse. *Indian J Pediatr.* 2001;68(6):571-572.
7. Dayapala A, Samarasekera A, Jayasena A. An uncommon delayed sequela after pressure on the neck. *Am J Forensic Med Pathol.* 2012;33(1):80-82.
8. Yadav J, Badkur DS, Arora A. Carotid sheath haematoma: a case report. *J Forensic Leg Med.* 2009;16(7):411-413.
9. Ramirez J, Petrone P, Kuncir E, Asensio J. Thyroid storm induced by strangulation. *South Med J.* 2004;97(6):608-610.
10. Sabo RA, Hanigan WC, Flessner K, Rose J, Aaland M. Strangulation injuries in children. part 1. clinical analysis. *J Trauma.* 1996;40(1):68-72.

11. Ramowski SK, Nystrom RJ, Chaumeton NR, Rosenberg KD, Gilchrist J. "Choking game" awareness and participation among 8th graders—Oregon, 2008. *MMWR.* 2010;59(1):1-5.

12. Russell P, Paulozzi L, Gilchrist J, Toblin R. Unintentional strangulation deaths from "the choking game" among youths aged 6-19 years --- United States, 1995--2007. *MMWR.* 2008;57(6):141-144.

13. Egge MK, Berkowitz CD, Toms C, Sathyavagiswaran L. The choking game: a cause of unintentional strangulation. *Pediatr Emerg Care.* 2010;26(3):206-208.

14. Andrew T, Macnab A, Russell P. Update on "the choking game". *J Pediatr.* 2009;155(6):777-780.

15. Feldman K, Simms R. Strangulation in childhood: epidemiology and clinical course. *Pediatrics.* 1980;65(6):1079-1085.

16. Shields L, Corey T, Weakley-Jones B, Stewart D. Living victims of strangulation. *Am J Forensic Med Pathol.* 2010;31(4):320-325.

17. Faugno D, Waszak D, Strack GB, Brooks MA, Gwinn CG. Strangulation forensic examination: best practice for health care providers. *Adv Emerg Nurs J.* 2013;35(4):314-327.

18. Christe A, Thoeny H, Ross S, et al. Life-threatening versus non-life-threatening manual strangulation: are there appropriate criteria for MR imaging of the neck? *Eur Radiol.* 2009;19(8):1882-1889.

19. Christe A, Oesterhelweg L, Ross S, et al. Can MRI of the neck compete with clinical findings in assessing danger to life for survivors of manual strangulation? a statistical analysis. *Legal Medicine.* 2010;12(5):228-232.

20. Sabo RA, Hanigan WC, Flessner K, Rose J, Aaland M. Strangulation injuries in children. part 1. clinical analysis. *J Trauma.* 1996;40(1):68-72.

STM Learning gratefully acknowledges the Training Institute on Strangulation Prevention, a project of Alliance for HOPE International, for allowing us to reproduce, in part or in whole, the chapter "Nonfatal Strangulation in Children."

Chapter 5

Bruises and Burns

Sylvia E. Britt, PhD, RN
Melanie Gibbons Hallman, DNP, CRNP, CEN, TCRN, FNP-BC, ACNP-BC
Shannon Polson, MSN, MSW, RN, LCSW, CNL, CWCN, PIP
Karen M. Coles, DNP, RN
Diana Faugno, MSN, RN, CPN, SANE-A, SANE-P, FAAFS, DF-IAFN
Charles E. Johnson, MD, FAAP
Gina M. French, MD
Patricia M. Speck, DNSc, ARNP, APN, FNP-BC, DF-IAFN, FAAFS, FAAN

The Skin

The skin, also called integument, forms a sensate barrier around the body to protect from infection and injury while simultaneously regulating both temperature and hydration. The skin consists of:

— Epidermis: An outer layer that is separated from an innermost layer, the dermis, by a structure called the basement membrane.

— Hypodermis (superficial fascia): Comprised of a system of blood vessels and adipose (fat) tissue; these collective layers rest on the hypodermis. Provides protection and nourishment to the outer skin layer and attaches itself to underlying structures.

Damage to skin is classified by type and reflective of the causative nature of the injury. Factors include[1]:

— Mechanical
— Chemical
— Bacterial
— Vascular
— Burn
— Radiation
— Moisture
— Infection
— Allergy
— Chronic inflammation
— Assault
— Intrinsic disease

(See **Table 5-1** for examples of skin injury.)

Table 5-1. Examples of Skin Injury and Conditions/Diseases That Mimic Injury

Neglect	Physical Abuse	Mimics of Abuse
— Moisture/chemical (eg, child left in a soiled diaper) — Bacterial/infection (eg, child not given access to proper medical care) — Burn (eg, child exposed to extreme sunlight during abandonment)	— Mechanical (eg, excoriation from choking/ physical struggle) — Vascular (eg, extravasation of blood from vessels broken during impact) — Burn (eg, from being left in extreme cold or exposed to extreme heat)	— Mongolian spots (see page 88)

Adapted from Bryant RA, Nix DP.[1]

— Injuries to the skin will vary in severity with the amount of force used, size of impact, and health of the child. They will also vary depending by the size, shape, temperature (ie, very hot, very cold) of the impacting object(s), and by the body surface(s) contacted.

— The relative force needed to leave an impact mark on a child's skin depends on the area impacted, skin thickness at point of impact, and underlying structures (ie, fat, muscle, bone).

— Legal (**Table 5-2**) and medical definitions (**Table 5-3**) of child physical maltreatment (CPM) do not necessarily agree.

— Temporary erythema (ie, redness from dilated blood vessels under the skin) after a light impact may not legally constitute maltreatment, but if the impact was an observed intentional slap to the face, the incident constitutes reportable CPM.

— The brain, head, and face are particularly vulnerable to serious injury from CPM.

Table 5-2. Federal Child Abuse Prevention and Treatment Act Definitions of Child Abuse
— "Any recent act or failure to act on the part of a parent or caretaker which results in death, serious physical or emotional harm, sexual abuse or exploitation."
— "An act or failure to act, which presents an imminent risk of serious harm."
Reprinted from US Department of Health and Human Services.[2]

Table 5-3. Medical Definition of Child Maltreatment
Tissue damage caused by a parent, guardian, or caregiver, for any reason, including reaction to an unwanted behavior, is child abuse and must be reported to proper authorities.
— Tissue damage includes bruises, burns, tears, punctures, fractures, rupture of organs, and disruption of functions.
— Impact, shaking, penetration, extreme heat or cold, or a caustic chemical or drug can cause tissue damage.
— The use of an instrument on any part of the body is child abuse.
Adapted from Ohio Chapter American Academy of Pediatrics Subcommittee, June 4, 1998.

— The skin may not show injury after a physical impact; therefore, tissue damage or functional change in underlying organs constitutes reportable CPM.

— Definitions must be established within a community as to what is reportable as CPM

— Requirement to report varies from state to state and profession to profession. Mandatory reporters typically include all those who have frequent interactions with children. If you suspect abuse, check your state mandatory reporting laws.[3]

Types of Blunt Injury

There are four main subdivisions of blunt injury[4]:

1. Scratches/grazes (abrasions): Removal of the outermost layer of skin by compressive and/or sliding force.
2. Bruises (contusions): Result from leakage of blood from vessels into tissues after sufficient force has been applied to distort soft tissues and tear one or more vessels.
3. Tears (lacerations): Result from blunt force, crushing, tearing, ripping, shearing, over stretching, severe bending, and pulling apart of soft tissues. They have ragged, variably irregular margins.
4. Bone fractures: A bone may fracture in different ways according to the amount of force and the fashion in which it was applied.

Bruises

— Bruises are damaged blood vessels from which blood cells escape and become distributed between layers of body tissue. Bruises appear more rapidly when tissue is thin or when superficial capillaries are leaking. Surface appearance is delayed when bruises occur between deeper structures (eg, between dermis and fascia, fascia and adipose tissues).

— The color of a bruise reflects the iron in hemoglobin, which changes with age and deoxygenation. The heme is degraded into biliverdin (green-blue bile pigment), bilirubin (orange-yellow pigment), and hemosiderin (red-brown in color).

— It is impossible to accurately date the age of a bruise from color alone,[5] but staging bruises is possible by describing the color. Staging is dependent on the depth of the bruise and clotting factors. Anticlotting medications and herbs, along with common pain relievers, impact continuous bleeding following trauma, exposing multiple stages of tissue healing (**Table 5-4**).

Table 5-4. Stages of Tissue Healing

Stage	Description
Onset	Blunt trauma results in capillary break and sealing, resulting in a brief white pallor. In the event of diminished blood flow, pallor persists, and visible necrosis follows.
Bleeding	Dependent on size and location of capillaries/vessels and the damage to the vessel, which results in hormonal cascade, resulting in a fibrinous clot that stops bleeding.
Inflammation	Cytokines act on a variety of cell functions, including cell reproduction, movement, scar tissue growth, and removal of dead cells, all while protected from further damage by inflammatory repair processes.
Proliferation	Wound rebuilds with firm scar tissue (granulation) and new blood vessels, and nerves grow into the area, resulting in a pinkish appearance (ie, neovascularization). Pain syndromes develop during this phase.
Maturation	Continuous remodeling and healing may take up to 2 years.

Adapted from Advance Tissue[6]; Allen GA, Glader B[7]; Hoffman R, Benz EJ Jr, Shattil SJ, et al[8]; Iannelli V[9]; Kaczor K, Pierce MC, Makoroff K, Corey TS[10]; Kliegman RM, Behrman RE, Jenson HB, Stanton BMD, Zitelli BJ, Davis HW.[11]

Bruises may not become visible for minutes, hours, or even a few days because it may take time for blood leaking from vessels beneath a layer of undisturbed fat or behind other structures to wind its way to the surface. In cases of shock arising from traumatic injury with significant blood loss, low blood pressure results in delayed bruising until restoration of blood pressure. With resumption of bleeding due to fluid volume restoration, it is possible to see new discoloration.[4]

— Color is influenced by children's skin color.[12,13]

— Caregivers may claim that bruising in children who bruise easily or have a hematological disease occurred during activities of daily life. Careful medical history reveals inconsistent injury with health status.[7,8,9,10,11]

— Prothrombin time, partial thromboplastin time (PTT), and a platelet count are needed on almost all children with bruises who may be CPM victims. With pattern bruises shaped like identifiable objects, or with other injuries prompting concern unrelated to easy bruising, these tests may be avoided.

— Conditions such as Von Willebrand disease may cause prolonged bleeding, but only in its most severe type. PTT is also prolonged in these cases.[14]

— Determination of bleeding time is rarely needed when the child has known preexisting blood-related diseases.

Common Tests for Children With Bruising

— Falls and injury: Not surprisingly, severe injuries can often lead to extensive bruising. Instead of simply looking at the size of a bruise, it is more important to think about whether or not the bruise is proportionate to the injury. For example, you would expect a much larger bruise if your child falls out of a tree than if he simply trips and falls on the grass.

— Child abuse: Bruising in infants, unexplained bruises, bruises in unusual places (eg, upper arms, hands, ears, neck, buttocks), and bruises in specific shapes (eg, large bite mark, cigarette burn, belt mark) may be signs of child abuse.[15]

— Von Willebrand disease: A common, though often mild, genetic bleeding disorder that can cause easy bruising, frequent nosebleeds, heavy menstrual bleeding, and bleeding after surgery.[16,17]

— Thrombocytopenia: Low platelet count that can be caused when platelets aren't being produced, are being destroyed, or when they are being sequestered in an enlarged spleen.[18]

— Idiopathic thrombocytopenic purpura (ITP): An autoimmune disorder that leads to the breakdown of platelets in the blood by antibodies and a low platelet count. Usually thought to be triggered by a recent viral infection, after which the young child develops large bruises and petechiae (ie, small purple dots under the skin).[19]

— Henoch-Schonlein purpura (HSP): An immune disorder that can cause abdominal pain, bloody stools, joint pain, and a distinctive rash on a child's arms, legs, and buttocks that looks like bruising (purpura).

— Hemophilia A (factor VIII deficiency) or hemophilia B (factor IX deficiency): Hemophilia is usually diagnosed before a child is 2 to 5 years old, when children may have easy bruising, bleeding in joints, or excessive bleeding after a cut or dental procedure.[20,21]

— Leukemia: In addition to easy bruising, bleeding, and a low platelet count, children with leukemia will usually have other signs and symptoms (eg, low red cell count, fever, weight loss).

— Vitamin K deficiency: Side effect of certain medications (eg, aspirin, seizure medicines, some antibiotics).[9,22]

Documentation

— Cases of CPM require a carefully recorded legal medical record, which may include drawings, color descriptions, measurements of marks, and photodocumentation.

— Photographs must include patient identification, often called bookends.

— Depending on the standard of practice of the medical examiner, photographs should include a minimum of 3 steps (oriented at a distance for identification of the child, oriented up close to the body with the body part and injury in focus, both with and without measuring tool) but may include up to 5 steps (oriented for identification of the child, oriented to body part injured, intermediate distance from injury site, and up close to the injury, all with and without a measuring tool). This is known as the "Rule of Thirds/Fourths/Fifths," depending on the number of photographs taken.

— For best representation of discoloration, use a blue or green background.

— Patient's pain level should be documented.

— Swelling may be difficult to photograph; however, comparison to another unaffected limb or side-lighting to demonstrate shadows highlights swelling. If the photographer is unable to capture swelling, measure and document the location and size of the area.

— A follow-up examination should be scheduled to demonstrate healing and reduction in swelling and pain.

Conditions That Mimic Abuse

(See **Table 5-5**.)

Table 5-5. A Variety of Skin Conditions May Mimic Child Physical Maltreatment

Coagulopathies
- Congenital
  - Hemophilia
- Acquired
  - Vitamin K deficiency
    - Liver disease
    - Binding by resins
    - Malnutrition
- Toxic
  - Salicylate poisoning

Connective tissue disorders
- Type I Ehlers-Danlos syndrome[24]

Chromosomal disorders
- Birthmarks
- Stork bites (bruises, pinch marks)
- Mongolian spots
- Pigmented nevi (bruises)
- Strawberry hemangiomas

Hypersensitivity vasculitis
- Stephens-Johnson syndrome[29]
- Hives
- Phytophotodermatitis (burn)

Other vascular-hematological conditions
- Schönlein-Henoch purpura[23]
- Platelet aggregation disorder
- Disseminated intravascular coagulation
- Blood dyscrasias

Neglect/accident
- Car restraint belt buckle burn (geometric burn)

Infectious diseases
- Chicken Pox scars (cigarette burns)
- Impetigo (cigarette burns)
- Monilia (burn)
- Scaled skin syndrome (burn)
- Purpura fulminans of meningococcemia
- Endocarditis
- Tinea corporis/ringworm (bite mark)
- Fifth Disease (rash looks like slap marks)[25]
- Chronic eczema (red rash)[26]
- Erythema multiforme[23,27]
- Haemophilus influenza type b (HIB)[28]

(continued)

Table 5-5. A Variety of Skin Conditions May Mimic Child Physical Maltreatment *(continued)*

Self-inflicted or factitial injury — Sucker bites/hickeys (pinch marks) — Bruise, burn, puncture — Banding — Cornelia de Lange — Lesch-Nyhan syndrome — Familial dysautonomia — Scars (from cutting) **Self-inflicted skin colorization** — Tattoo — Paint, crayon, dyes **Folk medicine practice** — Cao gio/coin rubbing (linear bruise or burn) — Moxibustion (burn) — Cupping (geometric round burn)	**Parasites** — Crab lice or other types of pediculosis (maculae ceruleae mimic bruises) **Miscellaneous** — Lichen sclerosis (in genital area may suggest trauma) — Valsalva (bilateral ecchymosis of eyes) — Forceful vomiting or coughing (petechial lesions on face) — Striae (linear marks along lower back, thighs, or abdomen may suggest lash marks) — Pressure from elastic bands or clothing (rope marks) — Poison ivy; linear streaks may resemble lash marks

— *Mongolian spots*: Birthmarks mainly ocurring in dark-skinned infants that range in color from bluish to greenish or gray to black (**Figure 5-1-a** through **e**). The spots usually occur on the lower back but may be on any body part and vary in size, shape, and number.[27] As the child grows, the spots will gradually disappear.[30]

— *Striae*: Red, purple, or white linear marks on the skin, which occur due to rapid growth in children of all sizes (**Figure 5-2**). Striae are not a result of abuse.[31]

— *Ringworm (tinea corporis)*: Common fungal skin infection caused by a warm, moist environment (**Figure 5-3**). The outline of tinea corporis may look like bite marks but is in fact a scaly red border of vesicles and pustules.[32]

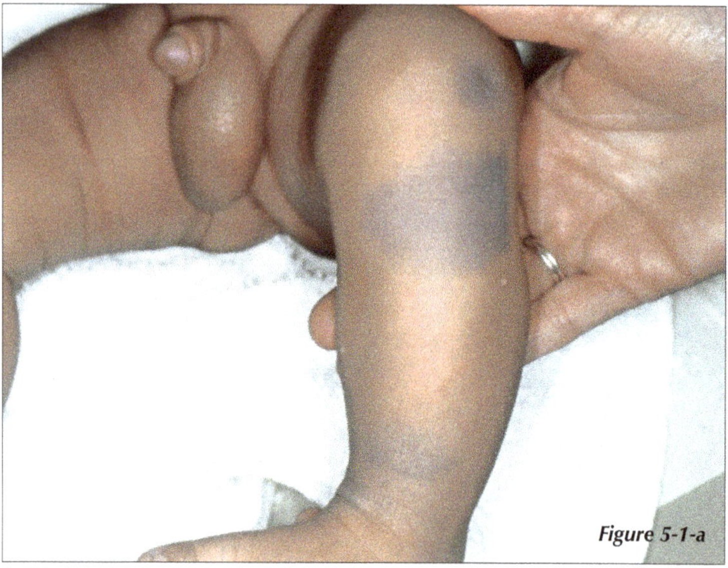

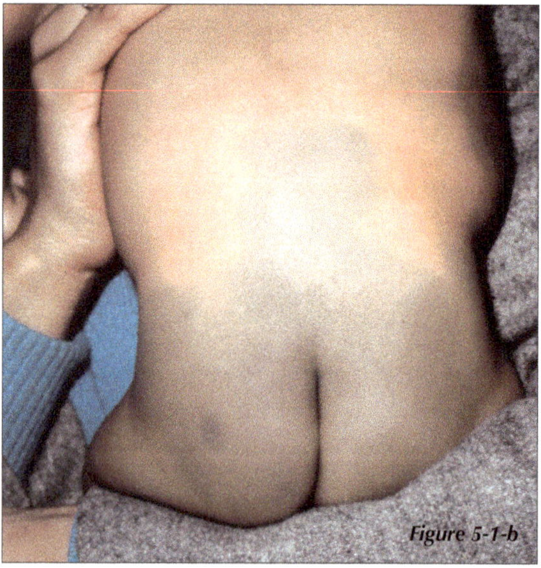

Figure 5-1-a. *The bruise-like marks on the lower leg of this pre-ambulating infant are Mongolian spots.*

Figure 5-1-b. *Mongolian spots on the buttocks of the same child.*

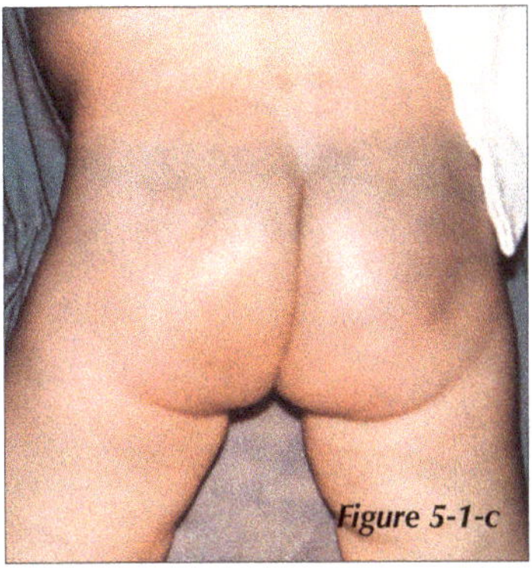

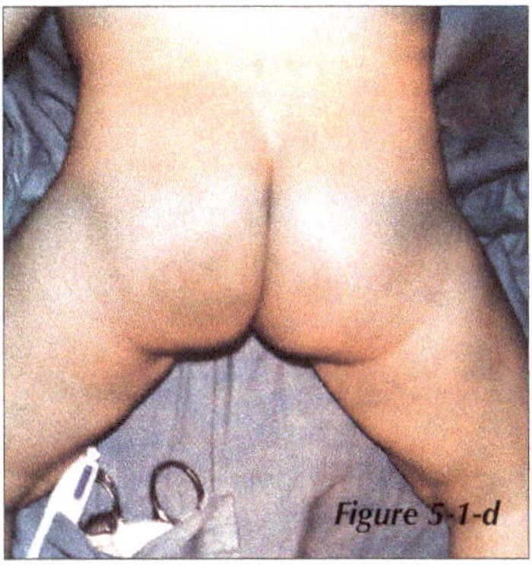

Figures 5-1-c and **d.** *The 11-month-old biracial boy was reported to the hotline by a new day care employee for bruising on his buttocks. The child was healthy and happy. The mother said that the discoloration was present from birth. The staff determined that the discoloration was a Mongolian spot. It involves the buttocks (c) and part of the left thigh (seen better on d).*

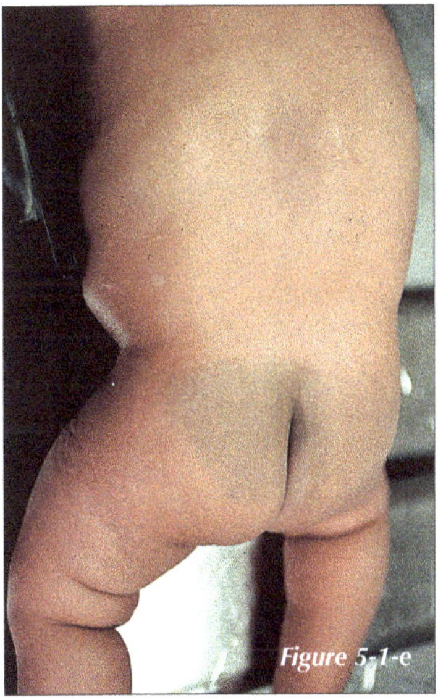

Figure 5-1-e. Mongolian spot.

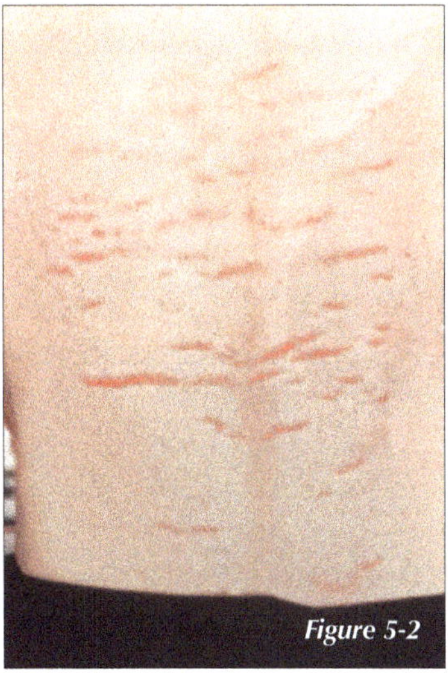

Figure 5-2. *Striae: linear marks on the back resulting from rapid weight gain and growth.*

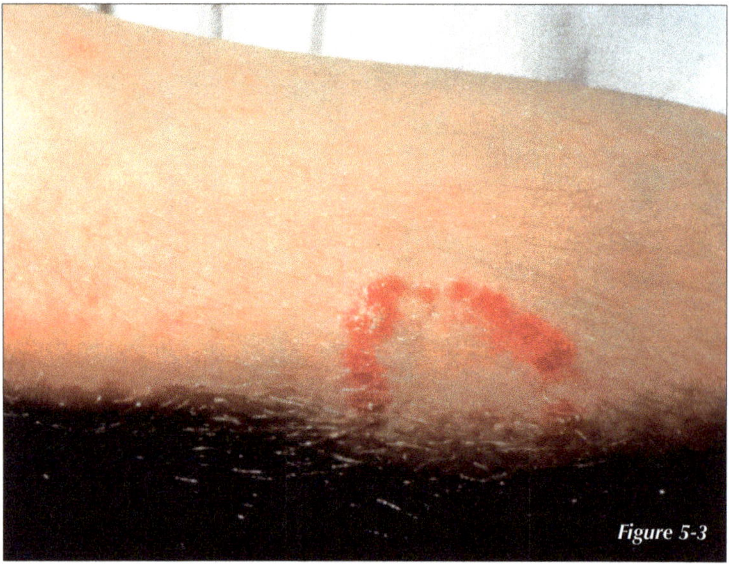

Figure 5-3. *Curved marks on the forearm resulting from ringworm.*

— ***Animal bite*:** Bites from dogs, cats, and humans have different shapes and types of tissue injury based on the dental anatomy and shape and size of the animal's teeth.[33] Animal bites are more elongated with tearing of tissue.[34]

— ***Cultural healing practices*:** Cao gio, or coining, is an Asian cultural healing practice in which a coin or the back of a spoon is used to rub heated herbal ointments over the skin along the spine, ribs, or head until reddened (**Figure 5-4**).[35]

— ***Scars or tattoos*:** Done for healing purposes, part of a cultural ritual, or for identification.[36]

— ***Falling against an object*:** Children fall against objects and imprint themselves with abrasions, erythema, or bruises on bony prominences. Imprints from falling show signs of less force than injuries sustained from abuse.[37]

— ***Poison ivy*:** The linear erythematous marks from contact with poison ivy can resemble an impact with a lash or hand (**Figure 5-5**), but vesicles, a raised border, and reports of itching and burning differentiate it from abuse.

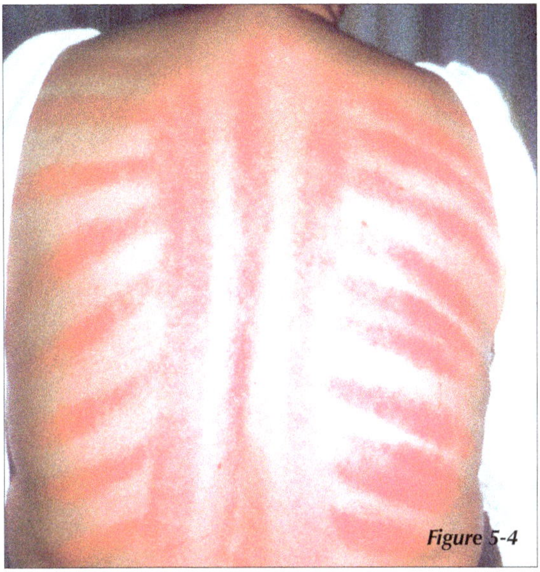

Figure 5-4. Cao gio.

Figure 5-5. Linear marks from contact with poison ivy.

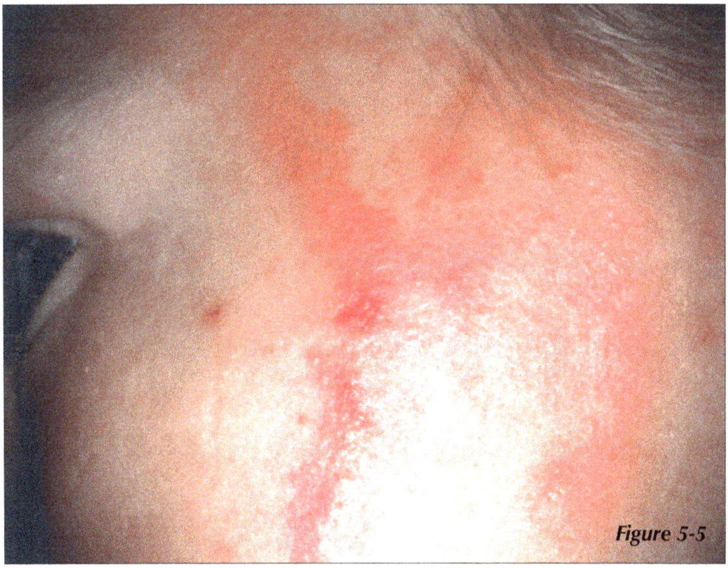

Assessment of Children Who Suffer Bruising or Burning

— The American Academy of Pediatrics defines significant trauma as any injury beyond temporary redness of the skin. One practical criterion often used is that any inflicted injury that lasts more than 24 hours constitutes significant injury (ie, physical abuse).[38]

— The buttocks and hips are the most frequently injured areas of the body. In children, these are unlikely to be life-threatening; however, the buttocks can pool a significant amount of blood, so an assessment of hypovolemic symptoms implying significant blood loss is warranted. A bruise or burn on any part of the body should be reported.

— In order of frequency, the following areas of the body may be abusively injured: face, arms, back, thighs, legs, scalp, eyes, chest, abdomen, hands or wrists, and neck.

— Fewer injuries involve the shoulders, ears, feet, genitalia, groin, perineum, nose, mouth, skull, brain, rectum, teeth, and kidneys.

— Facial injuries can damage the eyes, nose, mouth, teeth, ears, eardrums, and brain[39-43] and should be reported as child abuse.

— Physically maltreated children who require hospitalization show a pattern of injury focused on the head, neck, and hands that is observable even by nonphysicians.[44,45]

— School-aged children with injuries on clothed body areas may exhibit behaviors suggesting injury (eg, not being able to sit in class because of injuries to buttocks).

Developmental Indicators

— Developmental histories should be obtained with any childhood bruising or burning. Sources include recent well-child exams by primary care providers.

— Developmental landmarks help determine the probability of children actively participating in an injury such as a bruise or burn.[46]

1. Children begin rolling at age 3 months (50th percentile).
2. Children can get food into their mouths at age 5 months (50th percentile).
3. Children walk well at age 12 months (50th percentile).
4. Infants rarely bruise themselves before they are able to cruise (walk along furniture while holding onto it). If the child is not cruising, the child should not be bruising.[47]

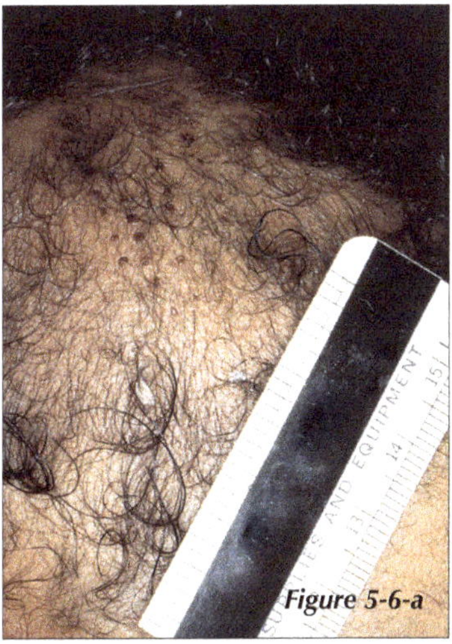

Patterned Injuries

— Intentional injuries can be identified by the patterns left on the skin (**Figures 5-6-a** and **b**). The injury may not surface for several days, but healing always begins with sparing at the point of impact, revealing the pattern.

Figure 5-6-a. *Patterned injury. Rows of punctate abrasions caused by a hair brush.*

Figure 5-6-b. *Loop marks caused by whipping with extension cord.*

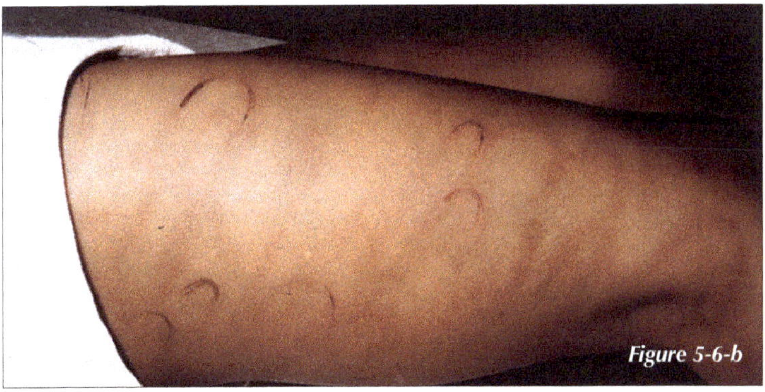

— Choice of instrument is influenced by parental experiences, children's size, and instrument availability.

— The hand is both the most common instrument used to strike children and a common "target organ."[45]

— A slap leaves a readily identifiable mark most often on the face or buttocks. With repeated strikes, the buttocks may have overlapping or coalescing marks (**Figure 5-7**). If instrumenrs are used, impact may result in hematomas, not visible but with significant blood loss.

— Belts, straps, and various household objects leave identifiable marks (**Figures 5-8-a** through **d** and **5-9-a** through **c**),[48] either a silhouette of the object if it has a large surface (eg, a paddle) or an outline if the object is narrow and blunt.

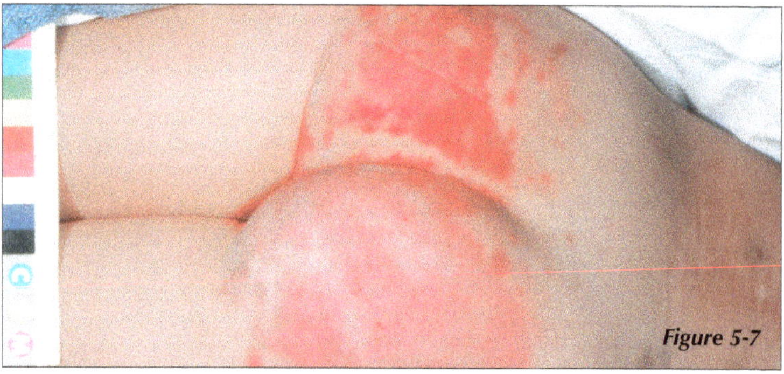

Figure 5-7. *Bruised buttocks resulting from repeated strikes with a hand. Note the finger outlines on the right buttock and that the groove between the buttocks has been protected.*

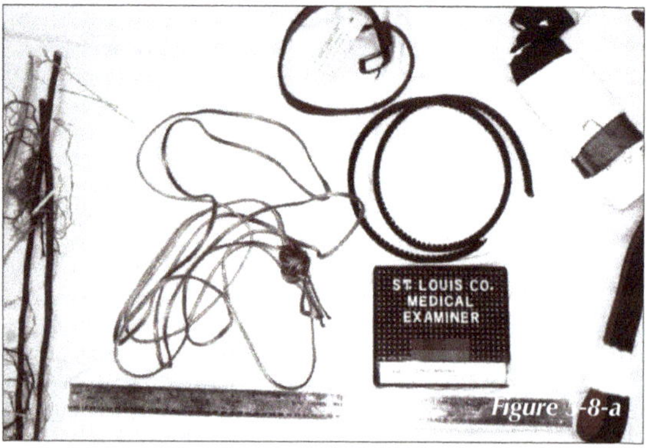

Figure 5-8-a. *Instruments used to beat the girl.*

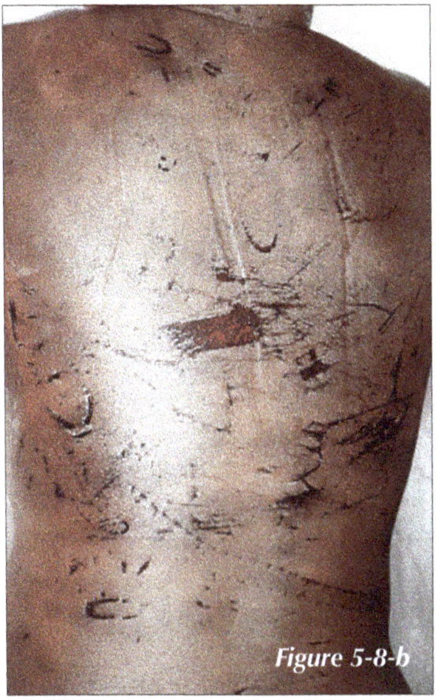

Figure 5-8-b

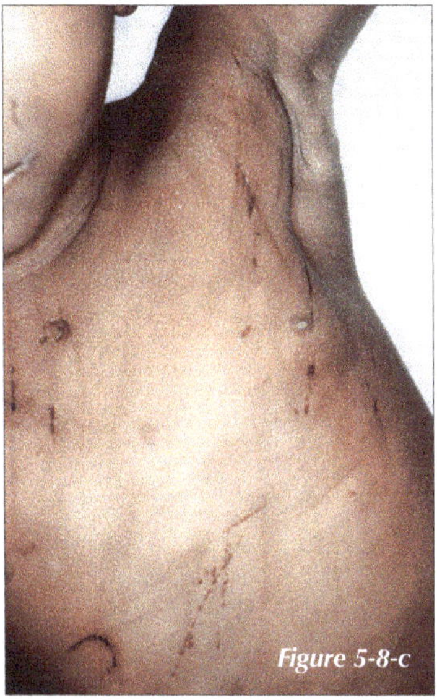

Figure 5-8-c

Figures 5-8-b and **c.** *Injuries include multiple abrasions and contusions of head, face, neck, chest, and abdomen. Patterned injuries of loops from belt marks and notches from the fan belt are recognizable.*

Figure 5-8-d

Figure 5-8-d. *Multiple abrasions and contusions of back and extremities.*

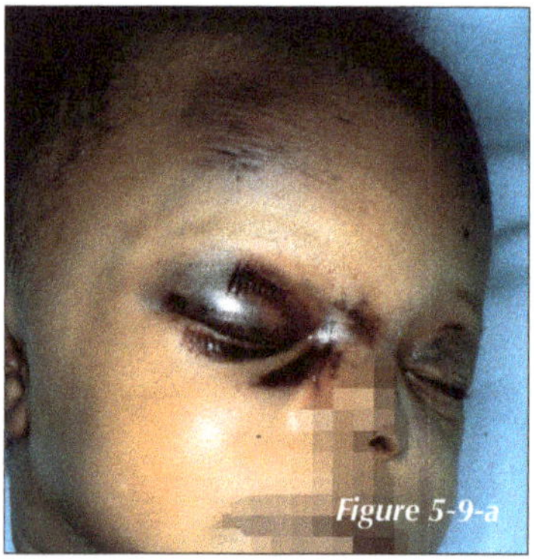

Figures 5-9-a, ***b***, *and* **c.** *Patterned injury and object used. Forehead marks by the straw, orbital injuries by metal banding.*

— Older children are more likely to be struck with instruments and can more readily escape, resulting in grab marks or evidence of being tied or restrained.

— Fingers, toes, and male genitalia of younger children may be intentionally bound with bands and hair.[49]

— Central ecchymosis, also called sucker bites or hickeys, can simulate a problem with hemostasis. Because they are inflicted by the perpetrator's mouth, they are typically bow-shaped (**Figure 5-10**).

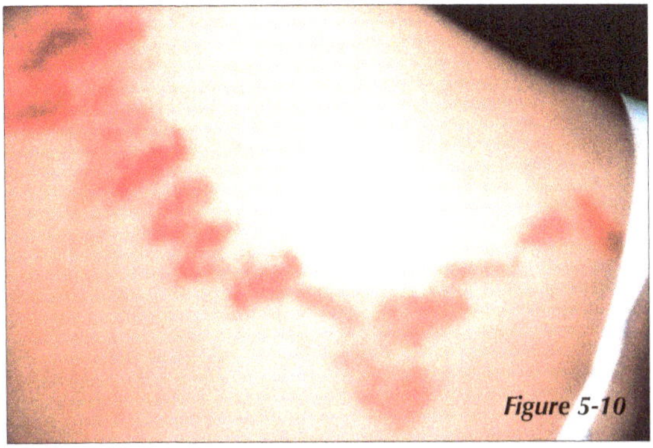

Figure 5-10. *Sucker marks on the back of an adolescent girl, made during sexual activity.*

— Abrasions of the eyelids, scalp bruising, and mouth contusions may result from intentional smothering and suggest intentional injury in children whose deaths are attributed to sudden infant death syndrome.[50,51]

— Sudden onset of seizures may present after intentional smothering has occurred.[51]

— Younger children may be smothered or shaken in an attempt to quiet or restrain them and, thus, are more likely to have facial abrasions, scalp bruising, and mouth contusions than older children.

— Older children may be strangled, exhibiting pattern bruising on the neck (**Figure 5-11**).

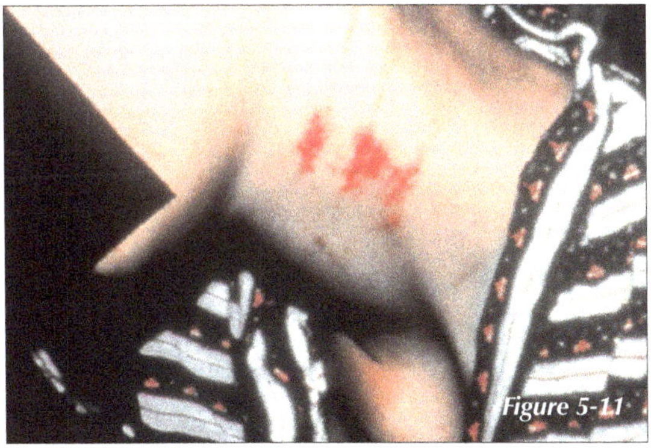

Figure 5-11. *Parallel marks compatible with a history of attempted strangulation by a caregiver. Note that the marks are an outline of the fingers and not a silhouette.*

— Neck bruising may be accompanied by "freckling" (ie, petechiae) of the facial skin, ear drum, and mucosal surfaces; bilateral conjunctival hemorrhage, frequently mistaken for hemorrhagic conjunctivitis; or significant bruising of the tongue.

— A hoarse voice may be mistaken for a sore throat, but in cases of strangulation, a hoarse voice may result from swelling of the larynx.

— Hospitalization is recommended for strangulation injury as persistent swelling results in a restricted airway.

— Symmetrical or mirrored marks are unusual.

1. If children are struck on the forehead or nose, bilateral ecchymosis may occur (also known as raccoon eyes).
2. Subconjunctival hemorrhages seldom occur from a blow to the nose or forehead. Look for strangulation injury.
3. Basal skull fractures may cause a panda-like blue discoloration around the eyes, as well as bleeding from the ears.
4. Children with bruises about both eyes with or without subconjunctival hemorrhages and no injury to the forehead or nose were probably struck on 2 occasions (**Figure 5-12**).

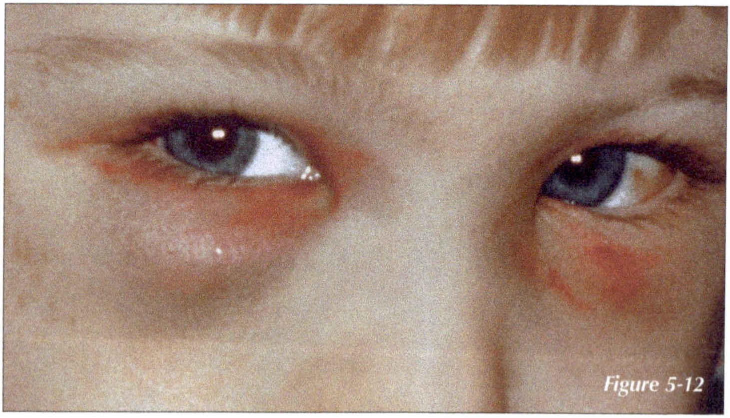

Figure 5-12. *Dual black eyes in a 4-year-old boy.*

Lack of Bruising

— Lack of visible bruising does not indicate absence of blunt trauma; rather, health, force, object, grazing, or direct, sharp, or rounded instruments will determine the resulting injury to internal organs and bones.

— Blows to the abdomen from a hand, fist, or instrument may not cause visible injuries because the abdominal skin collapses, injuring the bowel rather than the surface, especially at the ligament of Treitz where the bowel is bound to the spine, or spleen, a hollow viscous organ.[52]

  — Blows to the abdomen are the third most common injury in physically abused.

  — If a knee is used to crush the abdomen, marks are unlikely.

  — Children can die when abdominal injury goes unrecognized until there is irreversible shock and decline following trauma.[52]

— Caregivers may crush children's chests and fracture their ribs with a knee or an arm but leave no visible marks on the skin.

— Always consider what organs lay under marks from a blow.

1. If a child's abdomen evidences blunt trauma, radiographic abdominal studies are required.
2. If a child younger than 2 years has suffered blunt trauma, obtain a skeletal series. Oblique views of ribs improve identification of rib fractures of nonaccidental injuries (NAI).[53]
3. Consider radiographic brain studies, since the head can be a target of intentional trauma.
4. The American Academy of Pediatrics recommends a skeletal survey in all children under the age of 2 years in which physical abuse is a consideration. In children older than 2 years and up to 5 years should be considered on an individual basis.[54-58]
5. The Predicting Abusive Head Trauma (PredAHT) tool was effective in a validation study, suggesting it can help clinicians distinguish between abusive head trauma (AHT) and accidental head trauma.[59,60]
6. The 6 clinical features included in PredAHT are rib fractures, long bone fractures, apnea, seizures, retinal hemorrhage, and head/neck bruising.[61-63]

— Guardians and caretakers should be considered suspect when younger victimized children come to the attention of health care providers.

— Older children have the capacity to tell what happened in safe environments; therefore, the examiner should separate the child from the caregiver to obtain a history and complete a physical examination.

Falls

— Unconsciousness in conjunction with injuries to more than one area of the head indicate child abuse rather than a fall.

— Serious injuries are unusual in falls down stairs because the distances a child travels from stair to stair are short.

— Leading body surfaces over bony prominences are more likely to be injured in ambulating children.[64]

— Children rarely fall on belt buckles or other objects, and when they do, it rarely leaves a mark.

Sibling Involvement

The credibility of a history that a sibling caused the trauma must be checked by obtaining a detailed history, noting the developmental stage, mobility, and size of the child and the sibling; clothing worn; acceleration of the child; and objects (eg, table, stair edge, iron, door) that might have absorbed impact force before the final deceleration or landing (**Figure 5-13**). This history should be taken by a law enforcement investigator.

Burns

— The latest data on burn injuries to children shows[65,66]:

  — Burns are the third most frequent cause of injury ending in death, exceeded only by motor vehicle accidents and drowning.

  — Physical abuse or neglect is the cause of 10% to 20% of burn injuries.

  — The majority of burn injuries are scalds from hot liquids.

  — Scalds occur most commonly in children 0-4 years of age.

  — Contact burns from domestic appliances accounts for 40% of intentional burns.

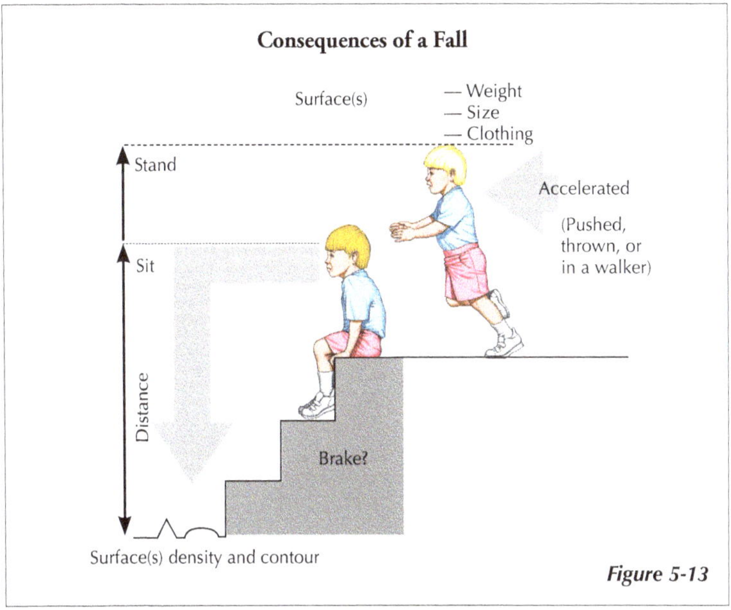

Figure 5-13. *Consequences of a fall down stairs.*

— The skin is the largest organ of the body and provides protection, sensation, thermoregulation, and secretion.[67] Burn injuries are painful, and without the protective mantle of the skin, nerve endings are exposed to stimulation.

— Abusive versus accidental burns can be identified based on body part(s) involved (**Figure 5-14**).

— Burns in children are more serious because their skin is more fragile (**Table 5-6**).

Burns are classified by depth of injury. Seriousness of a burn is determined by "depth (1st-degree, superficial and deep partial-thickness, and full-thickness) and the percentage of total body surface area (TBSA) involved."[71] **Table 5-7** demonstrates unique characteristics of burns and their classification according to degree.

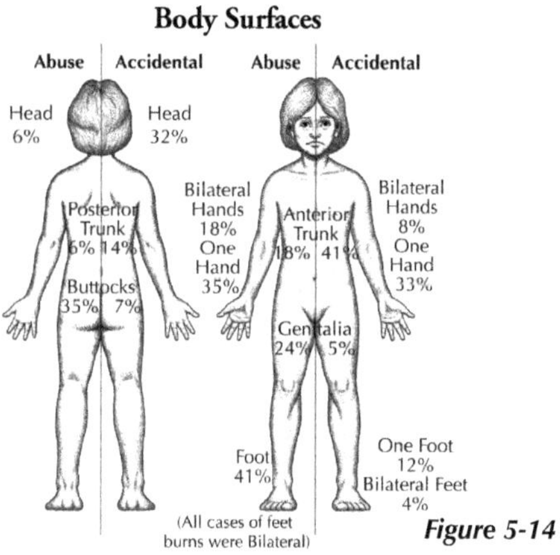

Figure 5-14. *Diagram of anterior and posterior body surfaces with the results of the Grossman Burn Center Study that was presented at the American Burn Association Annual Meeting in 1999. It represents the frequency of involvement of different body parts with a comparison between accidental and abusive burns.*

Table 5-6. Timing for Scald Burns Comparing Temperature to Injury Depth

Water Temperature (Fahrenheit)	Time to Receive First-Degree Burn	Time to Receive Second-Degree Burn	Time to Receive Third-Degree Burn	Time to Receive Fourth-Degree Burn
110 degrees	As tolerated	< 8 minutes	< 10 minutes	unknown
120 degrees	As tolerated	8 minutes	10 minutes	> 10 minutes
124 degrees	< 2 minutes	2 minutes	4 minutes	> 4 minutes
131 degrees	< 17 seconds	17 seconds	30 seconds	> 30 seconds
140 degrees	< 3 seconds	3 seconds	5 seconds	> 5 seconds
150 degrees	Instantaneous touch	< 1 second	1 second	> 1 second
>150 degrees	Approximate touch	Touch	>1 second	> 2 seconds

Data from Chundu K,[68] Burn Foundation,[69] Public Service Enterprise Group,[70] Wolf SE.[71]

Table 5-7. Classification of Burns

	First-Degree	Second-Degree	Third-Degree	Fourth-Degree
Depth	Epithelium superficial	Epithelium and dermal, including superficial, partial thickness, and deep partial-thickness	Epithelium, dermis, and into the underlying adipose tissue	Epithelium, dermis, including full thickness adipose and fascia, exposing muscle, bone, or other deep body parts
Cause	Sunburn, scald, flash flame	Scalds, flash, chemicals, sun	Contact with flames, hot surface, hot liquids, chemical, and electrical	Contact with flames, hot surface, hot liquids, chemical, and electrical
Pain	Painful, tender, sore	Very painful	Very little or no pain	Usually anesthetic or hypo-esthetic without pain; margins may be very painful as the depth lessens
Color	Pink to red; blanches white with light pressure	White or red or mottled red and white with oozing moisture, may include blisters	Acute leathery, dry, no elasticity; charred appearance with flash burns	White and pliable, black and charred, brown and leathery, or bright red, because of fixed hemoglobin in the subdermal region of the injury

(continued)

Table 5-7. Classification of Burns *(continued)*

	First-Degree	Second-Degree	Third-Degree	Fourth-Degree
Time Healing	2-5 days, expect peeling	5-21 days for superficial, 21-35 days for deeper injury	> 30 days if small areas; large areas need grafting	Long hospital stays with frequent surgeries to debris and apply skin graphs
Scar Formation	None, but may increase melanin deposition; this is damaged tissue	Fibrinogen deposition resulting in leather-like scarring	Fibrinogen deposition over large surfaces, creating contractures	Significant scarring and contractures over joints, loss of limb or body location (eg, nose, ears) and function, even with treatment

Adapted from University of New Mexico Hospitals.[72]

Scald Burns

Scald burn patterns help to identify the cause as accidental or abusive in nature.

— Splash burns are typically accidental, occurring when a hot liquid falls onto, is pulled toward, or thrown toward the child (**Figure 5-15**).

— Splash patterns in accidental immersions result as the child attempts to escape from hot liquid.

— Spill burns have a classic arrowhead shape.

— More extensive burn patterns may be caused by thick liquids (eg, grease, oils, syrups), which can reach higher temperatures than boiling water.

— Burn patterns of caustic liquids (acid or base) resemble those of hot liquids.

— Accidental scalds usually result from other liquids (eg, boiling water, coffee, soup).

— Abusive scald burns are largely caused by hot tap water.

— Sharp uniform margins of scald burns suggest abuse from forced immersion by the caregiver holding the child in hot liquid (**Figures 5-16-a** through **c**).

Figure 5-15. *Splash burn pattern.*

***Figure 5-16-a**, **b**, and **c**.* *Immersion burn patterns.*

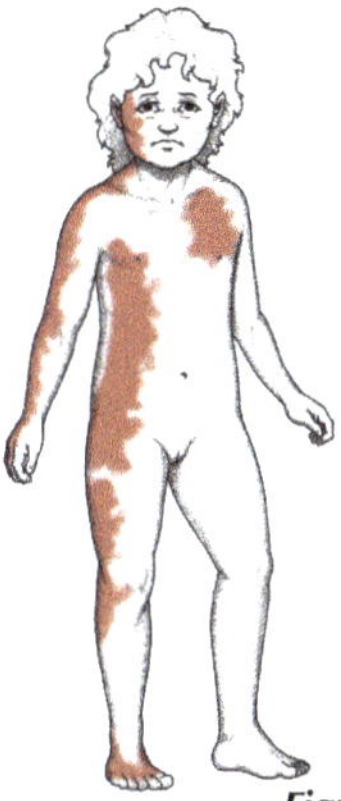

Figure 5-15

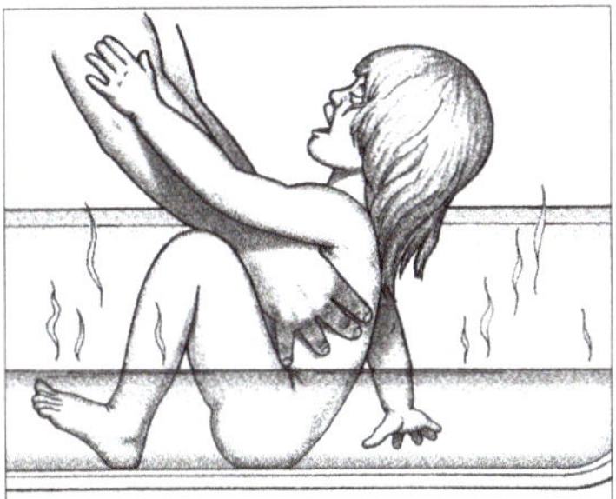

Figure 5-16-a

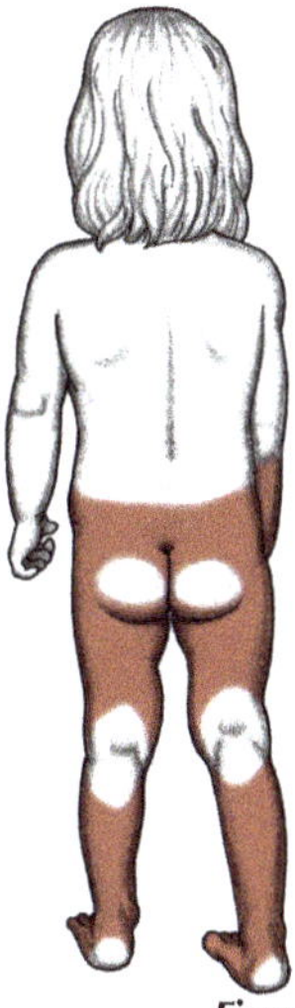

Figure 5-16-b

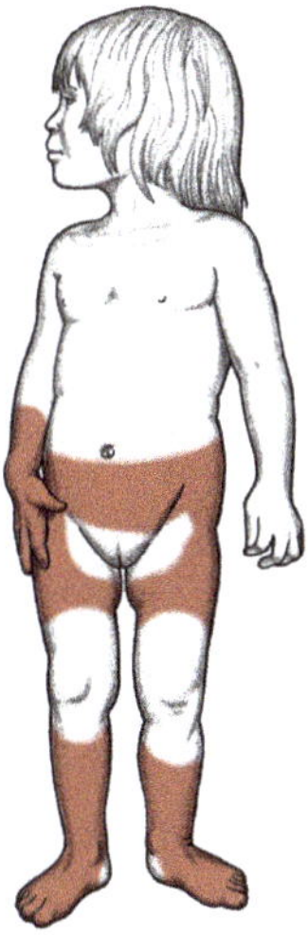

Figure 5-16-c

— Stocking-glove patterns on extremities with or without buttocks involvement suggest abuse (**Figures 5-17-a** and **b**, and **Figure 5-18**).

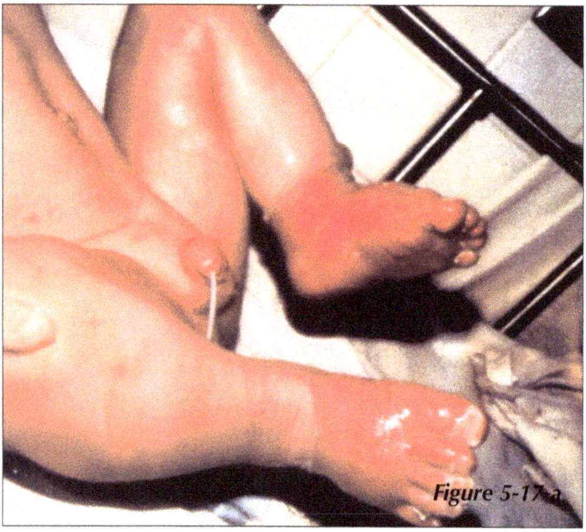

Figure 5-17-a. *Stocking pattern typical of immersion burns.*

Figure 5-17-b. *Glove pattern in immersion burn.*

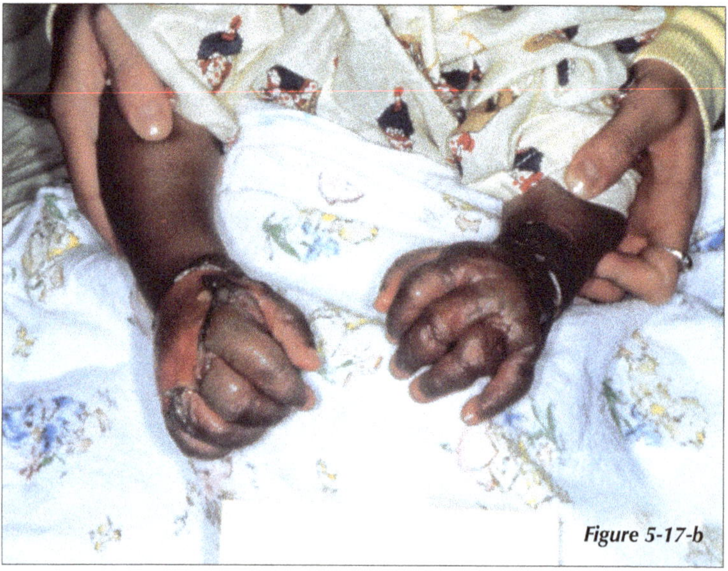

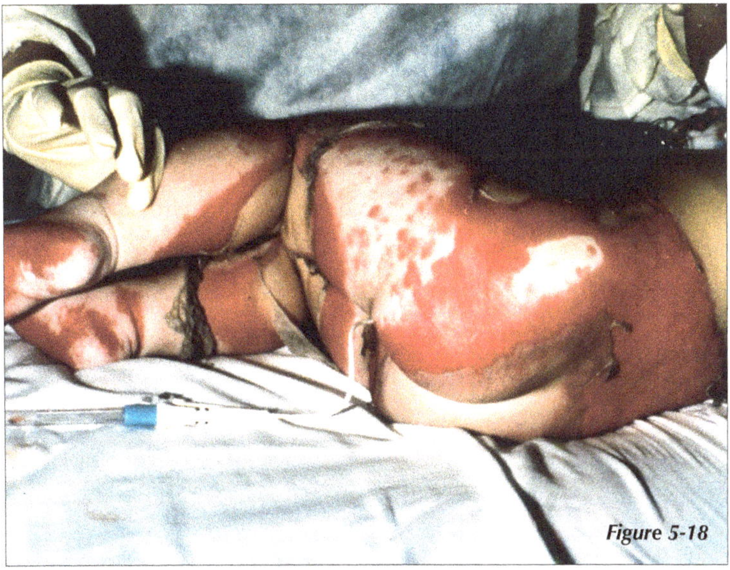

Figure 5-18. *The "doughnut"-shaped pattern on the right buttock is consistent with the lack of burns to the knees. The right buttock would be deeper in the water and against the cooler surface of the tub, whereas the left buttock would have been in the water and received burns to the entire surface. The distinct line of demarcation on the back trunk indicates the water level in the tub.*

— Skin surface sparing occurs within skin folds, when a diaper protects the area, or when a body area is pressed against the container of liquid.

— More severe burns occur when clothing is soaked and not removed.

Contact Burns: Intentional Non-scald Burns (INSB)

The most common reported intentional non-scald burns are contact burns[65]:

— An estimated 40% of contact burns occur from household items

— Causative agents include:

  — Cigarettes and cigarette lighters (**Figure 5-19**)

  — Hair dryers

  — Irons, curling tongs (**Figures 5-20-a** and **b**)

  — Microwaves

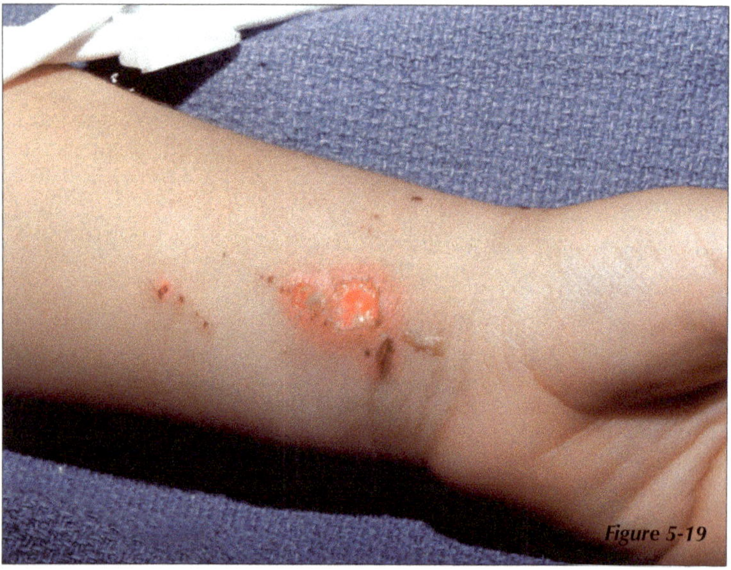

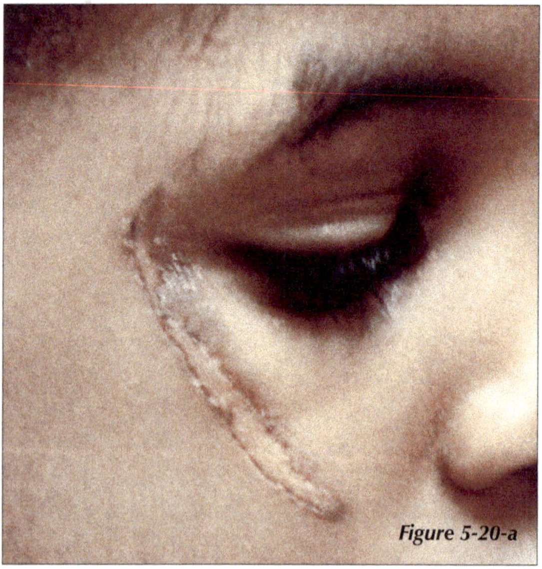

Figure 5-19. *Cigarette burn to a child's wrist.*

Figure 5-20-a. *Intentional curling iron burns inflicted by the boy's step-mother.*

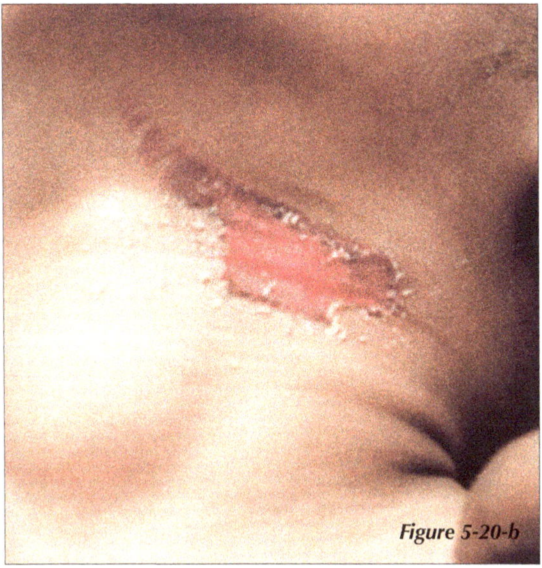

Figure 5-20-b. *Note the shape of the burn to the neck. This wound is the most recent.*

— Radiators, stoves, and heaters

— Miscellaneous agents: chemical burns, flame burns, heated knife, light bulb, hot grease, boiling oil, stun gun

— INSBs usually feature shape of causative agent, found on the trunk, limbs, and back of hand (palms of hands not usually involved)

— Assessment often reveals:

— New burn injuries with evidence of burns in various stages of healing including scarring

— Multiple INSBs may coexist with other types of trauma that may reflect abuse

Flame Burns

— Flame wounds tend to be severe and often involve the hand, potentially causing long-term disability from contractures or deep tissue damage.[71]

— Flame burns inflicted for punishment result from a burning match struck in the face or thigh of the victim.[73]

— Burns from matches or gas stoves may result from holding the child's hands, feet, or other body parts over the flames.[74]

Nonabusive Mimics of Burns

— Infectious diseases:

— ***Erysipelas***: Contagious infectious disease with redness and swelling of affected areas; may also have sharply demarcated bullous lesions (**Figure 5-21**).[75]

— ***Impetigo***: A contagious common skin infection among kids that produces blisters or sores on the face, neck, hands, and diaper area. Caused by *Staphylococcus aureus* or *Streptococcus pyogenes*, and more recently by methicillin-resistant *Staphylococcus aureus* (MRSA) (**Figure 5-22**).[76]

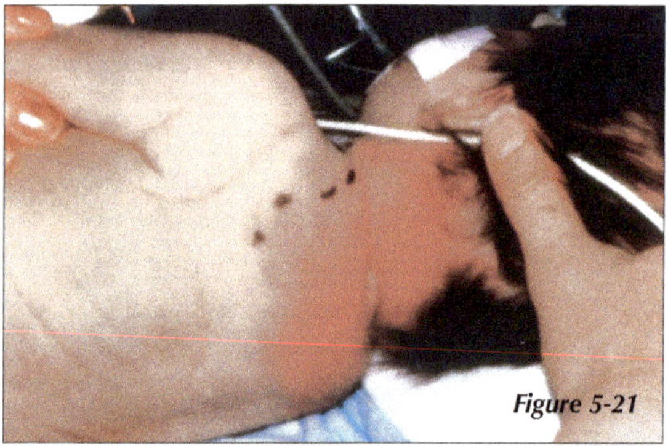

Figure 5-21. *Sharp, raised red lesion of erysipelas, a streptococcal infection.*

Figure 5-22. *Multiple circular crusting lesions of staphylococcal impetigo.*

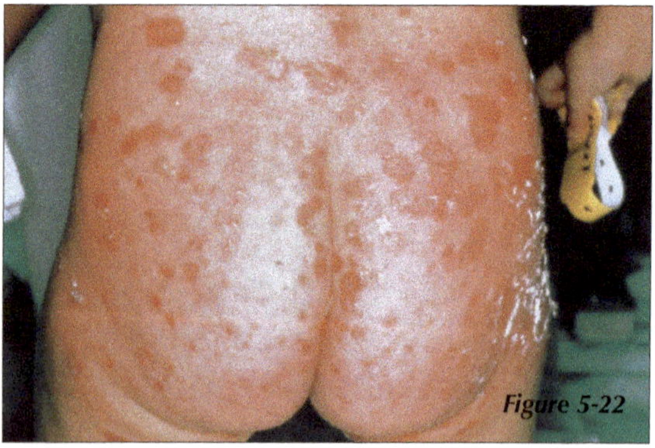

- *Staphylococcal scalded skin syndrome (SSSS)*: Staphylococcal disease presenting with superficial blistering to severe exfoliation, affecting almost the entire body.[77]
- *Phytophotodermatitis*: A phototoxic reaction that can occur at any age due to exposure to both a photosensitizing substance, such as lime or other citrus juices, and ultraviolet radiation. Classic examples are a handprint pattern on a child after exposure to lime juice while a parent was cooking and linear drip patterns presenting on a child's hands and arms after eating real juice ice pops.[78]

Differential Diagnosis for the Health Care Provider

- Diagnosis is based on history and physical exam.
- Order diagnostic laboratory tests.
- Obtain radiologic testing, including skeletal surveys and area-specific imaging, such as CAT Scans, ultrasounds, MRI scans, and other types of imaging specific to suspected organ injury.
- In the case of burns, perform a site visit to measure water temperature and/or see the layout of the environment described by the family. Site visit should be performed by law enforcement.
- Rule out medical causes and conditions.
- Use evidence-based scales to rule out abuse.

History

- Pay attention to the child's previous state of health, including development and behavior, and the details of the incident, including time, source of heat, supervision of the child, and location of others at the time of the incident.
- In the case of burns, note the child's age, whether tap water was the source of heat, bathroom-related histories, and histories requiring developmental skills beyond the child's age.[79,80]
- In the case of bruises, pay attention to the child's previous state of health, including development and behavior, and the details of the incident, including time, location, caregiver, and history.

PHYSICAL EXAMINATION OF BURNS

— Carefully measure and record the burned area and the depth of the burn(s).

— Describe the thermal injury as first, second, or third degree.

— Indicate the area covered by the burn as a percentage of body surface area and record it on age-corrected surface area charts (eg, Lund and Brower or Berkow charts).

— Be aware that depth of the burn cannot be accurately determined immediately after the burn. Repeat the exam 24 and 48 hours after the burn to completely assess the extent of involvement.

— If the injuries allow, directly observe the child's developmental capabilities to determine the credibility of the history.

— Suggestive findings include:

1. Burns on the back of the hand, buttocks, and feet.
2. Delay in seeking attention. Although, other factors may influence the decision not to seek immediate attention (eg, lack of transportation, lack of access to a phone, lack of money for transportation), and a burn may appear first as a simple injury and then evolve to vesicles, a classic finding in second-degree burns. Caregivers may not recognize the severity of the burn until after a nap, when the skin may come off a child as clothing or bedding is removed from contact with the skin surface.

REFERENCES

1. Bryant RA, Nix DP, eds. *Acute & Chronic Wounds: Current Management Concepts*. 4th ed. Saint Louis, MO: Mosby; 2011.
2. US Department of Health and Human Services. Definitions of child abuse and neglect in federal law. Child Welfare Information Gateway Web site. https://www.childwelfare.gov/topics/can/defining/federal/. Accessed September 1, 2016.
3. Child Welfare Information Gateway. *Mandatory Reporters of Child Abuse and Neglect*. Washington, DC: US Department of Health and Human Services, Children's Bureau; 2016. Child Welfare Information Gateway Web site. https://www.childwelfare.gov/topics/systemwide/laws-policies/statutes/manda/. Accessed February 28, 2017.

4. Besant-Matthews PE. Blunt and sharp injury handout – interpretation – documentation. *Journal of the Association of Firearm and Toolmark Examiners*. 1984;16(3):41-50.

5. Schwartz AJ, Ricci LR. How accurately can bruises be aged in abused children? Literature review and synthesis. *Pediatrics*. 1996;97:254-257.

6. Advanced Tissue. 6 steps of the wound healing process. Advanced Tissue Web site. https://www.advancedtissue.com/the-6-steps-of-the-wound-healing-process/. Accessed February 28, 2017.

7. Allen GA, Glader B. Approach to the bleeding child. *Pediatr Clin North Am*. 2002;49(6):1239-1256.

8. Hoffman R, Benz EJ Jr, Shattil SJ, et al, eds. *Hematology: Basic Principle and Practice*. 4th ed. Philadelphia, PA: Elsevier Health Sciences; 2004.

9. Iannelli V. Bruising and children who bruise easily: signs and symptoms of normal bruising. verywell Web site. https://www.verywell.com/bruising-symptoms-of-common-childhood-illnesses-2634329. Updated August 24, 2016. Accessed September 1, 2016.

10. Kaczor K, Pierce MC, Makoroff K, Corey TS. Bruising and physical child abuse. *Clin Pediatr Emerg Med*. 2006;7(3):153-160

11. Kliegman RM, Behrman RE, Jenson HB, Stanton BMD, Zitelli BJ, Davis HW. *Nelson Textbook of Pediatrics*. 18th ed. Philadelphia, PA: Saunders; 2007.

12. Sommers MS, Fargo JD, Baker RB, Fisher BS, Buschur C, Zink TM. Health disparities in the forensic sexual assault examination related to skin color. *J Forensic Nurs*. 2009;5(4):191-200.

13. Sugar NF, Taylor JA, Feldman KW. Bruises in infants and toddlers: those who don't cruise rarely bruise. *Arch Pediatr Adolesc Med*. 1999;153(4):399-403.

14. Montgomery RR, Scott JP. Von Willebrand disease. In: Behrman RE, Kleigman RM, Jenson HB, eds. *Nelson's Textbook of Pediatrics*. 16th ed. Philadelphia, PA: WB Saunders Company; 2000:1513-1515.

15. Iannelli V. Important facts, figures and examples of child abuse cases. verywell Web site. https://www.verywell.com/child-abuse-cases-and-stories-2633354. Updated April 13, 2016. Accessed September 1, 2016.

16. Cornforth T. What you should know about abnormal uterine bleeding. verywell Web site. https://www.verywell.com/abnormal-uterine-bleeding-3520365. Updated August 18, 2016. Accessed September 1, 2016.

17. Hayes K. What causes frequent bloody noses? verywell Web site. https://www.verywell.com/what-causes-frequent-bloody-noses-1192166. Updated April 20, 2016. Accessed September 1, 2016.

18. Eldridge L. Coping with thrombocytopenia (low platelets) during chemotherapy: symptoms, treatments, and coping with a low platelet count during chemo. verywell Web site. https://www.verywell.com/thrombocytopenia-low-platelets-chemotherapy-symptom-2249347. Updated August 16, 2016. Accessed September 1, 2016.

19. Kugler M. Idiopathic thrombocytopenic purpura (ITP): an autoimmune disease: what is ITP, is it hereditary and how is the disorder diagnosed and treated? verywell Web site. https://www.verywell.com/idiopathic-thrombocytopenic-purpura-itp-2860677. Updated February 29, 2016. Accessed September 1, 2016.

20. Kugler M. Christmas disease and hemophilia: inherited blood disorders. verywell Web site. https://www.verywell.com/christmas-disease-and-hemophilia-2860346. Updated June 12, 2014. Accessed September 1, 2016.

21. Yates A. Hemophilia. verywell Web site. https://www.verywell.com/understanding-hemophilia-401329. Updated November 20, 2015. Accessed September 1, 2016.

22. Wong C. Vitamin K: what you need to know about vitamin K. verywell Web site. https://www.verywell.com/all-about-vitamin-k-benefits-and-uses-89528. Updated January 7, 2016. Accessed September 1, 2016.

23. Mudd SS, Findlay JS. The cutaneous manifestations and common mimickers of physical child abuse. *J Pediatr Health Care*. 2004;18(3):123-129.

24. MayoClinicStaff. Ehlers-Danlos syndrome. Mayo Clinic Web site. http://www.mayoclinic.org/diseases-conditions/ehlers-danlos-syndrome/basics/symptoms/CON-20033656?p=1. Published August 20, 2015. Accessed September 1, 2016.

25. Centers for Disease Control and Prevention. Fifth disease. Centers for Disease Control and Prevention Web site. http://www.cdc.gov/parvovirusB19/fifth-disease.html. Updated November 2, 2015. Accessed September 1, 2016.

26. Skin conditions and eczema. WebMD Web site. http://www.webmd.com/skin-problems-and-treatments/guide/atopic-dermatitis-eczema. Accessed September 1, 2016.

27. Hornor G. Physical abuse: recognition and reporting. *J Pediatr Health Care*. 2005;19(1):4-11.

28. Immunization Action Coalition. *Haemophilus influenzae* type b (Hib) Photos. Immunization Action Coalition Web site. http://www.immunize.org/photos/hib-photos.asp. Updated July 18, 2016. Accessed September 1, 2016.

29. Stevens-Johnson syndrome (SJS). WebMD Web site. http://www.webmd.com/skin-problems-and-treatments/stevens-johnson-syndrome. Accessed September 1, 2016.

30. Gupta D, Thappa DM. Mongolian spots—a prospective study. *Indian J Dermatol Venereol Leprol*. 2013;79(4):469-478.

31. Mahesh M. Physiological striae in adolescence: not physical abuse. *Emerg Med J*. 2012;29(1):9.

32. Watkins J. Symptoms and treatment of ringworm infections. *British Journal of School Nursing*. 2014;9(3):144-146.

33. Kennedy SA, Stoll LE, Lauder AS. Human and other mammalian bite injuries of the hand: evaluation and management. *J Am Acad Orthop Surg*. 2015;23(1):47-57.

34. Hilton L. Cutaneous clues of child abuse. *Contemp Pediatr*. 2015;32(10):24-33.

35. wiseGEEK. In traditional Chinese medicine, what is coining? wiseGEEK Web site. http://www.wisegeek.org/in-traditional-chinese-medicine-what-is-coining.htm. Accessed September 1, 2016.

36. Jain A, Chen Y, Park U. Scars, marks & tattoos (SMT): physical atributes for person identification. Google Web site. https://www.google.com/webhp?sourceid=chrome-instant&ion=1&espv=2&ie=UTF-8#q=Scars+Marks+Tattoos+Physical+Attributes. Accessed September 1, 2016.

37. US Department of Justice, Office of Justice Programs, Office of Juvenile Justice and Delinquency Prevention. *Recognizing When a Child's Injury or Illness Is Caused by Abuse*. Washington, DC: US Department of Justice, Office of Justice Programs, Office of Juvenile Justice and Delinquency Prevention; 2014.

38. Committee on Child Abuse and Neglect, American Academy of Pediatrics. When inflicted skin injuries constitute child abuse. *Pediatrics*. 2002;110(3):644-645.

39. Levin AV. Ophthalmology of shaken baby syndrome. *Neurosurg Clin N Am*. 2002;13(2):201-211.

40. Grace A, Grace S. Child abuse within the ear, nose and throat. *J Otolaryngol*. 1987;16(2):108-111.

41. Tate RJ. Facial injuries associated with the battered child syndrome. *Br J Oral Surg*. 1971;9(1):41-45.

42. Manning SC, Casselbrant M, Lammers D. Otolaryngologic manifestations of child abuse. *Int J Pediatr Otorhinolaryngol*. 1990;20(1):7-16.

43. Obiako MN. Eardrum perforation as evidence of child abuse. *Child Abuse Negl*. 1987;11(1):149-151.

44. Forjuoh SN. Child maltreatment related injuries: incidence, hospital charges, and correlates of hospitalization. *Child Abuse Negl*. 2000;24(8):1019-1025.

45. Johnson CF, Kaufman KL, Callendar C. The hand as a target organ in child abuse. *Clin Pediatr*. 1990;29(2):66-72.

46. Frankenburg WK, Dodds JB. *Denver Developmental Screening Test*. Denver, CO: University of Colorado Medical Center; 1969.

47. Kemp AM, Dunstan F, Nuttall D, Hamilton M, Collins P, Maguire S. Patterns of bruising in preschool children—a longitudinal study. *Arch Dis Child.* 2015;100(5):426-431.

48. Johnson CF, Showers J. Injury variables in child abuse. *Child Abuse Negl.* 1985;9(2):207-215.

49. Johnson CF. Constricting bands: manifestations of possible child abuse. *Clin Pediatr.* 1988;27(9):439-444.

50. Boos SC. Constrictive asphyxia: a recognizable form of fatal child abuse. *Child Abuse Negl.* 2000;24(11):1503-1507.

51. Oral R, Koc F, Smith J, Sato Y. Abusive suffocation presenting as new-onset seizure. *Pediatr Emerg Care.* 2010;27(11):1072-1074.

52. Saxena AK. Pediatric abdominal trauma. Medscape Web site. http://emedicine.medscape.com/article/1984811-overview#a2. Updated August 14, 2015. Accessed September 2, 2016.

53. Meyer JS, Gunderman R, Coley BD, et al. ACR Appropriateness Criteria(®) on suspected physical abuse-child. *J Am Coll Radiol.* 2011;8(2):87-94.

54. Kemp AM, Maguire SA, Nuttall D, Collins P, Dunstan F. Bruising in children who are assessed for suspected physical abuse. *Arch Dis Child.* 2014;99(2):108-113.

55. Laskey AL, Stump TE, Hicks RA, Smith JL. Yield of skeletal surveys in children ≤ 18 months of age presenting with isolated skull fractures. *J Pediatr.* 2013;162(1):86-89.

56. Quigley AJ, Stafrace S. Skeletal survey normal variants, artefacts and commonly misinterpreted findings not to be confused with non-accidental injury. *Pediatr Radiol.* 2014;44(1):82-93.

57. Di Pietro MA, Brody AS, Cassady CI, Stolic A. Diagnostic imaging of child abuse. *Pediatrics.* 2009;123(5):1430-1435.

58. Warkentine FH, Horowitz R, Pierce MC. The use of ultrasound to detect occult or unsuspected fractures in child abuse. *Pediatr Emerg Care.* 2014;30(1):43-46.

59. Crowley LE, Morris CB, Maguire SA, Farewell DM, Kemp AM. Validation of a prediction tool for abusive head trauma. *Pediatrics*. 2015;136(2):290-298.

60. Pullin DA, Singleton MN. Child physical abuse: complex cases and guideline updates. Paper presented at: National Association of Pediatric Nurse Practitioners 37th Annual Conference; March 2015; Atlanta, GA.

61. Ernoehazy W. Haning injuries and strangulation. Medscape Web site. http://misc.medscape.com/pi/iphone/medscapeapp/html/A826704-business.html. Accessed September 2, 2016.

62. Pullen LC. Tool identifies clinical features predictive of child abuse. Medscape Web site. http://www.medscape.com/viewarticle/848655. Published July 27, 2015. Accessed September 2, 2016.

63. Sabo RA, Hanigan WC, Flessner K, Rose J, Aaland M. Strangulation injuries in children. part 1. clinical analysis. *J Trauma*. 1996;40(1):68-72.

64. Carpenter RF. The prevalence and distribution of bruising in babies. *Arch Dis Child*. 1999;80(4):363-366.

65. Kemp AM, Maguire SA, Lumb RC, Mann MK. Contact, cigarette and flame burns in physical abuse: a systematic review. *Child Abuse Rev*. 2014;23(1). doi: 10.1002/car.2278.

66. Toon MH, Maybauer DM, Arceneaux LL, et al. Children with burn injuries—assessment of trauma, neglect, violence and abuse. *J Inj Violence Res*. 2011;3(2):98-110.

67. Herndon DN. *Total Burn Care*. 3rd ed. Philadelphia, PA: Elsevier; 2007.

68. Chundu K. Pediatric burn: an overview. Maricopa Integrated Health System Web site. http://www2.mihs.org/WebsiteLink/AZBurn2012/Pediatric%20Burns2012.pdf. Accessed September 2, 2016.

69. Burn Foundation. Safety facts on Scald Burns. Burn Foundation Web site. http://www.burnfoundation.org/programs/resource.cfm?c=1&a=3. Accessed February 28, 2017.

70. Public Service Enterprise Group. Scalding from hot water. Public Service Enterprise Group Web site. https://www.pseg.com/home/education_safety/safety/scalding.jsp. Accessed February 28, 2017.

71. Wolf SE. Burns. Merck Manual Web site. http://www.merckmanuals.com/professional/injuries-poisoning/burns/burns. Accessed September 2, 2016.

72. University of New Mexico Hospitals. Burn classification. University of New Mexico Web site. http://hospitals.unm.edu/burn/classification.shtml. Accessed September 2, 2016.

73. Ramakrishnan KM, Mathivanan Y, Sankar J. Profile of children abused by burning. *Ann Burns Fire Disasters*. 2010;23(1):8-12.

74. Missouri Department of Social Services. Physical abuse. In: Missouri Department of Social Services, ed. *Child Welfare Manual*. Jefferson City, MO: Missouri Department of Social Services; 2014. Missouri Department of Social Services Web site. https://dss.mo.gov/cd/info/cwmanual/section7/ch1_33/sec7ch28.htm. Accessed September 2, 2016.

75. Davis L. Erysipelas. Medscape Web site. http://emedicine.medscape.com/article/1052445-overview#a4. Accessed September 2, 2016.

76. Impetigo. Kids Health Web site. http://kidshealth.org/en/parents/impetigo.html?WT.ac=ctg#catbacterial-viral. Accessed September 2, 2016.

77. King RW. Staphylococcal scaled skin syndrome. Medscape Web site. http://emedicine.medscape.com/article/788199-overview. Updated June 15, 2016. Accessed September 2, 2016.

78. Foods that contain psoralen. Heal With Food Web site. http://www.healwithfood.org/foods-that-contain/psoralen.php. Accessed September 2, 2016.

79. Montrey JS, Barcia PJ. Nonaccidental burns in child abuse. *South Med J*. 1985;78(11):1324-1326.

80. Hultman CS, Priolo D, Cairns BA, Grant EJ, Peterson HD, Meyer AA. Return to jeopardy: the fate of pediatric burn patients who are victims of abuse and neglect. *J Burn Care Rehabil*. 1998;19(4):367-376; discussion 366-367.

Chapter 6

Ophthalmic Manifestations and Oral Injuries

Joyce P. Williams, DNP, AFN-BC, FAAFS, FAAN
David A. Williams, DDS, MS, MPH
Diana K. Faugno, MSN, RN, CPN, SANE-A, SANE-P, FAAFS, DF-IAFN
Joseph Giangiacomo, MD
Lori D. Frasier, MD, FAAP
Patrica M. Speck, DNSc, ARNP, APN, FNP-BC, DF-IAFN, FAAFS, FAAN

Ophthalmic Manifestations

Ophthalmic abnormalities are present in about 5% of abused children,[1] with 75% to 90% of victims of shaken baby syndrome (SBS) having retinal hemorrhages.[2] The ocular manifestations linked to child abuse are listed in **Table 6-1**.

Table 6-1. Ophthalmic Findings in Cases of Child Abuse

Eyelids and Periorbital Area
— Adhesions from glue applications
— Cigarette burns
— Ecchymosis
— Laceration
— Crab lice (pediculosis of the eyelids and eyebrows)
Conjunctiva
— Conjunctivitis (chlamydia infection, gonorrhea, HIV retinitis)
— Hemorrhage
— Lacerations

(continued)

Table 6-1. Ophthalmic Findings in Cases of Child Abuse *(continued)*

CORNEA
— Laceration — Scars
ANTERIOR CHAMBER
— Heterochromia — Hyphema — Iridodialysis — Mydriasis
RETINA
— Commotio retinae — Detachment — Hemorrhage — Purtscher retinopathy — Retinal folds — Retinoschisis — Terson syndrome (retinal, preretinal, and vitreous hemorrhages in association with subarachnoid hemorrhage)
STRABISMUS
— Amblyopia — Esotropia — Exotropia — Paralytic
SHAKEN BABY SYNDROME
— Retinal hemorrhages (symmetric or asymmetric; unilateral or bilateral) — Hemorrhage predominantly in posterior pole; may be subretinal, intraretinal, neurofiber layer, preretinal, and vitreal
STRANGULATION AND SUFFOCATION
— Ranging from conjunctival petechiae to retinal hemorrhages bilaterally

— Every anatomical structure of the visual system can be affected[3] (**Figure 6-1**).

— The ability to identify child abuse as the cause of ophthalmic abnormalities rests on maintaining a high index of suspicion and asking appropriate questions of caregivers concerning the circumstances of injury.

Anatomy of the Eye

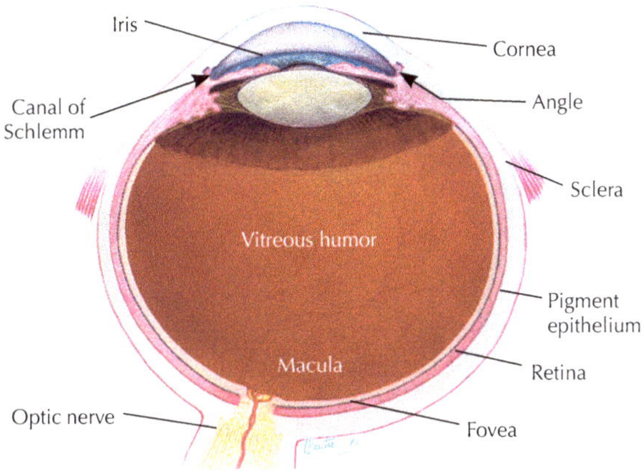

Figure 6-1

Figure 6-1. *Anatomy of the eye. Adapted from the National Eye Institute, National Institutes of Health, Bethesda, MD.*

— Consider physical abuse when an implausible history of unilateral cases of cataract, retinal detachment, or dislocated lens is given.

— The long-term ophthalmologic effects of child neglect include visual impairment caused by amblyopia, strabismus, optic atrophy, and atrophy of the visual cortex after neuronal injury.

— Perform an objective exam seeking disease processes to explain ophthalmic findings. When there is no medical diagnosis, referral to a pediatric ophthalmologist is essential for detection of subtle intraocular injury and findings.

Eyelids and Periorbital Area

— Ecchymoses, lacerations, and edema of the eyelids and periorbital area are vivid ocular clues of child abuse, specifically blunt trauma.

— Other signs include cigarette burns and adhesions of the upper and lower lids from application of a strong adhesive.[4]

— Pubic lice on the lashes or eyebrows may indicate child abuse but may also indicate transfer to the eyelashes and brows by exposure to bedsheets of infected adults.[5,6]

CONJUNCTIVA

— Subconjunctival hemorrhage and conjunctival laceration:

1. The subconjunctival hemorrhage results from a sudden increase in intrathoracic or intracranial pressure, as in blunt thoracic trauma, severe vomiting, Valsalva maneuver, or paroxysmal coughing.
2. Finding subconjunctival hemorrhage with no physiologic cause or known accidental trauma involving chest or neck compression may indicate strangulation during physical assault and abuse and could mimic hemorrhagic conjunctivitis (**Figure 6-2**).[7,8]

— Failure to recognize conjunctival findings associated with strangulation or closed head trauma may result in death of the child.

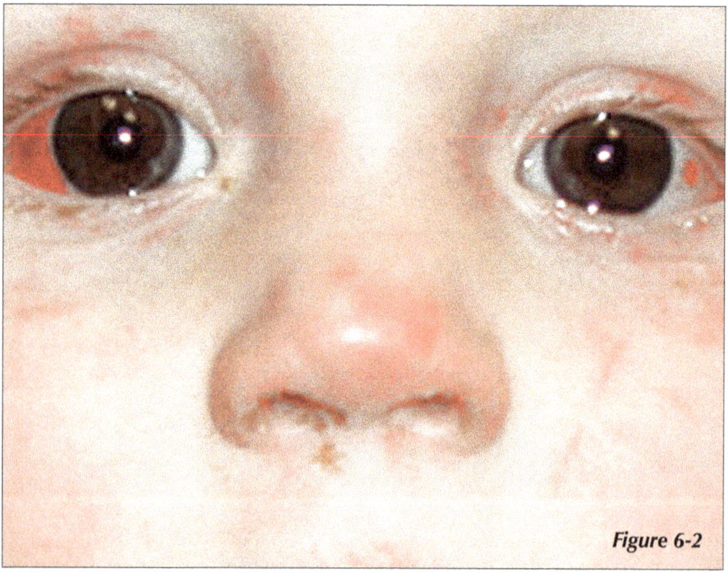

Figure 6-2. *Bilateral subconjunctival hemorrhages.*

— Conjunctivitis caused by sexually transmitted infection (STI)[9] is a red flag for sexual abuse in young children:

1. *Neisseria gonorrhoeae* conjunctivitis is characterized by copious mucopurulent discharge.
2. *Chlamydia trachomatis* infection manifests as acute or chronic conjunctivitis.
3. Both *N. gonorrhoeae* and *C. trachomatis* conjunctivitis can occur in neonates after passage through an infected birth canal.

— Eye infection can be caused by human immunodeficiency virus (HIV), although this is rare in child abuse, and it manifests as retinitis. Intravaginal transmission of HIV is also possible.

Cornea, Anterior Chamber, and Lens

— Corneal lacerations from sharp objects or corneal rupture from blunt trauma can indicate abuse and may cause scar formation and astigmatism.

— Breaks in Descemet's membrane usually result from blunt or penetrating trauma and can also produce astigmatism and scarring.

— The anterior chamber can be filled with blood (hyphema) after trauma. Nontraumatic etiologies must be excluded.

— Mydriasis (dilation of the pupil) can occur after rupture of the iris sphincter.

— Iridodialysis, the separation of the iris from its base, usually occurs after indirect impact trauma.

— Acquired heterochromia (ie, having different colored eyes) can occur nontraumatically, by accidental trauma, or through child abuse.

— In hemosiderosis, iron toxicity in the eye may develop from recurrent intraocular bleeding caused by abusive head trauma (AHT).

— Blunt head trauma can cause lens dislocation, cataracts, or other conditions, often in addition to hyphema or orbital ecchymosis and subconjunctival hemorrhage.

Retina

— Blunt force trauma to the retina may cause retinal detachment, commotio retinae, retinal hemorrhages, and vitreous hemorrhages that can lead to posttraumatic cataract or dislocated lens.

— Direct trauma to the globe and its surrounding tissue, either as a single event or as multiple events, may occur with AHT.

— Retinal hemorrhages are not unusual in neonates:

1. Between 30% and 59% of full-term infants have retinal hemorrhages at birth,[10,11] which appear as splintered, flame-shaped, dot, or blot and are rarely preretinal or vitreous. They occur with difficult deliveries, use of suction extraction, and rarely, cesarean section but usually resolve over several weeks.
2. With accidental trauma, retinal hemorrhages are usually few and small.
3. Infants with an underlying coagulopathy have hemorrhages in all retinal layers as well as the vitreous.
4. In rare cases of arteriovenous malformation or aneurysm, retinal hemorrhages may be as extensive as those seen with AHT.[12]
5. Other rare causes of extensive retinal hemorrhage are glutaric acidemia and galactosemia, each of which has a defined clinical spectrum differing from that of retinal hemorrhages linked to AHT.

Retinal Signs of Abusive Head Trauma

— Retinal hemorrhages are a hallmark of AHT.

— **Table 6-2** lists findings in cases of AHT.

— Note that intracranial and intraocular hemorrhage can occur in head trauma, birth trauma, coagulopathies, vascular disease, hypertension, diabetes, strangulation, arteriovenous malformation of the central nervous system (CNS), hypernatremia, and dehydration.

— With AHT, caregivers often do not report a clear history of trauma even with evidence of other injuries (eg, occult fractures of the long bones, ribs, and skull).

Table 6-2. Findings in Abusive Head Trauma

SYMPTOMS
— Lethargy
— Vomiting
— Seizures
— Apnea
— Respiratory arrest
— Cardiac arrest
SPECTRUM OF HEMORRHAGES
— Retinal hemorrhage with intracranial hemorrhage
— Retinal hemorrhage without other signs of abuse, such as bruising or occult fractures
— Intracranial hemorrhage without retinal hemorrhage
— Any combination of the above with external evidence of trauma
OCULAR PROGNOSTIC INDICATORS
— A sluggish pupil, minimal response, or absent pupil response
— Diffuse bilateral, retinal, or preretinal hemorrhages
CAUSES OF VISUAL LOSS FROM SHAKEN BABY SYNDROME
— Amblyopia
— Optic atrophy
— Choroidal retinal pigment epithelial disruption in macula
— Retinoschisis
— Cerebral cortical visual loss

— Mechanisms of injury in AHT:

1. CNS damage occurs when the cerebrum is whipped back and forth in the cranial cavity.[13]
2. Repetitive whiplash effect directly injures brain cells and tears the bridging cerebral veins, producing subdural hemorrhage.
3. Predisposing factors for CNS damage specific to infants include pliable skull, large brain closely positioned to the skull, relatively large surface area, shallow depth of subarachnoid space, incomplete myelinization, and short, narrow skull base coupled with weak and immature neck muscles.

4. AHT primarily occurs in small victims.
5. Substantial clinical, pathologic, and experimental evidence supports intraocular hemorrhage in AHT as a byproduct of repetitive forces stressing the retina, vitreous, and other structures.
6. In traumatic retinoschisis, repetitive shaking causes rapid acceleration and deceleration, producing a coup-contrecoup effect on the vitreoretinal interface.[14]
7. In infant eyes, firm attachments exist between the lens and the vitreous gel and retina. Forces transferred from these attachments cause significant traction on the retina, producing separation and hemorrhage in different retinal layers and on the inner surface of the retina, intraretina, or subretinal spaces (**Figure 6-3**).

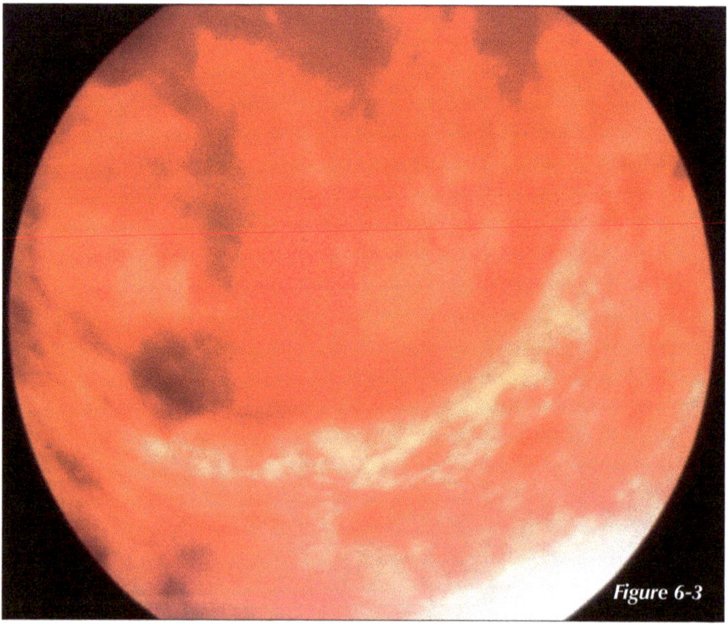

Figure 6-3. *Color funduscopic photograph of a 7-month-old child's retina showing hemorrhages at all layers of the retina as well as a macular fold along the inferotemporal vascular arcade. The latter finding is highly suggestive of SBS in a child of this age.*

8. Vitreous or retinal hemorrhage can also occur when increased intracranial pressure causes compression of the central retinal vein, resulting in intraocular hemorrhage, usually confined to the juxtapapillary and macular areas. However, central retinal vein occlusion should be easily distinguished from the retinal hemorrhages of SBS.

— For details regarding Terson syndrome or Purtscher disease, see Chapter 3, "Head Trauma."

Oral Injuries in Child Abuse

Injuries to the oral and perioral area occur as frequently as 50% to 75% in child abuse cases. These injuries may be incurred on hard or soft tissues.

Hard Tissue Injuries

Injuries to Teeth

- When forces are applied to the oral tissues, the teeth may be fractured or moved, or the supporting structures may be damaged.
  - Fractures to teeth may affect the enamel, the enamel and dentin, or the enamel, dentin, and pulpal tissue.
  - A critical finding when the fracture is observed is if there is bleeding from inside the tooth. This is an indication that the fracture includes the pulpal tissue, and a dentist should be consulted as soon as possible, as the vitality of the tooth has been compromised.
  - Where only the enamel or the enamel and dentin are fractured, there are concerns regarding the vitality of the tooth, but immediate referral is not necessary in most cases.
- Teeth may be moved completely out of the socket and mouth (avulsion) or may be moved within the socket in the direction of the force. This may be in any direction, including apical displacement.
  - If the tooth is avulsed and recovered, it should be placed in an isotonic liquid (eg, sterile saline, milk) and taken to the dentist for re-implantation. The tooth should not be cleaned in any way, as this can remove tissue remnants that, after re-implantation, may help the tooth to heal.

Injuries to Supporting Structures

— If the tooth is moved within the socket it may show signs of bleeding from the gingival tissue around the tooth.

— If radiographs are available, they may show widening of the socket around the tooth, or a fracture of the alveolar bone.

— It is best for a dentist to reposition the tooth, but if there is not a dentist readily available, the health care worker can reposition the tooth, using the adjacent teeth and the contralateral tooth as a guide.

— If the child can vocalize and states that his/her teeth "don't feel like they are coming together normally," then a fracture of the mandible or maxilla or dislocation of the temporomandibular joint should be suspected.

— In these cases a dentist or oral surgeon should be consulted.[15-19]

Soft Tissue Injuries

— Oral mucosa will react similarly to other mucosal tissues or skin, in that it can be lacerated, contused, incised, abraded, or burned.

— Sharp or hot objects being placed in the mouth or blunt objects inserted with force also may injure these tissues.

— STIs may be evident in the oral cavity, and underaged victims who are diagnosed with an STI are, by definition, abused.[18]

Lips

— Forces to the mouth most often cause lacerations or contusions to the lips.

— Blows to the mouth can cause lips to be cut with the child's teeth. Bruising or lacerations at the commissures (ie, corners) of the mouth or bruising of the upper lip at the midline may indicate the prior placement of a gag or pinching the lip to silence a child.

— The labial and lingual frenula may be torn as a result of a slap, forced feeding, or forcing some other hard object into the mouth. This type of injury is pathognomonic for abuse in the nonambulatory patient.

Tongue

The tongue can be damaged when it is caught between the arches of teeth during a blow to the face. In these cases, ensure that the patient has teeth that are consistent with the injury, as the tongue injury may not have been self-induced.

Hard and Soft Palate

— Injuries to the hard and soft palate may be unintentional if the child falls with an object in the mouth.

— Injuries suffered as abuse occur when an object is placed in the mouth or when an object is in the mouth when the child is struck.

— Indications of forced fellatio include contusions, abrasions, petechial hemorrhages, and/or ulcerations in the hard or soft palate or the posterior pharynx.[5,15,20]

Bite Marks/Pattern Injuries

Any clinical exam that identifies a circular, semicircular, or interrupted circular mark should be considered to be a bite mark until determined otherwise.

— The processing of the suspected bite mark/patterned injury should not interfere with the normal course of medical treatment for the patient, but care should be taken to preserve the mark as best as possible. For instance, if there is a suspected mark on the face, taping for a nasal tube should avoid the area.

Bite marks may be made by adults, children, or animals.

— The typical carnivores (eg, dogs, cats) have very sharp canine teeth and typically have a lesser intercanine distance (ie, distance between canine teeth). The bites of these animals have deep puncture wounds in the location of the canine teeth.

— The dental arches of children are much smaller than adults and the teeth themselves are smaller. Conversely, the adult arch is much larger with larger teeth.

— Typically, only the front 6 upper/lower teeth are involved in the bite, so it is difficult to identify the perpetrator beyond the child/adult determination.

— A dentist, trained as a forensic dentist (ie, forensic odontologist), should be called as soon as feasible in any case. If this is not possible, documentation should progress in a manner standard with any other injury.

 — Noninvasive procedures should be performed first. The wound should be drawn, followed by a written description and then photographed from 3 distances: (1) far, showing most of the patient; (2) medium, showing the location of the wound; and (3) near, showing just the wound.

 — The near photographs should be made with and without a scale. Ideally, an ABFO #2 ruler should be used, but if unavailable, other scales are adequate.

 — On areas that are curvilinear, such as the arm, both arches of the bite may not be maximally visible. In this case, the camera should be placed at right angles of the wound from at least 2 directions, with and without scale.

— Following noninvasive documentation, the area can be swabbed for DNA. Studies have shown that in the case of bite marks, saliva can remain on the skin for long periods of time in many hostile environments.

 — Procedure is to take a sterile swab from the collection kit, soak it in sterile water or saline and rub it over the area, rotating the swab to help "lift" potential epithelial cells from the perpetrator moving in a circular pattern starting at the center of the wound. This swab should then be set aside to dry.

 — A second dry swab rubbed over the area in the manner of the first swab then set aside to dry. Both swabs are then processed according to jurisdictional procedure.[21]

— Photography beyond the visible spectrum (ie, infrared, ultraviolet) can be used with success, particularly if there has been a great deal of time between injury and examination.

— The forensic odontologist may decide to excise the area around the wound in the case of a deceased patient, but the technique should only be undertaken by those familiar with the process and the evaluation of the final product.

Child Neglect

Dental neglect is defined by the American Academy of Pediatric Dentistry as the "willful failure of parent or guardian to seek and follow through with treatment necessary to ensure a level of oral health essential for adequate function and freedom from pain and infection." In children, it is the responsibility of the caregiving adult to ensure the health of the child.[22]

- — The most common form of oral neglect is failure to recognize and provide treatment for carious teeth.
- — This failure exceeds the non-esthetic black or brown spots on teeth and may lead to pulpal death, alveolar infections, or even death.
- — Baby bottle tooth decay is common in children who are put to bed with a bottle that includes a material that has fermentable sugar (eg, milk, formula, other liquids containing sugar). It usually affects the maxillary anterior teeth, but can go on to affect the posterior teeth.[5,23]

References

1. Altman RL, Forman S, Brand DA. Ophthalmologic findings in infants after an apparent life-threatening event. *Eur J Ophthalmol.* 2007;17(4):648-653.
2. American Academy of Pediatrics, Committee on Child Abuse and Neglect. Shaken baby syndrome: rotational cranial injuries—technical report. *Pediatrics.* 2001;108:206-210.
3. Odds of abuse associated with retinal hemorrhages in children suspected of child abuse. *J AAPOS.* 2009;13(3):268-272
4. Blinder KJ, Scott W, Lange MP. Abuse of cyanoacrylate in child abuse. case report. *Arch Ophthalmol.* 1987;105(12):1632-1633.
5. Charfi F, Ben Zina Z, Maazoun M, et al. Phthiriasis pubis palpebrarum in children. diagnosis and treatment [in French]. *J Fr Ophthalmol.* 2005;28(7):765-768.
6. Ryan MF. Phthiriasis palpebrarum infection: a concern for child abuse. *J Emerg Med.* 2014;46(6):e159-e162.
7. Andrew TA, Fallon KK. Asphyxial games in children and adolescents. *Am J Forensic Med Pathol.* 2007;28(4):303-307.

8. Christe A, Oesterhelweg L, Ross S, et al. Can MRI of the neck compete with clinical findings in assessing danger to life for survivors of manual strangulation? a statistical analysis. *Leg Med (Tokyo)*. 2010;12(5):228-232.

9. Lewis LS, Glauser TA, Joffe MD. Gonococcal conjunctivitis in prepubertal children. *Am J Dis Child*. 1990;144(5):546-548.

10. Smith WL, Alexander RC, Judisch GF, Sato Y, Kao SC. Magnetic resonance imaging evaluation of neonates with retinal hemorrhages. *Pediatrics*. 1992;89(2):332-333.

11. Ophthalmology Working Party of the Royal College of Ophthalmologists. Child abuse and the eye. *Eye*. 1999;13:3-10.

12. Weissgold DJ, Budenz DL, Hood I, Rorke LB. Ruptured vascular malformation masquerading as battered/shaken baby syndrome: a nearly tragic mistake. *Surv Ophthalmol*. 1995;39(6):509-512.

13. Giangiacomo J, Khan JA, Levine C, Thompson VM. Sequential cranial computed tomography in infants with retinal hemorrhages. *Ophthalmology*. 1988;95:295-299.

14. Greenwald MJ, Weis A, Oesterle CS, Friendly DS. Traumatic retinoschisis in battered babies. *Ophthalmology*. 1986;93:618-625.

15. Christian CW; Committee on Child Abuse and Neglect, American Academy of Pediatrics. The evaluation of suspected child physical abuse. *Pediatrics*. 2015;135(5):e1337-e1354.

16. Keels MA; Section on Oral Health, American Academy of Pediatrics. Management of dental trauma in a primary care setting. *Pediatrics*. 2014;133(2):e466-e476.

17. Malmgren B, Andreasen JO, Flores MT, et al. International Association of Dental Traumatology guidelines for management of traumatic dental injuries: 3. injuries in the primary dentition. *Dent Traumatol*. 2012; 28(3):174-182.

18. Naidoo S. The importance of oral and facial injuries in child abuse. *African Safety Promotion*. 2004;2(1):68-72.

19. Somani R, Kushwaha V, Kumar D, Khaira J. Child abuse and its detection in the dental office. *Journal of Indian Academy of Forensic Medicine*. 2011;33(4):361-365.

20. Kellogg N; American Academy of Pediatrics Committee on Child Abuse and Neglect. Oral and dental aspects of child abuse and neglect. *Pediatrics*. 2005;116(6):1565-1568.

21. Sweet D, Lorente M, Lorente JA, Valenzuela A, Villanueva E. An improved method to recover saliva from human skin: the double swab technique. *J Forensic Sci*. 1997;42(2):320-322.

22. American Academy of Pediatrics Committee on Child Abuse and Neglect; American Academy of Pediatric Dentistry. Guideline on oral and dental aspects of child abuse and neglect. *Clinical Practice Guidelines Reference Manual*. 2010;37(6):172-175.

23. Sujatha G, Sivakumar G, Saraswathi TR. Role of a dentist in discrimination of abuse from accident. *J Forensic Dent Sci*. 2010;2(1):2-4.

Chapter 7

Thoracoabdominal Injuries

Melissa L. Currie, MD
Cynthia J. Curtsinger, BSN, RN, CCM, CFN, SANE
Brooke E. Jones, MD, MSc, FAAP
Vinod B. Rao, MD, FAAP
Kirsten Bechtel, MD

Abdominal trauma ranks second only to head injuries as the most frequent form of fatal child abuse. Abusive thoracoabdominal trauma is most common in infants and young children. This type of injury carries significant risk for morbidity and mortality, with mortality from abusive abdominal injuries reported at 53% compared to 21% for accidental injuries.[1] Injuries, signs, symptoms, and clinical presentation may be subtle and easily overlooked.

Mechanisms of Injury

— Abusive thoracoabdominal injury usually results from an intrusive impact or rapid deceleration from impact when a child is thrown.

— Delay in seeking care should raise concern for abusive injury; however, delay may also be present in accidental injury.[2]

Thoracic Injuries

— The most common thoracic injuries in physically abused children are rib fractures.[3]

— Posterior rib fractures, or those close to the rib neck and head, result from levering of the posterior rib neck over the transverse spinous process as the rib cage is violently squeezed.[4] This squeezing fractures the inner cortex of the posterior rib neck and the posterolateral arc of the rib.

— With severe anterior and posterior compression of the thorax, the fracture line can extend to the anterior rib's articulation with the sternum.

— Anterior and lateral rib fracture may also occur as a result of a direct impact to the thorax.

— Sternal fractures can result from direct blows and are highly specific for abusive injury when no history of trauma is given. Sternal fractures do not occur with chest physiotherapy or cardiopulmonary resuscitation because infants' chests are highly compliant.[5-7]

— Clinically significant injury to the lungs and heart from child abuse is uncommon but can be seen with direct trauma to the chest.

— Pulmonary contusions, diffuse alveolar damage, pneumomediastinum, and multiple rib fractures can result from abusive chest compression or direct trauma to the chest (**Figures 7-1** and **7-2**).[8]

— Pneumothoraces may accompany rib fractures in older children.

— Although extremely rare, chylothorax can result from thoracic duct injury[9,10]

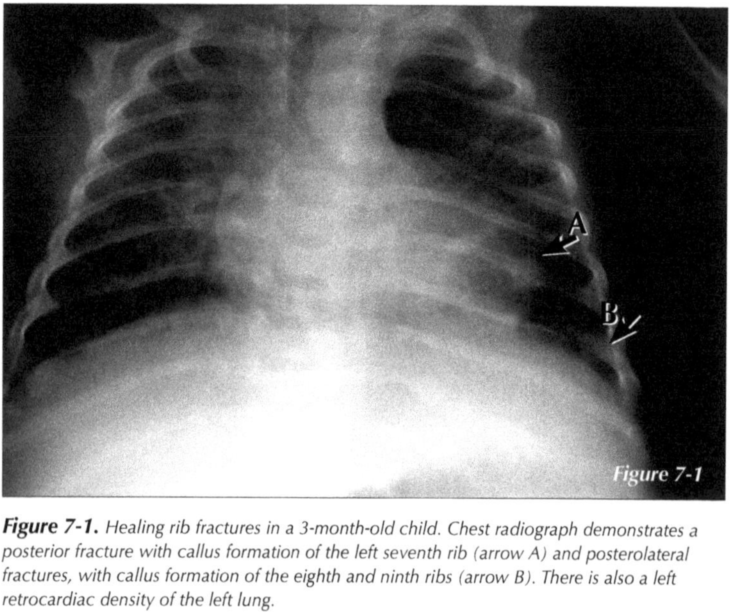

Figure 7-1. *Healing rib fractures in a 3-month-old child. Chest radiograph demonstrates a posterior fracture with callus formation of the left seventh rib (arrow A) and posterolateral fractures, with callus formation of the eighth and ninth ribs (arrow B). There is also a left retrocardiac density of the left lung.*

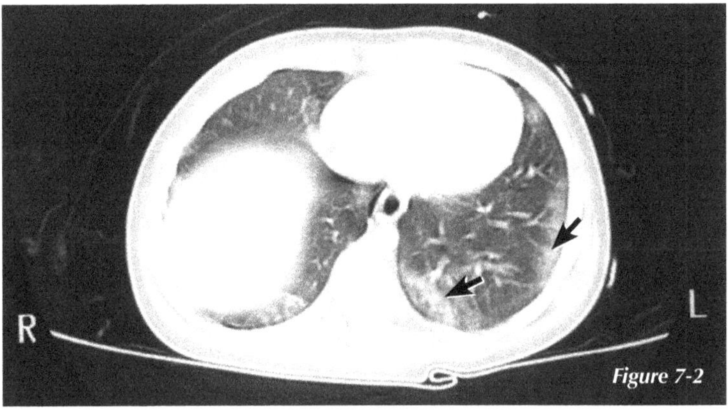

Figure 7-2. *Pulmonary contusions. CT scan of the chest of 3-month-old infant with healing left posterior and anterolateral rib fractures that demonstrates parenchymal contusions (arrows) at the base of the left lung.*

— Abusive blunt trauma to the anterior chest can cause commotio cordis, producing a disorganized cardiac rhythm and rapid cardiovascular collapse.[8] Abusive cardiac injuries are rare but frequently fatal.

— Blunt force diaphragmatic injury is sometimes seen at autopsy.

Abdominal Injuries

— With intrusive impact to the abdomen, the intestines and solid viscera are compressed.[11] The left lobe of the liver, pancreas, and small bowel are often injured by impacts to a child's epigastrium.[11,12] This is due to the positioning of the organs listed above, which lay between the impacting object and vertebral column.

— Traumatic bladder rupture caused by intrusive impact to the abdomen can occur,[13] and children may not be brought to medical attention for days following the injury.[1]

— The most common visceral injury in pediatric trauma is duodenal hematoma, which results when the duodenum is compressed between the abdominal wall and vertebral bodies.[14]

— Forceful slamming onto an upraised knee following a feeding has been reported to cause a rupture of the stomach along the greater curvature.[1]

— In abusive abdominal trauma, an intrusive impact to the anterior abdominal wall can cause perforation of the small intestine.

1. The mechanism of injury is either a rapid increase in intraluminal pressure or shearing of opposing intestinal surfaces.[1,11,15] Rapid deceleration, such as if a child were to be thrown against an object, can also injure the mesentery and disrupt intestinal vascular supply.[11]
2. Lacerations of the hepatoduodenal ligament, pneumatosis intestinalis, and portal vein gas can result from abusive abdominal trauma.[16,17]
3. Long-term sequelae are possible.[12]

— Impact to the right upper quadrant can injure the pancreatic head or uncinate process and descending and transverse portions of the duodenum.[18]

— Impact to the left upper quadrant may injure the pancreatic body or tail and the transverse and ascending portions of the duodenum.[18]

— Pancreatic pseudocyst is a healing process resulting from full or incomplete pancreatic transection as a result of blunt impact and takes weeks to become encapsulated.[19]

— Solid organ injury can occur, leading to medullary fat necrosis.[1,20,21]

— Forceful intrusive impacts to the abdomen can injure the left lobe of the liver. Liver injuries caused accidentally usually involve the right lobe's posterior segment, because it is surrounded by the ribs and spine and impacts against them in blunt abdominal trauma.[22]

— Isolated splenic and renal injuries rarely occur in abuse and are more commonly seen in accidental injury.[22,23]

— Fatal abusive abdominal injuries include intra-abdominal hemorrhage or peritonitis secondary to a ruptured hollow viscus (**Figures 7-3-a** and **b**). Abusive abdominal trauma may only be identified at autopsy (**Figure 7-4**).[11]

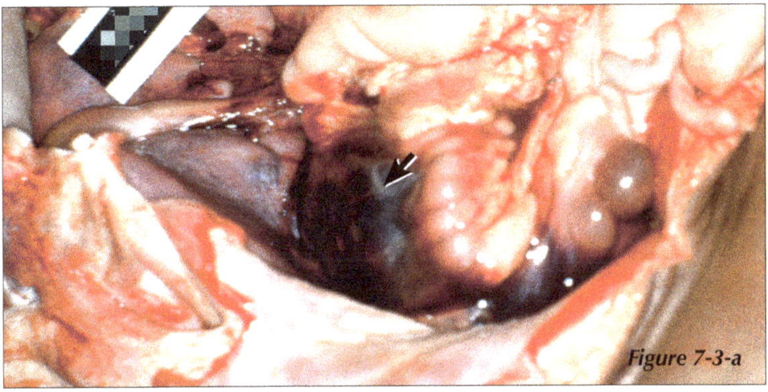

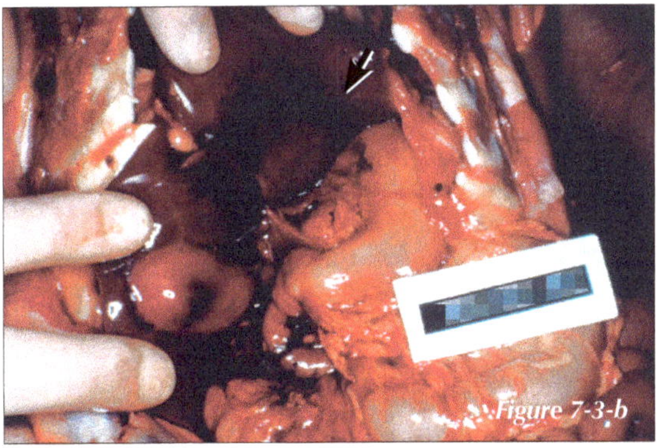

Figures 7-3-a and **b.** *Visceral bleeding in 2 cases of blunt trauma to the abdomen (arrows).*

Figure 7-4. *CT scan of the abdomen and pelvis demonstrating free intraperitoneal fluid between the bladder and rectum (arrows).*

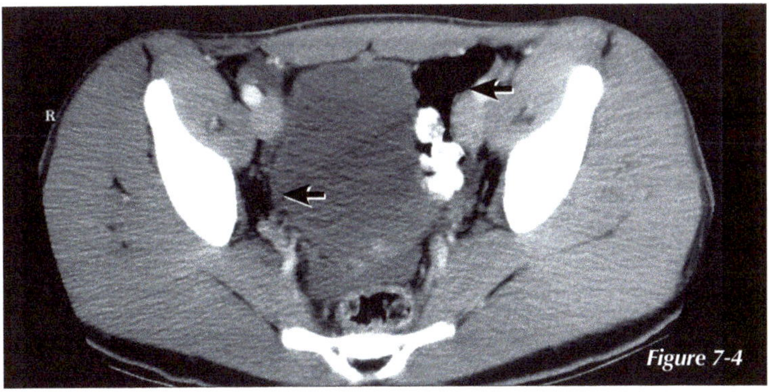

Medical Evaluation

History

— In cases of abusive injury, false, incomplete, or no histories are frequently given. Abdominal trauma may only be found during evaluation for injuries that are initiated for other concerns.

— Signs and symptoms, when present, can range from mild to severe, and may include decreased appetite, vomiting, abdominal pain, abdominal distension, hematochezia, hematuria, vaginal bleeding, dyspnea, apnea, hemodynamic instability, and/or cardiopulmonary arrest.

— History should be obtained from all individuals present at the time of the medical encounter, including all parents, children, and caregivers who were present at the time of the injury. It is important to speak to each person alone, including the patient, whenever possible.

Physical Examination

— Assess the stability of the airway, breathing, circulation, and mental status. Subtle alterations in level of consciousness, heart rate, and capillary refill time can be early signs of hypovolemia caused by myocardial injury, intra-abdominal hemorrhage, or peritonitis.

— A thorough physical examination should be performed.

— External evidence may be lacking because the chest or abdominal wall frequently yields to intrusive impacts without bruising. When present, abdominal distension and bruising are highly correlated with presence of intra-abdominal injury.[24]

— Less than 20% of patients with abusive abdominal trauma have evidence of bruising on physical examination.[22]

— The heart tones may be muffled during auscultation when there is myocardial injury with pericardial effusion.

— Tachycardia or bradycardia may indicate a myocardial injury.

— Children who have been physically abused may have occult intra-abdominal trauma with few or no localizing abdominal signs or symptoms.[25] Since abusive abdominal trauma may be occult, screening abdominal trauma laboratory studies may be warranted.

— The abdomen may be tender on palpation, but the source of the tenderness can be difficult to locate in young children.

— Extra-abdominal injury, including head injury, contusions, fractures, occult bony injury, genitourinary, and/or anal injury, can also be present, necessitating a thorough physical examination.

Laboratory Evaluation

— Laboratory screening tests may include creatine phosphokinase with myocardial bound fraction, troponin, lactate dehydrogenase, liver transaminases, amylase, lipase, urinalysis (bag specimen when screening for occult hematuria), and hemoccult.

— Laboratory values useful in detecting intra-abdominal injuries include:

1. Urinalysis with greater than 5 red blood cells (RBCs) per high-power field.[26]
2. Aspartate aminotransferase (AST) greater than 80 U/L or alanine aminotransferase (ALT) greater than 80 U/L.[27]
3. Low hematocrit and hemoglobin for age-based indices may warrant further investigation if other sources of blood loss are not identified.

— Finding an abnormal liver test justifies an abdomen and pelvis computed tomography (CT) scan with IV contrast.

— Diagnostic peritoneal lavage is rarely warranted in these patients and should be considered in consultation with a surgical service.

Diagnostic Imaging of Thoracic Injuries

— Plain radiographs:

1. Are best for detecting healing rib fractures with minimal radiation exposure. Acute rib fractures may be visualized on chest radiographs; however, they are usually not visible until callus formation occurs. Callus formation can be identified radiographically by 7 days (very rarely earlier) with nearly all having radiographic signs of bone healing by 10 to 14 days after injury (**Figure 7-5**).[28-30]

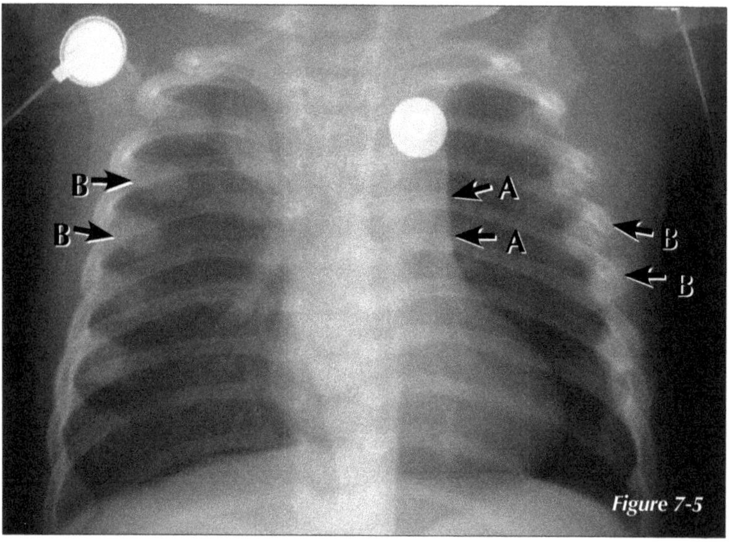

Figure 7-5. *Chest radiograph demonstrates a widened superior mediastinum (arrows A) and multiple bilateral rib fractures (arrows B).*

2. Can detect injuries such as pulmonary contusion, pneumothorax, hemothorax, cardiac contusion/rupture, and pericardial effusion (the latter two as evidenced by widened mediastinum).[22]

3. Can demonstrate a large cardiac image (cardiomegaly) indicating blunt cardiac rupture. The extent of blunt cardiac injury is determined using ultrasound, echocardiography, and angiography.[31]

Diagnostic Imaging of Abdominal Injuries

— Plain radiographs:

1. Can identify abnormalities from intestinal perforation with use of an upright abdominal or lateral decubitus view, depending upon the location of the perforation and volume of intraperitoneal air.

2. Intraperitoneal free fluid (blood or ascites) may appear as diffusely increased density or a central location of the bowel on supine abdominal views.

3. Intestinal intramural hematoma may not appear on plain radiographs. If the hematoma encroaches on the intestinal lumen, producing obstruction, plain radiographs may show a gas-filled stomach with little intraluminal air in the distal intestine. Intraluminal hematomas are best delineated on an upper gastrointestinal series, which outlines the mass.[11] Intestinal strictures caused by intramural hematomas or vascular injury may also be identified on an upper gastrointestinal series.

— CT scans:

1. Intra-abdominal injury is most rapidly diagnosed using CT scans with IV contrast, which detect intraperitoneal free fluid, solid organ injury, and life-threatening injuries.[11]
2. When intra-abdominal injury is suspected, a CT of the abdomen and pelvis should be ordered with the following considerations[32]:
   - — Perform with IV contrast
   - — Administer oral contrast for concerns of duodenal hematoma
   - — Late arterial phase/parenchymal imaging for concerns of solid organ injury
   - — Delayed, excretory phase imaging for concerns of genitourinary tract injury
3. The reliability of CT scans to detect intestinal injury is less clear.
4. The diagnosis of small-bowel and mesenteric injury is often made when other intra-abdominal injuries are found.
5. CT findings of small-bowel or mesenteric injury include free intraperitoneal fluid, thickened bowel wall, and extraluminal air.[33]
6. If free intraperitoneal fluid is found in more than one abdominal location, the likelihood of intestinal injury is 50%.[34]

— Ultrasound:

1. Utility is very limited from a forensic perspective.
2. Is inadequate for diagnosing subtle injuries that may be present and visualized on abdominal CT with IV contrast.[35]

3. The use of focused abdominal sonography for trauma (FAST) examination has been a growing clinical tool utilized in the emergent evaluation of patients suspected of abdominal trauma.
   - The FAST examination has the ability to provide quick, point-of-care information to guide acute management of patients in the emergency department setting with no radiation exposure, thereby potentially allowing reduction of abdominal CT use for patients with a low or moderate clinical suspicion of intra-abdominal injury.[36]
   - However, the FAST examination is not universally available and is operator dependent, requiring a trained, skilled provider.
   - The literature supports use of the FAST examination as an adjunct in evaluation for clinical decision-making; however, the poor sensitivity of the test suggests that it should not stand alone in determination of clinical actions.[36,37,38]

References

1. Maguire SA, Upadhyaya M, Evans A, et al. A systematic review of abusive visceral injuries in childhood—their range and recognition. *Child Abuse Negl.* 2013;37(7):430-445.
2. Wood J, Rubin DM, Nance ML, Christian CW. Distinguishing inflicted versus accidental abdominal injuries in young children. *J Trauma Acute Care Surg.* 2005;59(5):1203-1208.
3. Kleinman PK, Rosenberg AE, Tsai A. Skeletal trauma: general considerations. In: Kleinman PK. *Diagnostic Imaging of Child Abuse.* 3rd ed. Cambridge, UK: Cambridge University Press; 2015:23-52.
4. Kleinman PK. Bony thoracic trauma. In: Kleinman PK. *Diagnostic Imaging of Child Abuse.* 3rd ed. Cambridge, UK: Cambridge University Press; 2015:164-207.
5. Feldman KW, Brewer DK. Child abuse, cardiopulmonary resuscitation, and rib fractures. *Pediatrics.* 1984;73(3):339-342.
6. Kleinman PK, Schlesinger AE. Mechanical factors associated with posterior rib fractures: laboratory and case studies. *Pediatr Radiol.* 1997;27(1):87-91.

7. Gunther WM, Synes SA, Berryman HE. Characteristics of child abuse by anteroposterior manual compression versus cardiopulmonary resuscitation: case reports. *Am J Forensic Med Pathol.* 2000;21(1):5-10.

8. McEniery J, Hanson R, Grigor G, Horowitz A. Lung injury resulting from a nonaccidental crush injury to the chest. *Pediatr Emerg Care.* 1991;7:166-168.

9. Guleserian KJ, Gilchrist BF, Luks FI, Wesselhoeft CW, DeLuca FG. Child abuse as a cause of traumatic chylothorax. *J Pediatr Surg.* 1996;31(12):1696-1697.

10. Geismar SL, Tilelli JA, Campbell JB, Chiaro JJ. Chylothorax as a manifestation of child abuse. *Pediatr Emerg Care.* 1997;13(6):386-389.

11. Nimkin K, Kleinman PK. Visceral trauma. In: Kleinman PK. *Diagnostic Imaging of Child Abuse.* 3rd ed. Cambridge, UK: Cambridge University Press; 2015:563-607.

12. Shah P, Applegate KE, Buonomo C. Stricture of the duodenum and jejunum in an abused child. *Pediatr Radiol.* 1998;27(3):281-283.

13. Yang JW, Kuppermann N, Rosas A. Child abuse presenting as pseudorenal failure with a history of a bicycle fall. *Pediatr Emerg Care.* 2002;18(2):91-92.

14. Servaes S, Haller JO. Characteristic pancreatic injuries secondary to child abuse. *Emerg Radiol.* 2003;10(2):90-93.

15. Herr S, Fallat ME. Abusive abdominal and thoracic trauma. *Clin Pediatr Emerg Med.* 2006;7(3):149-152.

16. deRoux SJ, Prendergast NC. Lacerations of the hepatoduodenal ligament, pancreas and duodenum in a child due to blunt impact. *J Forensic Sci.* 1998;43(1):222-224.

17. Gurland B, Dolgin SE, Shlasko E, Kim U. Pneumatosis intestinalis and portal vein gas after blunt abdominal trauma. *J Pediatr Surg.* 1998;33(8):1309-1311.

18. Linsenmaier U, Wirth S, Reiser M, Körner M. Diagnosis and classification of pancreatic and duodenal injuries in emergency radiology. *Radiographics.* 2008;28(6):1591-1602.

19. Stringer M. Pancreatic trauma in children. *Br J Surg.* 2005;92(4):467-470.

20. Slovis TL, Berdon WE, Haller JO, Baker DH, Rosen L. Pancreatitis and the battered child syndrome: report of 2 cases with skeletal involvement. *Am J Roentgenol Radium Ther Nucl Med.* 1975;125(2):456-461.

21. Cohen H, Haller JO, Friedman P. Pancreatitis, child abuse, and skeletal lesions. *Pediatr Radiol.* 1981;10(3):175-177.

22. Herr SM. Abdominal and chest injuries in abused children. In: Jenny C. *Child Abuse and Neglect: Diagnosis, Treatment, and Evidence.* 1st ed. Saint Louis, MO: Elsevier Health Sciences; 2010:326-345.

23. Carter KW, Moulton SL. Pediatric abdominal injury patterns caused by "falls": a comparison between non-accidental and accidental trauma. *J Pediatr Surg.* 2015;51(2):326-328.

24. Hilmes MA, Hernanz-Schulman M, Greeley CS, Piercey LM, Yu C, Kan JH. CT identification of abdominal injuries in abused pre-school-age children. *Pediatr Radiol.* 2011;41(5):643-651.

25. Coant PN, Kornberg AE, Brody AS, Edwards-Holmes K. Markers for occult liver injury in cases of physical abuse in children. *Pediatrics.* 1992;89(2):274-278.

26. Homes JF, Sokolove PE, Brant WE, et al. Identification of children with intra-abdominal injuries after blunt trauma. *Ann Emerg Med.* 2002;39(5):500-509.

27. Lindberg DM, Shapiro RA, Blood EA, Steiner RD, Berger RP. Utility of hepatic transaminases in children with concern for abuse. *Pediatrics.* 2013;131(2):268-275.

28. Malone CA, Sauer NJ, Fenton TW. A radiographic assessment of pediatric fracture healing and time since injury. *J Forensic Sci.* 2011;56(5):1123-1130.

29. Prosser I, Lawson Z, Evans A, et al. A timetable for the radiologic features of fracture healing in young children. *AJR Am J Roentgenol.* 2012;198(5):1014-1020.

30. Sanchez T, Nguyen H, Palacios W, Doherty M, Coulter K. Retrospective evaluation and dating of non-accidental rib fractures in infants. *Clin Radiol.* 2013;68(8):e467-e471.

31. Rezende Neto JB, Diniz HO, Filho CS, Abrantes WL. Blunt traumatic rupture of the heart in a child: case report and review of the literature. *J Trauma.* 2001;50(4):746-749.

32. Meyer JS, Gunderman R, Coley BD, et al. ACR Appropriateness Criteria(®) on suspected physical abuse—child. *J Am Coll Radiol.* 2011;8(2):87-94.

33. Frick EJ Jr, Pasquale MD, Cipolle MD. Small-bowel and mesentery injuries in blunt trauma. *J Trauma.* 1999;46(5):920-926.

34. Hulka F, Mullins RJ, Leonardo V, Harrison MW, Silberberg P. Significance of peritoneal fluid as an isolated finding on abdominal computed tomographic scans in pediatric trauma patients. *J Trauma.* 1998;44(6):1069-1072.

35. Fox JC, Boysen M, Gharahbaghian L, et al. Test characteristics of focused assessment of sonography for trauma for clinically significant abdominal free fluid in pediatric blunt abdominal trauma. *Acad Emerg Med.* 2011;18(5):477-482.

36. Menaker J, Blumberg S, Wisner DH, et al. Use of the focused assessment with sonography for trauma (FAST) examination and its impact on abdominal computed tomography use in hemodynamically stable children with blunt torso trauma. *J Trauma Acute Care Surg.* 2014;77(3):427-432.

37. Scaife ER, Rollins MD, Barnhart DC, et al. The role of focused abdominal sonography for trauma (FAST) in pediatric trauma evaluation. *J Pediatr Surg.* 2013;48(6):1377-1383.

38. Schonfeld D, Lee LK. Blunt abdominal trauma in children. *Curr Opin Pediatr.* 2012;24(3):314-318.

Chapter 8

The Chemically Abused Child (Poisoning)

Kathy L. Bell, MS, RN
Robert T. Paschall, MD

The adult caregiver's intent when giving a child chemical substances determines, in part, if a chemical ingestion is abusive. An unintentional ingestion may be considered abusive if it results from supervisory neglect or child endangerment (ie, environmental safety neglect). Other factors, such as repetitive poisoning events with harm or risk of harm, are also considered.

NOTE: *Many substances with legitimate usage may be poisonous when improperly used or given or taken in an inappropriate dosage.*

Definitions

— ***Child***: Any person under 18 years of age.

— ***Ingestion***: Any means by which a substance gains systemic access to a child, including inhalation, injection, skin or mucous membrane contact, and swallowing.

— ***Intentional ingestion***: Occurring when a caregiver intended for the child to ingest a substance, although poisoning may not have been intended. Intentional ingestion can be abusive or nonabusive.

— ***Unintentional ingestion***: Perhaps most properly termed as exploratory ingestion.[1] Implies that the caregiver did not intend for the child to ingest a substance. It may be abusive when it results from supervisory neglect or endangerment or unintentional as a result of a nonabusive, non-neglectful "accidental ingestion." Even when reasonable precautions are taken and reasonable vigilance is exercised, children may still gain access to toxic or potentially toxic substances in their environment.

— ***Poisoning***: Any adverse outcome for a child exposed to a substance. Toxin and poison are used interchangeably in this chapter.

— ***Chemical abuse***: All intentional ingestions for abusive purposes and ingestions resulting from neglect.

— ***Chemically abused child***: A child who is harmed or threatened as a result of an act of commission or omission on the caregiver's part.

— ***Illicit substances***: Illegal substances used only for their mood-altering effects.

— ***Neglect***: Poisoning in which harm to the child results from lack of adequate supervision, endangerment, or both.

— ***Child endangerment***: A form of neglect in which conditions in the child's environment constitute a blatant disregard for the child's safety.

Epidemiology

— Statistics on exposures are compiled by the National Poison Data System (NPDS) of the American Association of Poison Control Centers (AAPCC).

— Children aged 1 to 5 years comprise nearly half of all poison exposures.

— Poisoning by cosmetics and personal care products leads the list of common substance exposures in children older than 6 years, followed by cleaning products and analgesics.

— Many exposures can be safely observed at home.

— Peak poisoning frequency occurs in 1-year-old and 2-year-old children.

— At age 13, girls account for the most serious exposures, often intentional overdoses.

— Typically, analgesics are related to the most serious consequences.

Intentional Abusive Poisoning

— Poisoning may be subtle or lack external signs, making diagnosis difficult, or a child might come to the emergency department with a relatively common event, such as experiencing a seizure.

— Children may appear stable and suddenly deteriorate.

— Determining the etiology of the event is crucial to the outcome of the visit.[1,2]

— Physical and sexual abuse may accompany intentional and unintentional ingestions in children.

— Major routes of ingestion:

1. Oral or via nasogastric or gastric tube
2. Parenteral (eg, intravenous, intramuscular, subcutaneous)
3. Mucosal (eg, ocular, oral, rectal, inhalation)
4. Integumentary absorption (ie, absorption through the skin)

— Motives for intentionally exposing a child to a potentially toxic substance:

1. Caregiver psychopathology
2. Facilitation of sexual abuse/assault
3. Discipline
4. Behavior modification
5. Amusement
6. Other (eg, personal gain, unorthodox childrearing practices)

Caregiver Psychopathology

— Caregiver psychopathology includes pediatric condition falsification (PCF), Munchausen syndrome by proxy (MSBP), and factitious disorder by proxy (FDBP). In recent literature, the common term for this disease process is medical child abuse (MCA).[3]

1. PCF involves caregivers harming children directly as well as indirectly by giving false information to medical providers, who respond unknowingly to false information and administer interventions that cause harm.
2. MSBP and FDBP pertain to the motive(s) of the caregiver to assume the role of the parent of a sick child for psychological gratification. This usually involves the mother, who deliberately falsifies a child's medical history, alters laboratory specimens, or induces illness or

injury in order to seek diagnostic and therapeutic interventions. Consider this disorder when caregivers' psychopathology includes fabrication, exaggeration, simulation, or induction of an illness in a child so they can assume the role of caring, vigilant caregivers to fulfill psychological needs.

Intentional ingestion resulting in poisoning of the child may be suspected in the situations listed in **Table 8-1**. (See also Chapter 14, "Medical Child Abuse/Munchausen Syndrome by Proxy.")

Table 8-1. Situations That Suggest Intentional Poisoning of a Child
1. The child is older than 6 years.
2. Multiple episodes of known or suspected "accidental" poisoning of a child or sibling.
3. Multiple substances are involved.
4. A single episode of suspected ingestion with no substance identified by caregivers or detectable by toxicology.
5. Known or suspected ingestion of a toxic substance in nonmobile infants.
6. Poisoning of children older than 3 years, unless clearly accidental.
7. Discrepancies between the clinical presentation and what a health care provider would expect based on history and laboratory reports.
8. Death of an index patient or sibling without a definitive cause.
9. Recurrent unexplained symptoms or signs that resolve when the primary caregiver is absent from the child and recur when the caregiver is present.
10. Symptoms of poisoning are episodic, with intervening periods of normalcy.
11. Clinical signs such as seizures, apnea, and altered level of consciousness observed only by the caregiver, with no independent or objective verification or observation.
12. Massive overdose.
13. Unusual poisonings from household substances such as salt, pepper, or water.

Facilitation of Sexual Assault or Abuse

— Drug- or alcohol-facilitated sexual assault can accompany voluntary or involuntary ingestion of a sedative-hypnotic drug, substance, or alcohol, which alter the victim's ability to consent or resist an assault.

— Alcohol (ethanol) is the most common substance detected in the toxicology results of sexual assault victims. Marijuana and benzodiazepines (eg, Xanax) are also found frequently.

1. The initial consumption of alcohol or drugs may be voluntary. When a sufficient level of intoxication is achieved, the unwanted sexual encounter occurs.

2. Drugs may be given overtly or covertly. Gamma-hydroxybutyrate (GHB) and flunitrazepam have been historically termed "date rape" drugs; however, many drugs and substances given in the right quantity and form can render a person vulnerable to a sexual assault.

3. Benzodiazepines have an exacerbated effect when taken with alcoholic beverages. Flunitrazepam (Rohypnol) is only one of many marketed benzodiazepines. The hypnotic effect begins in about 30 minutes and peaks at 2 hours. Victims suffer anterograde amnesia that lasts about 8 hours, complicating investigation of the incident.[4] Using the proper gas chromatography–mass spectroscopy assay, the drug is detectable in the urine for about 72 hours. Currently, a coating on the tablet makes it difficult to dissolve and turns the liquid blue when it does dissolve.

4. GHB is a Schedule 1 controlled substance, meaning that it has a high potential for abuse, has no currently accepted medical use in the United States, and lacks accepted safety for use under medical supervision.[5] It was formerly used in bodybuilding as an anesthetic and as a hypnotic agent. It is a naturally occurring endogenous compound found in most mammalian tissue, including the brain, where it is synthesized from the inhibitory neurotransmitter gamma-aminobutyric acid. GHB appears to function as a neurotransmitter or neuromodulator.[6] It is tasteless, colorless, and easily disguised in water and alcohol. Victims experience euphoria and uninhibited states at dosages of 1.5 g or more.[5] Dosages of 50 mg/kg can cause bradycardia, decreased car-

diac output, respiratory depression, seizures, coma, ataxia, nystagmus, myoclonus, and hypothermia. GHB acts synergistically with ethanol to depress the central nervous system and respiratory system. It begins to take effect in 15 to 30 minutes, peaks in 20 to 60 minutes, and has an elimination half-life of 30 minutes. The clinician must specifically request a GHB toxicology screen for it to be detected.

5. Bath salts and synthetic THC are relatively new to the sexual assault exam. Bath salts are synthetic forms of cathinone, a Schedule 1 controlled substance found naturally in the khat plant.[5] Synthetic THC is also known as K2 and spice. Both drugs can cause anxiety, hypertension, tachycardia, and hallucinations.[7]

— All patients suspected of being sexually assaulted should be asked about ingestion of alcohol, drugs, or potentially drug-containing drinks before the assault. If the patient is confused, has altered consciousness, is amnesic, or has had an unusual reaction to a known quantity of drugs or alcohol, drug- and/or alcohol-facilitated sexual assault should be suspected, and appropriate protocols for collection, preservation, and storage of samples should be followed.

— If ingestion occurred in the previous 24 hours, blood and urine should be collected. If ingestion occurred more than 24 hours prior, only urine should be collected. Check with the toxicology laboratory to ensure that the right samples are obtained and properly stored.

— In addition to evidence collected at the time of the sexual assault examination, law enforcement may collect glasses, bottles, or containers suspected of storing drugs.[5]

— Test results may not be available for several days.

Discipline

Caregivers may force children to ingest a noxious or potentially toxic agent as a disciplinary measure. Serious consequences arising from this practice include poisoning and death.

Behavior Modification

— Children whose behavior is challenging may be given sedating medication in an effort to control them.

— Other chemical restraint methods include blowing marijuana in children's faces and providing children with alcohol or a combination of alcohol and over-the-counter medication.

— Using over-the-counter medicines solely to modify or control children's behavior is suggestive of child abuse because it may endanger children's well-being.

Other Motives

— Children or animals may be given alcohol and drugs because adults find the effects amusing.

— Families who subscribe to unorthodox child-rearing practices may use nontraditional diets and folk medicines, leading to poisoning with toxic amounts of vitamins, herbal remedies, or heavy metals.

— Parents involved with drug culture may allow or encourage drug use, even by young children.[8]

Association With Physical Abuse

— Many familial and societal risk factors for intentionally or unintentionally exposing children to toxic agents are the same as the risk factors for physical abuse (eg, abusive disciplinary measures, poverty, caregiver drug use, impulsive anger-driven actions, misinformed attempts at behavior modification, unrealistic developmental expectations, multiplicity of life stressors).

— Perform a physical abuse evaluation appropriate for age and circumstances for any child suspected of being poisoned.

Unintentional Nonabusive Poisoning

— Children who gain access to and ingest potentially toxic substances are not usually considered victims of neglect, unless there is evidence for neglect in lack of supervision or endangering.

— Ideally, prenatal preparations for child safety, and later "upgrading" the safety level of the living environment at developmentally appropriate stages, preemptively childproof the environment and prevent unintentional poisoning and accidental physical injury.

— Anticipatory preparations for general child safety:

1. Adjusting the hot water heater thermostat to 120°F or less.
2. Installing doorway gates.
3. Ensuring that all medications are out of reach and in child-resistant containers.
4. Placing toxic materials in a locked area or one otherwise inaccessible to children.
5. Ensuring toxic materials are in their original, appropriately labeled containers.

— The Poison Prevention Packaging Act of 1970 instituted child-resistant caps on bottles of pharmaceuticals and other toxic substances and helped to substantially reduce morbidity and mortality due to poisoning in children.

— Situations leading to adverse outcomes:

1. Leaving the cap on a medication bottle loose or off makes its contents easily accessible to children.
2. Giving medication to children that is intended for another person and estimating the dose can result in adverse reactions or overdose.
3. Misunderstanding dosing instructions because of illiteracy, language barriers, poor education, or the belief that if a little of the medication is good, more is better, can cause caregivers to make dose administration errors.
4. Dilution errors, especially in mixing infant nutritional formula, can be serious:
    a. Hyponatremia occurs if water is mistakenly added to a ready-to-feed formula or if excessive volumes of water or flavored drinks are given instead of formula.
    b. Hyperosmolar diarrhea and dehydration occur if water is not added to a nutritional formula concentrate.

5. Living in inadequate housing with parents who have limited caregiving skills or with caregivers who lack knowledge about normal childhood development can create an unsafe environment.
6. Emotional disturbances (of child or parent), alcohol abuse and drug use, unemployment, chaotic lifestyle, or transient lifestyles can make caregivers distracted or volatile.
7. Living under any stressful circumstances can affect the normal behaviors of caregivers and children.

Dealing With Neglect and Endangerment

— Degrees of neglect are based on the number of neglect events and associated present harm or risk of future harm.

— Children may be endangered by having access to hazardous materials used to produce illicit substances, by the substances themselves, by a lack of supervision while caregivers are under the influence of drugs, and by the erratic inattentive behavior of caregivers under the influence of drugs.

— Child physical abuse and neglect and caregiver drug use are linked.

Methamphetamine

— Children exposed to methamphetamine manufacturing in the 1990s and early 2000s were exposed to multiple toxic ingredients. The ingredients used in its manufacture could be detected on every surface in the environment, including clothing, skin, and toys of children living in the home where the substance is produced. Some precursor chemicals could be absorbed through the skin and mucous membranes.

— Between 2008 and 2009, methamphetamine manufacturers employed a new method in which a 2-liter soft drink bottle is used in place of the conventional "lab." Using this faster, cheaper, and simpler method, users began making their own methamphetamine in small batches. This method can be very dangerous because improperly mixed methamphetamine can explode. In some parts of the country, this method's portability led to a downturn in the number of children exposed to manufacturing chemicals.

— In recent years, methamphetamine has been primarily accessible through Mexican drug trafficking organizations.[5] Although children may not be exposed to the manufacturing process, they are still at risk due to the presence and use of the drug itself.

— Many cases of childhood exposure to methamphetamine go unsuspected and unidentified, necessitating preventive efforts in identification.

— National medical experts have developed guidelines for initial response to children exposed to the manufacture and use of methamphetamine. (For more information, see National Guidelines for Medical Evaluation of Children Found in Drug Labs at http://www.nationaldec.org/user_files/18918.pdf).[9]

— Signs and symptoms of acute ingestion, inhalation, or contact with methamphetamine include agitation, anxiety, paranoia, psychotic behavior, confusion, hyperactivity, seizures, tachycardia and cardiac dysrhythmias, hypertension, hyperthermia, vasoconstriction, and pulmonary edema acutely, and over the long term, psychosis, movement disorders, strokes, cerebral hemorrhage, and chronic lung disease.

— The acids used in methamphetamine manufacture cause contact burns to the skin, eyes, respiratory system, and gastrointestinal (GI) organs.

— Toxic gases and flammable solvents are produced in manufacture, risking an explosion at the site with the potential for serious thermal and caustic burns.

— The solvents used can also produce serious health problems such as chemical hepatitis, renal failure, seizures, pancytopenia, and death.

— Methamphetamine use during pregnancy may place the unborn child at risk due to known systemic effects on the mother. The full effect on the unborn child is unknown but includes intrauterine growth delay and lethargy for weeks after birth.

— Infants born to methamphetamine-exposed mothers may go through withdrawal, experiencing jitteriness, irritability, irregular sleep patterns, poor feeding, hypertonia, tremors, and emitting high-pitched cries.

— Research projects assessing for current evaluations and long-term follow-up for children found living in methamphetamine laboratories are in development.

Caustic Ingestion

— Children who have ingested caustic chemicals used in methamphetamine and crack cocaine production exhibit chemical burns to the mouth and esophagus.[10] Outcomes range from minor injury to disability and death. Delayed death can occur, with the child eventually dying of complications of the caustic ingestion. Complications are usually related to injury of the oropharynx and esophagus.

— Recently, new forms of caustic dangers to children have surfaced in the form of common household products:

— Laundry detergent pods were first made available in 2012. Children under the age of 4, and especially those between 1 and 2 years of age, have experienced a variety of symptoms due to ingestion or bursting them open causing their skin and eyes to come into contact with detergent chemicals.[11] The most severe responses were those in cases of ingestion. Exposures have caused hospitalization, intubation, and in one case, death.

— Button-type lithium batteries present another new concern for parents. These batteries are found in remote controls, bathroom scales, reading lights, and greeting cards.[12] Children may put them in their mouths, swallow them, or insert them into their ears and noses. Generally, they pass without issue, but if not, serious exposures to the chemicals may occur.

— Unintentional poisoning is on the rise due in part to an increase in inappropriate use of prescription opioid medications.[13] Public health efforts to address this problem are taking shape in many communities in the form of education programs. Children are commonly exposed to antihyperlipidemics, oral hypoglycemic, and ß-blockers.[14]

— Out-of-hospital medication errors are another common cause of unintentional poisonings in children. Most result from taking or being given medication twice. Wrong medication, wrong dosage, and wrong units of measure were other reasons for medication errors.[15]

— Many parents are unaware of the hazards posed by electronic cigarettes. In small children, vomiting is the common symptom of ingesting nicotine. High doses may result in tachycardia, agitation, and seizure.[16] Electronic cigarette liquid is colorful, may be candy-flavored and scented, and there are currently no requirements for child-proof packaging. Less than a teaspoon can be fatal to small children.[17]

— Food and drinks are a potential source of poisoning in children. Water, nutmeg, energy drinks, alcohol, and food containing marijuana can, in toxic amounts, cause serious harm to a child.[18-22]

Evaluation

History of Present Illness

— Usually, caregivers find open bottles with some of their contents missing or empty bottles, and the children have a portion of the medication in their mouth, hands, or clothing.

1. Prudent caregivers seek medical attention immediately and may call a poison control center before arriving at the hospital. The container and its remaining contents should be brought with the child to the health care facility.

2. With an intentional poisoning for malicious intent, no information is usually given about the ingestion.

3. When the ingestion is a consequence of neglect, there is often no history of ingestion because the caregiver was neglectful or involved in illegal activities in the child's environment.

— If poisoning from an unknown source is possible, obtain a list of all medications and toxic materials accessible to the child. Alternatively, have family members or others search the places where the child has recently been for evidence of potentially toxic pharmaceutical and nonpharmaceutical agents.

— If abuse is suspected, a report to law enforcement is mandatory. Their involvement may provide relevant information from the residence or other locations where the child has recently been.

— **Table 8-2** lists clinical presentations of toxidromes and signs and symptoms of specific types of poisoning.

Table 8-2. Toxidromes

Toxidrome	Presentation	Vital Sign Changes	Causative Agents
Anticholinergic	Delirium Flushed skin Dilated pupils Urinary retention Decreased bowel sounds Memory loss Seizures "Hot as a hare, dry as a bone, red as a beet, blind as a bat"	Tachycardia Hyperthermia Hypertension	Antihistamines Scopolamine Jimson weed Angel trumpet Benztropine Tricyclic antidepressants Atropine
Cholinergic	Confusion Weakness Salivation Lacrimation Defecation Emesis Diaphoresis Muscle fasciculations Miosis Seizures	Bradycardia Hypothermia Tachycardia	Organophosphates Carbamates Mushrooms
Hallucinogenic	Disorientation Hallucinations Visual illusions Panic reaction Moist skin Hyperactive bowel sounds Seizures	Tachycardia Tachypnea Hypertension	Amphetamines Cannabinoids Cocaine Phencyclidine (PCP)

(continued)

Table 8-2. Toxidromes *(continued)*

Toxidrome	Presentation	Vital Sign Changes	Causative Agents
Opiate/ Narcotic	Altered mental status Unresponsiveness Miosis Shock	Shallow respirations Slow respiratory rate Bradycardia Hypothermia Hypotension	Opiates Propoxyphene Dextromethorphan
Sedative/ Hypnotic	Coma Stupor Confusion Sedation Progressive deterioration of CNS function	Apnea	Barbiturates Benzodiazepines Ethanol Anticonvulsants
Sympathomimetic	Delusions Paranoia, diaphoresis Piloerection Mydriasis Hyperreflexia Seizures Anxiety	Tachycardia Bradycardia (if pure alpha agonist) Hypertension	Cocaine Amphetamines Methamphetamines Phenylpropanolamine Ephedrine Pseudoephedrine Albuterol Ma huang

Reprinted with permission from Florida Poison Information Center Jacksonville. Toxidromes. Florida Poison Information Center Jacksonville Web site. http://www.fpicjax.org/Toxidromes.htm. Accessed June 23, 2013.

Clinical Laboratory Tests

— Initial basic laboratory tests may aid in diagnosing poisoning. The results are often available before toxicology screening reports, which can require more time than available to intervene.

— Basic clinical laboratory tests include measures of serum glucose, electrolytes, blood urea nitrogen (BUN), calcium, creatinine, liver enzymes, serum osmolality, and urine analysis done microscopically and using a dipstick.

— Results of these tests and others may direct initial therapy and lead to orders for specific toxicological tests.

— For patients with encephalopathic or other symptoms suggestive of poisoning, order extra blood to be drawn and urine collected early in the course. In anticipation of further testing for specific substances, save these body fluids in sufficient quantities and in appropriate containers.

— Be aware that laboratory test results can return to normal or baseline levels rapidly after ingestion, depending on the pharmacokinetics of the ingested substance and therapeutic interventions.

— Be aware of the detection capabilities of the toxicology laboratory.

— Turnaround time for routine toxicology screening and turnaround report time for specific detection methods. The time for receiving a report varies from hours to weeks depending on the specific test requested as well as the degree of sensitivity and specificity required.

— Sensitivities of detection tests vary considerably.

— Specify the type of specimen (urine, whole blood, serum, or gastric fluid), quantity required, and need for special containers and handling.

— Qualitative tests are done on urine and gastric fluid and quantitative tests on serum. Quantitative analysis for heavy metals is done on urine.

— Drugs may be detectable in blood soon after ingestion; however, most are concentrated in urine and remain present there for a longer time than in blood.

— Gastric contents may contain the unmetabolized parent drug, but gastric contents are not usually available for analysis unless the patient vomits spontaneously.

— Usually, a minimum of 50 to 100 mL of urine or gastric contents is required for toxicology screening.

— If ingestion occurred less than 12 hours before testing, obtain both urine and whole blood to increase detection rate. When in doubt, submit all available specimens for toxicology screening.

— Consult and collaborate with the toxicology laboratory or poison control center personnel to determine which specimen(s) to submit, substance(s) to be detected, and detection method needed. Consider:

1. Time of the ingestion.
2. Time sample was obtained.
3. Substance suspected of being ingested and/or patient's clinical presentation.

Radiographic Imaging

— Radiographic imaging may detect ferrous sulfate (iron) and enteric-coated tablets in a child's GI tract. Additionally, radiopaque foreign bodies that the child accidentally ingests, aspirates, or is forced to ingest may be seen in the GI or respiratory tract.

— A negative radiograph alone does not rule out ingestion or aspiration of these substances.

— Consider a skeletal survey in children younger than 2 years who may be chemically abused, particularly if physical abuse is also a possibility. Views recommended by the American Academy of Pediatrics Section on Radiology should be included in the skeletal survey.[23]

References

1. Calello D, Henretig F. Pediatric toxicology: specialized approach to the poisoned child. *Emerg Med Clin North Am*. 2014;32(1):29-52.

2. Finkelstein Y, Hutson JR, Freedman SB, Wax P, Brent J. Drug-induced seizures in children and adolescents presenting for emergency care: current and emerging trends. *Clin Toxicol (Phila)*. 2013;51(8):761-766.

3. Donaruma-Kwoh MM, Creamer LC, Giardino ER, Giardino AP, Pape J. When the Medical system is misused: the condition formerly known as Munchausen syndrome by proxy. In: Clements PT, Burgess AW, Fay-Hillier TM, Giardino ER, Giardino AP, eds. *Nursing Approach to the Evaluation of Child Maltreatment.* 2nd ed. Saint Louis, MO: STM Learning, Inc; 2014

4. Anglin D, Spears KL, Hutson HR. Flunitrazepam and its involvement in date or acquaintance rape. *Acad Emerg Med.* 1997;4(4):323-326.

5. US Department of Justice, Drug Enforcement Administration. *Drugs of Abuse: 2015 Edition.* Washington, DC: US Department of Justice, Drug Enforcement Administration; 2015. Drug Enforcement Administration Web site. https://www.dea.gov/pr/multimedia-library/publications/drug_of_abuse.pdf. Accessed September 13, 2016.

6. Ferrara SD, Frison G, Tedeschi L, LeBeau M. Gamma-hydroxybutyrate (GHB) and related products. In: LeBeau MA, Mozayani A, eds. *Drug-Facilitated Sexual Assault: A Forensic Handbook.* San Diego, CA: Academic Press; 2011:107-126.

7. Wood KE. Exposure to bath salts and synthetic tetrahydrocannabinol from 2009 to 2012 in the United States. *J Pediatr.* 2013;163(1):213-216.

8. Henretig F. The deliberately poisoned child. In: Levin AV, Sheridan MS, eds. *Munchausen Syndrome by Proxy: Issues in Diagnosis and Treatment.* New York, NY: Lexington Books; 1995.

9. National Alliance for Drug Endangered Children. National guidelines for medical evaluation of children found in drug labs. National Alliance for Drug Endangered Children Web site. http://www.nationaldec.org/user_files/18918.pdf. Accessed September 13, 2016.

10. Karasch S, Vinci R, Reece R. Esophagitis, epiglottitis, and cocaine alkaloid ("crack"): "accidental" poisoning or child abuse? *Pediatrics.* 1990;86:117-119.

11. Valdez A, Casavant M, Spiller H, Chounthirath T, Xiang H, Smith G. Pediatric exposure to laundry detergent pods. *Pediatrics.* 2014;134(6):1127-1135.

12. Mickalide A, Carr K. Safe Kids Worldwide: preventing unintentional childhood injuries across the globe. *Pediatr Clin North Am.* 2012;59(6):1367-1380.

13. Johnston B, Ebel B. Child injury control: trends, themes and controversies. *Acad Pediatr.* 2013;13(6):499-507.

14. Burghardt LC, Ayers JW, Brownstein JS, et al. Adult prescription drug use and pediatric medication exposures and poisonings. *Pediatrics.* 2013;132(1):18-27.

15. Smith M, Spiller H, Casavant M, Chounthirath T, Brophy T, Xiang H. Out of hospital medication errors among young children in the United States, 2002-2012. *Pediatrics.* 2014;134(5):867-876.

16. Lowry J. Electronic cigarettes: another pediatric toxic hazard in the home? *Clin Toxicol.* 2014;52:449-450.

17. Garbutt J, Miller W, Dodd S, Bobenhouse N, Sterkel R, Strunk R. Parental use of electronic cigarettes. *Acad Pediatr.* 2015;15(6):599-604.

18. David R, Ellis D, Gartner JC. Water intoxication in normal infants: role of antidiuretic hormone in pathogenesis. *Pediatrics.* 1981;68(3):349-353.

19. Ehrenpreis J, DesLauriers C, Lank P, Armstrong P, Leikin J. Nutmeg poisonings: a retrospective review of 10 years [*sic*] experience from the Illinois Poison Center: 2001-2011. *J Med Toxicol.* 2014;10(2):148-151.

20. Hoyte C. The toxicity of energy drinks: myth or reality? *Clin Toxicol (Phila).* 2013;51(8):729-730.

21. Donovan J. The burden of alcohol use: focus on children and preadolescents. *Alcohol Res.* 2013;35(2):186-192.

22. Onders B, Casavant MJ, Spiller HA, Chounthirath T, Smith GA. Marijuana exposure among children younger than six years in the United States. *Clin Pediatr (Phila).* 2016;55(5):428-436.

23. American Academy of Pediatrics, Section of Radiology. Diagnostic imaging of child abuse. *Pediatrics.* 2000;105:1345-1348.

Chapter 9

Neglect, Abandonment, and Failure to Thrive

Deborah A. Frank, MD
Angelo P. Giardino, MD, PhD
Mark D. Joffe, MD
Lakshmi Kolagotla, MD
Megan Sandel, MD
Ann L. O'Sullivan, PhD, FAAN, CPNP, CRNP
Steadman McPeters, DNP, CRNP, CPNP-AC, RNFA
Rosario V. Sanchez, MSN, RN, CCRN, CFN, SANE-A, D-ABFN

Definitions

In child-rearing, parents and caregivers may make errors in judgment that include acts of omission or commission. Neglect occurs when children's basic needs are not met, usually through caregivers' omissions. It is the most common form of child maltreatment and a major threat to the health and well-being of children. Whenever children are placed in a dangerous environment or situation, this constitutes neglect, even in the absence of actual harm. Often, it may not be clear if a mandatory report of neglect is warranted.[1]

- Clinically, neglect ranges from slightly less than adequate parenting (based on a generally accepted community standard) to severely dangerous omissions in care likely to cause death.[2]
- A child's age is a factor. In adolescence, parents' responsibilities diminish. Children's needs change as they are given more responsibility for their own care.
- **Table 9-1** lists the US federal government's categorization scheme for the forms of child neglect it recognizes.

Table 9-1. Types of Neglect

Physical Neglect

Abandonment
Desertion of a child without arranging for reasonable care or supervision. This includes cases where a child was not claimed within 2 days.

Expulsion
Blatant refusal of custody, such as the permanent or indefinite removal of a child from the home, without arranging for care by others or refusing to accept custody of a returned runaway.

Shuttling
Leaving the child in the custody of others for days or weeks at a time, possibly due to the unwillingness of the caregiver to maintain custody.

Nutritional neglect
Insufficient provision of food and nourishment, often evidenced by poor growth and undernutrition.

Clothing neglect
Insufficient provision of appropriate clothing, such as not having warm clothes or shoes in the winter.

Other
Includes inadequate hygiene and forms of reckless disregard for a child's safety and welfare, such as driving with the child while intoxicated or leaving a young child in the car unattended.

Medical Neglect

Denial of health care
Failure to provide or permit needed care as recommended by a competent health care professional for a physical injury, illness, medical condition, or impairment.

Delay in health care
Failure to seek timely and appropriate medical care for a serious health problem that any reasonable layman would have recognized as needing professional medical attention. Examples include not obtaining proper preventive medical or dental care, not obtaining care for a mentally ill or physically sick child, or not following medical recommendations.

Environmental Neglect

Lack of neighborhood safety, opportunities, and resources. Dangerous neighborhoods have been shown to have a harmful impact on children's development and mental health.

(continued)

Table 9-1. Types of Neglect *(continued)*

INADEQUATE SUPERVISION

Lack of appropriate supervision
Some states specify the amount of time children at different ages can be left unsupervised. The child's age, development, and situation need to be taken into account.

Exposure to hazards
Examples include safety hazards (poisons, small objects, electrical wires, stairs, drug paraphernalia), second-hand smoke (especially in children with pulmonary disorders), guns and other weapons, unsanitary household conditions, and lack of car safety restraints.

Inappropriate caregivers
Leaving the child in the care of someone who either is unable or should not be trusted to provide childcare, such as a young child, a known child abuser, or someone with a substance abuse problem.

EMOTIONAL NEGLECT

Inadequate nurturance/affection
Persistent, marked inattention to the child's needs for affection, emotional support, attention, or competence.

Chronic or extreme spousal abuse
Exposure to chronic or extreme spousal abuse or other forms of intimate partner violence (IPV).

Permitted drug or alcohol abuse
Encouragement or permission by the caregiver of drug or alcohol use by the child.

Other permitted maladaptive behavior
Evidence of chronic delinquency or criminally assaultive behaviors where the caregiver has reason to be aware of the existence and seriousness of the problem and does not intervene.

Isolation
Denying a child the ability to interact with peers or adults outside or inside the home.

NEWBORNS ADDICTED OR EXPOSED TO DRUGS

A number of states have statutory provisions requiring the reporting of substance-exposed newborns to Child Protective Services (CPS). Women who use drugs or alcohol during pregnancy can put their unborn children at risk for mental and physical disabilities.

HOMELESSNESS

Some states specifically omit homelessness from defining neglect, although homelessness is considered neglect with mismanagement of financial resources or when monies for rent are spent on drugs or alcohol, causing frequent evictions.

Adapted from Depanfilis D.[3]

— Professionals working in child maltreatment must rely on legal definitions of what constitutes neglect to guide practice and intervention decisions.[4,5]

— Understanding contributing factors is important, but neglect is best defined from the child's perspective.

— Law enforcement officers and prosecutors use legal definitions and standards to determine if they should become involved.

— Children must usually be at significant risk for severe bodily harm for the criminal justice system to become involved.

— Less severe forms of maltreatment are generally handled by CPS agencies without police or prosecutor involvement.[6]

— Most state statutes and research literature agree on 9 components of neglect[7]:

1. Inadequate food
2. Inadequate clothing
3. Inadequate shelter
4. Inadequate supervision
5. Inadequate medical care
6. Inadequate emotional care
7. Inadequate education
8. Exploitation
9. Exposure to unwholesome circumstances

— Basic needs that caregivers are to provide for children are[8]:

1. Food
2. Warmth
3. Clothing
4. Shelter and protection
5. Grooming and hygiene
6. Fresh air and sunlight

7. Activity and rest
8. Prevention from illness and accidents
9. Affection
10. Continuity of care
11. Security of belonging
12. Self-esteem
13. Opportunity to learn
14. Opportunity to achieve independence and success

— Neglect and child abuse are different forms of child maltreatment.

1. Neglectful parents are more disengaged from their children and have more negative interactions with them than abusive parents do.[9]
2. Neglectful mothers have a lower perception of personal and social adequacy and lower self-esteem than physically abusive mothers.[10]
3. Neglect is more detrimental to children's overall development than child abuse. Both neglect and emotional abuse may have a more profound negative long-term effect on academic performance, psychological distress, and psychopathology than physical abuse.[11-14]
4. Persistent, pervasive neglect seems especially deleterious to cognitive and psychological development.

— In models of human ecology, both parents and the community in general play a role in ensuring that the basic needs of children are met.[4] Ecologically based approaches to neglect seek to define a shared responsibility and to relate social factors that influence a caregiver's ability to provide care.[2]

Conceptual Model

— Five systems to understanding neglect (**Figure 9-1**) are[15,16]:

1. ***The microsystem***: Relationships within the actual family or caregiving unit.
2. ***The mesosystem***: Relationships between the child and community organizations that meet some of the child's needs.
3. ***The exosystem***: Relationships between family and community organizations that offer varying degrees of support for the family.

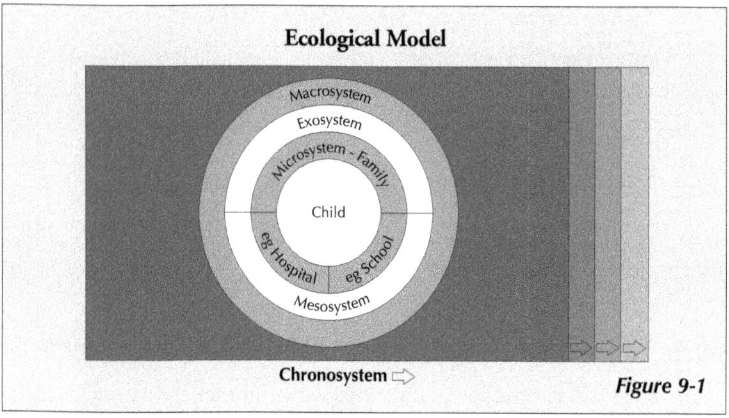

Figure 9-1. *Schematic of the Ecological Model. Adapted from Bronfenbrenner.*[15,16]

4. ***The macrosystem***: The overarching culture in which the microsystems, mesosystems, and exosystems operate within the society itself.
5. ***The chronosystem***: The temporal context in which actions and responses occur.

— No theory fully explains or predicts neglectful behavior, but research has identified risks associated with neglect.

— The overall risk of maltreatment increases approximately 2-fold for children with disabilities.

Dynamics of Neglect

Three categories of factors are often found in lives of neglected children:

1. ***Social factors***[17,18]: Poverty, social isolation, differences among ethnic and racial groups,[7,19,20] and the tendency for caregivers to perceive their neighborhoods and communities as more socially cold and isolated than do non-neglectful caregivers.[21-23]
2. ***Maternal and paternal factors***: Major affective disorders, alcoholism and/or drug abuse, lack of basic problem-solving skills and social competence,[24] youth, inexperience, and ignorance of the nutritional, developmental, and safety needs of children. Mothers with mental retardation or other developmental disabilities may need extra support to prevent neglect of their children.

3. ***Child factors***: Tendencies to be passive or quiet, as these children may be less demanding and, therefore, less likely to have their needs met; a poor fit between caregivers' personalities and children's temperaments; special needs.

Evaluation of Neglect in the Health Care Setting

The goal of the health care assessment is to collect growth parameters, perform routine assessment, and deliver a full range of primary care services. Screening for neglect generally unfolds in 2 phases: (1) screening for generic issues that commonly suggest the possibility of neglect and (2) more specific screening to explore aspects of the case that indicate a particular type or form of neglect.

Generic Screening

— Core issues are[25]:

1. Indications that basic needs are not being met in evaluations of general appearance, evidence of actual harm, risk of harm based on clinical situations, and a child's past medical history.
2. A pattern of caregiving that suggests the presence of neglect, such as lack of adherence to routine health care recommendations, past episodes of neglect, or previous CPS involvement.
3. Assessing potential contributing factors, especially parental coping strategies and the presence of domestic violence in family.
4. Assessing strengths and possible resources available to a child and family (eg, parental interest in child's well-being, other involved family members who are genuinely helpful, access to community-based family support programs).
5. Noting past successes and failures with previous interventions, including what did and did not work before, who was involved, and the reasons were for success or failure.
6. Obtaining prognostic information related to family motivation, capacity to change, and access to resources (eg, Does the family have a track record of accepting help and achieving goals? Is there a record of resistance to recommendations? Are resources available within the family and community?).

Specific Screening

— A medical history, physical examination, possible laboratory and diagnostic studies, and careful observation of the parent-child interaction are necessary.

— Incorporate reports by other disciplines, especially professionals who visit the child at home.

— Note specific issues related to a disability or special need that require more attention and understanding, such as using a medically trained sign language interpreter for a child with a sensory disability.

Role of the Health Care Provider

— If a screening identifies neglect, the health care provider should[26]:

1. Build a strong relationship with the family.
2. Provide ongoing education concerning child development.
3. Monitor the child's progress and serve on a support team that encourages the family to meet their challenges.

— Multidisciplinary team members teach the family skills in caring for children and provide educational experiences so the family can learn needed skills.

Types of Neglect

Medical Neglect

— Medical neglect is an identifiable pattern of apparent disregard for the importance of routine health care, which includes delay in seeking health care assessment at a reasonable point in an acute illness, failure to follow medical therapies as prescribed, failure to seek assistance for obvious developmental delays, and refusing appropriate medical care for treatable illness.

— Not all nonadherences are medical neglect:

1. In pediatrics, compliance rates range from 7% to 89% for short-term medical regimens and from 11% to 83% for long-term regimens.[27]
2. Reasons for noncompliance include forgetfulness, symptom improvement once treatment has begun, perceived ineffectiveness of treatment, misunderstanding instructions, child resistance, and the onset of side effects.

3. Assess the impact that noncompliance has on the child as well the pattern of adherence to prescribed regimen to distinguish noncompliance from medical neglect.
4. To avoid contributing to medical neglect, consider the medical knowledge and ability of caregivers and the family resources at their disposal. Ensure that caregivers understand the importance of the medical treatments and follow-up, and understand the family's resources so that noncompliance resulting from lack of finances or an inability to attend frequent office visits can be anticipated.
5. Address religion-based medical neglect. The religious exemption in the Child Abuse Prevention and Treatment Act Amendments of 1996 specifies that nothing in the Act should establish a federal requirement that parents or legal guardians provide a medical service or treatment that contradicts their religious beliefs.[28] State authorities may become involved to act in the best interests of a child and are permitted to deliver well-established medical services and treatments without labeling caregivers as neglectful or abusive. Most courts override parental religious practices when refused treatment is clearly superior to alternatives, significant complications of therapy are unlikely, or when failure to treat is expected to cause serious harm or death. The child must also be likely to enjoy a relatively normal life in the future, a provision that gives parents and guardians the right to refuse aggressive treatment for children who have severe disabilities or terminal illnesses. If children are old enough, they must also assent and/or consent to the therapy.[29]

— History determines the appropriateness of caregivers' responses. For existing illness, note:

1. Timelines for routine care.
2. Caregivers' responses to presence of symptoms and signs.
3. Reported adherence to medical regimens, supplemented by pharmacy records of filling prescriptions and, if appropriate, refill frequency.
4. Whether or not caregivers express concern and seem interested in the evaluation.
5. Whether or not caregivers ask appropriate questions about possible causes of the problem and treatments.

— During the physical examination:

1. Observe children's general appearances, looking for signs of neglect. For specific clinical conditions, conduct the physical examination based on what is visible.
2. Evaluate any delay in seeking treatment for new or acute symptoms.
3. Assess the state of disease control for chronic conditions, especially compared to what is expected when prescribed treatment is followed.
4. Evaluate children's general appearance and development for routine care.

— Laboratory tests ordered depend on a child's current condition.

Failure to Thrive

— Defined as a child who fails to grow as expected compared to peers of the same age and ethnicity, failure to thrive (FTT) is a symptom rather than a diagnosis. Traditionally FTT is considered ***organic*** or ***nonorganic***:

1. Organic FTT is growth failure ascribed to medical conditions.
2. Nonorganic FTT is attributed to parental neglect and sometimes referred to as maternal deprivation syndrome or hospitalism, which is the set of physical and mental effects that hospitalization or institutionalization has on a person and is especially visible in infants and children.

— Most cases of FTT result from a complex interaction of environmental and medical factors, referred to as "mixed" FTT.

1. Risk factors include poverty, emotional factors, parental factors, and children's factors (**Figure 9-2**).
2. Differential diagnosis ranges from major medical diagnoses such as human immunodeficiency virus (HIV) infection and cystic fibrosis to subtle organic etiologies such as oral motor deficits, obstructive sleep apnea syndrome, poor dentition, and food allergies. Erroneous health beliefs can contribute to FTT.

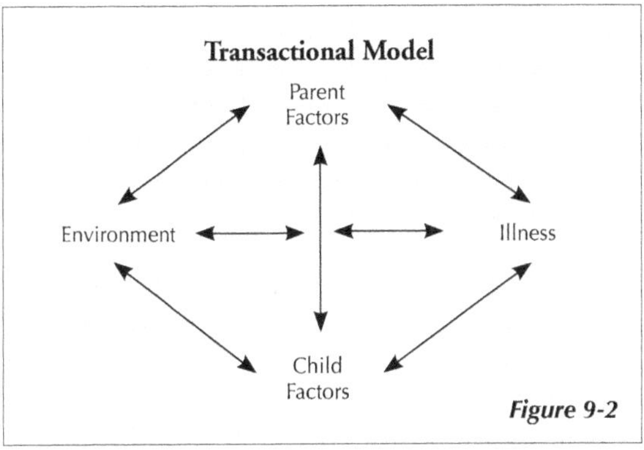

Figure 9-2. *The transactional model illustrates multiple cases of FTT, including both parent and child factors of environment and illness.*

Diagnosis

— A thorough prenatal history, noting gestational age, size at birth, perinatal complications, and course of the pregnancy is necessary.

— Obtain children's unclothed weight and plot it on standard growth grids (**Figures 9-3** through **9-12**). Note height and head circumference measurements and any signs that substantiate suspected diagnoses.

— Observe the parent-child interaction, noting disordered attachments:

1. Parent does not exhibit pleasure in the infant and may appear anxious or depressed. A mother may express less physical affection than would normally be expected.
2. Infant appears apathetic and engages in limited eye contact or vocalization.

Laboratory Evaluation

— Laboratory evaluation is guided by history and physical examination. The following are always required:

1. A complete blood count to diagnose iron deficiency anemia and rule out malignancy and eosinophilia
2. A lead screening to rule out lead poisoning
3. A urinalysis to screen for urinary tract infection, renal tubular acidosis, dehydration, and ketosis from malnutrition or diabetes

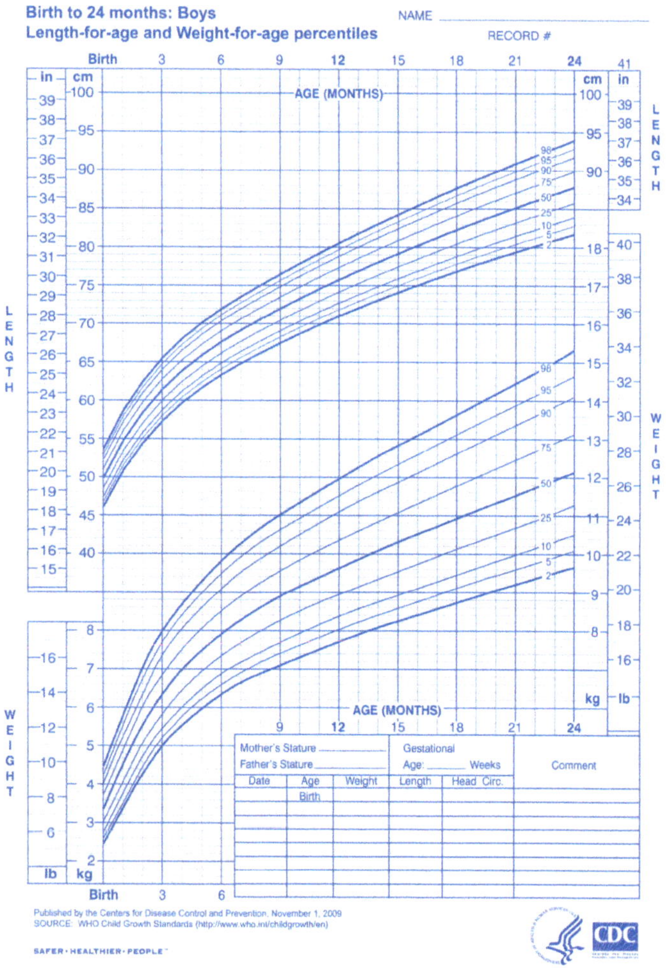

Figure 9-3

Figure 9-3. *Length- and weight-for-age percentiles for boys from birth to 24 months. Reprinted from Centers for Disease Control and Prevention.*[30]

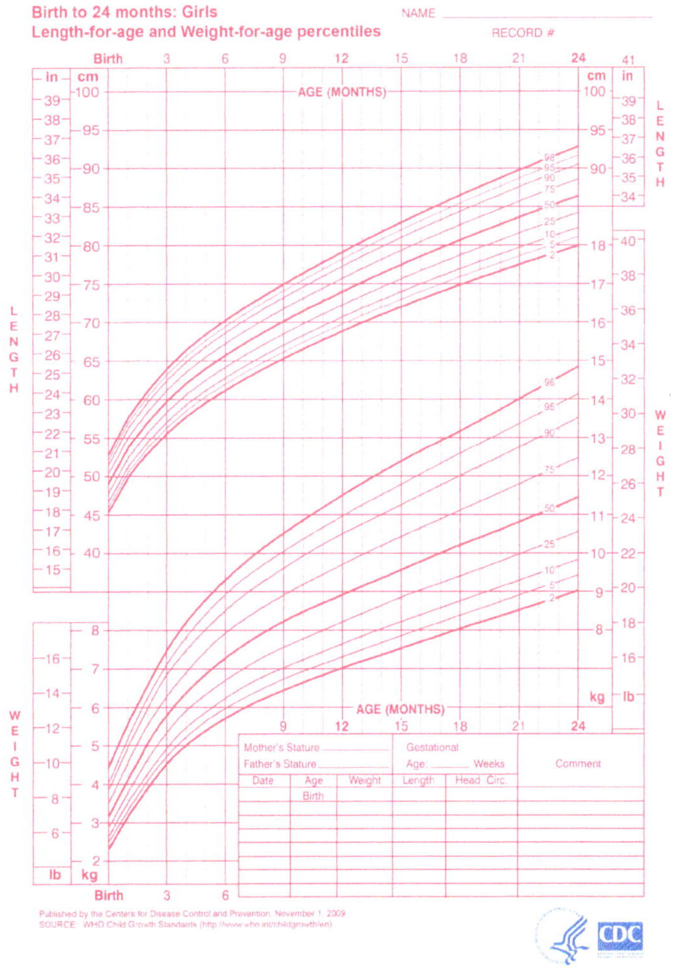

Figure 9-4

Figure 9-4. *Length- and weight-for-age percentiles for girls from birth to 24 months. Reprinted from Centers for Disease Control and Prevention.*[30]

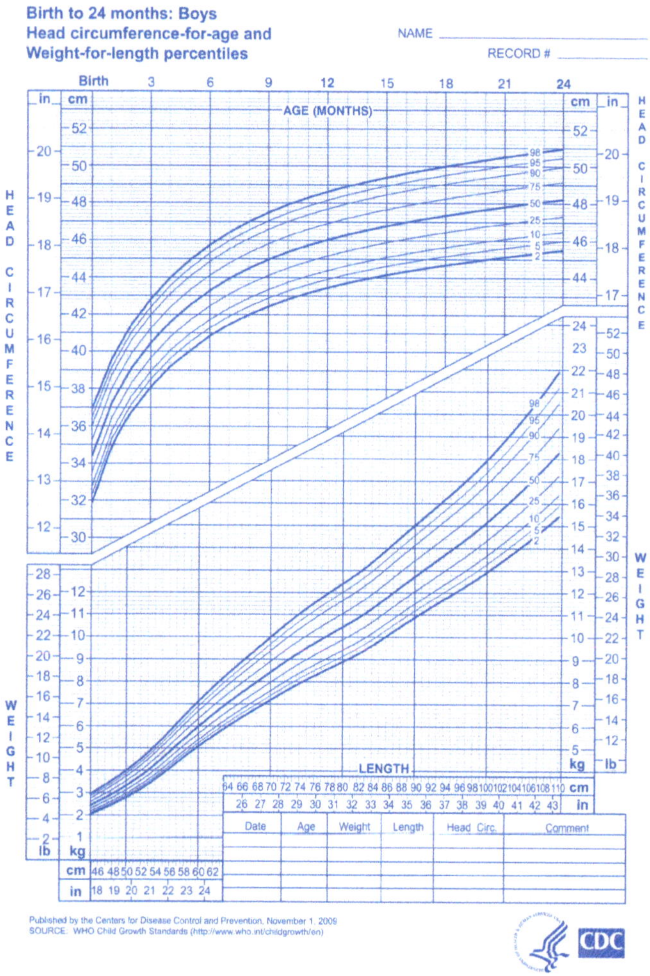

Figure 9-5. *Head circumference-for-age and weight-for-length percentiles for boys from birth to 24 months. Reprinted from Centers for Disease Control and Prevention.*[30]

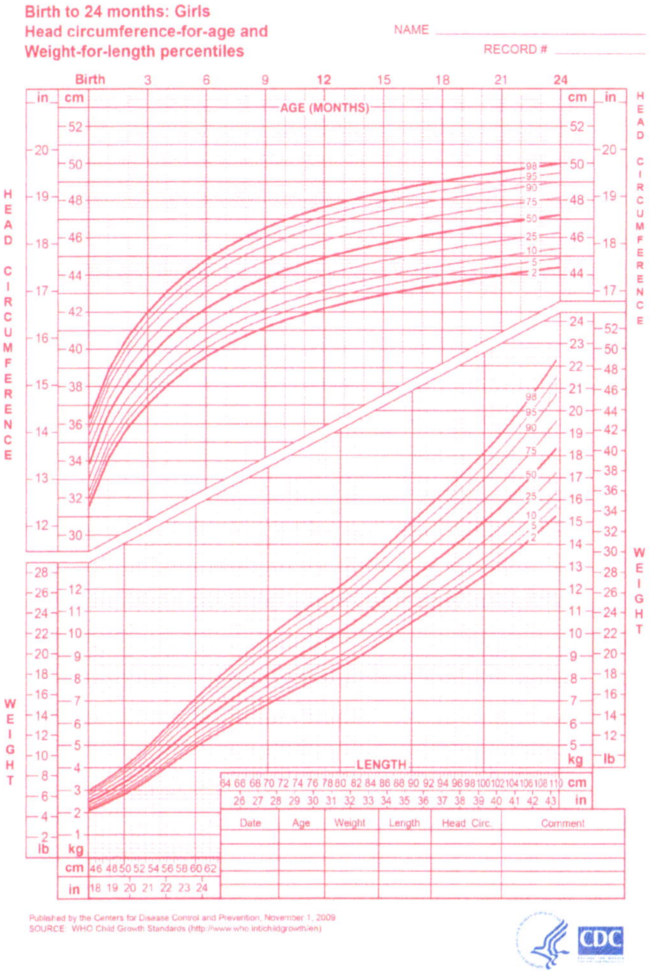

Figure 9-6

Figure 9-6. *Head circumference-for-age and weight-for-length percentiles for girls from birth to 24 months. Reprinted from Centers for Disease Control and Prevention.*[30]

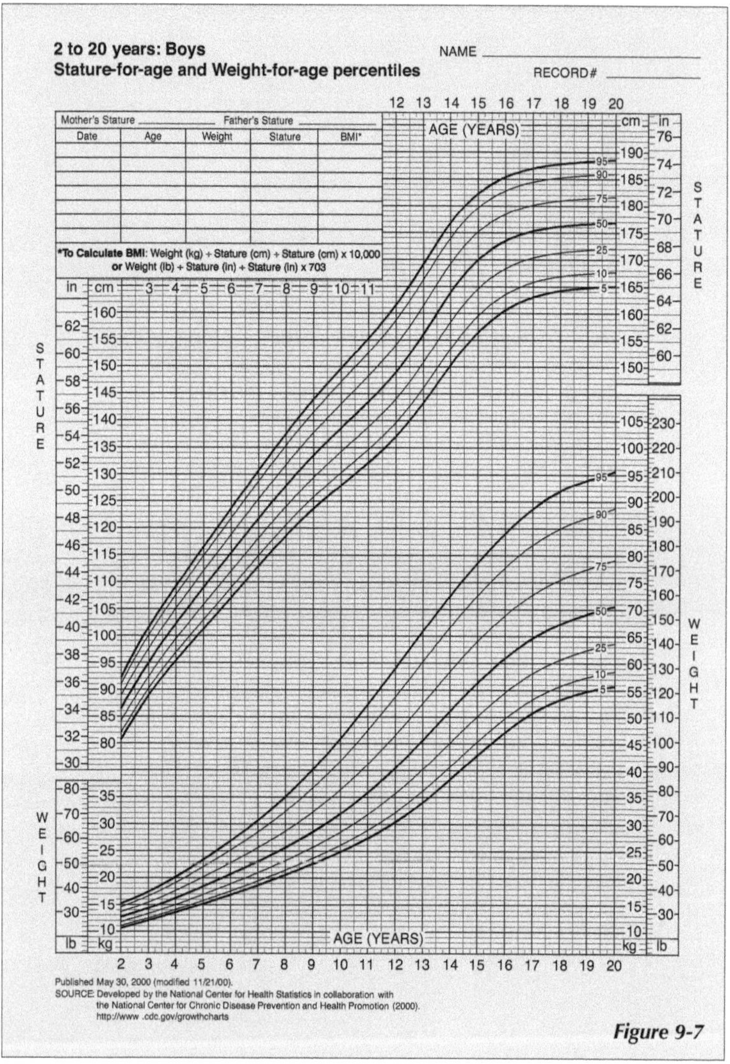

Figure 9-7. *Stature- and weight-for-age percentiles for boys from 2 to 20 years. Reprinted from National Center for Health Statistics, National Center for Chronic Disease Prevention and Health Promotion.*[31]

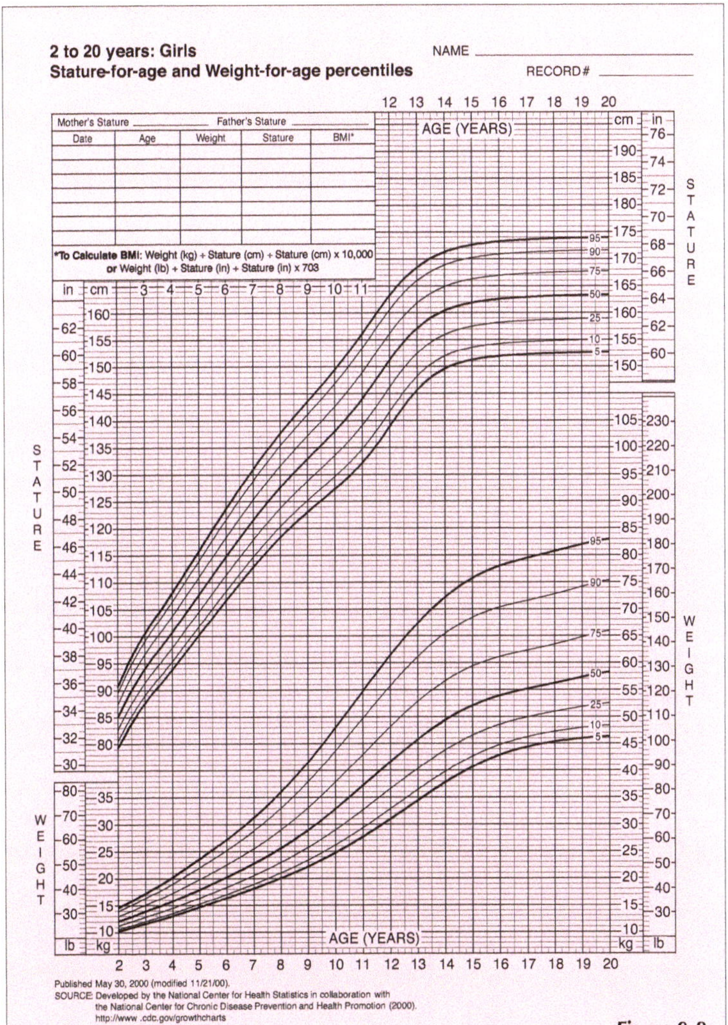

Figure 9-8

Figure 9-8. *Stature- and weight-for-age percentiles for girls from 2 to 20 years. Reprinted from National Center for Health Statistics, National Center for Chronic Disease Prevention and Health Promotion.*[31]

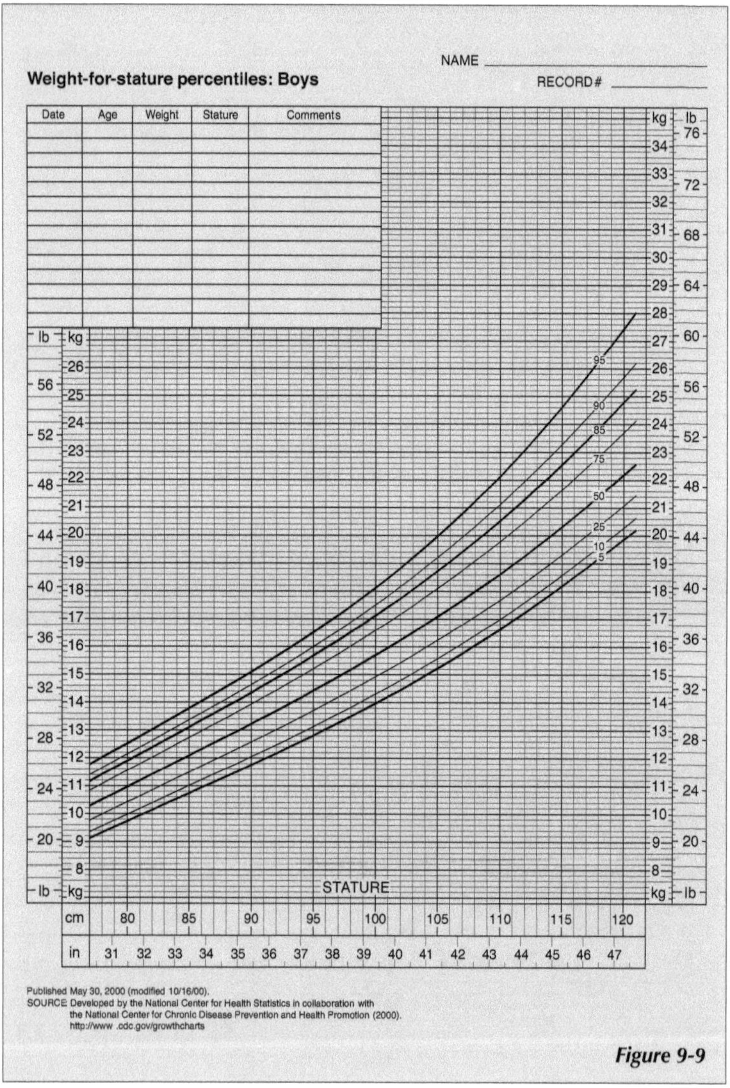

Figure 9-9. *Weight-for-stature percentiles for boys. Reprinted from National Center for Health Statistics, National Center for Chronic Disease Prevention and Health Promotion.*[31]

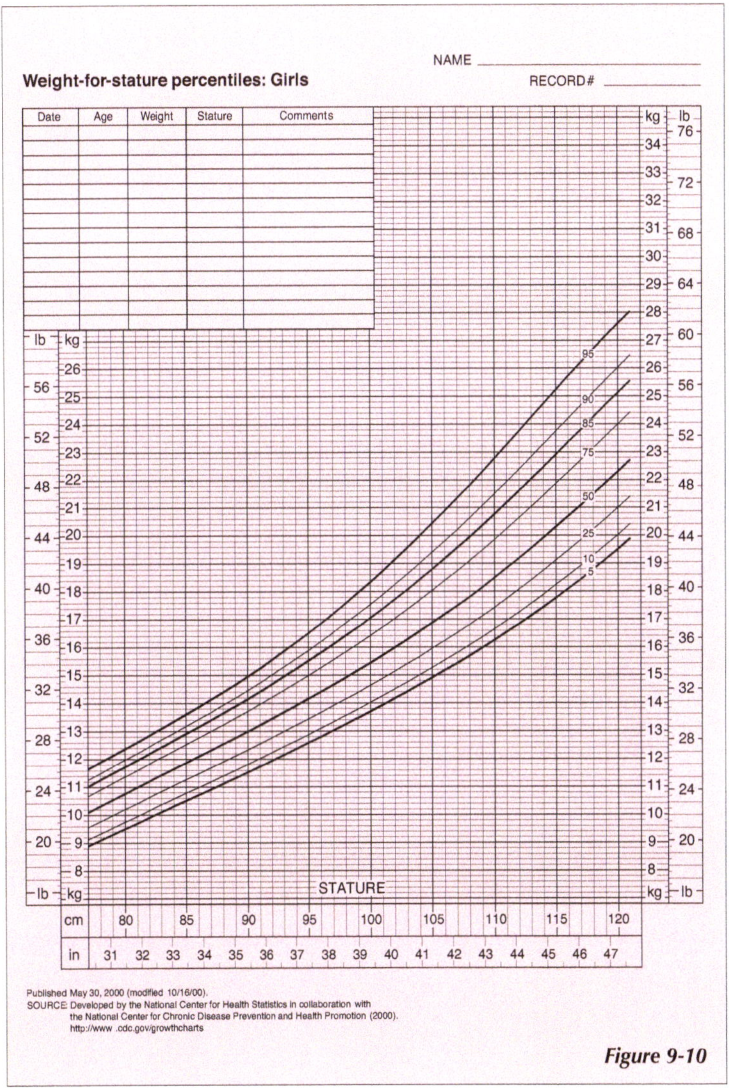

Figure 9-10. *Weight-for-stature for girls. Reprinted from National Center for Health Statistics, National Center for Chronic Disease Prevention and Health Promotion.*[31]

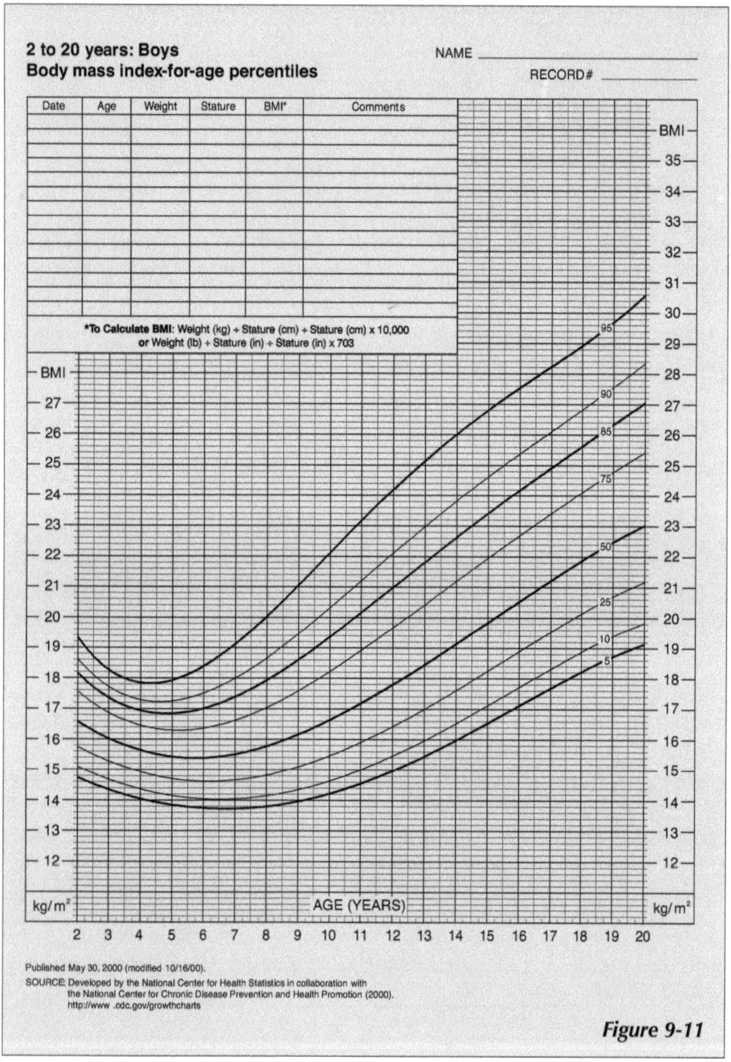

Figure 9-11. *Body mass index-for-age percentiles for boys from 2 to 20 years. Reprinted from National Center for Health Statistics, National Center for Chronic Disease Prevention and Health Promotion.*[31]

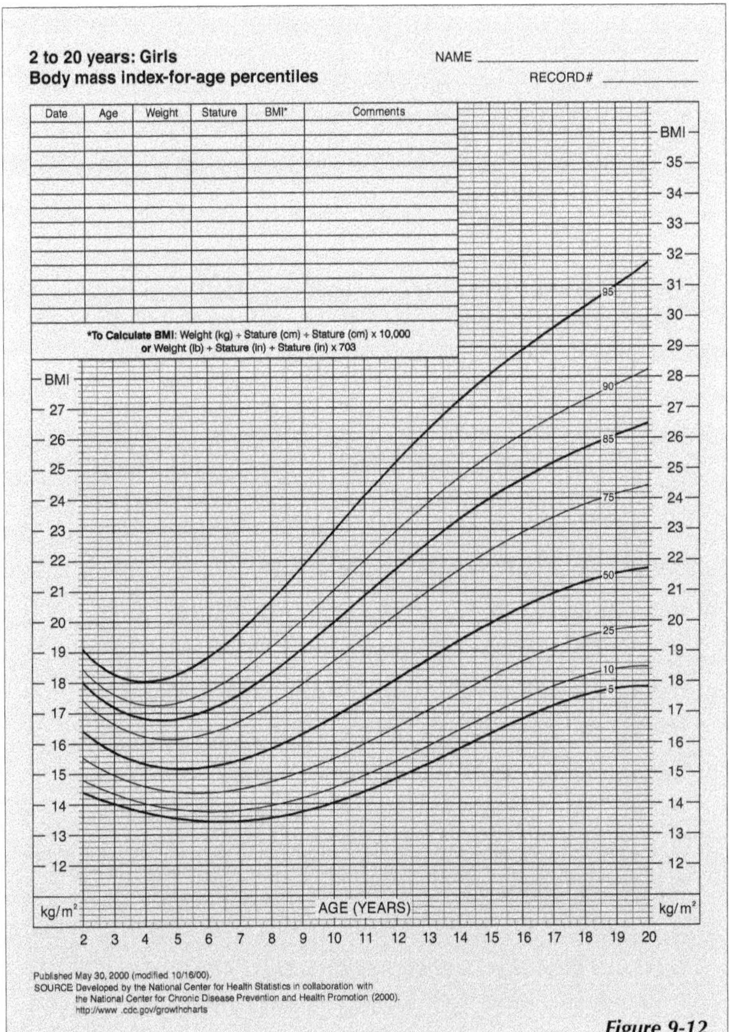

Figure 9-12

Figure 9-12. *Body mass index-for-age percentiles for girls from 2 to 20 years. Reprinted from National Center for Health Statistics, National Center for Chronic Disease Prevention and Health Promotion.*[31]

— Determine bone age in all children younger than 1 year whose weight is less than the fifth percentile for age but above the tenth percentile for height or length.[32] Bone age helps distinguish between constitutional short stature and endocrine or nutritional abnormalities.

1. In constitutional short stature, the bone age equals the chronologic age.
2. In endocrine or nutritional abnormalities, the bone age is less than the chronologic age.

— Assess children's degree of malnutrition and obtain total protein and albumin measurements. Provide emergency hospitalization for severely malnourished children. Allow less malnourished children to be managed at home if closely supervised outpatient therapy is available.[33]

— For severely malnourished children, obtain electrolyte, blood urea nitrogen, and serum creatinine levels for managing hydration and distinguishing acidosis and electrolyte abnormalities from metabolic or renal disorders. Also assess for rickets, measuring calcium, phosphorus, and alkaline phosphatase levels.

— For suspected syndromes, obtain a karyotype and genetic consultation.

— Perform a radioallergosorbent (RAST) test or skin testing for children with suspected allergies.

— Consider HIV and sweat testing, which identifies cystic fibrosis, for children with suggestive symptoms or family history.

— Consider celiac sprue in all children with FTT who do not respond to preliminary dietary intervention.

Treatment

— Successful treatment requires the collaborative efforts of medical, developmental, social work, and nutritional personnel.

— The current treatment approach is based on correcting the factors contributing to malnutrition and providing treatment for complications, including growth delay, impaired immunity, and deficits in cognitive and social development.[33]

1. Two manifestations of FTT that require urgent protective intervention are Munchausen syndrome by proxy (see Chapter 14, "Medical Child Abuse/Munchausen Syndrome by Proxy") and psychosocial dwarfism.
2. Surgical intervention via a gastrostomy tube can promote weight gain in children with chronic medical conditions.[34] Gastrostomy tube placement is associated with short-term infection[35,36] and long-term consequences such as delayed development and prolonged oral motor deficits. Weaning can require behavioral therapy[37] or hospitalization.

— An outpatient multidisciplinary team (ie, a pediatrician, nutritionist or dietician, social worker, and developmental specialist) approach is the preferred mode of treatment. Each professional performs an independent evaluation of the child; then, a treatment plan is tailored specifically to the family's needs.

— Parental acceptance of FTT as an interactional disorder and cooperation with treatment are associated with more positive case outcomes.[38]

— These children are at high risk for recurrent infection and require immunizations (eg, influenza and multivalent pneumococcal vaccine) in addition to those routinely given to children.

— Make referrals to other specialists as needed, but limit the number to avoid overwhelming the family.[33]

— Nutritional interventions are based on the initial evaluation.

1. Limit juice intake to 4 oz or less[39] and eliminate liquids that have little or no nutritional benefits, such as soda, fruit drinks, or tea.
2. Educate parents about choosing foods with high caloric density and good nutritional quality.
3. Modify dietary schedules to focus on offering 3 meals and 2 scheduled snacks daily, consuming solids before liquids, and eliminating grazing between meals.

— Social workers should determine whether adequate income exists to support the family's basic needs for food, shelter, clothing, and utilities. If it does not:

  — Help families obtain welfare; aid from Women, Infants, and Children; and/or food stamps as eligible.

  — Help families apply for assistance programs that pay heating bills, Section 8 vouchers, or supplemental security income.

  — Seek help from area food banks and charitable organizations.

— Early intervention or Head Start programs are appropriate for children with FTT to address the risk for developmental deficits.

— Assess problems in the family involving domestic violence, illnesses, or chronic diseases. Evaluate parental behaviors and the need for protection for children who have suffered inflicted injury or whose safety is jeopardized.

PHYSICAL NEGLECT

— Single episodes that point to a serious breach in acceptable parenting, or multiple episodes representing patterns that suggest a lack of reasonable supervision or little attention to creating and maintaining a safe environment, may signal physical neglect.

— When obtaining a history, look for indicators of exposure to avoidable and well-known environmental hazards. Use potential screening questions to identify risk-prone situations involving hygiene, clothing/shelter, housing, or custody/supervision.

— During the physical examination, note children's general appearance, cleanliness, and any parasitical infestations (**Figure 9-13**). Look for evidence of acute or healed injuries and check records for the history of each, as well as for evidence of environmental exposure. Note multiple bruises or scabs from old injuries or falls, unresolved tinea infections, extreme hunger at each visit, improper clothing for the season or environment, and excessively soiled clothing and/or filth in skin creases.

— Order laboratory tests as clinical findings suggest.

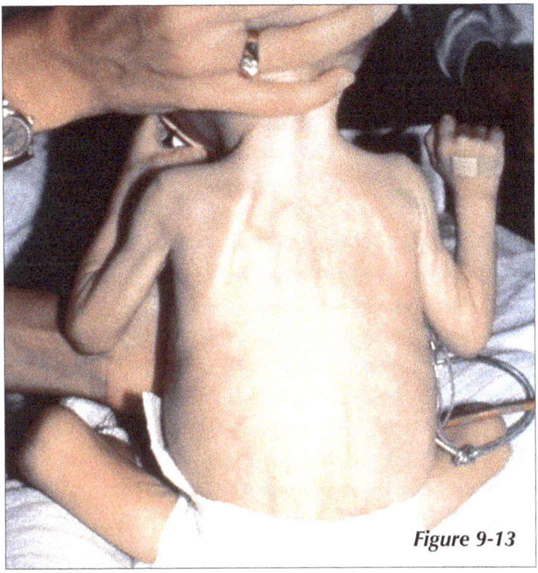

Figure 9-13. *Malnourished at 11 months, posterior view of infant shows loss of fat tissue, poor muscle tone, and hair loss.*

— Observe whether or not caregivers respond to children's natural curiosity about the environment in a supportive manner but also redirect children to safer activities when appropriate.

Abandonment

— Abandonment ranges from leaving a child with a temporary caregiver and not returning in a reasonable time frame to leaving the child alone, with or without the intent of having someone discover the child and provide care.[40]

— Children with chronic illnesses, premature infants, and other newborns who require prolonged hospitalization are at high risk for abandonment.

1. Parents may not have the opportunity to bond normally with these children because of the neonatal intensive care environment.
2. Older children with chronic illnesses and prolonged hospitalization may also be abandoned when parents do not show up at the time of discharge.
3. Children left where they may or may not be found are at significant risk of injury, illness, or death.

Table 9-2. Characteristics of Mothers Who Abandon Infants
— Young and unmarried
— Lack personal financial resources
— Fail to seek prenatal care throughout pregnancy
— Pregnant with first child
— In denial of the pregnancy and not telling anyone about it
— Living with their parents
— Fear the reaction of their families and partners
— Have other stressors, such as illegal immigration status or lacking health insurance
— Deliver their babies in nonhospital settings

— **Table 9-2** lists characteristics of mothers who abandon their infants.[41-43]

— "Safe Haven" laws are legislative efforts to provide parents, especially mothers, the option of safely abandoning their children with no risk of prosecution.[44] Although these laws vary by state, each state generally provides for young infants (typically younger than 30 days) to be safely brought to public places such as hospitals, fire departments, and police departments to be turned over to an adult with few or no questions asked and with no risk of prosecution for abandonment, provided that the child shows no signs of abuse.

Educational Neglect

— Parentally endorsed or tolerated truancy is a common form of educational neglect.[3] Truancy not supported by the family does not constitute educational neglect.

— School phobia, or refusal to attend school, can appear to teachers and school administrators to be educational neglect.

— Educational neglect also occurs when families fail to enroll children in school when they reach the age of compulsory education.[3]

— Children with special needs who require specialized services can be considered educationally neglected if caregivers do not reasonably attempt to assess and meet these needs.

— The consequences of educational neglect include academic underachievement, compromised employment potential, and social problems.

Neglect and Child Sex Trafficking

Childhood maltreatment, such as neglect and abandonment, are potential risk factors for trafficking victimization.

— In one study, 75% of commercially exploited children reported being abused and/or neglected; 55% had been abandoned by parents or guardians.[45] Related risk factors for trafficking and commercial sexual exploitation include:

  — Poor family functioning, parental substance abuse, and violence[46]

  — Death of a parent

  — Living in a divorced or single-parent home[47]

  — Previous interactions with the child welfare system or CPS, including out-of-home placement[46]

  — Disruptive family processes and maladaptive coping mechanisms (eg, substance abuse)[45,47]

— Trafficked and commercially exploited children who have experienced neglect or abandonment may remain captive due to the need for food, shelter, and relative safety.[45]

Interventions and Outcomes

— Interventions can have substantial, tangible, and enduring benefits[1,48] and are chosen based on the type of neglect that occurred, children's conditions, and family dynamics.

— Interventions for complex chronic conditions require 12 to 18 months or longer.

— Some cases can be managed by a physician and local CPS workers, but more complex cases benefit from involvement of an established multidisciplinary team.

— The goal is to have children's basic needs met in a way that fosters their ongoing health and well-being. Engage caregivers in understanding and meeting children's needs.

— If a child is believed to be in imminent danger, take immediate action to ensure the child's safety, including reporting to CPS.

— It may be necessary to hospitalize children in order for them to receive appropriate medical services and allow the CPS investigation to proceed. CPS determines to whom a child is discharged based on the findings of their investigation.

— Office-based interventions using outpatient settings are appropriate in less critical situations.

— School-based interventions should be implemented with the assistance of CPS.

— Clearly assess problems and determine the families' strengths and challenges in addressing the problems.

1. Communicate concern for children, show an interest in helping the caregivers and their families meet children's needs, and convey an understanding that the families care about what is best for their child.[49]

2. Explain the seriousness of the situation and communicate clearly that ultimately, action will be taken to ensure that children obtain everything they need.

3. Engage other disciplines to assist in treatment planning.

4. Maintain a working knowledge of the programs and resources available to help support children and their families.

5. Arrange for ongoing follow-up.

6. Clearly identify what it means to fail to meet appropriate milestones. If a caregiver fails to meet a child's needs, CPS may need to consider more disruptive solutions, including out-of-home placement.

— Specific interventions depend on the type of neglect that occurred, the amount of risk posed to children, children's developmental levels, caregivers' abilities, and types of services available.

1. ***Physical neglect***: Educate caregivers about child safety and avoidable environmental hazards. Provide follow-up office visits to reinforce anticipatory guidance. Assess children's well-being and provide additional age-appropriate information as children grow. Provide home services to ensure follow-through.
2. ***Medical neglect***: Identify medical conditions and educate parents about signs and symptoms they need to know and address. Make sure they understand how and when to seek health care, what constitutes an emergency, the importance of sticking to the treatment plan, connections to community resources, and which components of routine care cannot be ignored. Schedule follow-up visits and stress that failure to keep these appointments is a serious indication that the family cannot care for a child. Employ a case management approach for complex medical conditions that require the input of several different health care providers.
3. ***Follow-up***: Assess what steps are needed for the family to understand the circumstances that led to neglect. Identify family strengths essential to long-term solutions.

— Also address the problems of the neglectful parent or caregiver.

1. Make sure the intervention is structured and goal directed, modeling the organization needed.
2. Provide treatment for depression, addiction, family conflicts, and other personal problems.
3. Provide training in parenting skills, especially for young, inexperienced parents and those who have children with special needs. Include training in stress reduction, impulse control, money management, job placement, and marital counseling.[50]
4. Family therapy that includes extended family members may be more effective than individual therapy.

— See **Table 9-3** for information on outcomes.

Table 9-3. Outcomes of Neglect	
Areas Affected	— Physical health — Psychological adjustment — Intellectual, social, behavioral, and effective development
Factors	— Child's developmental level when the neglect occurred — Type, severity, and chronicity of the neglectful behavior
Adverse Neuropsychological Effects	— Cognitive deficits — Academic underachievement — Depressed affect — Behavior problems — Poor peer relations — Subsequent alcoholism, drug abuse, and criminal convictions — Premature death
Successful Interventions	Providing food supplementation and emotional support to mothers and children improves affect, peer relations, and problem-solving skills. Positive long-term outcomes may be more influenced by developmental stimulation than nutritional assistance.

References

1. Goldman J, Salus MK, Wolcott D, Kennedy KY. *A Coordinated Response to Child Abuse and Neglect: The Foundation for Practice*. Washington, DC: US Dept of Health and Human Services, Administration for Children and Families; 2003.
2. Dubowitz H, Black M, Starr RH, Zuravin S. A conceptual definition of child neglect. *Crim Justice Behav*. 1993;20:8-26.
3. DePanfilis D. *Child Neglect: A Guide for Prevention, Assessment, and Intervention*. Washington, DC: US Dept of Health and Human Services, Administration for Children and Families; 2006.
4. National Clearinghouse on Child Abuse and Neglect Information. *In Focus: Acts of Omission—An Overview of Child Neglect*. Washington, DC: US Dept of Health and Human Services, Administration for Children and Families; 2001.

5. Ludwig S. Defining child abuse: clinical mandate—evolving concepts. In: Ludwig S, Kornberg AE, eds. *Child Abuse: A Medical Reference*. New York, NY: Churchill Livingstone; 1992:1-12.

6. Pence D, Wilson C. *Team Investigation of Child Sexual Abuse: The Uneasy Alliance*. Thousand Oaks, CA: Sage Publications; 1994.

7. Rose SJ, Meezan W. Variations in perceptions of child neglect. *Child Welfare*. 1996;75:139-160.

8. Hobbs CJ, Hanks HB, Wynne JM. Neglect. In: Hobbs CJ, Hanks HG, Wynne JM, eds. *Child Abuse and Neglect: A Clinician's Handbook*. New York, NY: Churchill Livingstone; 1993:147-159.

9. Bousha DM, Twentyman CT. Mother-child interactional style in abuse, neglect and control groups: naturalistic observations in the home. *J Abnorm Psychol*. 1984;93:106-110.

10. Christensen MJ, Brayden R, Dietrich MS, McLaughlin FJ, Sherrod KB, Altemeier WA. The prospective assessment of self-concept in neglectful and physically abusive low-income mothers. *Child Abuse Negl*. 1994;18:225-232.

11. Kendall-Tackett KA, Eckenrode J. The effects of neglect on academic achievement and disciplinary problems: a developmental perspective. *Child Abuse Negl*. 1996;20:161-169.

12. Widom CS. Childhood victimization and the development of personality disorders. unanswered questions remain. *Arch Gen Psychiatry*. 1999;56:607-608.

13. Melchert TP. Clarifying the effects of parental substance abuse, child sexual abuse, and parenting caregiving on adult adjustment. *Profess Psychol Res Pract*. 2000;31:64-69.

14. Brunner R, Parzer P, Schuld V. Dissociative symptomatology and traumatogenic factors in adolescent psychiatric patients. *J Nerv Ment Dis*. 2000;188:71-77.

15. Bronfenbrenner U. Ecology of the family as a context for human development: research perspectives. *Dev Psychol*. 1986;22:723-742.

16. Bronfenbrenner U. Interacting systems in human development: research paradigms—present and future. In: Bolger N, Caspi A, Downey D, Moorehouse M, eds. *Persons in Context: Developmental Processes*. New York, NY: Cambridge University Press; 1989:25-49.

17. Daro D, McCurdy K. *Current Trends in Child Abuse Fatalities and Reporting: The Results of the 1991 50-State Survey*. Chicago, IL: National Center for the Prevention of Child Abuse; 1992.

18. Klerman LV. *Alive and Well? A Research and Policy Review of Health Programs for Poor Young Children*. New York, NY: National Center for Children in Poverty. Columbia University School of Public Health; 1991.

19. Rose SJ. Reaching consensus on child neglect: African American mothers and child welfare workers. *Child Youth Serv Rev*. 1999;21:463-479.

20. Dubowitz H, Klockner A, Starr RH, Black MM. Community and professional definitions of child neglect. *Child Maltreat*. 1998;3:235-243.

21. Garbarino J, Crouter A. Defining the community context for parent-child relations: the correlates of child maltreatment. *Child Dev*. 1978;49:604-616.

22. Garbarino J, Sherman D. High-risk neighborhoods and high-risk families: the human ecology of child maltreatment. *Child Dev*. 1980;51:188-198.

23. Garbarino J. The price of privacy in the social dynamics of child abuse. *Child Welfare*. 1977;56:565-575.

24. Daro D. *Confronting Child Abuse: Research for Effective Program Design*. New York, NY: The Free Press; 1988.

25. Dubowitz H, Giardino A, Gustavson E. Child neglect: guidance for pediatricians. *Pediatr Rev*. 2000;21:111-116.

26. McCleery JT, Pinyerd BJ. Nursing evaluation and treatment planning. In: Bross CD, Krugman RD, Lenherr MR, Rosenberg DA, Schmitt BD, eds. *The New Child Protection Team Handbook*. New York, NY: Garland Publishing; 1988:127-135.

27. Matsui DM. Drug compliance in pediatrics: clinical and research issues. *Pediatr Clin North Am*. 1997;44:1-14.

28. Child Welfare Information Gateway. *Definitions of Child Abuse and Neglect*. Washington, DC: US Department of Health and Human Services, Children's Bureau; 2016. Child Welfare Information Gateway Web site. https://www.childwelfare.gov/pubPDFs/define.pdf. Accessed March 23, 2017.

29. Bross DC. Medical care neglect. *Child Abuse Negl.* 1982;6:375.
30. Centers for Disease Control and Prevention. WHO growth standards are recommended for use in the U.S. for infants and children 0 to 2 years of age. Centers for Disease Control and Prevention Web site. https://www.cdc.gov/growthcharts/who_charts.htm. Updated September 9, 2010. Accessed April 25, 2017.
31. National Center for Health Statistics, National Center for Chronic Disease Prevention and Health Promotion. Clinical growth charts. Centers for Disease Control and Prevention Web site. https://www.cdc.gov/growthcharts/clinical_charts.htm. Accessed March 24, 2017.
32. Frank DA. Failure to thrive. In: Dershowitz R, ed. *Ambulatory Pediatric Care.* 3rd ed. Philadelphia, PA: Lippincott-Raven; 1999:903-907.
33. Frank DA, Drotar D, Cook J, Kasper D, Bleiker J. Failure to thrive. In: Reese R, Ludwig S, eds. *Child Abuse: Medical Diagnosis and Management.* 2nd ed. Baltimore, MD: Lippincott Williams and Wilkins; 2001:307-338.
34. Kang A, Zamora SA, Scott RB, Parsons HG. Catch-up growth in children treated with home enteral nutrition. *Pediatrics.* 1998;102:951-955.
35. Jarnagin WR, Duh Q, Mulvihill SJ, Ridge JA, Schrock TR, Way LW. The efficacy and limitations of percutaneous endoscopic gastrostomy. *Arch Surg.* 1992;127:261-264.
36. Kadakia SC, Sullivan HO, Starnes E. Percutaneous endoscopic gastrostomy or jejunostomy and the incidence of aspiration in 79 patients. *Am J Surg.* 1992;164:114-118.
37. Benoit D, Wong EE, Zlotkin SH. Discontinuation of enterostomy tube feeding by behavioral treatment in early childhood: a randomized controlled trial. *J Pediatr.* 2000;137:498-503.
38. Ayoub CC, Milner JS. Failure to thrive: parental indicators, types, and outcomes. *Child Abuse Negl.* 1985;9:491-499.
39. Smith MM, Lifshitz F. Excess fruit juice consumption as a contributing factor in nonorganic failure to thrive. *Pediatrics.* 1994;93:438-443.

40. Child Welfare League of America. *The Nature of Baby Abandonment.* Washington, DC: Child Welfare League of America. Available at: www.cwla.org/programs/baby/babyaboutpage.htm. Accessed December 5, 2003.

41. Oberman M. Mothers who kill: coming to terms with modern American infanticide. *Am Criminal Law Review.* 1996;34:1-110.

42. Meyer CL, Oberman M, White K, Rone M, Batra P, Proano T. *Mothers Who Kill Their Children: Understanding the Acts of Moms from Susan Smith to the "Prom Mom".* New York, NY: New York University Press; 2001.

43. Zoller ML. *Abandoned Baby Laws: Is the Solution Worse Than the Problem?* Richmond, VA: Virginia Department of Public Health; 2003.

44. Child Welfare Information Gateway. *Infant Safe Haven Laws.* Washington, DC: Child Welfare Information Gateway; 2013. Child Welfare Information Gateway Web site. https://www.childwelfare.gov/pubPDFs/safehaven.pdf. Accessed March 23, 2017.

45. MD Hampton, Shade K. The experiences of adolescent victims of commercial sexual exploitation in the United States: a qualitative systematic review protocol. *JBI Database System Rev Implement Rep.* 2015;13(8):110-119.

46. Salisbury EJ, Dabney JD, Russell K. Diverting victims of commercial sexual exploitation from juvenile detention: development of the InterCSECt screening protocol. *J Interpers Violence.* 2015;30(7):1247-1276.

47. Choi KR. Risk factors for domestic minor sex trafficking in the United States. *J Forensic Nurs.* 2015;11(2):66-76.

48. Urquiza AJ, Winn C. *Treatment for Abused and Neglected Children: Infancy to Age 18.* Washington, DC: US Dept of Health and Human Services, Administration for Children and Families; 1994.

49. Schmitt B, ed. *The Child Protection Team Handbook.* New York, NY: Garland STPM; 1977.

50. Lutzker JR, Rice JM. Project 12-ways: measuring outcome of a large in-home service for treatment and prevention of child abuse. *Child Abuse Negl.* 1984;8:519-524.

10

Chapter

Sexual Abuse

Diana K. Faugno, MSN, RN, CPN, SANE-A, SANE-P, FAAFS, DF-IAFN
Susan B. Patton, DNSc, PPCNP-BC, AFN-BC, FAANP, FAAN
Steadman McPeters, DNP, CRNP, CPNP-AC, RNFA
Rosario V. Sanchez, MSN, RN, CCRN, CFN, SANE-A, D-ABFN
Martin A. Finkel, DO, FACOP, FAAP
Lawrence R. Ricci, MD
Joyce Wientzen, LCSW
Patricia M. Speck, DNSc, ARNP, APN, FNP-BC, DF-IAFN, FAAFS, FAAN

— Sexual abuse is defined as the exposing of children to sexual experiences inappropriate for their level of physical and emotional development.

— Sexual abuse may involve use of force or threats, but not all sexual abuse is coercive. Offenders may bribe, ploy, or deceive to gain access to children.

— Offenders may build trust with nonoffending parents or guardians with the intention of abusing a child.

— Sexual abuse is always initiated for the offending adult's sexual gratification.[1]

— Research has shown that girls are abused more often than boys, whereas boys are more likely to be killed or seriously injured by their abusers.[2]

  — The Children's Bureau report *Child Maltreatment 2010* found that 9.2% of abused children were sexually abused (1 in 5 girls and 1 in 20 boys).[3]

  — Boys may be less likely to report abuse, which might account for lower reported rates of abuse.

- To date, the literature about abusers suggests an association between childhood sexual abuse and adult sexual offending behaviors.[4,5]
  - Conversely, a 2016 prospective study of sexually abused males demonstrated little association between their abuse in childhood and adult offending behavior (with 14.8% of maltreated boys being subjects of official notifications for sexual abuse and 3% of those sexually abused boys going on to commit sexual offenses). There was, however, a significant association between childhood sexual abuse and adolescent prostitution.[6]
  - Polyvictimization (ie, exposure to multiple types of maltreatment) has been significantly associated with sexual offending, violent offending, and general (ie, nonsexual, nonviolent) offending.[6]
- Children of all ages may be sexually abused.
  - In a study conducted by Finkelhor and colleagues,[7] adolescents aged 14 to 17 years were found most likely to be sexually victimized. Nearly 1 in 6 adolescents (16.3%) had been sexually abused the year prior to the study and more than 1 in 4 (27.3%) had been sexually abused during their lifetimes.
- Shame or guilt may discourage children from disclosing abuse.
- Children with diminished familial supervision and support or living in chaotic family environments (ie, domestic violence, addiction, parental incarcerations) may be at higher risk for abuse.[8-11]
- Forensic evidence and/or medical histories are the most abundant forms of evidence for child sexual abuse.
- Less than 5% of all children who disclose sexual abuse will present with physical findings diagnostic for sexual abuse.[12]
- A supportive medical examination, incorporating trauma-informed care principles and using nonblaming language appropriate for the child's stage of development, has great therapeutic value.[13]
- The initial primary impact of sexual abuse is biological and psychological, with changes to the brain resulting from dysregulation of the fight or flight responses.[14-16]

— The long-term impact of toxic stress is biological, emerging as chronic disease and potentially robbing the victim of as much as 20 years of life.[11,17]

— Adverse childhood experiences (ACEs) or Adverse Childhood Experiences–International Questionnaire (ACE-IQ) scores, used as vital signs at each provider contact, provide an opportunity to identify childhood polyvictimizations and intervene to mitigate the impact of the toxic events (T. Smith, C. Knight, P. M. Speck, unpublished data, 2017).

Overview

Risk Factors for Perpetration

Researchers have identified 6 categories of risk factors for the perpetration of child sexual abuse[18,19]:

1. Family risk factors (eg, history of abuse, poor family functioning and harsh discipline, poor family attachment/bonding)
2. Externalizing behaviors (eg, aggression/violence, anger/hostility, substance abuse, nonviolent criminality, paranoia/mistrust)
3. Internalizing behaviors (eg, history of mental illness, anxiety and mood disorders, low self-esteem)
4. Social deficits (eg, poor social skills, loneliness, difficulties with trust of self or environment, including intimate relationships)
5. Sexual problems (eg, deviant sexual interest, victimization)
6. Attitudes tolerant of adult-child sex and minimizing perpetrators' culpability

Symptoms

— No constellation of signs, symptoms, or behaviors reliably indicates sexual abuse, except the presence of certain sexually transmitted infections (STIs) or pregnancy.[19]

— The American Medical Association (AMA) *Diagnostic and Treatment Guidelines* describe many possible symptoms of sexual abuse:

— Physical symptoms can include headache, abdominal pain, genital pain, and pain on urination.

— Behavioral symptoms can include temper tantrums, aggression, sleep disturbances, appetite disturbances, phobias, withdrawal, depression, self-injury, substance abuse, school problems, and sexual behavior problems.[20-22] Behavioral complaints, especially if related in time to victimization, may reflect current abuse.[23]

— Both types of symptoms occur with other stresses, and no symptom is independently diagnostic of child sexual abuse.

Disclosure

Disclosure is a process with distinct phases: denial, tentative disclosure, active disclosure, recantation, and reaffirmation.[24] (See Chapter 11, "The Sexual Abuse Interview," for more information.)

Role of the Health Care Provider

Mental Health Providers

— The clinical therapist serves as a child advocate and assesses developmental status and social and emotional functioning.

— The therapist's goal is to form clinical impressions and make clinical treatment decisions. Once a diagnosis is established, sexual abuse-specific treatment follows.

Medical Care Providers

— Primary care providers are likely to care for sexually abused children in their practices, where they receive preventive health care and treatment for a variety of conditions (a setting in which symptomatology secondary to abuse is not common).

— Children aged < 2 years without a primary care provider are 4 times more likely than children with a care provider to experience confirmed/suspected physical abuse.[25]

— Most children do not require emergency care following abuse.[26]

— It is important for primary care providers to know how to respond to and evaluate the sexually abused child, when to refer the child for evaluation by other professionals, when to report cases to appropriate investigative agencies, and how to counsel nonoffending parents to decrease long-term deleterious effects of abuse.[27]

— Child Advocacy Centers (CACs) unite professionals and agencies in a multidisciplinary team (MDT), facilitating a child-focused approach to abuse. The literature supports the use of CACs as a cost-effective, child-friendly resource for abused children.[28]

— The medical forensic examination is a focused, impartial analysis of a child's physical, developmental, social, and psychological condition, including documentation of what is seen and said during evaluation.

— The medical diagnosis of sexual abuse is based on detailed analysis of history and anogenital findings.[29,30]

1. Most sexually abused children, even those who have been sexually penetrated, present with normal anogenital findings.[31-33] Anogenital tissues heal quickly and completely after many types of anal and genital trauma.[32]
2. Patient history plays a key in the medical diagnosis of sexual abuse. A history of injury, particularly in young children who describe pain and bleeding, without visible signs of injury does not rule out abuse; likewise, findings of penetration without a history does not rule out penetration.
3. As the child matures, estrogen masks former visible injury.[7,34]

— **Table 10-1** lists findings indicative of sexual abuse.[35]

Table 10-1. Medical Examination Findings Indicative of Sexual Abuse

— Semen or sperm

— Pregnancy

— Fresh genital or anal injuries (eg, lacerations, abrasions, contusions, transactions, avulsions, hematomas, ecchymosis, petechiae, bite marks) with no adequate accidental explanation

— Significant hymenal and vaginal disruption transecting the hymenal base between 3 o'clock and 9 o'clock, whether healed or acute, with or without a history

— Syphilis or gonorrhea not acquired perinatally

— Human immunodeficiency virus (HIV) infection not acquired perinatally or intravenously

Data from Bays and Chadwick.[36]

— Medical forensic evaluations are indicated:

1. To identify recent or old trauma and obtain specimens for STI tests or trace evidence.[37]
2. To treat injuries and infection.
3. To reassure the child and family of physical integrity.
4. To make recommendations for mental health treatment.

— For suspected sexual abuse, include a developmental and behavioral assessment, a careful search for other forms of abuse, and an evaluation of sexual maturity.

— Magnifying and illuminating instruments for anogenital examinations include: headlight and magnifying loop, digital cameras, video/colposcope, and colposcope-replacing mounted camera.[36,38]

— Speculum or digital vaginal or rectal examinations are rarely needed in prepubertal children.[38] If trauma or forensic evidence indicate need, consider an examination under anesthesia or conscious sedation. Use of anesthesia is rarely necessary.

— For the rare physical injury requiring medical intervention[39]:

  — Clinical forensic examinations are conducted after surgical emergency treatment.

  — Reconstruction of injuries is usually only possible with a multidisciplinary approach.

  — The provider will determine whether or not to take photodocumentation prior to treatment.

  — Focused, detailed photos of injuries, including measuring devices for scale, meet quality criteria for forensic evidence.

  — Photodocumentation is stored unedited for use as forensic evidence.

Impact of Sexual Abuse and Treatment

— The psychological effects of child sexual abuse can be short-term or long-term. For victims of child sexual abuse, depression and other mental health conditions can persist over a lifetime.[11,40]

— Evidence continues to emerge about ACEs (eg, physical, sexual, and emotional abuse; neglect; household violence) and polyvictimization (ie, multiple and chronic toxic stress from adverse experiences).[41]

  — ACEs are associated with structural changes in brain functioning (one source of behavioral and emotional outcomes such as addictive behaviors, suicide attempts, depressive episodes, sleep disturbances, and high-risk behavior).

  — ACEs and polyvictimization, particularly in infancy and childhood, are emerging as pivotal elements in long-term health sequelae (eg, obesity, hypertension, diabetes, autoimmune disease) and significant expenditures in the health and criminal justice systems.

— Sexually abused children often experience sexual behavior problems.[40,42] Characteristic symptoms of problematic sexual behavior include[43]:

  — Behavior that does not respond to limits. Most behaviors diminish after sufficient limits are set.

  — Apparent interest in sexual behavior but not in other activities normal for a child's age.

  — Complaints from other children that a child's sexual behavior is upsetting or uncomfortable for them.

  — Sexual behaviors that increase in intensity and frequency with time.

  — Coercing other children into sexual behavior using bribes, threats, and manipulations.

  — Sexual behavior accompanied by a sense of shame or embarrassment rather than the normal lighthearted response of children.

Legal and Reporting Issues

— All states have laws specifying the age at which an individual can consent to sexual contact (usually between 14 and 18 years).[44]

— Every state mandates that certain individuals (eg, physicians, nurses) report suspected child abuse to law enforcement and/or Child Protective Services (CPS). (See Chapter 1, "Introduction to Child Maltreatment," for more information on mandated reporting.) State laws protect reporters who act in good faith from civil suits. For guidelines to the decision to report child sexual abuse, refer to Table 2 of the American Academy of Pediatrics' "Guidelines for the Evaluation of Sexual Abuse of Children" (available online at http://pediatrics.aappublications.org/content/pediatrics/103/1/186.full.pdf).

Child Sex Trafficking

— Children who have experienced prior abuse (eg, physical, sexual, emotional), have a history of homelessness (eg, runaways), and/or lack social support are at greater risk for recruitment by traffickers, who exploit vulnerability.[45]

— There is a positive connection between childhood sexual abuse and risk for child sex trafficking.[46]

— Early intervention is necessary to promote resiliency and prevent long-term negative consequences.[47]

Vulnerability

— As many as 87.5% of trafficked children may have histories of prior or early sexual and/or physical abuse.[46-48]

— Feelings of low self-esteem, unworthiness, and shame associated with sexual abuse exacerbate vulnerability.[46]

— The average age of trafficked children is 12 to 14 years.[49]

— The following characteristics make children especially vulnerable to trafficking.[49-51]

1. Children are vulnerable to deception and coercion, especially when alone or unsupervised. Traffickers may exert control over children by means of intimidation or exploitation of children's emotional and physical dependence on adults.

2. Children are not physically strong enough to fight off traffickers. They are easily intimidated and may lack awareness of impending danger.
3. In the eyes of some criminal justice professionals, children lack credibility (especially runaways, troubled children, and those with a history of drug abuse and/or prior dealings with law enforcement). Traffickers and pimps may intentionally place children in criminal situations, resulting in a criminal record. As a result, these children may appear less credible to authorities and, therefore, are less likely to be identified as victims.

— Pronounced severity of childhood sexual abuse puts children at greater risk for sex trafficking. Severe sexual abuse may include[48]:

— Longer duration

— Physical or emotional force

— Penetration

— Abuse by a father or father figure

Factors

— Traffickers invest a great deal of time and effort in grooming children. For the trafficker, it is especially advantageous for children to view him/her as a "caretaker."

— Trafficked children with a history of abuse may feel a deep sense of betrayal by family that discourages them from attempting to escape their traffickers. This is especially true children who have experienced the following:

— Domestic violence

— Neglect

— Sexual abuse committed by a family member

— Prior history of sexual abuse may lead children into prostitution for survival sex (ie, to meet daily needs for food, shelter, drugs).[46]

The Medical Examination

— Medical professionals must be able to competently interpret findings in medical examinations and determine their significance for CPS, law enforcement, and prosecuting agencies.

— Before the examination begins, always allow children to share any concerns about their bodies. Answer all questions they might have related to the examination.

PRELIMINARY ACTIONS

— Determine what information is needed, obtain information, and identify the source of the information.

1. Review details of the case with the referring party, including preliminary written reports, videotaped interviews, face-to-face meetings with CPS, and law enforcement personnel. Oftentimes, law enforcement and CPS provide this information to the health care provider.
2. Meet with accompanying adults without the child present to determine what caregivers know about the presenting concerns. Obtain a complete medical history and detailed review of symptoms, with special attention to the genitourinary and gastrointestinal systems whenever possible.
3. Explain to caregivers what will happen during the visit, assuring them that there will be an opportunity to explain the results of the examination, answer questions, and describe steps to follow. Many parents fear that their child will experience pain during this examination and often assume their child's examination will be like an adult's anogenital examination. Reassure parents that the examination is different for children, particularly if the child is prepubertal or peripubertal.

— Gather pertinent data from children and caregivers in a nonjudgmental and empathetic manner. Document their histories verbatim to accurately reflect the clinical history.

— Ask age-appropriate questions to develop a chronological timeline leading up to the disclosure or suspicion of sexual abuse. Note idiosyncratic details provided by the child or anything the child observed.

  — Using developmentally appropriate language, explain to the child that you are concerned about his/her well-being. Then, explain that the examination will be similar to the experience of going to the doctor when they are sick (**Box 10-1**).

Box 10-1. Example Pre-exam Statement to a Child Patient
"Sometimes kids have worries or concerns about their bodies. I want you to think about any worries or concerns you have, because after we talk, I'm going to take a look at you from head-to-toe to make sure you're okay. I'll also answer any worries you might have and want to talk about."

— No 2 children will relate their experiences in the same way or with the same level of detail and clarity. Individual characteristics (eg, interviewer behavior and gender, family relationships, community influences, cultural and societal attitudes) determine whether, when, and how children disclose abuse.

1. Obtain a history to determine a care plan for evaluation, testing, treatment, evidence collection, and documentation.
2. Open-ended questions that tap into the 5 senses will elicit accurate answers (**Table 10-2**).

Table 10-2. Exam Questions for the Child Patient

- "How old are you?"
- "Do you know why you are here today?"
- "Do you hurt anywhere?"
- Regarding the abusive incident:
  - "What did you see?"
  - "What did you smell?"
  - "What did you hear?"
  - "What did you feel?"
  - "What did you taste?"

3. Ask about symptoms associated with urination or defecation after contact. When temporally related to a specific event, and in the absence of alternative preexisting conditions, a history of dysuria after genital fondling or genital-genital contact confirms with medical certainty superficial trauma to the periurethral and vestibular structures.

4. Ask simple, open-ended questions, addressing only one subject per question (eg, "Tell me more about that."), in order to elicit more information from the child.[52]

— A child's history is critical to understanding an abusive event and often is the only available evidence. Follow these steps to determine if the questioning method used to obtain previous medical history was appropriate:

1. Look at the history. Ignore the questions asked and only read the answers.

2. If the child only answered "Yes" or "No" or offered only 2-word responses, the method of questioning needs refinement.

3. If by reading only the answers you can understand the child's concerns, the questions were appropriately open-ended.

— A forensic interview conducted by a trained specialist (either before or after the medical examination) is encouraged. Structured forensic interview protocols improve the quality of investigative interviews.[53]

Indications for and Timing of a Physical Examination

In cases of suspected sexual abuse, a physical examination should be performed as soon as possible. The patient's needs must be met, and children should not have to undergo multiple examinations. Because the perspectives of CPS and law enforcement personnel may differ, the forensic medical provider should take the lead in determining the need for and timing of the physical examination.

— Determine whether or not an immediate examination is needed based on:

1. When something last happened.

2. Whether any of the things that happened hurt the child.
3. Whether the suspect has had access to the child within the time frame for evidence collection.

— If a child states that he/she was touched within the past 72 to 120 hours, conduct the examination immediately or as soon as possible.

— DNA testing is now very sensitive. It is possible to obtain positive results from swabs taken in acute examination. Follow your community protocol and forensic laboratory recommendations based on capacity for or access to DNA detection and analysis.

— When the history suggests the potential to collect trace evidence and/or seminal products, collect and preserve them immediately.

  — Seminal products will be detected from crime scene investigation samples or retrieved from clothing or bed sheets, rather than the child's body.

  — The presence of or risk for an STI or pregnancy is an indication for immediate examination.[54]

— If a child states that abusive contact occurred more than 120 hours (5 days) prior and does not complain of significant discomfort, defer examination until the next available appointment.

— Injury may be visible for weeks, even if pain is diminished.[32,33]

— Most examinations of children who complain of or are suspected of being sexually abused are not medical emergencies, but they are urgent from the perspective of CPS and law enforcement.

— Allow children to make decisions during the examination process and respect the child's desires. If a child is not emotionally ready for the examination and there is no absolute medical urgency to conduct it, defer the examination until another day.

— Do not physically restrain children. If a child will not cooperate, conduct the examination under anesthesia or with conscious sedation.

Preparing the Child for the Physical Examination

— Anticipate a child's and family's fears and anxieties about the examination. Identify and address both realistic and unrealistic concerns.

1. Young children are usually worried about shots and needles. If shots or needles are necessary, consider delaying tests or sample collection or bring the child back on another day.
2. Mothers of prepubertal children are usually worried that the child will undergo a speculum examination.

— Do not underestimate the degree of distress that children and parents may have as they approach the anogenital examination.

1. Conduct the anogenital examination only as part of a complete head-to-toe examination, indicating that all parts of the body are important and all parts will be checked.
2. Use the components of the physical examination that precede the anogenital examination to build rapport with and gain the trust of children.
3. Explain to children what they should anticipate feeling during the examination to demystify the experience and reduce anxiety. An age-appropriate movie can be used as a distraction for the child.
4. If possible, conduct the examination using video or digital media documentation so children can observe the examination if they want to. Before positioning children for the genital examination, permit them to see their belly buttons or fingernails on the monitor.
5. Be aware that prepubertal children usually want parents or caregivers to accompany them during the examination, whereas adolescents usually request that parents not be present. If the caregivers are not in the room, a male or female assistant (depending on the patient's gender and availability) should be present, positioned at the head of the examination table.
6. Provide patients with choices when possible and respect their preferences.

Examination Positions and Techniques for Female Children

Examination positions and techniques depend on a girl's age, history provided, and degree of cooperation.

Prepubertal Girls

— Determine whether or not to have the child sit on her mother's lap or independently on the table in the supine frog-leg position. Choose the position most comfortable for the child and most conducive to cooperation (**Figures 10-1-a** and **b**).

— Use the knee–chest position to improve visualization of the hymenal membrane edge, with gravity permitting the hymenal tissue to fall forward while upward and lateral traction is exerted (**Figure 10-2**).

— Once the girl is in the frog-leg position, use labial separation and labial traction to enhance the view of the vestibular structures (**Figures 10-3-a** and **b**).

1. In both techniques, grasp the individual labia between the index finger and thumb and exert both lateral and downward traction to open up the vaginal vestibule.
2. Use labial techniques whether the child is in the supine frog-leg or the lithotomy position.

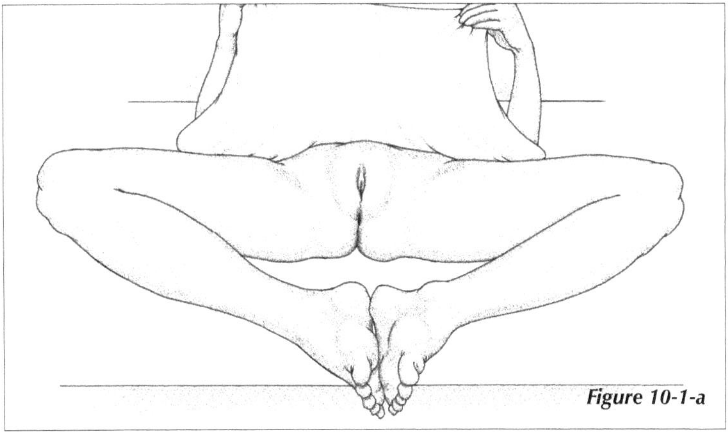

Figure 10-1-a. *A child examined in the supine frog-leg position.*

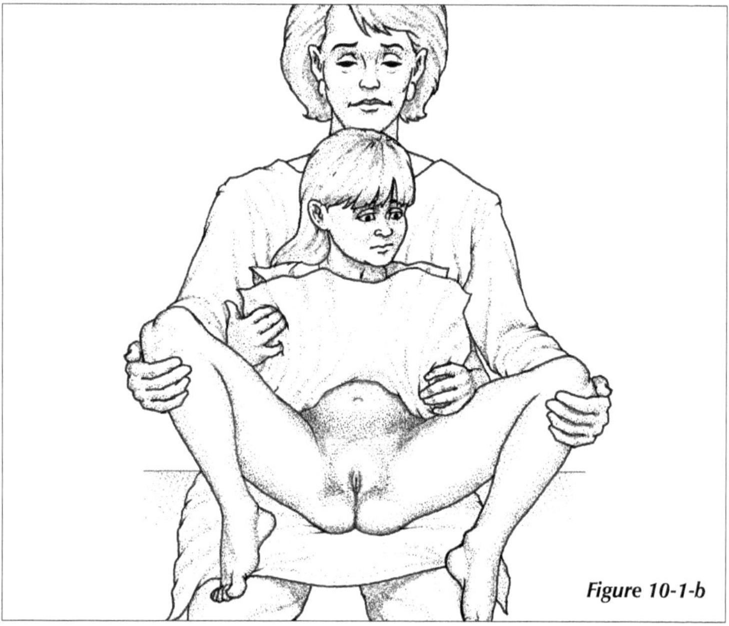

Figure 10-1-b. *A genital examination can also be performed with the patient in the frog-leg position while sitting on the caregiver's lap.*

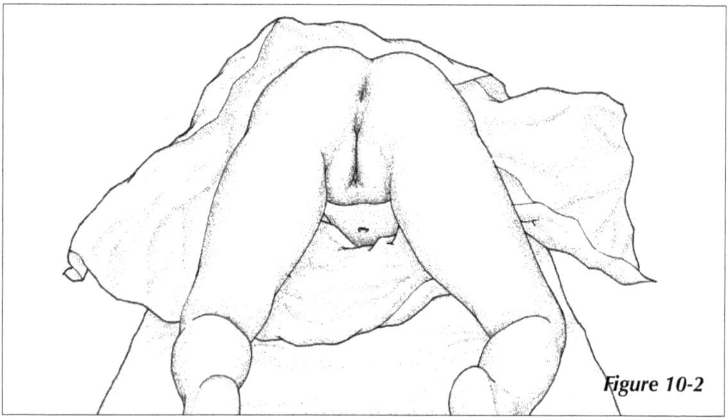

Figure 10-2. *A child examined in the prone knee-chest position.*

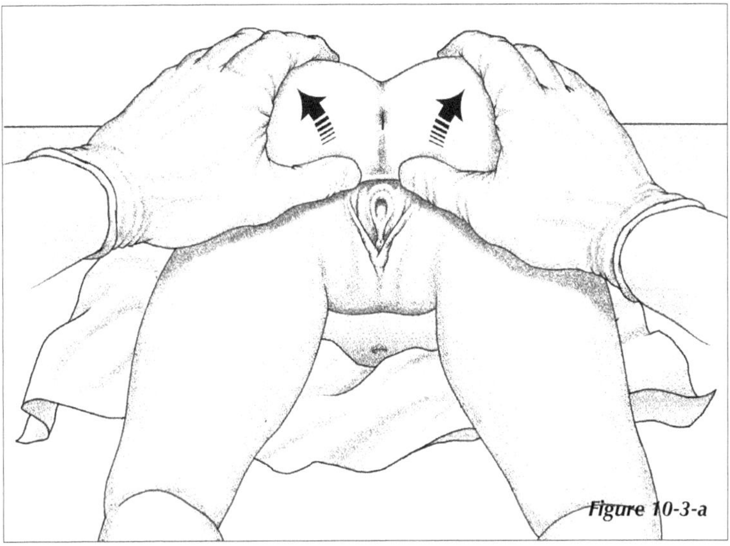

Figure 10-3-a. *Labial separation and traction in the genital examination of a girl in the prone knee-chest position.*

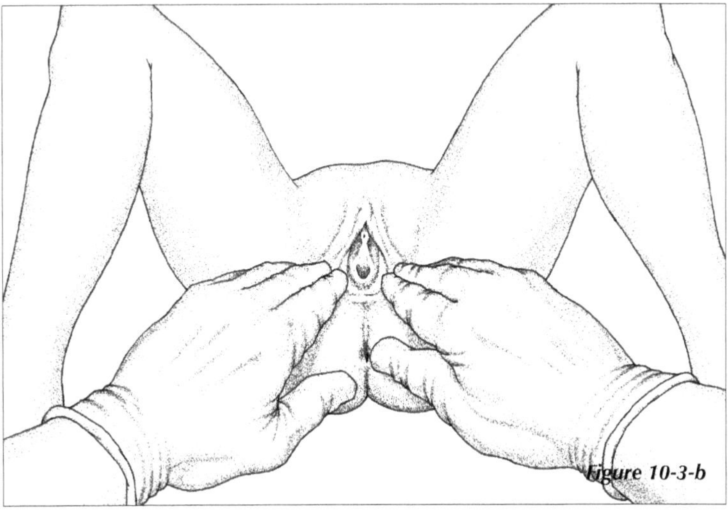

Figure 10-3-b. *Genital examination of the female in the supine frog-leg position with labial separation and traction.*

3. When the moist redundant hymenal tissue is folded or adhered to itself, instill a few milligrams of saline solution into the vestibule and vagina. The saline solution "floats" the hymenal tissue, reducing cohesion, and helps to define the hymen's appearance. Confirm all findings in both the knee-chest and the supine frog-leg position. If saline is used, consider collection of the droplets (by swabbing) to confirm time since exposure. In the event of DNA detection from the internal mucosa, the historical narrative should be revisited.
4. In prepubertal children, do not use a cotton-tipped swab to lift the edge of the hymenal membrane, because it may be tender to touch due to the lack of estrogen effect. Characteristics of a lack of estrogen effect include reddening with visible vessels, translucency, flatness, crescentic or annular hymen, and pain without discharge. If discharge present, consider foreign body or urine from incontinence.

— A speculum examination is usually not needed and rarely indicated in the prepubertal or peripubertal child. When needed, conduct the speculum examination under conscious sedation or anesthesia, with full awareness of risk for iatrogenic injury.

— Document all iatrogenic injury, regardless of underlying conditions.

Older Girls or Adolescents

— Characteristics of estrogen effect in peripubertal and pubertal females include thickened, pink hymenal tissue (occasionally with white margins); folded tissue; crescentic or annular hymen; stretchiness; and cyclic discharge ranging from creamy (early cycle), clear (mid-cycle), and curdled (late cycle).

— Examination techniques include:

— Cover a GYN/rectal 6-inch cotton-tipped swab with the finger of a large colored glove. Place the covered swab behind the hymenal membrane, moving it along the rim to visualize the entire tissue (**Figures 10-4-a** through **c**).

— Use a gloved finger to lift the margin of the hymen and palpate transections for firm scar tissue.

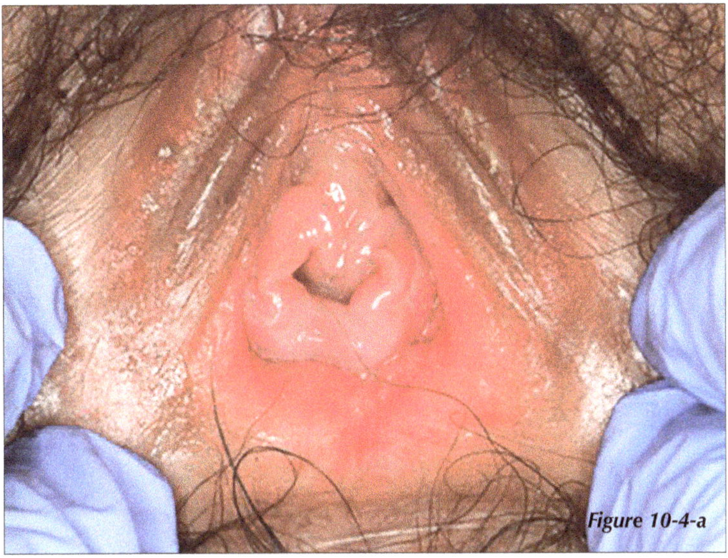

Figure 10-4-a

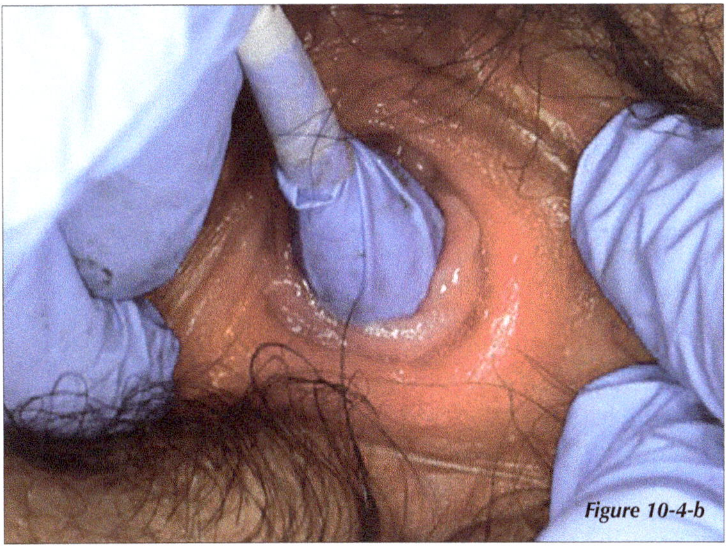

Figure 10-4-b

Figure 10-4-a through **c.** *15-year-old female showing use of a covered swab.*

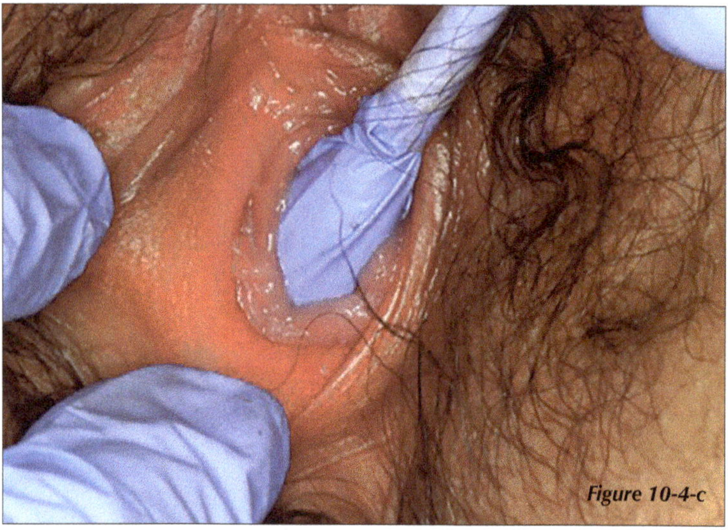

***Figure 10-4-a** through **c.** 15-year-old female showing use of a covered swab.*

— As a last option, pass an uninflated Foley catheter through the hymenal orifice, inflate the balloon within the vagina with 10 to 20 ccs of air, and exert traction so the membrane's edge is laid out on the convex surface of the balloon.

— Perform a traditional adult gynecologic examination using a speculum. Use a speculum if the female patient has had a previous menses or if you are using conscious sedation (**Table 10-3**).[55]

— If using conscious sedation with the peripubertal girl with visible estrogen effect, introduce a small vaginal speculum to provide access to the transverse hymenal orifice diameter to determine if it is large enough to permit introduction of a foreign body. Adult vaginal speculums measure 35 mm wide, which is less than the diameter of the average adult erect penis.

Examination Positions and Techniques for Male Children

— Note the appearance of the genitalia and inspect the penis for bruising, swelling, erythema, lesions, rashes, and/or other irregularities.

Table 10-3. When to Use a Speculum

Situation	Speculum Use
Menarchal female consenting to the speculum examination	Yes
Child under general anesthesia or conscious sedation	Yes
Child is uncooperative or unable to tolerate speculum	No
Premenarchal child with lack of estrogen	No
Child of any age who refuses the speculum examination	No

— Note if the penis is circumcised.

— Record Tanner stage.

— Testes should be palpated to ensure descension and lack of masses or tenderness.

— Note any trauma, lesions, or rashes.[56,57]

— Inspect the anus with gentle traction to both sides of the anal opening.

  — The tone of the anus should be assessed for laxity in the absence of stool in the rectum.

  — Anal dilation is a dynamic sign and measuring maximum anal dilation during the examination is difficult. Further research is needed to assess the significance of anal findings with respect to abuse, and the impact of examination positions, techniques, and other factors on the frequency of these findings.[58]

  — The anal rugae should be carefully checked for fissures or tears, lesions, bruising, bleeding, or ulcerations.

  — Due to the potential for retraumatizing the child, digital rectal examination is only recommended if medically. If a child is having trouble sitting or walking, a rectal inspection should be performed.

— Watch for symptoms of STIs including penile discharge and genital warts.

Review of Genital and Anal Anatomy

Terminology

— "Normal" does not convey the varied appearance of anogenital structures in children.

— The terms vulva, pudenda, and perineum lack specificity; avoid using them as sole descriptors to record genital appearance.

— ***External genitalia*** or ***pudendum feminium*** covers all components of the visible external genital structures, including the labia minora, clitoris, vestibule of the vagina, bulb of the vestibule, Skene's and Bartholin's glands, and vaginal orifice.

— ***Perineum*** refers to the area between the thighs bounded by the posterior aspects of the labia majora and minora and anus in females and the scrotal sac and anus in males.

Vagina

— The vagina extends from the inner aspect of the hymen to the anterior and posterior fornix.

— Hymenal membrane separates the vestibule from the vagina. Structures in front of hymenal membrane are vestibular. Vaginal structures begin with inner aspect of hymen.

— The entrance to vagina is through the hymenal orifice. Objects entering the vagina must have passed through this orifice.

— The muscular canal of the vagina comprises 3 layers, with the innermost mucosal surface being the vaginal epithelium. The muscular vagina is traversed circumferentially by vaginal rugae (in the presence of estrogen). Prominent intravaginal columns line the longitudinal axis of the vagina and traverse the vaginal rugae on both anterior and posterior walls. Smooth vaginal walls imply a lack of estrogen effect.

— The posterior vaginal column may abut the inner aspect of the hymenal membrane and produce a small projection or bump on the edge of the membrane, not to be confused with a hymenal tag or injury.

Vaginal Vestibule

— The vaginal vestibule (ie, introitus, pudendum feminium) is the space external to the hymenal membrane enclosed by labia minora and majora. Being as the structure is internal, hairless, and covered with mucous membrane, use of the term "external genitalia."

— The vestibular borders are:

1. Lateral: labia minora
2. Superior/anterior: clitoris
3. Posterior/inferior: fossa navicularis and posterior fourchette

— The fourchette is formed by the posterior joining of labia minora. In young girls, labia minora resemble butterfly wings and do not extend to join posteriorly until girls approach puberty, reflecting the effects of estrogen.

— The concave area between the posterior attachment of the hymen and the fourchette is the fossa navicularis. It is defined by the fossa.

— Labia majora join posteriorly to form a nondescript border variously known as the posterior commissure, Hart's line, and posterior fourchette.

— Perforations within the vestibule:

1. Urethra
2. Paired periurethral ducts or Skene's glands
3. Vaginal (hymenal) orifice
4. Paired greater vestibular ducts or Bartholin's glands

— The vaginal vestibule is most commonly penetrated in child sexual abuse. Genital-to-genital contact limited to the vestibule is vulvar coitus. During genital fondling of a prepubertal girl, the finger may or may not penetrate beyond the vestibule.

— DNA and cellular evidence is located under the fingernails of the abuser.

Hymenal Membrane

— The hymenal membrane is the external surface covered by the urogenital sinus epithelium.

— It attaches to the lateral and anterior walls of the vagina and posteriorly to the floor of the vagina.

— The hymen is present at birth in all but a few congenital malformations. Absence of a hymen does not exist as a congenital anomaly without other major urogenital malformations.

— Terms used to describe the hymen's appearance are annular, crescentic, fimbriated, septate, and cribriform[59] (**Figures 10-5** through **10-22**). Appearance within the basic orifice types is highly variable.

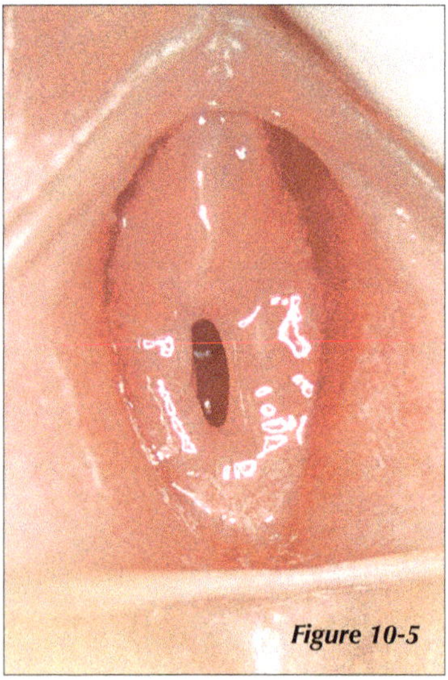

Figure 10-5. *Annular configuration of the hymenal orifice. Vascularity of the mucosa of the vestibule demonstrates slight injection surrounding the attachment of hymenal membrane to walls of the vagina and is normal.*

Figure 10-6. *Crescentic hymenal orifice with slight redundancy to tissues between the 11 o'clock and 1 o'clock positions.*

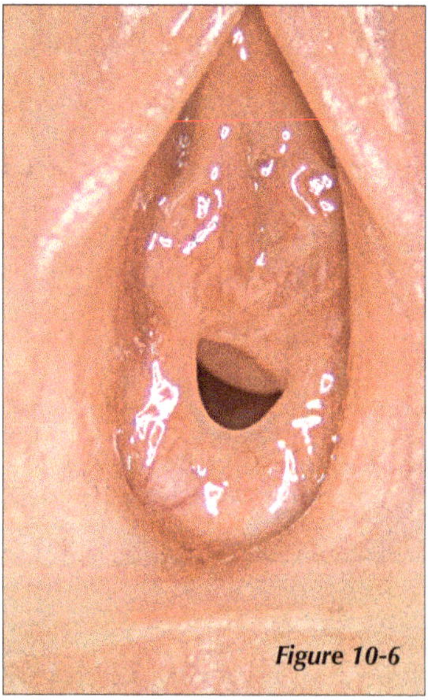

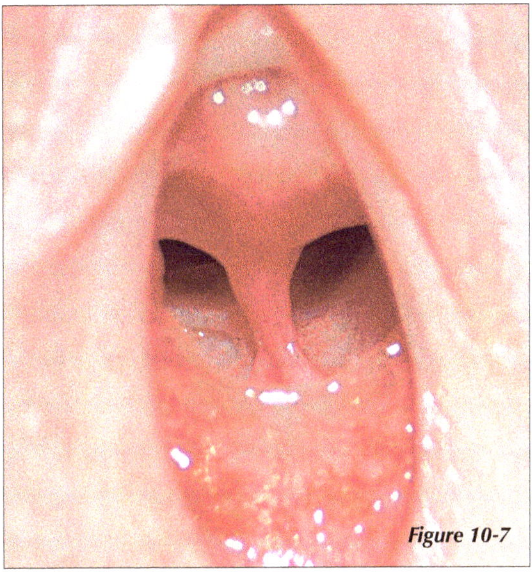

Figure 10-7

Figure 10-7. *Intravaginal longitudinal septum intersects hymenal orifice and vagina. This congenital defect may be associated with upper genital urinary tract anomalies and should be investigated in early adolescence.*

Figure 10-8. *Septate hymen bisecting hymenal orifice in the plane of the hymen without intravaginal extension.*

Figure 10-9. *Using only the traction and separation technique, redundant tissue surrounding the hymenal orifice restricts visualization of orifice.*

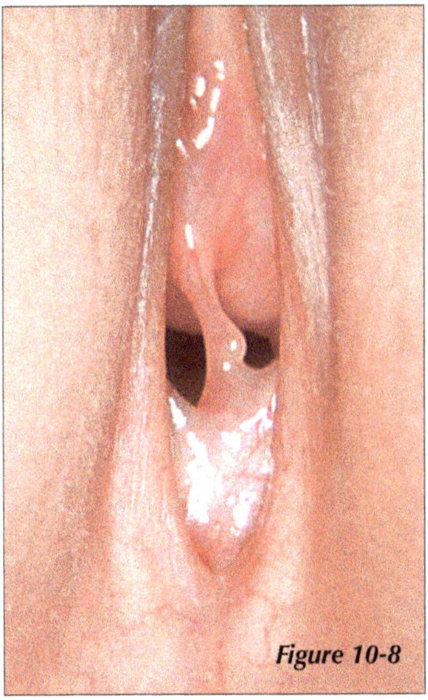

Figure 10-8

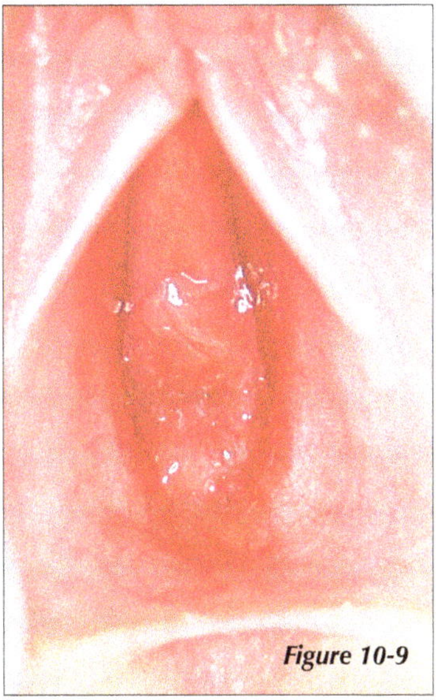

Figure 10-9

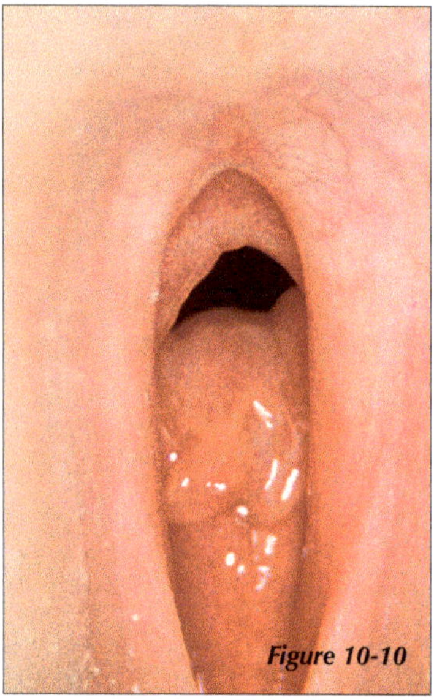

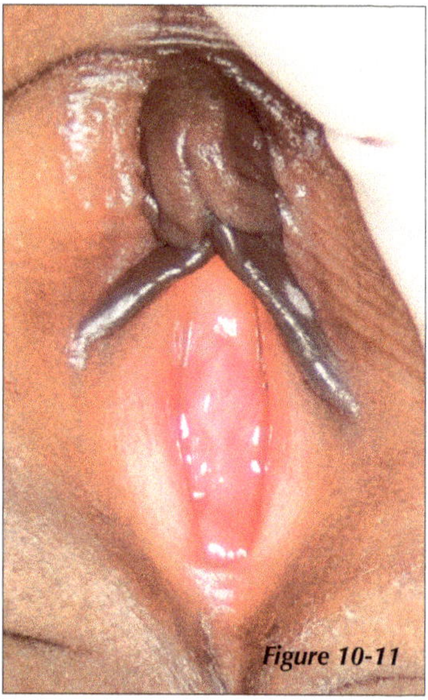

Figure 10-10. *Knee-chest position allows redundant tissue to fall forward, covering the urethra and allowing visualization of the crescent-shaped hymenal orifice.*

Figure 10-11. *Hymenal orifice not visualized with labial separation alone.*

Figure 10-12. *Labial traction affords unfolding of redundant tissue, which enhances visualization of the annular orifice, intravaginal content, and the urethra.*

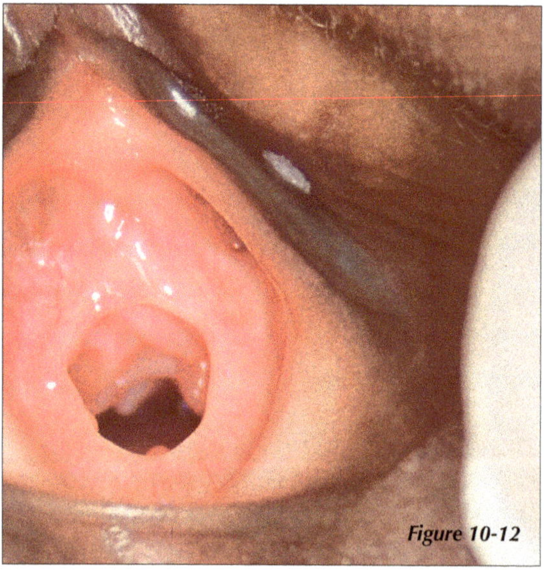

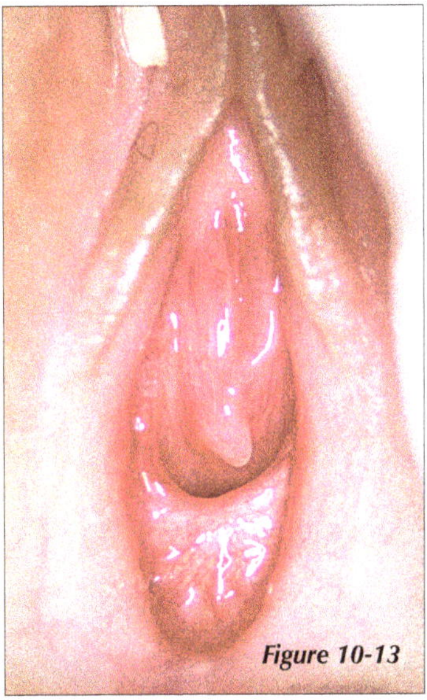

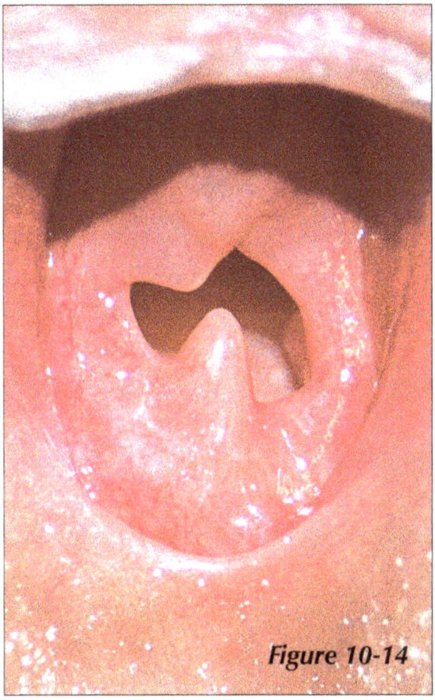

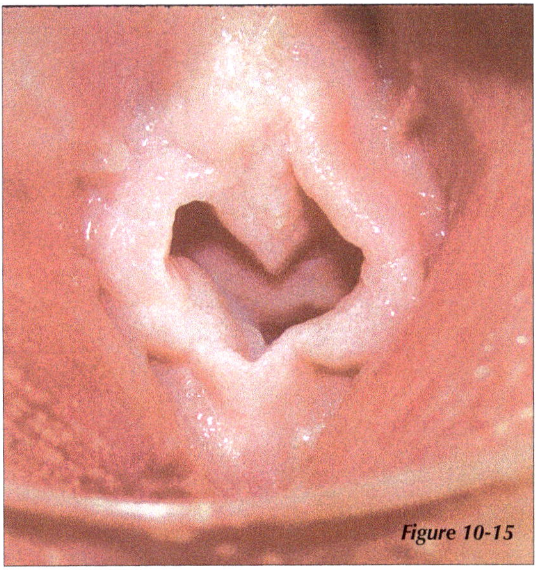

Figure 10-13. *The anterior tag present below urethra is a normal anatomic variation.*

Figure 10-14. *Prominent projection of hymenal tissue at the 6 o'clock position represents an external reflection of a posterior longitudinal intravaginal column.*

Figure 10-15. *Estrogenized annular hymen with slight redundancy and elasticity. Prominent anterior column.*

Figure 10-16. *Redundant estrogenized hymen with labial separation does not allow visualization of hymenal orifice.*

Figure 10-17. *With additional traction the crescentic appearance is visualized.*

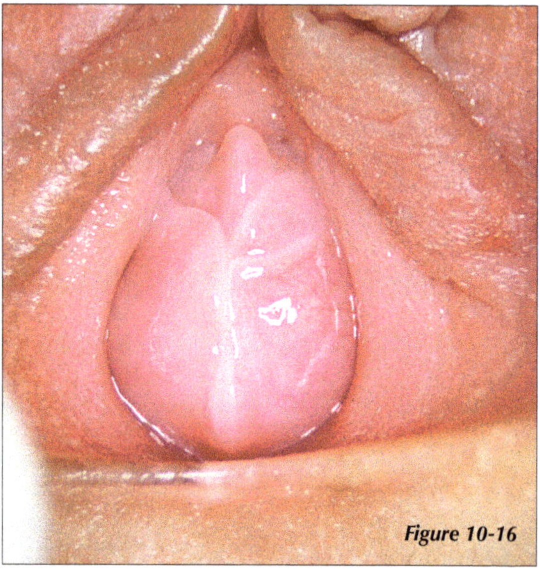

Figure 10-16

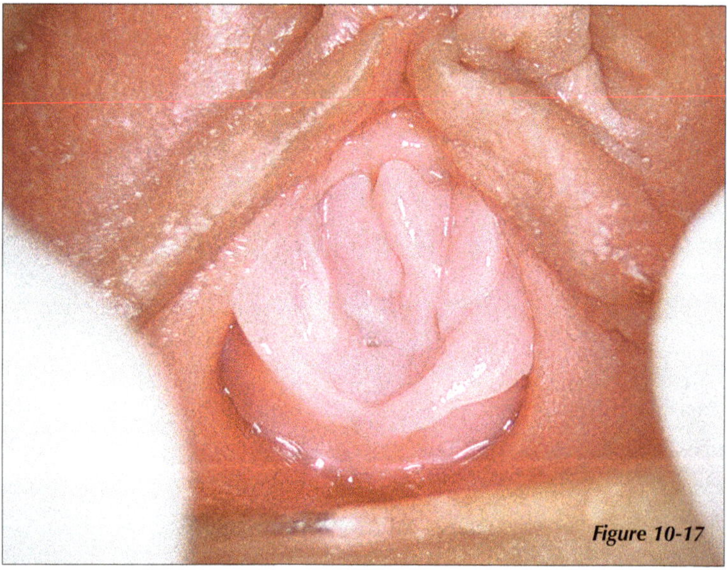

Figure 10-17

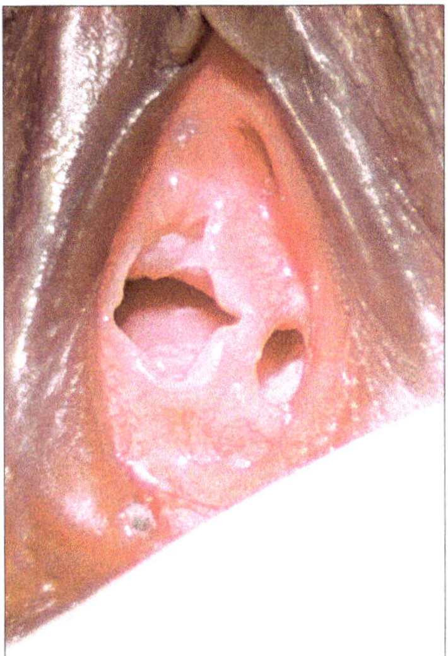

Figure 10-18

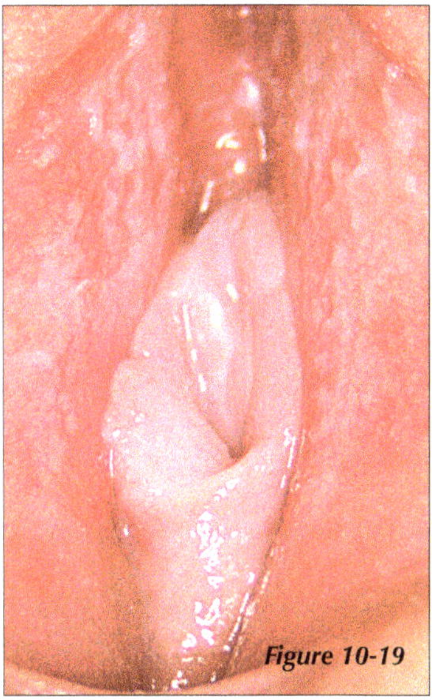

Figure 10-19

Figure 10-18.
Septate hymen in pubertal girl. Tampons should not be used until septum is interrupted surgically.

Figure 10-19.
Sleeve-like configuration of hymenal membrane in prepubertal girl. Hymen demonstrates estrogen effect.

Figure 10-20.
Annular configuration of estrogenized hymen in Tanner Stage II girl.

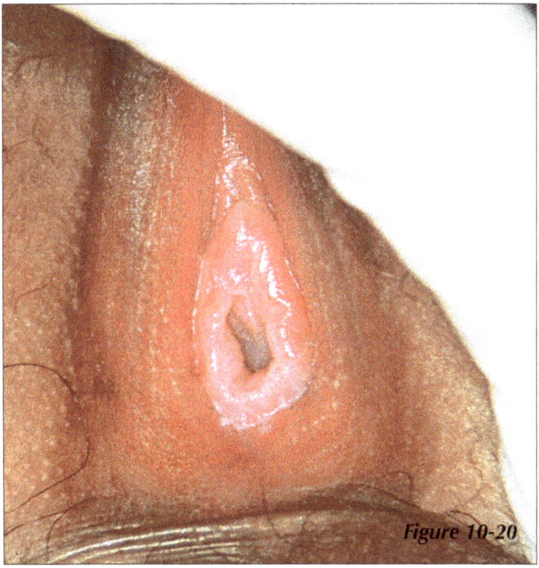

Figure 10-20

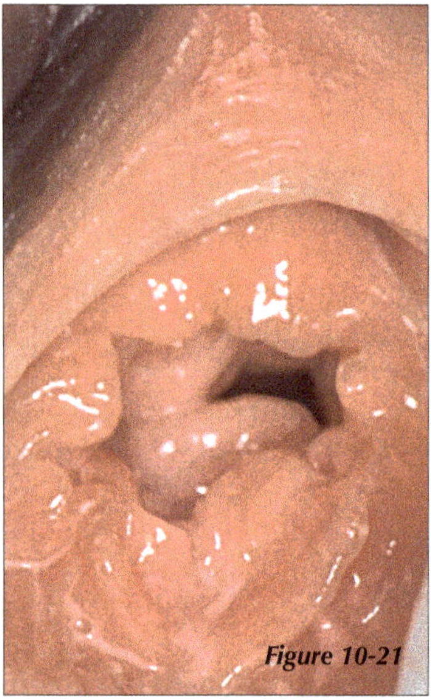

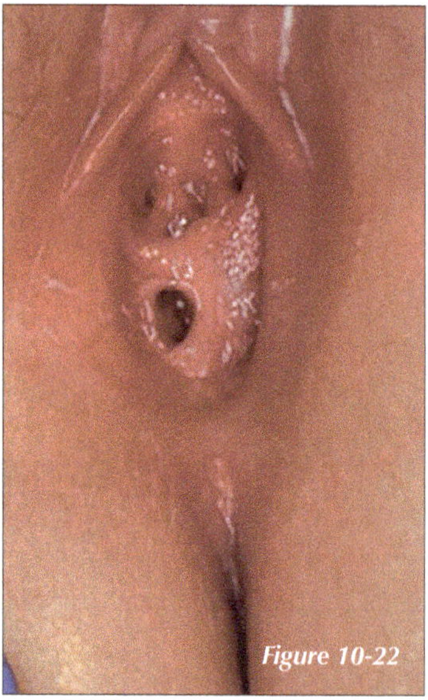

Figure 10-21. *Fimbriated appearance of hymenal edge with labial traction. Fimbriation or scalloping of edge circumferentially provides greater distensibility to orifice. Scalloped appearance does not represent multiple small partial transections.*

Figure 10-22. *Asymmetrical annular hymen in a 6-year-old female.*

— Failure of cannulization produces an imperforate hymen that appears clinically as either mucocolpos in prepubertal children or hematocolpos at puberty. This is a rare occurrence.

— Hymenal appearance is influenced by maternal estrogen in newborns; then, the hymen involutes until puberty,[60] when estrogen thickens the hymenal membrane, reduces the vascularity of tissues, produces a pinkish-white appearance, and increases elasticity and distensibility.

— The Hymen Estrogen Response Scale (HERS) is a useful tool for evaluating changes to the hymen and surrounding structures related to developmental and cyclical changes throughout the life span (**Table 10-4**).[61]

— Variability of vascular patterns of unestrogenized tissues makes it unlikely to have diagnostic value alone. Diagnosticians have difficulty distinguishing between normal vasculature and hypervasculature and erythema.

Table 10-4. Hymen Estrogen Response Scale and Scoring

Variable	0	1	2	Score
Color	Red	Pink	White	
Lubrication	None/scant clear	Scant white caked	Clear to white mucous	
Distensibility	None/flat	Some folds/ scallops	Redundancy/ layers	
Sensitivity	Painful to touch	Sensitive to touch	No pain to touch	
Thickness	Thin, translucent flat	Areas of thickening, some translu-cent margins	Thick, without translucency	

HERS Score Total

Variable	HERS Interpretation
0-1	No estrogen effect (NEE)
2-4	Early transition (ET)
5-7	Late transition (LT)
8-10	Full estrogen effect (FEE)

Reprinted with permission from PM Speck © 1998, rev. 2002, 2007, 2017.

— The linea vestibularis is a distinct midline area of decreased vascularity involving the fossa and fourchette that pales with traction. New examiners often misidentify the linea vestibularis as a scar. Palpation of this area along with a history of bleeding and pain would help differentiate a scar from linea vestibularis.

1. Before interpreting a midline avascular area as scar tissue, be sure that labial traction is not enhancing the blanched appearance of the linea vestibularis.

2. Genital trauma can produce scar tissue that appears avascular when healed but is readily differentiated from midline blanching linked to labial traction. Many scars are not midline. Midline findings in the perineal area is nonspecific and may be related to straddle injury.

3. Lymphoid follicles are small, translucent ovoid bumps in the fossa that occasionally must be differentiated from vesicles or cysts (**Table 10-5**).

Table 10-5. Genital Findings in Nonabused Girls

GENITAL FINDINGS

— Erythema of the vestibule (56%)
— Periurethral bands (50.6%)
— Labial adhesions (38.9%)
— Lymphoid follicles on the fossa navicularis (33.7%)
— Posterior fourchette midline avascular areas (25.6%)
— Urethral dilation
— With labial traction (90.5%)
— With supine separation (79.3%)

HYMENAL FINDINGS

— Mounds (33.8%)
— Projections (33.3%)
— Septal remnants (18.5%)

INTRAVAGINAL FINDINGS

— Vaginal ridges (90.2%)
— Rugae (88.7%)

UNUSUAL FINDINGS*

— Posterior fourchette friability (4.7%)
— Anterior hymenal clefts (1.2%), (1 child)
— Notches of the hymen (1.2%), (1 child)
— Hymenal septa (2.5%), (2 children)
— Vaginal discharge (2.5%), (2 children)
— Foreign body (1.2%), (1 child)

**The major concern in a study of this type is the lack of certainty about whether the sample contains only nonabused children. The children were screened for behavioral indicators but were not interviewed.*
Note: The cervix was visualized without a speculum in 69% of the children during the knee-chest examination.
Adapted from McCaan J, Wells R, Simon M, Voris J.[62]

— Hymenal examination aims to determine whether or not the hymenal opening is sufficient to allow the introduction of the object stated to have been introduced or, if not, what can explain the discrepancy between the report and findings. Specific measurements are of limited value (**Table 10-6**).[63]

Table 10-6. Transhymenal Diameters

Age	Mean Diameter Range
Preschool children (2 years to 4 years 5 months)	3.9 to 5.2 mm (overall range: 1 to 8.5 mm)
Early school (5 years to 7 years 11 months)	4.2 to 5.6 mm (overall range: 1 to 9 mm)
Preadolescent (8 years to Tanner stage II)	5.7 to 7.3 mm (overall range: 3 to 11 mm)

Adapted from McCann J, Wells R, Simon M, Voris J.[62]

— Without estrogen, the hymenal membrane has limited elasticity and distensibility, so penetration readily produces injury, pain, and slight bleeding. The thin hymen, when injured, necrotizes and the tissue sloughs.

— Pubertal (estrogenized) hymens are more elastic and distensible, so it is more likely that the hymenal orifice will accommodate an object with no significant residual effect. Thicker estrogenized tissue tears but remains visible after injury.

Male Genitalia

Figures 10-23-a and **b** depict normal male anatomy. Document the aspects listed in **Table 10-7**.

Anus

— The anal verge overlies the subcutaneous tissue of external anal sphincter, beginning at the most distal portion of the moist anoderm and extending to the exterior margin of the anal skin.

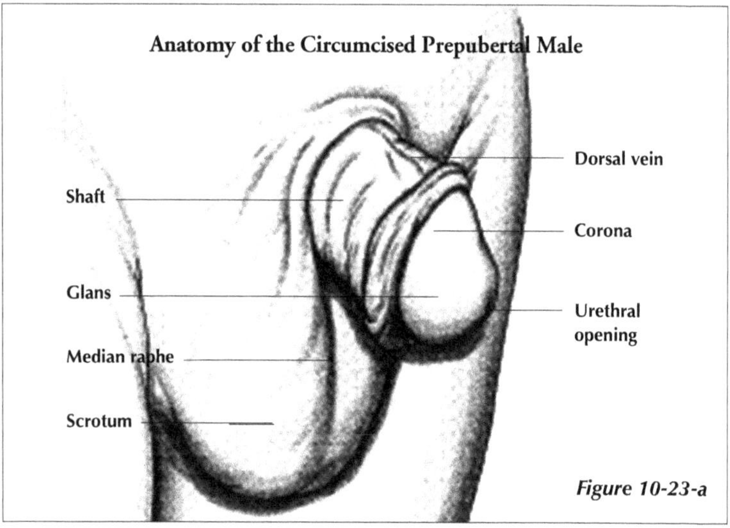

Figure 10-23-a. *Anatomy of the circumcised prepubertal male.*

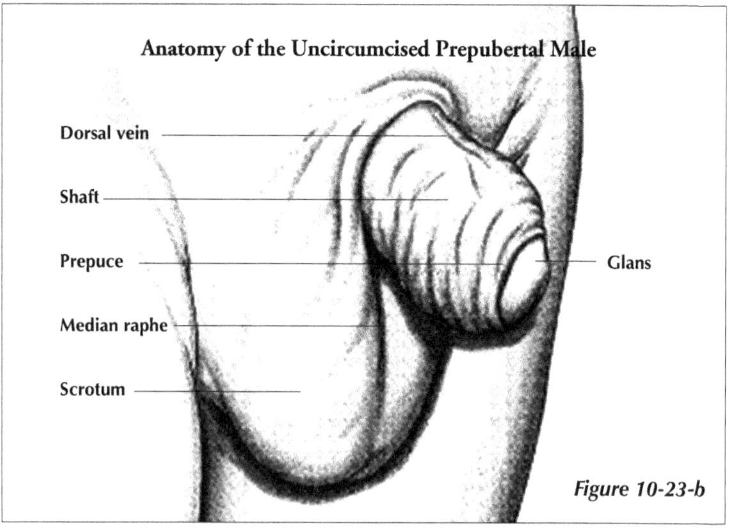

Figure 10-23-b. *Anatomy of the uncircumcised prepubertal male.*

Table 10-7. Medical Examination of Male Genitalia
1. Tanner stage
2. Circumcision status
3. Retractability of foreskin if uncircumcised
4. Appearance of glans and frenulum
5. Urethral discharge/stigmata of STIs
6. Signs of injury to glans or shaft of penis
7. Location of testis
8. Signs of scrotal trauma
9. Presence of hernias
10. Inguinal adenopathy

— The external hemorrhoidal plexus of perianal space is within the loose connective tissue surrounding external anal orifice.

— The anoderm extends from internal aspect of the anal verge to the pectinate or dentate line. The internal margin of the anoderm interdigitates with the ampulla of the rectum. A scalloped appearance comes from alternating rectal sinuses and columns and is called the pectinate or dentate line. The anoderm is devoid of hair, sebaceous glands, and sweat glands, so penetration may cause superficial trauma. Trauma is experienced as a painful, burning sensation with the passing of stool.

— Rugae are symmetrical, circumferentially radiating folds formed by relaxation of corrugator cutis ani muscle (**Figure 10-24**). Diagnostic residua from trauma to anal verge tissue are infrequent.

— Scrutinize the gluteal cleft and perineal tissues. Superficial abrasions of the gluteal cleft occur after genital-to-anal contact. With this type of trauma, children complain of discomfort when wiping themselves but not with bowel movements. Children may interpret downward pressure over the anal verge that creates dilation as penetration of the anal canal.

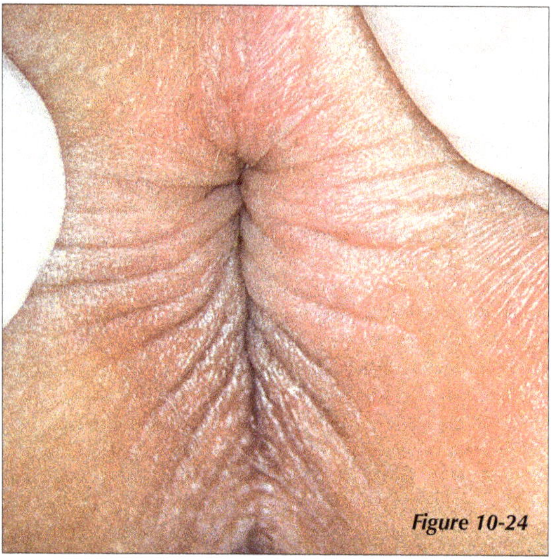

Figure 10-24. *Symmetrical radiating rugal folds of normal atraumatic anus.*

— Functionally, the anus dilates routinely to allow the passage of stool and could readily admit an object the size of a penis with minimal or no residual findings if lubrication is used.

— Variables determining the presence of residua from genital-to-anal contact are:

1. Degrees of force and restraint.
2. Degree of a child's cooperation.
3. Size of object introduced relative to anal anatomy

— Diagnostic residual evidence from consensual anal intercourse is infrequent.[64]

— Report of a burning sensation while passing stool after anal penetration is diagnostic of trauma to the anoderm.

— Check children's histories for insight into whether or not a child had contact with potentially infected ejaculate and is at risk for STIs.

— Today, it is possible to identify offenders through DNA found in the anal folds and in feces.

Interpreting Residual Effects From Sexual Contact

— Diagnostic categories in the AAP statement are:

1. Concerning but in isolation not diagnostic (eg, abrasions or bruising of the inner thighs and genitalia, scarring or tears in the labia minora, enlargement of the hymenal opening, perineal body scars).
2. More concerning but in isolation not diagnostic (eg, scarring, tears, or distortion of the hymen or anus; decreased or absent hymenal tissue; scarring of the fossa navicularis; injury to or scarring of the posterior fourchette; anal lacerations).
3. Diagnostic with medical certainty (eg, semen and sperm with positive DNA identification, positive culture for gonorrhea or positive serology for syphilis or HIV with no history of congenitally acquired infection).

— If acute or healed genital or anal injury is found, obtain a complete history about the injury.

— Note especially the size and type of the penetrating object and the circumstances under which the event occurred; degree of discomfort; number of episodes of contact; associated symptoms and observations; whether or not treatment was sought and received; time between last alleged contact and examination.

— If history suggests an accidental mechanism, a third party usually observed the injury, medical attention is sought immediately, the scene inquiry confirms the injury's plausibility, and the history and pattern of injury are compatible.[65,66]

Examining and Interpreting Anal Findings in Male and Female Victims

— When evaluating a child's anus and rectum, practitioners may employ various positions (eg, prone knee–chest, supine knee–chest, lateral decubitus), but the prone knee–chest position may present difficulties, especially if it is suspected that the child experienced penetration in this position.

— For chronic anal abuse without acute external abnormalities, anoscopy is not routinely recommended due to triggering of the actual event. Do not use an anoscope without conscious sedation, particularly if the child reports an acute sexual assault event.

— Digital rectal examination provides little helpful information.

— If the anus dilates when the buttocks are separated, search for stool. Reflex anal dilation with stool in or recently evacuated from the rectal ampulla is normal.

— When anal verge tissue shows acute injury, anoscopy can detect internal lacerations, petechiae, and bruising of the anorectal canal. Seminal products can also be collected during the procedure.

1. External findings do not always portend the absence of more internal injuries.
2. Clinical history must guide the decision to use or not use anoscopy.
3. Include children's spontaneous descriptions of their experiences.

Patterns of Trauma

Provide both written and photographic documentation of the pattern and extent of acute injuries.

— Digital photographic documentation should be considered mandatory in all child sexual abuse examinations. It is a valuable resource for peer evaluation and educational purposes.

— Extragenital signs of injury (eg, ligature, bite marks, grasp marks) are best seen with digital imaging using a standard reference (eg, American Board of Forensic Odontology No. 2 ruler, coin).[67,68]

— The most significant factors determining extent of injury are degree of force, object used to inflict injury, overall health and condition of the individual, and type of contact.

Penetration

— The medical definition of penetration is "passing into the deeper tissues or into a cavity."[69] ***Vaginal penetration*** implies introducing an object through the labia and hymenal orifice and into the posterior portion of the vagina.

— The legal definition of penetration is "insertion of the male part into the female parts to however slight an extent; and by which the offense is complete without proof of an emission."[70]

— With vaginal penetration, acute examination reveals obvious residual signs such as a laceration to the membrane's edge that extends to the vaginal floor.

— Most hymenal lacerations after vaginal penetration occur between the 5 o'clock and 7 o'clock positions with the child in a supine position, but they can occur anywhere between the 3 o'clock and 9 o'clock positions.

— Forceful penetration can lacerate the fossa navicularis and lateral walls of the vagina or possibly perforate the posterior fornix into the peritoneal cavity.[71,72]

— Lacerations after vaginal penetration that extend to the base of the attachment of the hymen to the posterior vaginal floor may extend through the fossa and fourchette and into the perineal body. This can be assessed with the child under anesthesia (**Figure 10-25**).

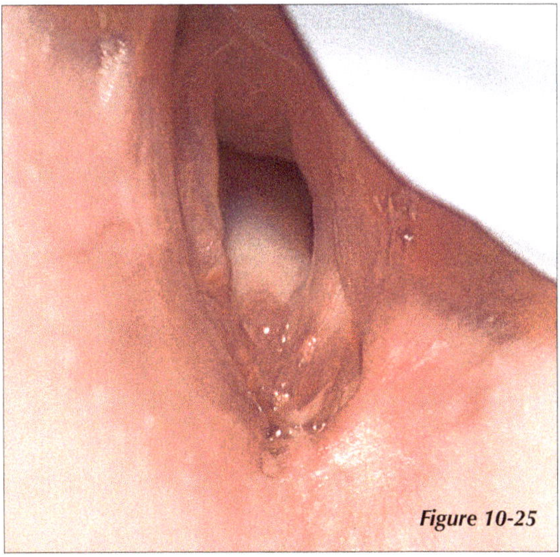

Figure 10-25. *Acute penetrating transection of the posterior fourchette, fossa navicularis, hymenal membrane, and proximal vagina.*

Genital Fondling

— Genital fondling of girls:

1. The hand is usually placed over the mons pubis and the index and third finger separate the labia and enter the vaginal vestibule.
2. Typically, the structures that form the vaginal vestibule are rubbed, causing acute signs of erythema, superficially denuded mucosa, abrasions or scratches, and lacerations and edema of the inner aspects of the labia minora, periurethral area, posterior fourchette, and fossa navicularis.
3. Typically, serious trauma is not found, but a sharp fingernail forcefully introduced into the vagina can significantly injure the posterior portion of the hymen, fossa, fourchette, or vagina.

— Children who are fondled can experience trauma to the periurethral area or complain of dysuria.

Vulvar Coitus

— Vulvar coitus can cause abrasions and bruising of the inner aspects of the labia minora, clitoral hood, periurethral area, and with downward pressure, the posterior fourchette. Posttraumatic dysuria can also occur.

— Girls can perceive genital-to-genital contact via vulvar coitus as penetration.

— Vulvar coitus does not usually injure the hymenal orifice.

Accidental Injuries

Usually, the patterns of trauma and history suggest the cause of accidental injuries to the genitalia.[73,74]

— Most accidental injuries occur when children fall on a horizontal bar of a bicycle, jungle gym, or picket fence and suffer a unilateral crush injury of the clitoral hood and labia minora between the bar and the inner aspect of the thigh.

— Boys who fall on an object or are kicked and injure their genitals usually incur trauma to the scrotum and inguinal region.[66,75]

— Masturbation-related injury (eg, localized erythema, superficial abrasions) typically appears in the frenulum area, resulting from tugging or rubbing. Masturbation is unlikely to result in any genital injury.[76]

Labial Agglutination

— Labial agglutination is common in prepubertal children[77] and reproductive-aged adolescents on long-term estrogen-suppressing birth control. It involves the thin, unestrogenized, highly vascular mucosal tissues of the inner aspect of the labia minora joining together following tissue breakdown in an agglutination process. The etiology is usually nonspecific (eg, incontinence) but requires injury to the labial margins for the fusion of tissue.

— Depending on the degree of fusion, agglutination can inhibit the ability to examine the hymenal membrane and internal structures and may obstruct urinary and menstrual outflow.

— Chronic moisture, conditions of the vulva, and injury resulting from abuse are known to cause adhesions.

— Agglutination has been associated with sexual abuse as well.[78-80]

— Estrogen cream can be used to obtain medical dehiscence.[81] Do not use "gentle traction" because it causes denuded edges that are painful and quickly readhere, not to mention the pain associated with genital manipulation. The authors suggest conscious sedation when surgically separating labial adhesions that prevent micturition, followed by application of estrogen cream for weight (ie, dosage calculated according to weight of the patient).

Extragenital Trauma

Extragenital signs of trauma are infrequent in child sexual abuse because perpetrators usually do not intend to physically harm the child and preferentially use deceit, coercion, or threats to ensure cooperation. When extragenital trauma is found, the sexual interaction usually involves rape, implying the use of restraint and force.[82]

— Children forced to perform fellatio can suffer tears to the labial frenulum and petechiae of the palate.

— Signs of restraint may be seen around the wrists and ankles.

— Grasp marks may appear as bruising of the extremities or, if the child was strangled, the neck.

— Bite marks can be present on the neck, breasts, buttocks, or inner thighs.[83,84]

Sodomy and Genital-to-Anal Contact Without Penetration

— *Freaking* is the most common form of genital-to-anal contact and involves rubbing the dorsal side of the penis shaft between the gluteal cleft over the external anal verge tissues, causing pressure perceived as penetrating into the anorectal canal. In such cases, the child may complain of feelings of needing to evacuate the rectum.

— Superficial abrasions can occur when the shaft is rubbed between the buttocks over the natal cleft, causing the child discomfort when wiping.

— Trace evidence and seminal products are collected from the inner thighs, buttocks, or back as well as anything that the child or perpetrator used to clean the child after ejaculation. Today, it is also possible to recover touch DNA.

— Significant DNA evidence on the child may be trapped in the anal folds for extended periods of time. Such evidence should be collected for analysis.

Interpretation of Healed and Healing Injuries

— Healed residual effects are infrequent.[85]

— Superficial injuries to genital and anal tissues heal via regeneration of labile cells[86]:

1. Thrombosis and inflammation
2. Regeneration of epithelium over a denuded surface
3. Multiplication of new cells
4. Differentiation into new epithelium

— The process proceeds at a rate of about 1 mm per 24 hours and is complete in 48 to 72 hours, with differentiation of new epithelium in 5 to 7 days.[86]

— More serious lacerating injuries leave residual signs.

1. Deep wounds heal by repair, which includes forming granulation tissue.
2. After the first steps of regeneration, organization of the coagulated blood and eventual formation of granulation tissue and wound contraction occur.
3. Macrophages begin to digest the fibrin clot and capillaries proliferate from the wound margins, leading to formation of an amorphous gelatinous matrix that acts as a substrate for collagen fibrils.
4. This neovascularization is a self-limited phenomenon that starts in the first days after injury and continues until full contraction.[86]
5. Mature granulation tissue develops over several months, with the scar changing from red to pink to pale and finally to white.
6. Scars can distort the genital tissue appearance. Healed well-delineated acute lacerations can be a fraction of their initial size.

— When scar tissue is present, it signals significant trauma, and a history reflective of significant injury should coexist.

— In very young children, a history may not be available. Clinical observations must be trusted.

— Describe all wound characteristics. Photograph all nongenital injuries and all anogenital examinations with or without injury. Photography is mandatory in cases of child sexual abuse.

Sexually Transmitted Diseases

(See Chapter 12, "Sexually Transmitted Diseases.")

Forensic Evidence

(See Chapter 17, "DNA and Evidence Collection.")

Medical Conditions That Mimic Child Sexual Abuse

(See **Table 10-8**.)

Table 10-8. Medical Conditions That Mimic Child Sexual Abuse
— Infectious processes localized to the anogenital area
— Vulvovaginitis
— Anogenital conditions with primary anogenital involvement
— Anogenital conditions with systemic or extragenital involvement
— Anogenital conditions that have primary systemic or extragenital conditions
— Acquired structural abnormalities
— Neoplasms, either primary or secondary, with genital tract manifestations
— Congenital anomalies

The Forensic Medical Record

— The medical record in child sexual abuse cases may be kept separate from the general forensic medical record, either in an effort to protect the integrity of the case or as a matter of historical policy. Access, and even parental access, to the medical records of adolescents and children is a controversial issue. The medical forensic record may or may not be subject to HIPPA, depending on jurisdictional legal interpretations.

1. Obtain the medical history, including a detailed review of systems and an appropriate developmental and social history. Typically, the parent or guardian will have this information.
2. Document the medical history and any visual findings.
3. Document the child's demeanor (eg, whether he/she is sitting still, playing with a teddy bear, sleeping).
4. Accurately record the exact words used by the child to describe the abusive event. Use quotation marks to indicate an exact quote. Speak to the child and parent(s)/guardian(s) using the child's words. Do not introduce new words to the child.
5. Document the child's physical condition.

— Document the clinical evaluation.

1. Record the forensic medical history verbatim.
2. Follow standardized forms to assist questioning. Craft questions that are developmentally appropriate and follow a style that is not leading or suggestible.
3. Obtain photodocumentation even if the examination does not demonstrate diagnostic findings.
4. When acute signs of injury are identified, conduct follow-up examinations with photodocumentation to record healing and residual findings.
5. Collaborate with and provide records to the primary care provider, who in many instances will facilitate for medical care, mental health care, and coordination of community resources.

Formulating a Conclusion

— Significant historical details include:

— The child's demeanor in evaluation

— Presence or absence of acute or chronic genital and/or anal trauma

— Presence of extragenital trauma

— Presence or absence of STDs

— The evaluation of collected evidence by a forensic laboratory for supporting DNA evidence

— History guides evaluation. In the absence of history and other supporting evidence, physical findings stand alone.

References

1. Finkelhor D. Current information on the scope and nature of child sexual abuse. In: Behrman R, ed. *The Future of Children*. Los Altos, CA: Center for the Future of Children; 1994:31-54.
2. Sedlak AJ, Schultz D, Wells SJ, Lyons P, Doueck HJ, Gragg F. Child protection and justice systems processing of serious child abuse and neglect cases. *Child Abuse Negl*. 2006;30(6):657-677.

3. US Department of Health and Human Services; Administration for Children and Families; Administration on Children, Youth and Families; Children's Bureau. *Child Maltreatment 2010.* Washington, DC: US Department of Health and Human Services; Administration for Children and Families; Administration on Children, Youth and Families; Children's Bureau; 2011.
4. Seto MC, Lalumiere ML. What is so special about male adolescent sexual offending? a review and test of explanations through meta-analysis. *Psychol Bull.* 2010;136(4):526-575.
5. Jespersen AF, Lalumiere ML, Seto MC. Sexual abuse history among adult sex offenders and non-sex offenders. a meta-analysis. *Child Abuse Negl.* 2009;33(3):179-192.
6. Leach C, Stewart A, Smallbone S. Testing the sexually abused sexual abuser hypothesis: a prospective longitudinal birth cohort study. *Child Abuse Negl.* 2016;51:144-153.
7. Finkelhor D, Turner H, Ormrod R, Hamby SL. Violence, abuse, and crime exposure in a national sample of children and youth. *Pediatrics.* 2009;124(5):1-13.
8. Finkelhor D, Turner H, Hamby S, Ormrod R. *Polyvictimization: Children's Exposure to Multiple Types of Violence, Crime, and Abuse.* Washington, DC: US Department of Justice, Office of Justice Programs, Office of Juvenile Justice and Delinquency Prevention; 2011.
9. National Center for Victims of Crime. Child sexual abuse statistics. National Center for Victims of Crime Web site. http://victimsofcrime.org/media/reporting-on-child-sexual-abuse/child-sexual-abuse-statistics. Accessed April 18, 2017.
10. US Department of Justice, Office of Justice Programs, Office of Juvenile Justice and Delinquency Prevention. *How the Justice System Responds to Juvenile Victims: A Comprehensive Model.* Washington, DC: US Department of Justice, Office of Justice Programs, Office of Juvenile Justice and Delinquency Prevention; 2005.
11. Puetz VB, Parker D, Kohn N, Dahmen B, Verma R, Konrad K. Altered brain network integrity after childhood maltreatment: a structural connectomic DT study. *Hum Brain Mapp.* 2017;38(2):855-868.

12. Heger A, Ticson L, Velasquez O, Bernier R. Children referred for possible sexual abuse: medical findings in 2384 children. *Child Abuse Negl.* 2002;26(6-7):645-659.
13. Substance Abuse and Mental Health Services Administration. *Trauma-Informed Care in Behavioral Health Services.* Rockville, MD: Substance Abuse and Mental Health Services Administration; 2014.
14. Anda RF, Felitti VJ, Bremner JD, et al. The enduring effects of abuse and related adverse experiences in childhood: a convergence of evidence from neurobiology and epidemiology. *Eur Arch Psychiatry Clin Neurosci.* 2006;256(3):174-186.
15. McEwen BS. Sex, stress and the hippocampus: allostasis, allostatic load and the aging process. *Neurobiol Aging.* 2002;23(5):921-939.
16. Xiong R, Zhang L. Role of the hypothalamic-pituitary-adrenal axis in developmental programming of health and disease. *Front Neuroendocrinol.* 2013;34(1):27-46.
17. Jackson AM, Deye K. Aspects of abuse: consequences of childhood victimization. *Curr Probl Pediatr Adolesc Health Care.* 2015;45(3):86-93.
18. Whitaker DJ, Le B, Karl Hanson R, et al. Risk factors for the perpetration of child sexual abuse: a review and meta-analysis. *Child Abuse Negl.* 2008;32(5):529-548.
19. Huffhines L, Tunno AM, Cho B, et al. Case file coding of child maltreatment: methods, challenges, and innovations in a longitudinal project of youth in foster care. *Child Youth Serv Rev.* 2016;67:254-262.
20. Krugman RD. Recognition of sexual abuse in children. *Pediatr Rev.* 1986;8(1):25-30.
21. Hunter RS, Kilstrom N, Loda F. Sexually abused children: identifying masked presentations in the medical setting. *Child Abuse Negl.* 1985;9(1):17-25.
22. Rogers D. Physical aspects of alleged sexual assault. *Med Sci Law.* 1996;36(2):117-122.
23. Paradise JE. The medical evaluation of the sexually abused child. *Pediatr Clin North Am.* 1990;37(4):839-862.

24. Sorenson T, Snow B. How children tell: the process of disclosure in child sexual abuse. *Child Welfare*. 1991;70(1):3-15.

25. Stockwell MS, Brown J, Chen S, Irigoyen M. Is there a relationship between lacking a primary care provider and child abuse? *Ambul Pediatr*. 2007;7(6):439-444.

26. Smith DW, Letourneau EJ, Saunders BE, Kilpatrick DG, Resnick HS, Best CL. Delay in disclosure of childhood rape: results from a national survey. *Child Abuse Negl*. 2000;24(2):273-287.

27. Jenny C, Crawford-Jakubiak JE; Committee on Child Abuse and Neglect. The evaluation of children in the primary care setting when sexual abuse is suspected. *Pediatrics*. 2013;132(2):558-567.

28. Formby J, Shadoin AL, Shao L, Magnuson SN, Overman LB. *Cost-Benefit Analysis of Community Responses to Child Maltreatment: A Comparison of Communities With and Without Child Advocacy Centers*. Huntsville, AL: National Children's Advocacy Center; 2006.

29. Cantwell HB. Vaginal inspection as it relates to child sexual abuse in girls under thirteen. *Child Abuse Negl*. 1983;7(2):171-176.

30. Kerns DL, Ritter ML, Thomas RG. Concave hymenal variations in suspected child sexual abuse victims. *Pediatrics*. 1992;90(2 pt 1):265-272.

31. Kellogg ND, Menard SW, Santos A. Genital anatomy in pregnant adolescents: "normal" does not mean "nothing happened." *Pediatrics*. 2004;113(1 pt 1):1000-1011.

32. McCaan J, Miyamoto S, Boyle C, Rogers K. Healing of hymenal injuries in prepubertal and adolescent girls: a descriptive study. *Pediatrics*. 2007;119(5):e1094-e1106.

33. McCaan J, Miyamoto S, Boyle C, Rogers K. Healing of nonhymenal genital injuries in prepubertal and adolescent girls: a descriptive study. *Pediatrics*. 2007;120(5):1000-1011.

34. Adams JA, Zuckerman AL. Genital complaints in prepubertal girls. Medscape Web site. http://emedicine.medscape.com/article/954024-overview#a2. Updated March 22, 2016. Accessed April 18, 2017.

35. McCann J, Voris J, Simon M, Wells R. Perianal findings in prepubertal children selected for nonabuse: a descriptive study. *Child Abuse Negl.* 1989;13(2):179-193.

36. Bays J, Chadwick D. Medical diagnosis of the sexually abused child. *Child Abuse Negl.* 1993;17(1):91-110.

37. Theodore AD, Runyan DK. A medical research agenda for child maltreatment: negotiating the next steps. *Pediatrics.* 1999;104(1 pt 2):168-177.

38. American Academy of Pediatrics Committee on Child Abuse and Neglect. Guidelines for the evaluation of sexual abuse in children: subject review. *Pediatrics.* 1999;103(5 pt 1):186-191.

39. Verhoff MA, Kettner M, Lászik A, Ramsthaler F. Digital photo documentation of forensically relevant injuries as part of the clinical first response protocol. *Dtsch Arztebl Int.* 2012;109(39):638-642.

40. Berliner L, Elliott DM. Sexual abuse of children. In: Meyers JEB, Berline L, Briere J, Hendrix CT, Jenny C, Reid TA, eds. *The APSAC Handbook on Child Maltreatment.* 2nd ed. Thousand Oaks, CA: Sage Publications; 2002:55-78.

41. Substance Abuse and Mental Health Services Administration. Adverse childhood experiences. Substance Abuse and Mental Health Services Administration Web site. https://www.samhsa.gov/capt/practicing-effective-prevention/prevention-behavioral-health/adverse-childhood-experiences. Accessed May 28, 2017.

42. Kendall-Tackett KA, Williams LM, Finkelhor D. Impact of sexual abuse on children: a review and synthesis of recent empirical studies. *Psychol Bull.* 1993;113(1):164-180.

43. Johnson TC. *Understanding Your Child's Sexual Behavior: What's Natural and Healthy.* Oakland, CA: New Harbinger Publications; 1999.

44. Myers JEB. *Legal Issues in Child Abuse and Neglect Practice.* 2nd ed. Thousand Oaks, CA: Sage Publications; 1998.

45. Varma S, Gillespie S, McCracken C, Greenbaum VJ. Characteristics of child commercial sexual exploitation and sex trafficking victims presenting for medical care in the United States. *Child Abuse Negl.* 2015;44:98-105.

46. Greenbaum VJ. Commercial sexual exploitation and sex trafficking of children in the United States. *Curr Probl Pediatr Adolesc Health Care.* 2014;44(9):245-269.

47. Chung RJ, English A. Commercial sexual exploitation and sex trafficking of adolescents. *Curr Opin Pediatr.* 2015;27(4):427-433.

48. Choi KR. Risk factors for domestic minor sex trafficking in the United States. *J Forensic Nurs.* 2015;11(2):66-76.

49. McClain NM, Garrity SE. Sex trafficking and the exploitation of adolescents. *J Obstet Gynecol Neonatal Nurs.* 2011;40(2):243-252.

50. Newby A, McGuinness TM. Human trafficking: what psychiatric nurses should know to help children and adolescents. *J Psychosoc Nurs Ment Health Serv.* 2012;50(4):21-24.

51. Cole J, Sprang G. Sex trafficking of minors in metropolitan, micropolitan, and rural communities. *Child Abuse Negl.* 2015;40:113-123.

52. DeLago C, Deblinger E, Schroeder C, Finkel MA. Girls who disclose sexual abuse: urogenital symptoms and signs after genital contact. *Pediatrics.* 2008;122(2):e281-e286.

53. Lamb ME, Orbach Y, Hershkowitz I, Esplin PW, Horowitz D. *Tell Me What Happened: Structured Investigative Interviews of Child Victims and Witnesses.* Hoboken, NJ: John Wiley & Sons; 2008.

54. Christian CW, Lavelle JM, De Jong AR, Loiselle J. Forensic evidence findings in prepubertal victims of sexual assault. *Pediatrics.* 2000;106(1):100-104.

55. Spencer M. Iatrogenic hymenal injury. *Top Emerg Med.* 2005;27(1):89.

56. Honor G. Medical evaluation for child sexual abuse: what the PNP needs to know. *J Pediatr Health Care.* 2011;25:250-256.

57. Scrandis DA, Watt M. Child sexual abuse in boys: implications for primary care. *The Journal of Nurse Practitioners.* 2014;10(9):706-713.

58. Adams JA, Kellogg ND, Farst KJ, et al. Updated guidelines for the medical care of children who may have been sexually abused. *J Pediatr Adolesc Gynecol.* 2016;29(2):81-87.

59. Berenson AB, Heger A, Andrews S. Appearance of the hymen in newborns. *Pediatrics.* 1991;87(4):458-465.

60. Berenson AB, Grady JJ. A longitudinal study of hymenal development from 3 to 9 years of age. *J Pediatr.* 2002;140(5):600-607.

61. Speck PM, Lee ED. Hymen estrogen response scale (HERS) reliability study. *End Violence Against Women International and Office for Victims of Crime Notebook.* Addy, WA: End Violence Against Women International; 2011:28-29.

62. McCann J, Wells R, Simon M, Voris J. Genital findings in prepubertal girls selected for nonabuse: a descriptive study. *Pediatrics.* 1990;86(3):428-439.

63. Paradise JE. Predictive accuracy and the diagnosis of sexual abuse: a big issue about a little tissue. *Child Abuse Negl.* 1989;13(2):169-176.

64. Eckert WG, Katchis S. Anorectal trauma. medicolegal and forensic aspects. *Am J Forensic Med Pathol.* 1989;10(1):3-9.

65. Bond GR, Dowd MD, Landsman I, Rimsza M. Unintentional perineal injury in prepubescent girls: a multicenter, prospective report of 56 girls. *Pediatrics.* 1995;95(5):628-631.

66. Kadish HA, Schunk JE, Britton H. Pediatric male rectal and genital trauma: accidental and nonaccidental injuries. *Pediatr Emerg Care.* 1998;14(2):95-98.

67. Deming JE, Mittleman RE, Wetli CV. Forensic science aspects of fatal sexual assaults on women. *J Forensic Sci.* 1983;28(3):572-576.

68. Vale GL. Dentistry, bite marks and the investigation of crime. *J Calif Dent Assoc.* 1996;24(5):29-34.

69. Stedman TL, ed. *Stedman's Medical Dictionary.* 25th ed. Baltimore, MD: Williams & Wilkins; 1990.

70. Black HC. *Black's Law Dictionary.* 5th ed. Saint Paul, MN: West Publishing; 1979.

71. Hoffman RJ, Ganti S. Vaginal laceration and perforation resulting from first coitus. *Pediatr Emerg Care.* 2001;17(2):113-114.

72. Bhagat M. Coital injury presenting in a 13 year old as abdominal pain and vaginal bleeding. *Pediatr Emerg Care.* 1996;12(5):354-355.

73. Dowd MD, Fitzmaurice L, Knapp JF, Mooney D. The interpretation of urogenital findings in children with straddle injuries. *J Pediatr Surg.* 1994;29(1):7-10.

74. Waltzman ML, Shannon M, Bowen AP, Bailey MC. Monkeybar injuries: complications of play. *Pediatrics.* 1999;103(5):e58.

75. Donald TG, Ludwig S. Pediatric male rectal and genital trauma: accidental and nonaccidental injuries. *Pediatr Emerg Care.* 1998;14(6):452-453.

76. Meyer TL, Cheng TL. Unveiling the secrecy behind masturbation. *Pediatr Rev.* 2002;23(4):148-149.

77. Muram D. Treatment of prepubertal girls with labial adhesions. *J Pediatr Adolesc Gynecol.* 1999;12(2):67-70.

78. Berkowitz CD. Sexual abuse of children and adolescents. *Adv Pediatr.* 1987;34:275-312.

79. Berkowitz CD, Elvik SL, Logan MK. Labial fusion in prepubescent girls: a marker for sexual abuse? *Am J Obstet Gynecol.* 1987;156(1):16-20.

80. McCann J, Voris J, Simon M. Labial adhesions and posterior fourchette injuries in childhood sexual abuse. *Am J Dis Child.* 1988;142(6):659-663.

81. Omar HA. Management of labial adhesions in prepubertal girls. *J Pediatr Adolesc Gynecol.* 2000;13(4):183-185.

82. Cartwright PS. Factors that correlate with injury sustained by survivors of sexual assault. *Obstet Gynecol.* 1987;70(1):44-46.

83. Wright FD, Dailey JC. Human bite marks in forensic dentistry. *Dent Clin North Am.* 2001;45(2):365-397.

84. American Academy of Pediatric Dentistry, Ad Hoc Work Group on Child Abuse and Neglect. Oral and dental aspects of child abuse and neglect. *Pediatrics.* 1999;104:348-350.

85. Finkel MA. Anogenital trauma in sexually abused children. *Pediatrics.* 1989;84(2):317-322.

86. Edwards LC, Dunphy JE. Wound healing. I. Injury and normal repair. *N Engl J Med.* 1958;259(5):224-233.

Chapter 11

The Sexual Abuse Interview

Diana K. Faugno, MSN, RN, CPN, SANE-A, SANE-P, FAAFS, DF-IAFN
Karmie Johnson, DNP, RN, PMHNP-BC
Shannon Polson, MSN, MSW, RN, LCSW, CNL, CWCN, PIP
Rosario V. Sanchez, MSN, RN, CCRN, CFN, SANE-A, D-ABFN
Susan K. Reichert, MD, FAAP
Terry Chianello, MA, MSW, LCSW
Mary T. Rourke, PhD
Patricia M. Speck, DNSc, ARNP, APN, FNP-BC, DF-IAFN, FAAFS, FAAN

Trauma-Informed Care

— Trauma-informed care, which arose from the mental health literature, has the following characteristics[1]:

1. ***Realizes*** the widespread impact of trauma and understands potential paths for recovery
2. ***Recognizes*** the signs and symptoms of trauma in clients, families, staff, and others involved with the system
3. ***Responds*** by fully integrating knowledge about trauma into policies, procedures, and practices
4. Seeks to actively ***resist retraumatization.***[1]

— A trauma-informed approach can be implemented in any type of service setting or organization.

— Trauma-informed care is distinct from trauma-specific interventions or treatments designed to address the consequences of trauma and to facilitate healing.

— There are 6 key principles to trauma-informed care, which are not a prescribed set of practices or procedures:
  1. Safety
  2. Trustworthiness/transparency
  3. Peer support
  4. Collaboration/mutuality
  5. Empowerment/voice and choice
  6. Cultural, historical, and gender issues
— These principles are not a prescribed set of practices or procedures. They are generalizable across settings where terminology and use are specific to the location.
— Trauma-specific intervention programs generally recognize the following:
  — The patient's need to be respected, informed, connected, and hopeful regarding their own recovery
  — The interrelation between trauma and physical health (eg, behavioral and addictive disorders, depression, anxiety) in victims and the nonoffenders that lead to chronic disease and early death
  — The need to work with victims in a collaborative setting
— Trauma-informed interviews of children create safe environments where they can use their words or pictures to describe experiences.
— The younger the child (ie, < 4 years), the more likely they can answer questions related to the senses (ie, sight, hearing, smell, taste, touch).
— Older children with repeated assaults may be unable to remember specific events, but they can provide sensory/seasonal information to providers. This information is useful for understanding triggering of sensations in the medical or forensic interview (**Table 11-1**).
  — ***Forensic interview*:** A structured conversation with a child intended to elicit detailed information about an event or events the child may have experienced or witnessed. The purpose of a forensic interview is to obtain information from a child that may be helpful in a criminal investigation.
  — ***Medical forensic history*:** Specific questions asked of patients by examiners for the medical forensic evaluation, including the child's medical history and a history of the event in question.

Table 11-1. Contrasting Forensic and Clinical Interviews

Forensic Interviews	Clinical Interviews
The goal is to gather reliable and accurate information, when appropriate.	The goal is to assess and provide treatment.
Focus is on finding facts. Accuracy of events is important.	The focus is therapeutic. The perception and impact of events is important.
Key principles are objectivity, neutrality, and the elimination of bias.	Key principles are empathy, support, and establishing a therapeutic alliance.
Court is the client.	Child is the client.
Consent to obtain outside information and disclose information is obtained and understood prior to interview.	Client must consent before external verification and sharing of information.
Interviews are formal and restrictive.	Interviewing can be based on multiple strategies.
Confidentiality is restricted.	Traditional confidentiality is employed.
Competency of client is questioned.	Client competency is not a primary concern.
Interview is recorded.	Interview is private.

Reprinted with permission from Center on Child Abuse and Neglect. The Differences Between Forensic Interviews & Clinical Interviews. *Norman, OK: University of Oklahoma Health Sciences Center; 2000.*

— ***Clinical interview***: A tool that helps physicians, psychologists, and researchers make an accurate diagnosis of a variety of mental illnesses. There are 2 common types: structured clinical interviews and clinical diagnostic interviews.

Issues Related to Interviewing Children

— To verbally inquire about sexual abuse, all medical practitioners need to add sensitivity, caution, and a few basic ground rules of easily learned techniques to the history-taking skills they already possess.

- — Create a safe environment.
- — Pose nonleading, open-ended questions.
- — Remain objective.
- — Ask enough questions to develop a reasonable medical conclusion, as circumstances allow.
- — Do not appear startled or surprised by anything revealed.
- — Pursue responses with additional clarifying inquiries.
- — Communicate neutral but active listening.

— Be prepared to work cooperatively with law enforcement, child protective services (CPS), and other agencies to determine the type of interviews needed and how each party will contribute to the process.

— Reporting suspected child abuse to CPS is mandated throughout the United States and Canada. The provider should consider the facts in each individual case, but the threshold for reporting suspected abuse is low.

— The responsibility to investigate the occurrence of abuse does not fall to the health care provider, but intervening on behalf of client safety does.[2]

— Consider the number and nature of other interviews planned for a child and do not expand inquiry into areas already explored if they do not affect your medical diagnosis.

— While statements made to most individuals are considered hearsay and are not admissible in court testimony, the medical hearsay exception allows statements made to a health care provider during an encounter in which the provider will contribute to or develop the medical diagnosis, which is admissible in court.

— Health care providers can also testify to statements made spontaneously during the interview or evaluation. Providers should document the circumstances for of the spontaneous disclosure (eg, "As I separated the labia minora, the patient said, 'That is where he touched.'").

Caregiver History

— Have caregivers complete a prepared questionnaire or conduct an interview over the phone or in person. Verbal interviews are best conducted without children present.

— If more than one parent or caregiver is present, interview them separately when possible.

— Obtain the following information in the caregiver interview:

1. The child's past medical history
2. Ongoing medical problems and medications
3. Whether the child took medication on the day of the evaluation
4. Depending on the child's age, a history of birth trauma, prematurity, developmental disorders, seizures, attention deficit/hyperactivity disorder, or learning difficulties
5. Any hospitalizations, major accidents, or injuries the child sustained as well as any negative experiences in a health care setting
6. Past history of physical, sexual, or emotional abuse
7. Family medical history, including history of chaos, death, divorce, or other adverse experiences in the parent's childhood
8. Whether the child or other children are in contact with individuals who may have abused others in the past

— Perform a careful and comprehensive review of systems (ROS), paying close attention to signs and symptoms that may relate to sexual abuse.

1. Question caregivers and older children as to whether they have ever noted any bleeding, pain, lesions, or discharge from the child's anogenital areas.
2. Note any history of sexually transmitted diseases or pregnancy.
3. Ask the child for the names they use for various body parts and the names or nicknames of key people and pets in his/her life. Use those names during the interview. Do not introduce new language to the child or parent/guardian.

— Gather a social history to identify health and safety concerns.

1. Inquire about family/household dynamics and structure. Review family discipline practices.
2. Ask about the child's school and/or daycare situations and social relationships.

— Ask how the abuse has affected the caregivers and family to obtain insight into a child's presentation and statements or lack of disclosure.

— Ask about support systems for family members and encourage them to consider interventional services.

— In a nonjudgmental way, ask if the child has been exposed to sexual materials and activities.

1. Ask about the family's habits regarding privacy and nudity in the home.
2. Ask if they have observed sexualized behaviors, preoccupation with sexual matters, and/or excessive masturbation exhibited by the child.

— Inquire about other worrisome behaviors, especially behavioral changes, changes in sleep patterns, secondary enuresis, encopresis, nightmares, eating disturbances, variations from normal attitudes and moods, and unexplained changes in levels of participation and interests.

— For older children and teens, ask about risk-taking behaviors, eating disorders, suicidal tendencies, substance use, and voluntary sexual involvement.

Disclosure Process

— Typically, children do not directly or immediately disclose abuse. They often have difficulty disclosing something that would get someone else in trouble.[3]

— Disclosures are more likely to occur after an extended period, when the offender is no longer present, or after an emotionally upsetting incident. It is important to note the source of disclosure if it did not occur spontaneously.[2]

— Factors that influence a child's ability and willingness to disclose sensitive information include:

1. Response of the caregiver (usually the mother)[4]
2. Perpetrator's use of threats/coercion or bribes, even when the promised consequences seem unrealistic or minimal to an adult[5-7]
3. The dynamics of the victim-offender relationship[3,8,9]
4. The degree to which the child feels responsible for negative consequences to the offender or family
5. The age of the child

— Different factors influence disclosures in younger and older children.

1. Disclosures of preschool children are usually accidental and spontaneous.
2. Older children and teens may be prompted by conversations with peers in whom they have confided or who tell them about their own abuse and support them in coming forward.

— The phases of disclosure are denial, tentative disclosure, active disclosure, recantation, and reaffirmation.[10]

— Consistency issues:

1. Consistency is important when assessing a child's statements about abuse, but not all inconsistencies indicate unreliability. Rather, they may reflect memory recall disturbances.
2. Sensory core details are often consistent, whereas peripheral nonsensory data may vary.
3. Providing either more or less information is not considered a contradiction. Journals for older children help them recall specific incidences that can provide prosecutorial information.
4. Remember that if the sexual abuse occurred on many occasions, the child may be unable to give a concise description of an individual episode and instead may combine elements from several episodes into a description of a single event.[11]

— Lack of disclosure during the medical examination or discrepancies in the information obtained do not necessarily indicate that abuse did not occur.[10,12,13]

— (See **Table 11-2** for criteria for assessing a child's statements.)

Developmental Considerations

— Estimate a child's developmental level to determine how to communicate effectively; however, do not use a child's age as the sole basis for determining the child's cognitive capabilities. Anxiety and trauma can cause cognitive and emotional regression.

Table 11-2. Criteria to Consider When Assessing Allegations of Child Sexual Abuse

- — Circumstances of the disclosure
  - — Spontaneity
  - — Environment at time of disclosure
  - — Timing of disclosure, triggers for disclosure
  - — Threats, bribes, or coercion
  - — Reaction of significant others to child's disclosure
- — Consistency of core details
- — Idiosyncratic or rich details
- — "Child's-eye view"
- — Use of nonverbal means (gestures, drawings, figures) to describe abusive incidents
- — Description of sexual matters advanced for developmental age
- — Emotional state of child at time of disclosure and when discussing the abuse

Adapted from Kuehnle.[14]

- — Children's language skills can vary tremendously. Pay attention to the length of spontaneous words and sentences as well as the complexity of the grammatical constructions.[15] Tailor your language to match the child's.
- — Pay attention to a child's vocabulary to gauge what the child understands and to pick up any idiosyncratic words used.
- — Assess the child's ability to listen to questions and process information.
- — Do not overestimate cognitive processing skills when children use advanced vocabulary or long, grammatically complex sentences. Expressive and receptive language skills reflect children's comprehension of their personal experience and do not necessarily reflect accurate or commonly accepted use of language.
- — Use simple, clear, medically unsophisticated language and use the child's words to communicate with him/her.

— Avoid compound statements and questions.

— Keep sentences relatively short and convey only 1 idea or question at a time. For example:

— "Why are you here with me today?"

— "What color is this block?"

— "What is the name of your school?"

— Children who are highly anxious have difficulty with abstract terms.

1. Use concrete terms, precise language used by the child, and proper names instead of pronouns.
2. In follow-up questions, repeat in the child's terms for any items or people to with he/she referred.
3. Young children have difficulty with relational terms (eg, more than, less than); therefore, avoid asking questions that require these comparisons.

— Communicating the timing of an incident is hard for young children. Time may be communicated in light and dark, cold and hot, in and out of school, and in relation to holiday activities.

1. Children younger than 10 or 11 years are developmentally incapable of accurately pinpointing when an event occurred.
2. Provide children with concrete anchors to help them define a time frame (eg, daytime, nighttime, what grade they were in, where they lived, holidays or seasons of the year).
3. Do not expect children younger than 10 years to accurately communicate the number of times an event or action occurred.[16] Even a child who has consistently given clear, compelling details of sexual abuse may guess and/or offer an implausible/contradicting response when asked a developmentally inappropriate question.

— Identifying basic abilities in a brief developmental assessment does not translate into children having the ability to describe a sexual abuse experience in adult language.

Patient Emotional and Comfort Issues

— Anxiety can negatively influence children's ability to connect with health care providers, divert their attention, and decrease their memory efficiency.[17] Recognize such anxiety and work to create a safe environment.

— Minimize outside disruptions.

— Reduce the apparent power difference between child and health care provider.

— Ensure the medical forensic evaluation space is as comforting and child-friendly as possible.[17]

— It is preferable to interview and examine children without caregivers present, because children might be influenced by hearing their caregiver's concerns about suspected abuse.[2]

1. It is not uncommon for children and parents to object to being separated. Approach both with compassion and supportive explanations. For example, "I am going to talk with your daughter for a little while before I start the examination. Most kids do well with this. If there are any problems, I will come get you."
2. Verbally commit to respecting parents' rights and decisions, unless children have been removed from parental custody.
3. Remain neutral and nonjudgmental toward the family.
4. If there is substantial resistance to separation, conduct the initial part of the interview with parents present. Once a rapport is established and expectations are more apparent, parents and children are likely to have less anxiety about separating.
5. Some children may experience separation anxiety and resist being interviewed alone. In such cases, facilitate the separation and communicate their parents' support of the process. Give children some control by offering to modify the examination process whenever they are uncomfortable.
6. Reassure children that if they need their parents to be present as the examination proceeds, the parents will be asked to join you.

7. Caution parents that they are not to answer for children or to actively participate in the process, unless specifically requested to do so.
8. Watch for physical movement cuing the child to stop cooperating. Separate the adult from the child and report the attempted influence to CPS.

Interview Models

Develop a standardized approach to questioning children about sexual abuse.

— NICHD Protocol:

1. Developed by researchers at the National Institute of Child Health and Human Development and available online (most effective with required training).[18]
2. Improves the detail and accuracy of information given.[19]
3. NICHD Protocol is the only systematically evaluated forensic interview protocol for children.[19]
4. Three phases include (1) introduction, (2) rapport-building, (3) substantive or free recall.

— Traces of the cognitive interview and narrative elaboration models are used in current approaches to interviewing.[20]

— Recommendations support a flexible yet comprehensive interview format that is a composite of several research-based models.[21]

Incorporating Interviewing Skills Into the Medical Forensic Examination

— Begin the evaluation in an interview area separate from the examination room or in the examination room, with the child seated in a chair at your eye level.

— Remove distractions from the room (eg, few toys, table and chair only, child-friendly colors).

— Transition to the physical examination area and complete the patient interview during the examination process.

— Continue to ask questions about the child's knowledge of his/her body.

— Use the language that the child uses.

Introduction and Building Rapport

— Begin by greeting the patient.

— Create a comfortable atmosphere while conveying what is expected from the patient.

— Inform the child that you will be asking a lot of questions so you can take better care of him/her. Remind the child that he/she knows more than anyone about his/her body. This helps to empower the child and communicates respect for what he/she has to share.

— Tell the child that he/she can answer questions in various ways (ie, giving a correct response, if possible; asking for clarification, if necessary; saying "I don't know." or "I don't remember.").

— When a child appears reluctant to answer verbally, offer the options of writing answers or drawing pictures in response to your questions.

— Rapport building:

1. Begin with several focused, fact-finding questions (eg, ask for age, grade in school, interests, activities). Use these to gauge a child's communication style and cognitive capabilities.
2. Alternately, ask questions that invite children to respond in a less structured manner (ie, the free-running narrative approach), which can produce more comprehensive results. In an unstructured manner, engage children in discussions of a benign life event to establish a communicative connection.[22]
3. In addition to or instead of asking routine questions about school, ask children to talk about what happens in their favorite class or to describe a recent field trip.
4. Use the free-running narrative approach to convey to children that they will be doing the talking and the adult will be doing the listening.

— Continue building a safe environment and rapport during the evaluation as you engage patients, listen to their answers, and ask them further questions to develop an understanding of what they have experienced.

— Avoid trying to put children at ease by empathizing and making consoling but biased statements, such as saying the offender is bad or does bad things or should go to jail.

Collecting Substantive Information

— Collect information about children's health, activities, social circumstances, and safety as well as abuse-related issues.

— Obtain a thorough history from children, tailored to each child's age and developmental capabilities and reflecting his/her own perspective.

— Ask questions about each individual body part as you examine them.

— Maintain this interview style to convey to children that later questions about the genital and anal areas are part of a normal procedure and to give them practice discussing specific information about body parts.

1. For all bodily orifices, ask the child "Has anything happened here that made you uncomfortable?" If he/she responds positively, say "Tell me more." or ask "What happened next?" Asking "Did someone touch you there?" is leading, and the child may feel compelled to answer in the affirmative, even if it never happened.
2. If a child describes being injured on a certain part of the body, clarify the circumstances under which the injury occurred and, if inflicted, by whom it was inflicted.
3. If a child describes an injury or inappropriate touch, invite the child to point to, on his or her own body or on a drawing of a body, the exact place of contact. This is more specific than words alone.[14]
4. The use of anatomically correct dolls is controversial and is not usually advisable in the medical forensic interview setting, unless the health care provider has had extensive special training with these dolls and can discriminate appropriate circumstances for their use.[21,23]

Types of Questions

— Interview questions can be viewed along a continuum of degrees to which they draw on recall versus recognition memory.

— Memory is reconstructed, not in a logical order after trauma.

1. It is more difficult for individuals to access a memory without being offered any cues (recall) than it is to recognize something after cues or choices are given.[24]

2. Questions that rely on recall memory are open-ended and require longer explanatory responses from older children but may not be answered by younger verbal children.
3. Questions that tap recognition memory elicit brief answers (often yes or no).
4. Calling on recall memory is strongly encouraged in child abuse evaluations because it is considered less suggestive. However, building on memory reconstruction occurs with statements like "Tell me more." or questions like "Is there anything else?" Using the language of the child allows for clarifying questions to confirm the statements from the child.

— Categories of questions include open-ended, clarifying, focused, leading, accusatory, and coercive questions (**Table 11-3**).

Table 11-3. Types of Questions Used in Interviews of Suspected Child Abuse Victims

Type of Question	Characteristics	Examples
Open-ended	— Draws mainly upon recall memory — Accuracy is thought to be maximized — Optimal starter questions; follow with clarifiers	— "Tell me why you came in to see me today." — "Tell me all about why you are here." — "And then what happened?"
Specific or focused	— Both recall and recognition memory are tapped — Reasonable accuracy — Appropriate when used to clarify responses to open-ended questions	— "Who hit you there?" — "Did anyone touch you in a private area? Anyone else?"

(continued)

Table 11-3. Types of Questions Used in Interviews of Suspected Child Abuse Victims *(continued)*

Type of Question	Characteristics	Examples
Multiple choice	— Draws mainly upon recognition memory — Accuracy may be improved if an unspecified alternative is included — Appropriate as a clarifying question	— "Did that happen in the bedroom, the bathroom, or somewhere else?" — "Did she hit you one time or more than one time?"
Yes/no	— Forces a choice; younger children may simply choose first or last options — May be less reliable — Best used for clarification or in head-to-toe review of systems, returning to open-ended query if child gives affirmative response	— (After child has stated that she had been touch on her private parts): "Point to it." — (Once she points): "Did that hurt you?" — "Have you ever been hurt on your private parts?"
Leading	— Suggests that there is only one acceptable response — Format of question generally includes an act, an actor, and a tag — Accuracy questionable — Should never be used	— "Your dad hit you, right?" — "No one has ever done anything to hurt your bottom, have they?" — "Tell me about when your brother hurt you."
Coercive	— Evokes emotion, secondary gain, not necessarily memory retrieval — Accuracy severely compromised — Inappropriate; should never be used	— "Tell me who did that to you, and I'll let you go back to see your mommy in the playroom."

— Not all types of questions are equally effective. Tailor inquiries to the child's age, emotional state, level of cooperation, and communication style.

— Generally, start the interview with open-ended questions, then prompt further recall with more open-ended follow-up questions.

— If clarification is needed, ask more specific questions.

1. Focused, clarifying questions direct the flow of conversation.
2. Restate a point of information that the child has shared to highlight the issue and clarify that both of you are discussing the same thing.
3. Use focused or direct questions strategically to obtain a specific piece of information that follows from what has already been shared.
4. Use direct questions to draw out a reluctant child who has not responded to open-ended inquiry or to determine if the child is more willing to discuss a sensitive subject.
5. After the point is made, quickly return to open-ended questions.

— Optimally, the interview process will have a back-and-forth, dynamic rhythm in which open-ended queries are followed by more open-ended questions or by clarifying questions that are then followed by more open-ended questions (**Figure 11-1**).

— While examining a child's body, inquire directly about past events affecting each area. If the child has any complaints, immediately offer an open-ended prompt to access his/her recall memory. When that inquiry is complete, continue the body survey questions.

— Include questions about spanking when examining children's back and buttocks. This can lead to a discussion of disciplinary methods. Ask if anyone is ever punished or spanked in the family and compare the information with that provided by the caregiver(s).

— Intermittently ask questions aimed at identifying whether children have been threatened or bribed.

— Ask children if they know what a secret is to ascertain whether they understand the concept. Ask if they have any secrets or have been told by someone to keep a secret.

Sexual Abuse Interview Flow

Open-ended question	Evaluator:	"How come you are here today?"
	Child:	"My dad hurt me."
Clarifying question	Evaluator:	"Where did he hurt you?"
	Child:	"He hurt me on my body."
Open-ended question	Evaluator:	"Can you tell me more about that?"
	Child:	"He hit me on my face, then on my back and my stomach."
Clarifying question	Evaluator:	"What did your dad hit you with?"
	Child:	"He hit me with a belt."
Open-ended question	Evaluator:	"Then what happened?"
	Child:	"He made me get on the bed."
Open-ended question	Evaluator:	"What happened after he made you get on the bed?"
	Child:	"Then he touched me."
Clarifying question	Evaluator:	"Where did he touch you?"

Figure 11-1

Figure 11-1. *Sample flow of interview questions.*

— To stimulate their memory, use some direct questions that offer children multiple answers. Bear in mind the child's age, because children have some difficulty remembering several choices, especially if the choices are embedded in lengthy questions.

— If considerable open-ended inquiry has not introduced the topic of abuse and concern remains, ask a focused question about one factor that may be related to the current abuse circumstances.[12]

— Using a laundry-list approach (ie, asking the same question about various individuals, situations, locations) is another option.

— When a child indicates that he/she does not know why he/she is being evaluated or is unwilling to discuss abuse-related topics through general inquiry, make a broad statement acknowledging that some children you have seen have been hurt by someone or have been touched in a way that was uncomfortable or private. This let them know it is OK to talk about such matters with their health care provider. This approach is not a shortcut to be used at the beginning of every child abuse evaluation; it is best saved for times when the concern about abuse is high and a child is evasive or seems unfocused.

— Whether or not children respond by disclosing abuse, continue taking the history, alternating open invitations for narrative descriptions of events and concerns with focused clarifying questions, as appropriate.

CLOSURE

— When the examination and history are complete, invite the child to ask questions and add any information you may not have addressed. Thank or commend the child for participating in the examination and interview, but do not offer praise for the content of any disclosures made.

— During the interview, the child should be assessed for possible mental health problems. If symptoms of a mood disorder or posttraumatic stress disorder are identified, appropriate mental health treatment and referral should be considered and discussed.[2]

— Using developmentally appropriate terms, review significant findings with children and reassure them about their bodies and their health.

— If more tests, visits, or interviews are anticipated, tell older children and caregivers about them and offer to address any concerns they have. For younger children, tell caregivers in the presence of the child.

— When counseling is recommended, introduce the idea and enlist children's cooperation.

— Let children know that you will be discussing findings with parents, investigators, caseworkers, and others. Particularly with teens, address issues of confidentiality and determine if the teen wants to participate in the parental debriefing.

— For children of all ages, explore whether they feel safe in their environment and whether they feel they are believed and supported. If children feel they are in danger or will face negative consequences as a result of their disclosure of abuse or participation in the examination, document their fears and communicate them to law enforcement and/or CPS.

— End the interaction with an offer to be available to children if more questions or concerns arise or if they want to discuss anything else.

Documentation

— Thoroughly document children's and caregivers' histories, physical examination findings, and lab results. Follow local forms/protocols.

— Preserve the unique information gained during the medical forensic evaluation interview as comprehensively as possible.

— Record everything needed to adequately remember the case for competent testimony in court, taking into consideration the common lag before most cases go to trial (months to years).

— Indicate the specific source of all information.

— Document whether a child was interviewed alone or with others and indicate who was present.

— Include direct quotations, especially from the patient. Note pertinent questions asked to provide context for the child's responses.

— Include your observations of the child's demeanor, apparent emotional state, body language, and behavior during the interview and examination.

— Take careful notes during the medical forensic evaluation. Remember that notes are part of the medical record and are not to be discarded.

— It is common practice for trained forensic interviewers (non–health care providers) to audiotape or videotape interviews of suspected child abuse victims.[23,25]

— Clinical interviews, such as those conducted by a health care provider are not expected to be recorded and without permission may violate client privacy under the Health Insurance Portability and Accountability Act (HIPAA).

- Given the relatively low incidence of physical or lab findings diagnostic for abuse, assert that a patient's normal physical examination findings are consistent with and, in fact, expected findings for the history given.
  - With advances in forensic laboratory testing, future laboratory evidence may provide answers, even when the child presents with no physical findings.
- It may be useful to comment on the healing process and affirm that it is anticipated that any physical trauma incurred as a result of the abuse would have resolved by the time of the current examination.
  - There is continued debate as to whether to bring a child in for evidence collection following disclosure for 2 reasons.
    - Institutions need systems to provide round-the-clock support.
    - The best predictor for finding evidence is recent access by the accused.
- If the history, interview, observations, physical examination, and lab findings are inconsistent with a medical diagnosis of abuse, ensure that conclusions reflect that determination.
- When clarity is uncertain, it is wise to state that more information is needed or that based on the information available at the time of the evaluation abuse cannot be ruled out.
- If other risk factors were identified during the medical evaluation, mention these in the report and recommend that interventions be taken to address them.

Sexual Abuse Interviewing and Child Sex Trafficking

- Child sex trafficking victims should be interviewed according to the guidelines of trauma-informed care.[26]
- After positive identification of the trafficking victim, it is imperative that the health care provider understands the child's vulnerabilities regarding their perception of the crime. Many children do not identify as trafficking victims.

— Use of clear, developmentally precise language is imperative.

— Insensitivity and overly direct questioning may be traumatic and may cause the child to retreat into his/her experiences.

Rapport-Building

— It is important to make the child feel comfortable to build rapport with him/her.[27,28]

— Dress like a "normal person" (no white coat or badges).

— Offer a drink and/or blanket.

— Ask if the child is hungry.

— Ask about the child's feelings.

Key Questions

— For a disclosure of child sex trafficking:

— "Tell me what happened to you."

— Never say "Tell me your story." because it implies distrust.

— For no disclosure, the following questions can be modified for the child's age and developmental level[27]:

— "Tell me what brings you today."

— "Can you come and go when you want?"

— "Has anyone threatened your family or friends?"

— "Have you ever been physically harmed in any way?"

— "What are your living conditions like? Do you have a bed, room, and bathroom?"

— "Have you ever been deprived of food, water, or medical care?"

— "Is anyone forcing you to do things you do not want to do?"

— "Has anyone forced you to perform sexual acts against your will?"

— "Have you ever had to exchange sex for something you needed or wanted?"

— "Do you feel safe talking to me right now?"

— "Are there times when you don't feel safe where you live?"

— Be honest and do not make promises you cannot keep.

— Refer the child to CPS.

References

1. Substance Abuse and Mental Health Services Administration. Trauma-informed approach and trauma-specific interventions. Substance Abuse and Mental Health Services Administration Web site. https://www.samhsa.gov/nctic/trauma-interventions. Accessed May 4, 2017.
2. Jenny C, Crawford-Jakubiak JE, Christian CW, et al. The evaluation of children in the primary care setting when sexual abuse is suspected. *Pediatrics*. 2013;132(2):e558-e567.
3. Milne L, Collin-Vézina D. Disclosure of sexual abuse among youth in residential treatment care: a multiple informant comparison. *J Child Sex Abus*. 2014;23(4):398-417.
4. Lawson L, Chaffin M. False negatives in sexual abuse interviews. *J Interpers Violence*. 1992;7:532-542.
5. Faller KC. Disclosures in cases of sexual abuse. *Natl Child Advocate*. 2002;4:6-10.
6. Faller KC. The role relationship between victim and perpetrator as a predictor of characteristics of intrafamilial sexual abuse. *Child Adolesc Soc Work*. 1989;6(3):217-229.
7. Sauzier M. Disclosure of sexual abuse. for better or worse. *Psychiatr Clin North Am*. 1989;12(2):445-471.
8. Elliott DM, Briere JN. Forensic sexual abuse evaluations of older children: disclosures and symptomatology. *Behav Sci Law*. 1994;12(3):261-277.
9. Summit RC. The child sexual abuse accommodation syndrome. *Child Abuse Negl*. 1983;7(2):177-193.
10. Sorenson T, Snow B. How children tell: the process of disclosure in sexual abuse. *Child Welfare*. 1991;70(1):3-15.
11. Bauer PJ, Fivush R. Constructing event representations: building on a foundation of variation and enabling relations. *Cogn Dev*. 1992;7(3):381-401.

12. Faller KC. The characteristics of disclosure among children who may have been sexually abused. *Child Maltreat.* 1999;4(3):217-227.

13. Keary K, Fitzpatrick C. Children's disclosure of sexual abuse during formal investigations. *Child Abuse Negl.* 1994;18(7):543-548.

14. Kuehnle K. *Assessing Allegations of Child Sexual Abuse.* Sarasota, FL: Professional Resources; 1996.

15. Lamb M, Sternberg KJ, Esplin PW. Conducting investigative interview of alleged sexual abuse victims. *Child Abuse Negl.* 1998;22(8):813-823.

16. Walker AG. *Handbook on Questioning Children: A Linguistic Perspective.* Washington, DC: American Bar Association Center on Children and the Law; 1994.

17. Saywitz K, Camparo L. Interviewing child witnesses: a developmental perspective. *Child Abuse Negl.* 1998;22(8):825-843.

18. Lamb ME, Orbach Y, Hershkowitz I, Esplin PW, Horowitz D. A structured forensic interview protocol improves the quality and informativeness of investigative interviews with children: a review of research using the NICHD Investigative Interview Protocol. *Child Abuse Negl.* 2007;31(11):1201-1231.

19. Harris S. Toward a better way to interview child victims of sexual abuse. National Institute of Justice Web site. https://www.nij.gov/journals/267/pages/child-victim-interview.aspx. Accessed May 4, 2017.

20. Newlin C, Steele LC, Chamberlin A, et al. *Child Forensic Interviewing: Best Practices.* Washington, DC: US Department of Justice, Office of Justice Programs, Office of Juvenile Justice and Delinquency Programs; 2015.

21. Poole DA, Lamb ME. *Investigative Interviews of Children: A Guide for Helping Professionals.* Washington, DC: American Psychological Association; 1998.

22. Hlavka H, Olinger S, Lashley J. The use of anatomical dolls as a demonstration aid in child sexual abuse interviews: a study of forensic interviewers' perceptions. *J Child Sex Abuse.* 2010;19(5):519-553.

23. Bourg W, Broderick R, Flagor R, Kelly DM, Ervin DL, Butler J. *A Child Interviewer's Guidebook.* Thousand Oaks, CA: Sage Publications; 1999.

24. Morgan K, Dorgan K, Hayne H. Body maps do not facilitate older children's report of touch. *Scand J Psychol.* 2013;54(1):51-55.

25. Ceci S, Bruck M. *Jeopardy in the Courtroom: A Scientific Analysis of Children's Memory.* Washington, DC: American Psychological Association; 1995.

26. Reeves E. A synthesis of the literature on trauma-informed care. *Issues Ment Health Nurs.* 2015;36(9):698-709.

27. Chung RJ, English A. Commercial sexual exploitation and sex trafficking of adolescents. *Curr Opin Pediatr.* 2015;27(4):27-433.

28. Cecchet SJ, Thobum J. The psychological experience of child and adolescent sex trafficking in the United States: trauma and resilience in survivors. *Psychol Trauma.* 2014;6(5):482-493.

Chapter 12

Sexually Transmitted Diseases

Ashton Tureaud Strachan, DNP, RN, CRNP, FNP-C
Samuel Strachan, MD, FAAP
Aimee Chism Holland, DNP, WHNP-BC, FNP-C, RD
Andrew Sirotnak, MD, FAAP

General Principles

— Sexually transmitted diseases or infections (STDs/STIs) in prepubertal children or adolescents can manifest as specific complaints localized to the genitourinary tract, as incidental or unexpected examination finding or laboratory confirmation, or as a first clinical indication of sexual assault or abuse. Nonvenereal causes of vulvovaginitis are also found in children (**Table 12-1**).

— The prepubertal or preadolescent vagina differs from the adult vagina in pH, mucosa, glands, and general anatomy. These differences affect the mode of transmission, symptoms, diagnostic evaluation, and treatment for STDs (**Table 12-2**).

— Evaluate STDs in the context of clinical history and presentation. The risk of transmission and development of infection associated with abuse or assault depend on:

1. Prevalence of STDs in the general population or community
2. The type or manner of abuse or assault
3. Mode of delivery of the organism
4. Infectivity of the organism
5. The sexual development of the child or adolescent
6. The possibility of preexisting colonization or prior abuse
7. The time of the examination in relation to the abuse or assault

Table 12-1. Causes of Vulvovaginitis in Children

Cause	Infective Agent or Condition
Bacterial infections	— *Bacteroides* spp — *Corynebacterium diphtheriae* — *Enterobius vermicularis* — *Escherichia coli* — *Haemophilus influenzae* — *Haemophilus* pneumonia — *Klebsiella pneumoniae* — *Shigella sonnei* — *Staphylococcus aureus* — *Streptococcus pneumoniae* — *Streptococcus pyogenes*
Helminthic infections	— *Ascaris lumbricoides* (round worms) — *Enterobius vermicularis* (pinworms) — *Trichuris trichuria* (whipworms)
Viral infections	— *Molluscum contagiosum* — Varicella zoster (chickenpox)
Other causes	— Allergy — Chemical irritation (soaps, bubble bath) — Ectopic ureter — Foreign bodies — Lichen sclerosis et atrophicus — Mechanical irritation (tight underwear) — Poor hygiene — Rectovaginal fistula — Trauma

Adapted from Anderson B, Thimmesch I, Aardsma N, Terrell M, Carstater S, Schober J[1] *and Jenny C.*[2]

Table 12-2. Differences Between Female Adults and Female Children Affecting the Diagnosis

CHARACTERISTIC	ADULTS	CHILDREN	EFFECT ON DIAGNOSIS AND TREATMENT
Vaginal pH	< 4.5 (acidic)	6.5 to 7.5 (alkaline)	Vagina supports a different flora.
Normal vaginal flora	Lactobacilli	Gram-positive cocci and anaerobic gram-negative species are more common; flora resembles that of postmenopausal women	Cocci and gram-negative organisms can cross-react with immunofluorescent stains for *Chlamydia trachomatis*.
Vaginal mucous glands	Present	Absent	Child's vagina is probably a more hostile environment to some pathogens (eg, *Trichomonas vaginalis*) because of a lack of mucus.
Vaginal mucosa	Stratified squamous epithelium	Columnar epithelium	Pathogens such as *Neisseria gonorrhea* and *C. trachomatis* infect columnar epithelium and cause vaginitis in children and cervicitis in adults.
Vaginal length	11-12 cm	4 to 5 cm	Cuboidal mucosa closer to to the external genitalia might increase the likelihood of organisms entering the vagina without actual penile penetration.
Vaginal anatomy	Thick protective labia; elastic, distensible structure	Comparatively thin labia; rigid, nonelastic, and thin-walled vagina	Sexual penetration is probably more likely to cause bleeding and mucosa disruption in children, possibly increasing the likelihood of infection with HIV.

Adapted from Matytsina L, Greydanus D, Gurkin Y[3]*; Green KA, Zarek SM, Catherino WH*[4]*; Wald ER.*[5]

— STD evaluation in abused children considers individual sexual abuse or assault history, examination findings, and STD epidemiology specific to the community or environment of the child (**Table 12-3**).

Table 12-3. Sexual Abuse Cases With an Increased Probability of Contracting an STD
— Child has signs or symptoms of an STD or a genital infection that can be sexually transmitted.
— There is a high prevalence of STDs in the community or location where the offense occurred.
— The perpetrator is known to have an STD.
— The perpetrator is at high risk to have an STD.
— There is a history of penetration or ejaculation.
— Physical examination shows acute trauma with mucosal injury.
— Siblings or household members are either known to have an STD or signs or symptoms of an STD.

— Cultures remain the standard test for bacterial pathogens because the tests are sensitive and specific.

— Direct immune fluorescence, enzyme immunoassays (EIAs), and newer DNA amplification tests for causative organisms are not sufficiently assessed in prepubertal children and should not be used.

— Ligase chain reactions are widely used in adolescents and adults for STD screening.

— Clear recommendations for using STD screening methods in sexually abused prepubertal children are unavailable.

— Before submitting specimens for laboratory tests, ensure specimens are correctly labeled and chain of custody issues are addressed.

— Follow the American Academy of Pediatrics (AAP) and Centers for Disease Control and Prevention (CDC) guidelines for STD evaluation (**Table 12-4** and **Table 12-5**).

Table 12-4. Centers for Disease Control and Prevention Recommended Laboratory Evaluation of Sexually Abused Prepubertal Children

— Visual inspection of the body and oral, genital, and perianal areas for genital warts and ulcerative lesions

— Cultures for *Neisseria gonorrhea* from the pharynx, vagina, and anus. Cervical specimens are not recommended for prepubertal girls. A meatal specimen is adequate when penile discharge is present.*

— Cultures for *Chlamydia trachomatis* from anus and vagina. Urethral specimen in boys only if discharge is present. Pharynx cultures are not recommended because the yield is low and some laboratories cannot distinguish between *C. trachomatis* and *C. pneumoniae.*

— Wet mount and culture of vaginal swab specimen for *Trichomonas vaginalis*†

— Herpes simplex virus culture of any suspicious pharynx, vaginal, or perianal lesions

— Serology for syphilis, HIV, hepatitis Bs-Ag if risk factors or supporting epidemiological case evidence are present

— Collection of serum sample to preserve for subsequent analysis and comparison

— **Evaluation at 2-week follow-up:** If indicated or symptomatic, repeat cultures and wet mount in children who did not receive prophylactic therapy.

— **Evaluation at 12-week follow-up:** Repeat serology for syphilis, HIV, hepatitis B.

* *If initial sexual exposure is acute or recent, follow-up cultures are recommended 2 weeks later because sufficient quantities of organisms may not have developed to yield positive cultures.*

† *Significance of clue cells or other indicators of bacterial vaginosis in the absence of a vaginal discharge or as an indicator of sexual exposure in prepubertal girls is not clear.*

Adapted from Centers for Disease Control and Prevention.[6]

Table 12-5. Prophylaxis After Sexual Victimization of Preadolescent Children and Adolescents*

Sexually Transmitted Diseases	Children[7]	Adolescents[‡6]
Neisseria gonorrhoeae	For children who weigh < 45 kg, the recommended regimen is Ceftriaxone 125 mg IM single dose.[§] For children weighing ≥ 45 kg and who are ≥ 8 years old, the recommended regimen is Ceftriaxone 250 mg IM single dose[§] ***PLUS*** Azithromycin 1 g PO single dose.	Ceftriaxone 250 mg IM single dose ***PLUS*** Azithromycin 1 g PO single dose ***OR*** Cefixime 400 mg PO single dose§ ***PLUS*** Azithromycin 1 g PO single dose
Chlamydia trachomatis	For children who weigh < 45 kg, the recommended regimen is Erythromycin 50 mg/kg per day, divided into 4 doses for 10 to 14 days. For children weighing > 45 kg who are younger than 8 years old, the recommended regimen is Azithromycin 1 g PO single dose. ***OR*** Doxycycline 100 mg twice daily for 7 days.	Azithromycin 1 g PO single dose ***OR*** Doxycycline 100 mg twice daily for 7 days
Trichomoniasis and bacterial vaginosis	Metronidazole 2 g PO single dose	Metronidazole 2 g PO single dose ***OR*** Tinidazole 2 g PO single dose

(continued)

Table 12-5. Prophylaxis After Sexual Victimization of Preadolescent Children and Adolescents* *(continued)*

Sexually Transmitted Diseases	Children[7]	Adolescents[‡6]
Prevention of hepatitis B virus infection	Begin or complete the hepatitis B virus immunization, if not fully immunized.	Hepatitis B virus immunization at time of initial examination, if not fully immunized, and completion of the second dose 4 weeks after the first dose and the third dose 5 months after the second dose. If sexual partner has acute HBV infection, HBIg 0.06 mL/kg IM should be given, as well.
Human immunodeficiency virus (HIV)	Consider offering post exposure prophylaxis (PEP) for HIV, depending on circumstances and risk factors for HIV. Consult infectious disease specialist.	Consider offering post exposure prophylaxis (PEP) for HIV, depending on circumstances and risk factors for HIV. Consult infectious disease specialist.
Human papillomavirus (HPV)	HPV immunization at time of initial examination, if not fully immunized and the child is greater than 9 years old. Completion of the second dose 2 months after the first dose and the third dose 4 months after the second dose (ie, 6 months after the first dose).	HPV immunization at time of initial examination, if not fully immunized, and completion of the second dose 2 months after the first dose and the third dose 4 months after the second dose (ie, 6 months after the first dose).

**Drug dosage recommendations listed herein are those of the authors and are not endorsed by the US Public Health Service or the US Department of Health and Human Services.*

†*Consider emergency contraception and administration of emergency and contraceptive pills and antiemetic.*

§N. gonorrhoeae *has shown increasing resistance to single-dose oral cefixime administration and as such should not be considered first-line therapy unless IM ceftriaxone is not available.*[8]

Adapted from Green K, Zarek S, Catherino W[4]*; Centers for Disease Control and Prevention*[6]*; American Academy of Pediatrics.*[7]

— Use an experienced reference laboratory and be familiar with the laboratory's procedures for culture and confirmatory testing. Know which tests may be referred to other laboratories for completion.

— Know the local, state, or public health laboratory or department that tracks the community epidemiology of STDs and other reportable diseases.

— Prophylactic antibiotic treatment is usually not recommended for prepubertal children because the infection rates are low and typically symptomatic.

— Offer adolescents screening for acute sexual assault STD prophylaxis, HIV post-exposure prophylactic (PEP) therapy, and counseling about pregnancy, if needed (see **Table 12-5**).

— Perform only tests that appear medically necessary and minimize physical and emotional trauma.

Bacterial STDs

Gonorrhea

— Gonorrhea is the second most common STD.[6]

— This STD is caused by the gram-negative intracellular, oxidase-positive diplococcus *Neisseria gonorrhoeae* (**Figure 12-1**). The organism is fragile, will not grow without proper culturing, and infects only humans. It infects columnar and pseudostratified epithelia, causing endocervical infections in adolescents and adults. Lack of endocervical glands in a prepubertal child makes ascending infection and cervical infection rare.

Clinical Presentation

— Isolating *N. gonorrhoeae* in a culture from a prepubertal child indicates sexual abuse.[7]

— Finding gonorrhea in children is diagnostic for sexual abuse (**Figure 12-2**).

— Resistant strands of *N. gonorrhoeae* may exist, thus making treatment complicated.[6]

— A confirmed positive test result for a culture must be reported to authorities for investigation, even if the child does not disclose sexual abuse.

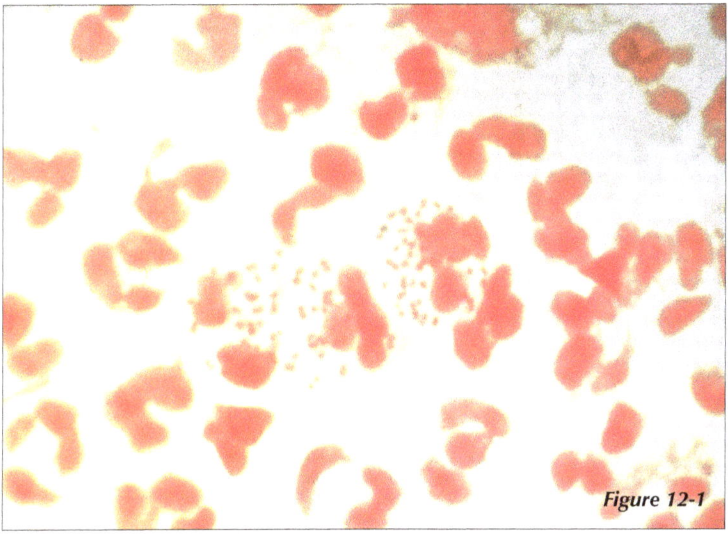

Figure 12-1. *Intracellular gram-negative diplococcus of* Neisseria gonorrhoeae.

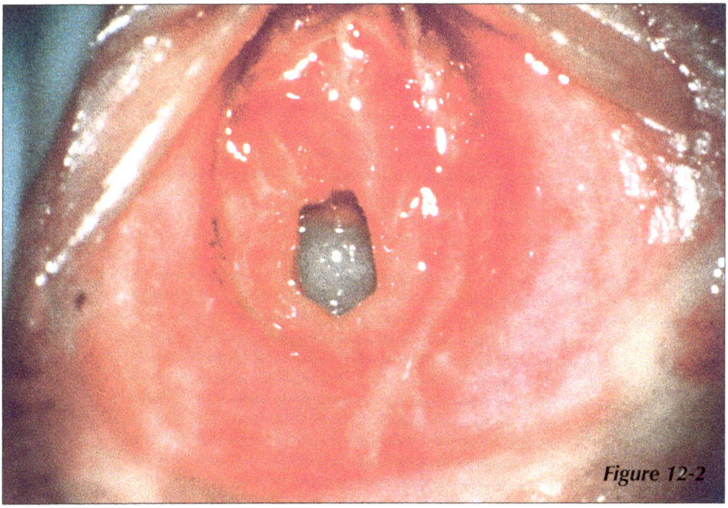

Figure 12-2. *Vaginal discharge in a 6-year-old girl who disclosed attempted penile penetration with ejaculation. Culture positive for* Neisseria gonorrhoeae.

— The incubation period of a gonorrhea culture is about 1 week.

— Gonorrhea may be asymptomatic or present as urethritis, vulvovaginitis, cervicitis, pelvic inflammatory disease (PID), proctitis, pharyngitis, or epididymitis.

— Bacteremic spread to secondary sites in adolescents and adults can cause arthritis, myocarditis, perihepatitis, dermatitis, meningitis, or endocarditis.

— Prepubertal children and adolescents may be asymptomatic with pharyngitis, but vulvovaginal and penile infections are usually symptomatic, with discharge, perineal pruritus, dysuria, urethritis, or proctitis symptoms in males.[7]

— Infection at more than one site is common. In female patients, both vaginal and rectal cultures will often test positive.

Laboratory Diagnosis

— The AAP recommends tests when epidemiologically indicated or when the history or physical findings suggest the possibility of oral, genital, or rectal contact.[7]

— Take samples for bacterial cultures from boys based on the clinical history and disclosure of sexual abuse.

— Accurate diagnosis of gonorrhea depends on culture using a gonococcal selective media, with confirmatory tests to properly identify *N. gonorrhoeae* and prevent misidentification of other organisms.

Treatment

(See **Table 12-5**.)

Chlamydia

— Chlamydia, caused by *Chlamydia trachomatis*, is the most common bacterial STD in the United States. Chlamydia infections may pose several consequences, such as PID, infertility, transmission to newborns, and coinfection with other STDs.[6]

1. *C. trachomatis* is an obligate intracellular organism with multiple serotypes and must be grown in a live tissue culture (**Figure 12-3**).

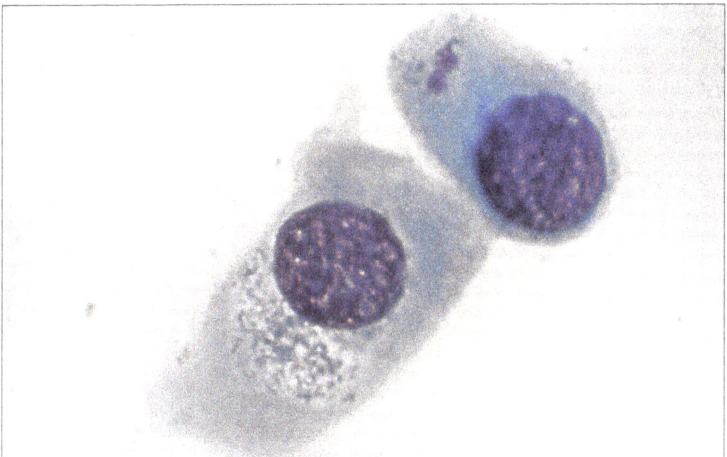

Figure 12-3

Figure 12-3. *Intracellular bodies of* Chlamydia trachomatis *seen on Giemsa stain before fluorescein antibody staining.*

2. Serotypes L1, L2, and L3 cause lymphogranuloma venereum (LGV) and are more frequently found in cases of men who have sex with men (MSM). Serotypes D through K cause conjunctivitis, pneumonia, urethritis, cervicitis, vaginitis, and salpingitis.[9]

3. Direct contact with an infected individual is required. No cases of fomite transmission have been reported.

— Chlamydia is most frequent among minority women, especially adolescents.[6] It is not very prevalent among sexually abused children.[1]

Clinical Presentation

— Infections in children can be perinatally acquired. Risk of transmission is 50%. Infections affect the conjunctiva, nasopharynx, rectum, and vagina.

— Neonatal conjunctivitis is the most common clinical presentation.[6]

— Colonization of the vagina and rectum that is acquired at birth can last for up to 3 years.[6]

— Adult females usually have cervicitis, but asymptomatic infections are common. Mucopurulent discharge may be present. Urethritis can develop in men or women, but men may not have discharge or symptoms.

— Adult complications include PID, salpingitis, perihepatitis, endometritis, epididymitis, proctitis, Reiter's syndrome, infertility, and sterility.

— Routine diagnosis of chlamydia in children is based on sexual abuse history, physical examination, and laboratory tests can be difficult in children.

1. Consider preexisting infection in very young children.
2. Most children have no symptoms or discharge, although discharge may be seen in prepubertal girls (**Figure 12-4**).
3. Coinfection with *N. gonorrhoeae* and multisite infection with chlamydia is common in adolescents and adults but is also found in prepubertal children.[6]

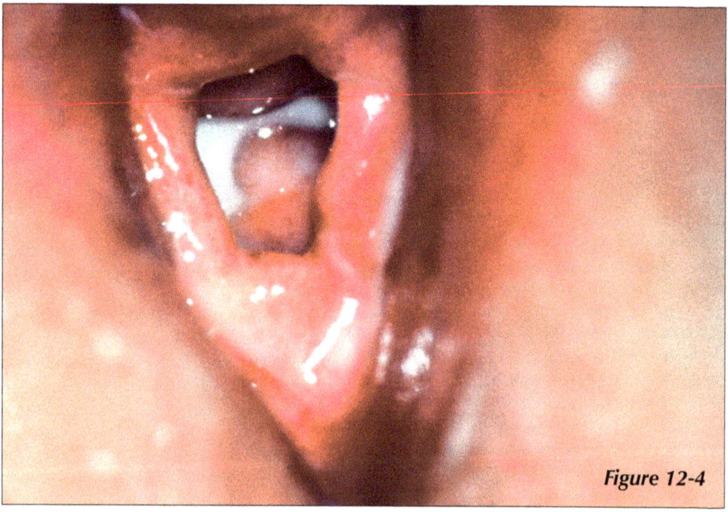

Figure 12-4. *Vaginitis with purulent discharge caused by* Chlamydia trachomatis *in a prepubertal girl with no disclosure of sexual abuse.*

Laboratory Diagnosis

— In pediatric cases, proper handling of specimens and use of standard culture techniques are essential to recovering the organism in children.

— Nucleic acid amplification test (NAAT) may be used to detect chlamydia in urine and vaginal specimens in young females. For young male patients, a culture is still the preferred method for testing. In both male and female patients, cultures are preferred for extragenital site testing.[6,10]

1. Use proper transport media with either polyester or calcium alginate swabs.
2. Be vigilant about the laboratory procedures followed when a specimen is submitted.

Treatment

(See **Table 12-5**.)

Syphilis

— Children can be infected with *Treponema pallidum* in utero or it can be acquired through direct contact with syphilis sores. Congenital syphilis, transmitted transplacentally, is far more common in children than acquired syphilis, which is almost always transmitted from abuse by an infected adult.

— Primary and secondary syphilis rates are highest among African American, non-Hispanic individuals and males compared to females.[7]

— Syphilis may be the sole indicator of sexual abuse in cases where it is acquired.[7]

Clinical Presentation

— *T. pallidum* is a spirochetal organism with an incubation period of about 3 weeks. Primary and secondary stages occur in children. Adults are more likely to progress to tertiary and latent phases.

— Primary syphilis manifests as a macule that evolves into a papule, which then erodes with a sharply defined border (**Figure 12-5**).

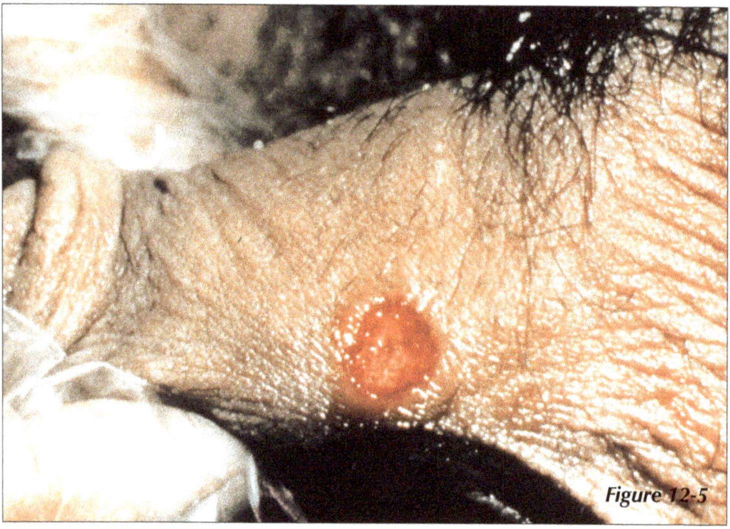

Figure 12-5. *Primary syphilis chancre in an adolescent male.*

1. The lesion contains serous material and is infectious.
2. The chancre is painless and is associated with nonsuppurative regional adenopathy. It heals without therapy in 3 to 8 weeks.
3. In children, these lesions may be mistaken for anal fissures or cellulitis.[7]

— Secondary syphilis can occur in children who live in areas of high disease prevalence and are not treated during primary syphilis. It develops about 4 to 8 weeks after the chancre appears.[7]

1. Lesions include:
   a. A nonpruritic maculopapular rash on the palms and soles (**Figure 12-6**).
   b. Classic flat-surfaced or raised perianal lesions (condyloma lata).
   c. Mucosal lesions and enlarged nontender lymph nodes.[6,7]
2. Skin lesions contain the organism and are a source of spread of the infection.
3. Alopecia, periostitis, hepatomegaly, and acute glomerulonephritis can occur.[7]

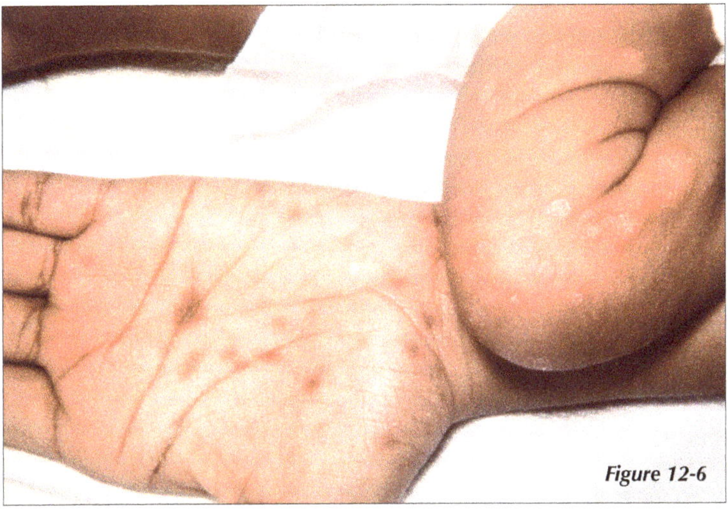

Figure 12-6. *Palmar rash seen in secondary syphilis in this child's mother. (Photograph courtesy of Louis M. Bell, MD; Philadelphia, PA.)*

— Tertiary syphilis refers to cardiac, neurological, ophthalmic, and auditory involvement as well as the gummatous lesion.

— Latent syphilis refers to those periods after infection when patients are seropositive but demonstrate no other evidence of disease.

Laboratory Diagnosis

— Use of selective criteria for testing is prudent and cost-effective.

1. Because syphilis can infect and potentially kill a developing fetus, the CDC recommends that all pregnant women be screened at the first prenatal visit.[11]
2. The definitive diagnosis for syphilis is made by the presence of spirochete lesions on microscopic darkfield examination on exudate, discharge, or tissue sample and serologic testing.[7]
3. Blood tests, such as the venereal disease research laboratory (VDRL) or rapid plasma reagin (RPR) may be used but run the risk for false negative in early primary or late acquired syphilis.[7]
4. Criteria for performing selective screening for children are listed in **Table 12-6**.

Table 12-6. Criteria for Selective Screening for Syphilis in Children
— Children with evidence of other STDs — Children with a history of unusual exanthema or genital or perianal lesions — Children with a parent, family member, or perpetrator with syphilis or HIV infection — Children living in an area where there is a high incidence of adult disease — Adolescent victims and those who are sexually active — Foreign-born children — Children who may have been inadequately treated for congenital syphilis

— Other causes of false positive result rates are low but occur in patients with viral infections, atopic dermatitis, pneumonia, connective tissue disease, tuberculosis, and endocarditis.

— Perform specific treponemal tests to confirm results.

1. Tests include the fluorescent treponemal antibody absorption (FTA-ABS) test and the microhemagglutination assay-*T. pallidum* (MHA-TP).
2. The FTA-ABS and MHA-TP tests remain positive for life.

— For children diagnosed with syphilis after the newborn period, perform a cerebrospinal fluid (CSF) test for neurosyphilis and consult an infectious disease specialist.

Treatment

— For acquired syphilis (including primary disease) and secondary syphilis in early stages, treat with benzathine penicillin G 50 000 units/kg intramuscularly (IM), up to the adult dose of 2.4 million units in a single dose.

— It is recommended in those with a penicillin allergy to undergo skin testing and desensitization and receive treatment.[7,11]

— Children allergic to penicillin and nonpregnant adolescents should follow a regimen of doxycycline 100 mg orally twice a day for 2 weeks or tetracycline 500 mg orally 4 times a day for 2 weeks.

— In individuals that use the nonpreferred treatment of penicillin, close follow-up should be performed to ensure adequate treatment.[7]

— Based on high rates of treatment failure and increased risk of neurological complications, the CDC recommends prolonged treatment with benzathine penicillin G for HIV-infected individuals with syphilis.[11]

Bacterial Vaginosis

— Bacterial vaginosis (BV) is the most frequent cause of vaginitis discharge in adults.

— BV can be diagnosed in children but is not a clear indicator of sexual activity or abuse.

— BV has morbidity implications in pregnant women.

— BV is characterized by decreased hydrogen peroxide–producing lactobacilli and increased anaerobes (*Prevotella* spp, *Mobiluncus* spp, *Bacteroides* spp, *Gardnerella vaginalis*, and *Mycoplasma hominis*).[7]

— Females with BV should be evaluated for other STDs, and ensure up-to-date status on the HPV and Hepatitis B vaccinations.[7]

— *Gardnerella vaginalis* is not a diagnostic marker of sexual activity or abuse. If diagnosed, perform an evaluation.

— The clinical significance of finding *G. vaginalis* in males is unclear. Treating male sex partners of infected adult women does not prevent recurrence of BV.[7]

Clinical Presentation and Laboratory Diagnosis

BV usually manifests as a foul-smelling, thin, whitish/gray, noninflammatory discharge (**Figure 12-7**). Diagnostic testing includes:

1. ***KOH Whiff test.*** The pH is > 4.5, and a fishy odor is present before or after adding 10% potassium hydroxide (KOH).
2. ***Wet mount testing.*** Clue cells (granulated epithelial cells studded with small coccobacilli) are noted microscopically.

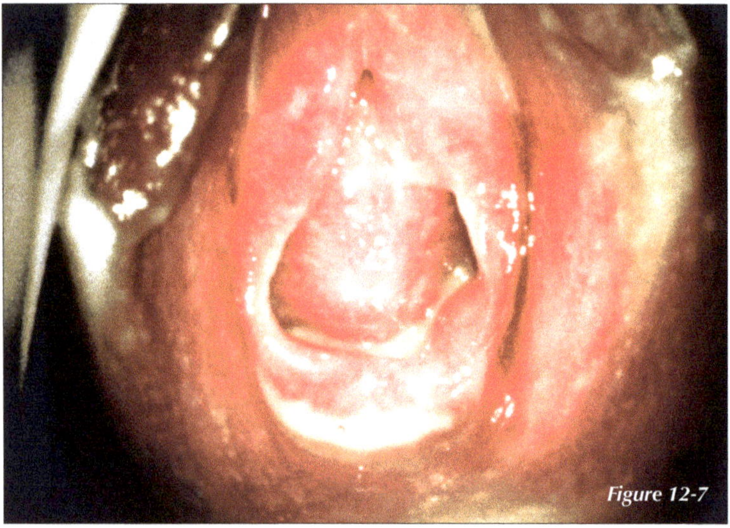

Figure 12-7. *Profuse, thin, gray discharge in a 7-year-old girl with bacterial vaginosis.*

Treatment

(See **Table 12-5**.)

Trichomonas

— *Trichomonas vaginalis* is a flagellated protozoan that causes trichomoniasis.

— *Trichomonas*, BV, chlamydia, and gonorrhea are common STDs transmitted after sexual assault.[12]

— For those individuals with HIV, an increased risk of PID is associated with concurrent infections of trichomoniasis, or BV.[7]

Clinical Presentation

— Adult women characteristically have a diffuse, malodorous, yellow-green, or frothy discharge and vulvovaginal irritation. On examination, females may also have a "strawberry cervix."[6]

— Most males are asymptomatic but have symptoms of urethritis. Untreated infections can progress to salpingitis or prostatitis in males.

— Perinatal infections are usually found in urine samples of infants and can persist for up to 1 year if untreated.

— After infancy, finding *T. vaginalis* in prepubertal and nonsexually active girls strongly suggests sexual abuse.[7]

— No cases of fomite transmission have been reported.

Laboratory Diagnosis

— *T. vaginalis* is a motile protozoan (**Figure 12-8**), but subjective analysis of a wet mount microscope slide is relatively insensitive. NAAT is encouraged if Trichomonas is not identified on a wet mount.[13]

— Adult patients with clinical presentations that are consistent with trichomonas infections typically receive standard treatment based on that suspicion.

— *Trichomonas hominis*, a commensal species, is a bowel organism that can be misdiagnosed as *T. vaginalis* but can be differentiated by an experienced laboratory technician by the length of the undulating membrane. *Trichomonas tenax* is a related species associated with oral gingivitis.

Treatment

(See **Table 12-5**.)

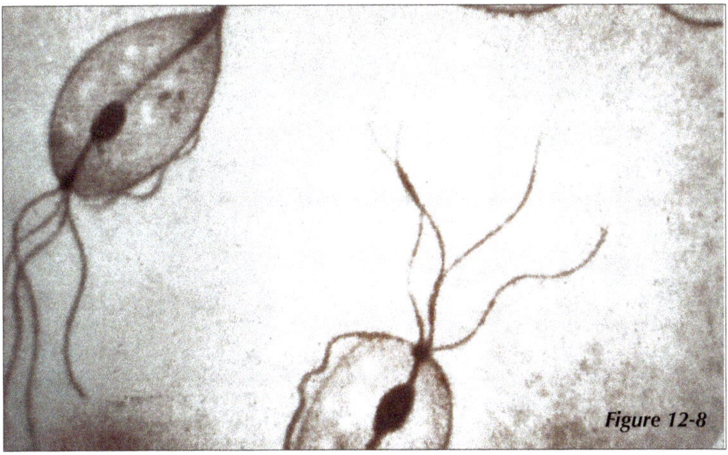

Figure 12-8. *The flagellated protozoan* Trichomonas vaginalis.

Genital Mycoplasmas

— In adults, colonization or asymptomatic infections with genital mycoplasmas correlate with sexual activity.

— Adults have both asymptomatic colonization and genitourinary tract infections.[14]

— Colonization with both *Mycoplasma hominis* and *Ureaplasma urealyticum* is not a significant marker for sexual abuse in children.[13]

— *Mycoplasma genitalium* has been linked in male urethritis and is consistently found more often in females with PID than non-PID females.[6]

— Currently no diagnostic test has been cleared by the FDA for testing of *M. genitalium*.[6]

— The lack of a cell wall makes beta-lactam antibiotics an ineffective treatment option. Antibiotics of choice are macrolides, tetracyclines, and fluoroquinolones.[15] Curative management will generally occur when treating urethritis, cervicitis, or PID.[6]

Other Uncommon Bacterial Sexually Transmitted Diseases

— Chancroid:

1. Chancroid is endemic in some regions of Africa, but very few cases are found in the United States.
2. The disease is caused by *Haemophilus ducreyi*, spread by direct contact with an infected source, and diagnosed clinically by painful genital ulcers and inguinal adenopathy.
3. Identification on specific culture media is approximately 75%.[16] Polymerase chain reaction (PCR) assays provide specific diagnosis but the testing is not available in most laboratories.
4. Chancroid is an important cofactor for HIV transmission, and up to 10% of patients are coinfected with syphilis or herpes simplex virus (HSV).[6]
5. Treatment for adults is azithromycin 1 g oral single dose; ceftriaxone 250 mg IM single dose; ciprofloxacin (18 years and older) 500 g orally twice daily for 3 days; or erythromycin base 500 mg orally 4 times daily for 7 days.

6. Single-dose, directly observed therapy is preferred.
7. The evidence of a chancroid in an infant or child is strong evidence for sexual abuse.

— Granuloma inguinale (donovanosis):

1. Granuloma inguinale is a rare disease caused by the intracellular gram-negative *Klebsiella granulomatis* (formerly known as *Calymmatobacterium granulomatosis*). It is endemic to some tropical countries.[7]
2. Painless, beef-red, vascular genital ulcers bleed on contact.[7]
3. Culture is difficult. Seeing dark-stained intracytoplasmic Donovan bodies on tissue biopsy confirms the diagnosis. Culture lesion for *H. ducreyi* to rule out chancroid.
4. Long-term treatment is needed to heal the ulcers; relapse is common and treatment should continue until all lesions are healed.
5. The preferred treatment is doxycycline 100 mg orally twice a day for a minimum of 3 weeks. Alternatively, trimethoprim-sulfamethoxazole (1 double-strength tablet orally twice a day for a minimum of 3 weeks), ciprofloxacin (750 mg twice a day for a minimum of 3 weeks), or erythromycin (base 500 mg orally 4 times a day for a minimum of 3 weeks) may be used.[6,7]

— Lymphogranuloma venereum:

1. Lymphogranuloma venereum is a rare disease in the United States caused by the invasive serovars L1, L2, and L3 subtypes of *C. trachomatis*.
2. Self-limited genital or anal ulcers develop at the infection site in 3 to 12 days, with a clinical presentation of tender unilateral inguinal or femoral lymphadenopathy after 2 to 6 weeks.
3. Homosexual men may have proctocolitis or inflammation of the perirectal and perianal lymphatic tissues. Fissures and strictures in these areas can occur.[6]
4. Diagnosis is made by exclusion of other causes of genital ulcers and inguinal adenopathy and serology for LGV.

5. Treatment involves aspiration of buboes to prevent ulcers, which may cause scarring. Doxycycline 100 mg orally twice a day for 3 weeks or erythromycin base 500 mg orally 4 times a day for 3 weeks is needed.

Viral Sexually Transmitted Diseases

Human Immunodeficiency Virus Infection and Acquired Immunodeficiency Syndrome

— Infection is caused by the human RNA retrovirus HIV type 1, which is more common worldwide, or HIV type 2, which is more common in West Africa.[16]

— It is recommended that infants born to HIV-infected mothers be tested at birth, 2 to 3 weeks, 1 to 2 months, and 4 to 6 months of age. A final antibody test at 12 to 18 months can reassure the clearance of maternal antibodies.[17]

— It is estimated that nearly 20% of untreated HIV-infected children die before age 4.[6]

— The World Health Organization (WHO) recommends initiating antiretroviral therapy (ART) in all infants, children, and adolescents who have HIV.[18]

— Acquired immunodeficiency syndrome (AIDS) in children and adolescents ranges from symptomatic HIV-seropositive status to an immunocompromised host at risk for opportunistic infections.

— Common clinical findings include fever, lymphadenopathy, sore throat, rash, hepatosplenomegaly, parotitis, progressive neurological disease, recurrent diarrhea, and malignancies.[6]

— Side effects of antiretroviral drug therapies complicate chronic care for children with AIDS.

— **Table 12-7** lists the most common AIDS-defining conditions in children.

Laboratory Diagnosis

— Routine standard of care in pediatric HIV is serologic testing (EIA), HIV PCR, HIV viral load, and HIV cultures.

— Monitor circulating CD4 lymphocyte count and CD4 to T-suppressor CD8 cell ratios and correlate with course of infection and treatment.

Table 12-7. AIDS-Defining Conditions Most Commonly Reported to the CDC for Children Older Than 13 Years

— Bacterial infections (multiple or recurrent)
— Candidiasis of bronchi, trachea, lungs, or esophagus
— Cervical cancer (invasive)
— Coccidioidomycosis (disseminated or extrapulmonary)
— Cryptococcosis (extrapulmonary)
— Cryptosporidiosis [chronic intestinal (>1 month's duration)]
— Cytomegalovirus retinitis (with loss of vision)
— Encephalopathy (HIV-related)
— Herpes simplex: chronic ulcers (>1 month's duration) or bronchitis, pneumonitis, or esophagitis (onset at age >1 month)
— Histoplasmosis (disseminated or extrapulmonary)
— Isosporiasis [chronic intestinal (>1 month's duration)]
— Kaposi sarcoma
— Lymphoid interstitial pneumonia or pulmonary lymphoid hyperplasia complex
— Lymphoma (Burkitt, immunoblastic, primary of brain)
— Mycobacterium avium complex or *Mycobacterium kansasii* (disseminated or extrapulmonary)
— Mycobacterium tuberculosis of any site (pulmonary, disseminated, or extrapulmonary)
— Mycobacterium (other species or unidentified species; disseminated or extrapulmonary)
— *Pneumocystis jirovecii* pneumonia
— Pneumonia (recurrent)
— Progressive multifocal leukoencephalopathy
— Salmonella septicemia (recurrent)
— Wasting syndrome attributed to HIV

Reprinted from Centers for Disease Control and Prevention.[19]

— Repeat testing at 3, 6, 12, and possibly at 18 months; symptoms can be delayed. Consult the CDC Revised Surveillance Case Definition for HIV.[7,17]

— Testing children who are being evaluated for sexual abuse or assault may require informed consent by state and local law as well as hospital regulations.

1. Maintain confidentiality in all cases.
2. Legal issues may complicate the testing of suspected perpetrators of sexual assault.

— **Table 12-8** lists risk factors for transmission of HIV to the pediatric victim; use this to decide who should be tested for HIV.[7]

1. Review all cases of sexual abuse or acute sexual assault for these risk factors.
2. Consider testing the victim after careful discussion with the child and parent or guardian (**Table 12-9**).

Table 12-8. Risk Factors for Hepatitis B and HIV Transmission in Child Sexual Abuse or Assault
— Sexual contact that is physically traumatic, impairs mucosal barrier integrity (oral, vaginal, or anal receptive intercourse), or is without condom protection
— Genital or oral mucosal lesions, ulcers, bleeding
— Promiscuous sexual activity or prostitution
— Illicit drug use that can impair judgement or lower threshold for sexual aggression
— Intravenous drug use or sharing needles
— Social risk factors (eg, poverty, alcoholism, transient adults in the home environment, developmentally delayed or handicapped child, mentally ill caregiver or guardian)

Adapted from Sirotnak.[20]

Table 12-9. Suggested Guidelines for HIV Transmission Testing in Child Sexual Abuse or Assault

SITUATION IN WHICH TO ENCOURAGE OR PURSUE HIV TESTING IN A CHILD OR ADOLESCENT

— Child has signs or symptoms of HIV/AIDS infection.

— Child has another sexually transmitted disease.

— Parent or guardian is anxious and requests testing even if patient is at low risk for infection.

— Patient requests HIV testing.

— There is a confirmed or suspected sexual contact that is physically traumatic, impairs mucosal barrier integrity (oral, vaginal, or anal receptive intercourse), or is without condom protection.*

— Evidence of foreign body fluid is found on examination (semen, blood, saliva).

— Alleged assailant is HIV seropositive or has a clinical profile consistent with HIV/AIDS infection, such as having a disease or condition common in an immunocompromised host (eg, tuberculosis).

— There are multiple alleged assailants or a single unknown assailant.

— Alleged assailant is at risk of being infected with HIV.

COMMON RISK FACTORS

— Engaging in intravenous drug use, especially if sharing needles or equipment

— Engaging in sex for money or drugs

— Promiscuity or multiple sex partners

— Engaging in male-male sexual activity, especially if without condom protection

— Having received blood transfusion or blood products before mandatory blood testing for HIV began

— Having sex or sharing intravenous drug needles or equipment with any individual who may have engaged in any of the above

— Having other sexually transmitted disease(s)

**The disclosure of the victim should not be used as a criterion alone when considering testing because of the possibility of incomplete disclosure, which is common in children, or omission of information by a victim.*

Treatment

— Offer antiretroviral therapy to HIV-infected children. Initiation depends on various clinical, immunological, and virological criteria.[6,21] Consult infectious disease specialists.

— **Table 12-10** lists the estimated risk of transmission of HIV per episode and type of exposure.[22,23]

Table 12-10. Estimated Likelihood of HIV Transmission During Unprotected Sex or Contaminated Needle Exposure When the Source Is HIV Infected

Exposure	Likelihood of Transmission (per 10 000 exposures)
Receptive anal intercourse	10 to 30
Receptive vaginal intercourse	8 to 20
Needle-sharing injection	67
Percutaneous (healthcare workers)	30
Insertive anal intercourse	3
Insertive vaginal intercourse	3 to 9

Adapted from Bamberger JD, Waldo CR, Gerberding JL, Katz MH.[22]

— With appropriate diagnostic testing and timely treatment, clinical symptoms of HIV-1 and occurrence of AIDS-defining illnesses now are rare among children in the United States and other industrialized countries. The number of reported pediatric AIDS cases has decreased significantly since the mid-1990s, primarily as a result of prevention of mother-to-child transmission of HIV.[7]

— Use postexposure antiretroviral prophylaxis (PEP) according to a careful assessment of the details of the assault, the risk factors for HIV, the availability of consultation guidance for the clinician and support services for the victim, and the level of patient compliance.

Herpes Simplex Virus

— Genital herpes is caused by infection with HSV, a double-stranded, enveloped DNA virus with 2 subtypes (HSV-1 and HSV-2).

1. Infections with HSV-1 usually involve the oral mucosa, face, and skin above the waist.
2. Infections with HSV-2 usually involve the genitalia, perineum, and skin below the waist through sexual transmission (**Figure 12-9**). However, an increase in the number of HSV-1 infections in the anogenital area has been observed.[6,7]
3. Many individuals infected with HSV-2 are undiagnosed and may spread the virus unknowingly.[6]
4. Fomite transmission in children is unproved.
5. In cases of neonatal transmission of HSV, nearly 85% are a result of perinatal transmission, and 10% are of postnatal cause.[24]

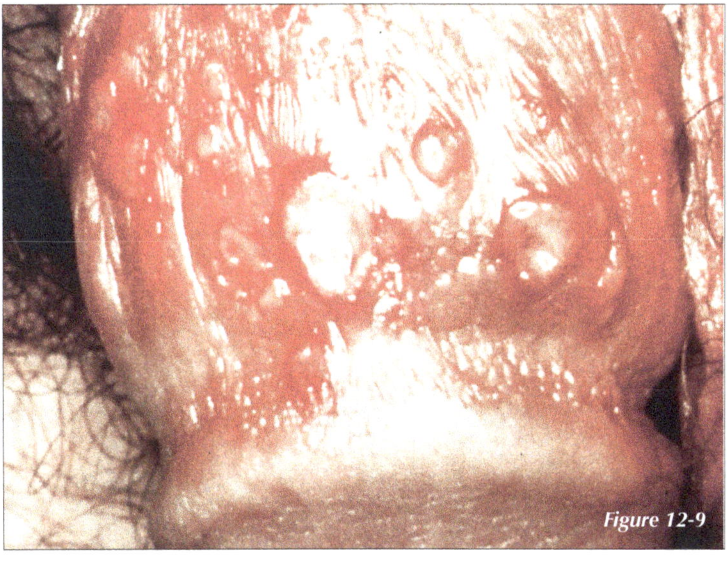

Figure 12-9. *Primary herpes in a male. (Photograph courtesy of Centers for Disease Control and Prevention; Atlanta, GA.)*

Clinical Presentation

— HSV is transmitted by close contact with an infected individual.

— The incubation period is 2 days to 2 weeks.[7]

— After the neonatal period, the HSV infection can be seen as localized skin or eye disease, localized or disseminated central nervous system disease, or fulminant multisystem organ disease.[25]

— HSV in childhood is primarily a localized disease.

1. HSV-1 usually results from contact with infected oral lesions or secretions that can be autoinoculated to other sites. It is frequently transmitted by infected persons who are asymptomatic shedders.
2. HSV-2 infection of the genitalia and perianal areas usually results from sexual contact.
3. Transmission by sexual contact is the most common source of genital herpes,[26] but autoinoculation from an oral source in children is also documented.

— The actual risk of acquiring HSV after assault is unknown.[27]

— Childhood herpes usually presents as gingivostomatitis, with painful vascular lesions of the lips, oral mucosa, and pharynx. Spread to the skin of the face and other areas, eyes, and fingers may occur (**Figure 12-10**).[7]

1. HSV may also precipitate erythema multiforme.
2. Genital lesions manifest in children as in adults, with itching and swelling followed by painful vesicles that develop and ulcerate in several days. Vesicles often group pathognomonically together.
3. Lesions are usually seen on the vulva, vagina, cervix, penis, scrotum, rectum, and anus. Severe perianal infections are associated with pain, bloody discharge, and fever.[26]
4. Primary infections last 10 to 21 days.

— Severe localized lesions and disseminated HSV infection, especially involving the central nervous system, occur in immunocompromised hosts and can be life threatening or fatal.

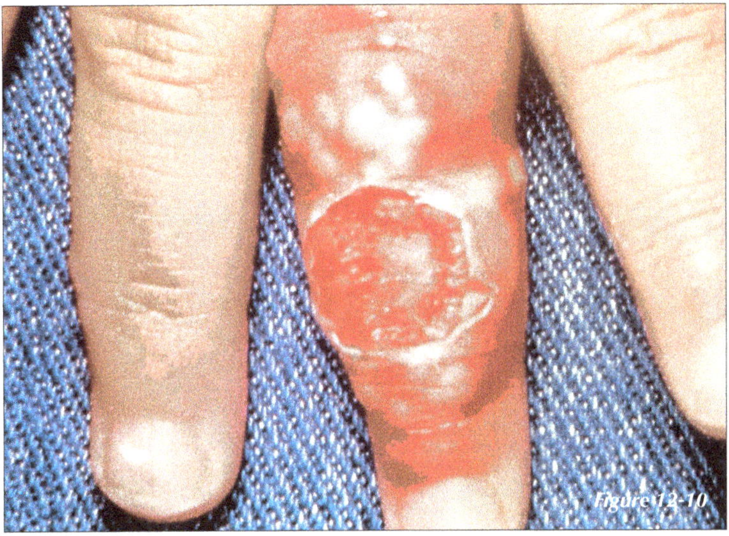

Figure 12-10. *Herpetic whitlow in a toddler with HSV-1 gingivostomatitis who chewed her finger.*

— Recurrence of genital HSV usually manifests with milder symptoms, less viral shedding, and less severe vesicular lesions on the penis, scrotum, vulva, cervix, and perianal area.

Laboratory Diagnosis

— Testing is done based on culture of suggestive lesions. Cytopathic changes usually occur within 3 days of tissue culture inoculation.

— For confirmatory testing, include fluorescent antibody staining and enzyme immunoassays.

1. Rapid diagnostic tests are as specific as culture but not as sensitive, and they are not appropriate for use as the primary diagnostic method.
2. PCR is a very sensitive tool for identifying HSV DNA, especially in CSF, but does not identify the type.[28]
3. PCR and viral cultures should be typed to determine which strand of HSV is the causative agent.[6]

4. Typing may be helpful in cases where the perpetrator is identified with herpes.

5. Serum may be obtained late in the disease course or recurrent infection may boost precipitating titers.

Treatment

— When oral acyclovir therapy is started within 6 days of the onset of disease, the duration of illness and viral shedding is shortened by 3 to 5 days. Valacyclovir and famciclovir are effective in adults, but neither is approved for children.

— Treatment guidelines for children with genital herpes are not available.

1. The AAP recommends acyclovir 40 to 80 mg/kg per day divided in 3 or 4 doses for 5 to 10 days (maximum 1 g/day) for primary genital herpes.

2. The dose for recurrent genital and cutaneous or ocular herpes is 1000 to 1200 mg/day in 3 to 5 divided doses for 5 days and must be started within 2 days of symptom onset to be of benefit.

3. Chronic suppressive therapy may employ lower doses but may not be beneficial.

4. Topical acyclovir (5%) ointment does not shorten the duration of symptoms or viral shedding.

5. Prophylaxis for HSV and treatment of localized, progressive, or disseminated HSV (varicella) in an immunocompromised host requires higher doses and longer terms of therapy.[6]

Human Papillomavirus

— Human papillomavirus is the most common viral STD, resulting in most sexually active individuals becoming infected at least once in their lifetime.[6]

— Most HPV infections are self-limiting and resolve without symptoms.

— HIV-seropositive men and women may have both severe human papillomavirus (HPV) infection and a higher prevalence of precancerous cervical lesions.[6]

— Over 100 types of HPV are known, with just under half infecting the genital area.[6]

— HPV infects epithelial cells, which undergo transformation and proliferation.

— Transmission is by direct contact with infected skin or mucous membranes.

1. Sexual transmission of anogenital warts in children has been demonstrated.
2. Because HPV is also perinatally transmitted, there is an inherent difficulty evaluating the source of infection in a very young child with warts.

— Perinatally acquired HPV occurs, but lesions may not develop until months after the initial exposure.

— The exact incubation period for HPV in infants after perinatal exposure is not known but is estimated to be at least several months.

— HPV lesions in infants and young children may resolve spontaneously and then reappear, making it hard to determine exactly when the actual HPV exposure occurred.

— Nonsexual transmission by autoinoculation, direct contact to the genital and perianal area, can result in the spread of lesions.[7]

— There is no increased incidence of anogenital warts in a child or family with common warts.[29]

— Before sexual abuse or assault is ruled out, perform a careful family, social, and medical history, especially if children are preverbal and cannot be interviewed concerning abuse.

— Children beyond infancy but prepubertal that present with anogenital lesions should be examined for sexual abuse.

— Evaluating an older child or adolescent for sexual abuse or assault includes a careful visual inspection of oral, genital, and anal mucosa for HPV lesions.

— Consider HPV vaccination in children of appropriate age range.

Clinical Presentation

— Make the diagnosis visually.

1. The classic condylomata acuminata lesions are soft, irregular, flesh-colored growths. They can be typical flat lesions or friable, soft exophytic lesions. They can range from millimeters to several centimeters with a cauliflower-like appearance (**Figure 12-11**).[7]
2. Penile (frenulum, coronal sulcus, and meatus) and scrotal lesions can be raised or flat and have either white or pigmented macules.
3. Females have similar lesions on the labia and vagina.
4. Lesions on the anus, rectum, and perianal areas occur in both sexes and can present with burning, local pain, itching, and bleeding (**Figure 12-12**).[7]
5. Anoscopy may be needed to diagnose internal lesions, which are found more often in patients who have had receptive anal intercourse.
6. Secondary ulceration and infection can occur, especially in young children.

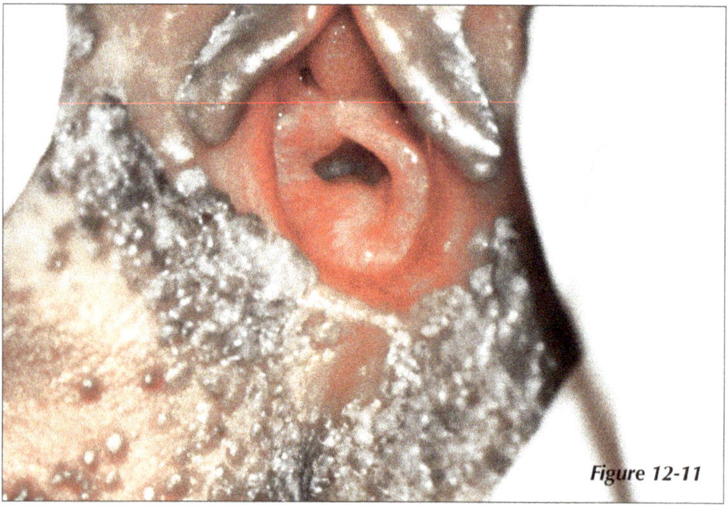

Figure 12-11. *Genital condyloma acuminata caused by HPV in a 2-year-old girl. Mother has seen these lesions for several months.*

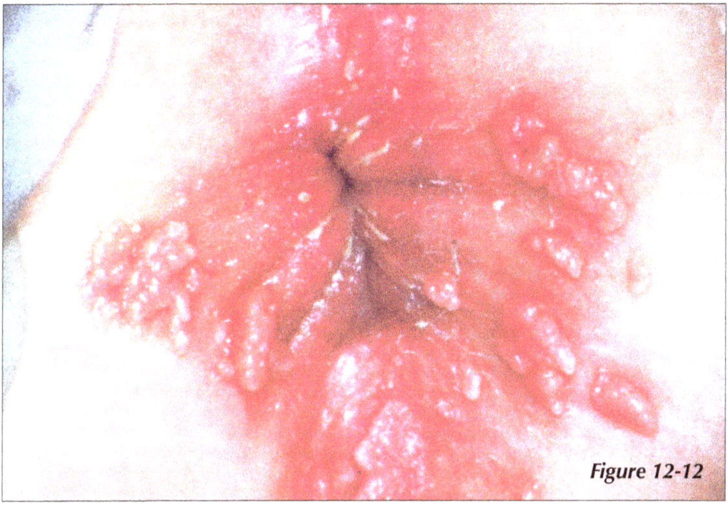

Figure 12-12. *Perianal condyloma acuminata caused by HPV in a 4 year old with no disclosure of sexual abuse.*

7. Lesions can be unapparent in the vagina, on the cervix, and on the perineum.
8. Specific types of HPV cause genital tract dysplasia and both cervical and anorectal cancer.
9. Follow up on children and adolescents with anogenital HPV carefully.

— The diagnosis of cervical lesions and microwarts on the vulvar mucosa can be enhanced using colposcopy and by applying 3% to 5% acetic acid, which turns the lesions white.

1. HPV cannot be cultured, but biopsy of any suspicious wart-like lesion can be diagnostic.
2. Syphilis, molluscum contagiosum, and sebaceous glands of the vulva and prepuce may be mistaken for HPV lesions.
3. Subtyping of HPV lesion biopsies is available and may be considered in cases highly suggestive of sexual abuse, although this information has limited forensic value.

Treatment

— Most nongenital warts resolve spontaneously, but many persist for years.

— No known optimal treatment for genital and anal warts or standard of care guideline exists.

— Treatment is directed at eradicating symptomatic lesions.

1. Some lesions spontaneously regress, but many recur even after treatment.
2. No current evidence suggests that removal of warts decreases infectivity or affects the development of cervical cancer.

— Treatment of genital and anal warts is guided by the available treatment resources, patient preferences, age and degree of symptoms in the child, and experience of the clinician (**Table 12-11**).

Hepatitis Viruses

— Hepatitis B virus (HBV) can cause a serious acute viral illness that leads to chronic liver disease, including cirrhosis and liver cancer, and, in some cases, extreme illness and death.

— Hepatitis B vaccine became available in 1981, but many adolescents and young adults (who are at highest risk for sexually transmitted HBV) are not immunized.

— Chronic HBV infection occurs in as many as 90% of infants infected by perinatal transmission.

— The prevalence of HBV in sexually abused children is unknown.

— Risk factors for HBV transmission are similar to those for HIV (see **Table 12-8**).

— HBV is transmitted through blood or body fluids of hepatitis B surface antigen (HbsAg)-positive individuals.

— Rates of transmission during heterosexual or homosexual activity and needle sharing drug abuse are high.

— Close personal contact in household and care settings can occur via mucous membrane contacts.

Table 12-11. Treatment of Genital/Anal Warts in Children, Adolescents, and Adults

Treatment	Wart Location	Duration of Treatment	Side Effects	Precautions and Contraindications*
Podofilox 0.5% gel (patient applied)	External genital (not mucous membranes)	Twice daily for 3 days followed by none for 4 days; cycle repeats no more than 4 times; limit to < 0.5 mL or 10 cm2 of skin	Local swelling, itching, and pain	NOT tested for safety in children and not for use in pregnant women
Imiquimod 5% cream (patient applied)	External genital, perianal	3 times/week for up to 16 weeks		NOT tested for safety in children and not for use in pregnant women
Trichloro-acetic (TCA) or bichloro-acetic acid (BCA) 80% to 90%	External genital, perianal, vaginal, and anal	As frequently as 3 times/week; use of baking soda or talc to absorb excess acid	Local swelling, discomfort, and pain; damage to adjacent tissue	May be too painful in very young child or those with many lesions
Podophyllin resin 10% to 25% (in a compound tincture of benzoin)	External genital, perianal, vaginal, urethral meatus	Limit to < 0.5 mL or 10 cm2 of skin or 2 cm2 of vaginal mucosa per session, wash after 1 hour initial and 4 to 6 hours subsequent, repeat weekly if needed	Local swelling and pain; vaginal application may cause some systemic absorption	NOT for use in pregnancy; not for use in oral, cervical, or anal canal; careful use in young children recommended; potentially neurotoxic

(continued)

Table 12-11. Treatment of Genital/Anal Warts in Children, Adolescents, and Adults *(continued)*

Treatment	Wart Location	Duration of Treatment	Side Effects	Precautions and Contraindications*
Cryotherapy with liquid nitrogen or with cryoprobe	External anal, genital; external exophytic or cervical (cryoprobe); urethral meatus; oral warts	Repeat application every 1 to 2 weeks; topical or local anesthesia helpful	Localized pain, blister, necrosis	Too painful in infants, very young child, or with many lesions; vaginal perforation or fissures with cryoprobe use
Surgical removal (electrosurgery, sharp or shave excision, laser ablation)	External genital, anal, oral; large numbers of warts or failed topical therapy	Usually single removal	Painful, anesthesia necessary; some local tissue damage and residual hypopigmentation	Needs experienced clinician, equipment; hemostasis
Interferon (efficacy and recurrence rates comparable to those with other modalities)	External genital, anal	Subcutaneous, IM, or intralesional injections weekly, up to 3 weeks		Systemic reactions possible; not recommended for routine treatment of HPV; hematological and liver function abnormalities

**Child may need vaginoscopy or anoscopy in severe cases. Adolescents and adult women with exophytic cervical warts must have high-grade squamous intraepithelial lesion excluded before treatment and should be managed in consult with an expert.*

Adapted from Muram D, Stewart DC[29] *and Centers for Disease Control and Prevention.*[30]

— Fomite transmission can occur.

— Diagnosis is made by serology for HBV infection (**Table 12-12**).

— There is no effective treatment for acute HBV infection. Chronic carriers must be followed to monitor for liver disease.[7]

— PEP is the most effective way to prevent acute disease and HBV transmission.

1. PEP with HBV vaccine, hepatitis B immunoglobulin (HBIG), or both can prevent infection after exposure.
2. Sexual exposure during consensual activity or assault that disrupts mucosa integrity or causes bleeding carries the highest risk of HBV infection.

Table 12-12. Diagnostic Serological Tests for Hepatitis B Virus Antigens and Antibodies

HBV Factors	HBV Antigen or Antibody	Purpose for Testing
HBsAg	HBV surface antigen	Identify acutely or chronically infected persons (used in the vaccine)
Anti-HBs	Antibody to HBsAg after immunization	Identify resolved infection and determine immunity
HBeAg	HBVe antigen	Identify infected persons at increased risk of transmitting HBV
Anti-HBe	Antibody to HBVe antigen	Identify infected persons with lower risk for transmitting HBV
Anti-HBc	Antibody to HBcAg (not present after immunization)	Identify acute, resolved, or chronic HBV infection
IgM anti-HBc	IgM antibody to HBcAg	Identify acute or recent HBV infections

Adapted from American Academy of Pediatrics.[7]

3. If a partner or assailant has acute HBV infection, administer Hepatitis B Immune Globulin (HBIg) 0.06 mL/kg IM single dose as well as HBV vaccine.
4. If the HBV status of the assailant is unknown or if it is a high-risk source, treat the unimmunized victim in the same manner.
5. Assess victims or partners who are immunized for an adequate response to the vaccine by screening anti-HBsAg antibodies before initiating HBIg or PEP.[7]

— Other hepatitis viruses are reviewed in **Table 12-13**.

Miscellaneous STDs and Other Conditions

(See **Table 12-14**.)

Table 12-13. Hepatitis Virus Disease Spectrum

Hepatitis Type	Infective Agent	Transmissions Route	Chronic Disease	Immunoprophylaxis for High-Risk Groups and Postexposure
A	RNA picorna-virus	Fecal-oral Homosexual sex Drug injection	No	HAIg vaccine
B	DNA hepadna-virus	Blood, body fluids Heterosexual sex Homosexual sex Drug injection Transfusion	Yes	HBIg vaccine
C	RNA flavivirus	Blood and blood products (before 1987) Drug injection, nasal drug use Hemodialysis High-risk sexual activity	Yes	Children 3 to 17 years of age: peginterferon and ribavirin. Rates of undetectable HCV for 6 or more months are 38% to 50% for genotypes 1 and 4 and 80% to 100% for types 2 and 3.

(continued)

Table 12-13. Hepatitis Virus Disease Spectrum *(continued)*

Hepatitis Type	Infective Agent	Transmissions Route	Chronic Disease	Immunoprophylaxis for High-Risk Groups and Postexposure
D	RNA genome particle and delta protein	Requires HBV as helper virus with same routes as HBV	Not by D alone, but will hasten B	None, but protect against B
E	RNA non-enveloped spheri-cal genus Hepevirus	Fecal-oral (greater in adults that in children) Water contamination Transfusion	No	HEIg exists but is not proven to be effective
G	RNA flavivirus (HGV and GBV-C)	Blood Coinfects with HBV and HCV Organ transplants Drugs, dialysis, homosexual sex	Yes	None

Table 12-14. Miscellaneous STDs and Conditions

Condition	Cause	Transmission	Treatment	Considerations
Pediculosis pubis	*Phthirus pubis* (crab lice)	Close physical contact	Permethrin Lindane	May be adult STD; decontaminate environment
Scabies	*Sarcoptes scabiei*	Close physical contact	Permethrin Ivermectin (adults only) Lindane (second line)	May be adult STD; decontami-nate environment

(continued)

Table 12-14. Miscellaneous STDs and Conditions *(continued)*

Condition	Cause	Transmission	Treatment	Considerations
Molluscum contagiosum	Molluscipox-virus	Close physical contact, sexual contact, and fomites	Self-limiting but genital lesions should be treated. Mechanical removal of lesion; topical peeling agents; freezing	Decontaminate environment; autoinoculation
Proctitis	Gonorrhea, chlamydia, syphilis, LGV, HSV	Anal intercourse	Ceftriaxone PLUS Doxycycline, Acyclovir if genital lesions identified Abstain from sexual inter-course.	Predominantly homosexual disease
Procto-colitis	*Campylobacter* sp, *Shigella* sp, *Entamoeba histolytica*, LGV, CMV	Anal intercourse and fecal-oral contact	Depends on infective agent Supportive care Abstain from sexual intercourse.	Predominantly homosexual disease Anoscopy, sigmoidoscopy, stool culture, and examination
Enteritis	*Giardia lamblia*, opportunistic pathogens in HIV	Anal intercourse and fecal-oral contact	Depends on infective agent Supportive care	Predominantly homosexual disease Anoscopy, sigmoidoscopy, stool culture, and examination

REFERENCES

1. Anderson B, Thimmesch I, Aardsma N, Terrell M, Carstater S, Schober J. The prevalence of abnormal genital findings, vulvovaginitis, enuresis and encopresis in children who present with allegations of sexual abuse. *J Pediatr Urol.* 2014;10(6):1216-1221.
2. Jenny C. Sexually transmitted diseases and child abuse. *Pediatr Ann.* 1992;21(8):497-503.
3. Matytsina L, Greydanus D, Gurkin Y. Vaginal microbiocoenosis and cytology of prepubertal and adolescent girls: their role in health and disease. *World J Pediatr.* 2010;6(1):32-37.
4. Green KA, Zarek SM, Catherino WH. Gynecologic health and disease in relation to the microbiome of the female reproductive tract. *Fertil Steril.* 2015;104(6):1351-1357.
5. Wald ER. Gynecologic infections in the pediatric age group. *Pediatr Infect Dis.* 1984;3(suppl 3):S10-S13.
6. Centers for Disease Control and Prevention. 2015 sexually transmitted disease treatment guidelines. *MMWR Morb Mortal Wkly Rep.* 2015;64(3):1-81.
7. American Academy of Pediatrics. Sexually transmitted diseases. In: Kimberlin DW, ed. *Red Book: 2015 Report of the Committee on Infectious Diseases.* 30th ed. Elk Grove, IL: American Academy of Pediatrics; 2015:896-904.
8. Centers for Disease Control and Prevention. Update to CDC's *Sexually Transmitted Diseases Treatment Guidelines, 2010*: oral cephalosporins no longer a recommended treatment for gonococcal infections. *MMWR.* 2012;61(31):590-594.
9. Martin-Iguacel R, Llibre JM, Nielsen H, et al. Lymphogranuloma venereum proctocolitis: a silent endemic disease in men who have sex with men in industrialised countries. *Eur J Clin Microbiol Infect Dis.* 2010;29(8):917-925.
10. Seña AC, Hsu KK, Kellogg N, et al. Sexual assault and sexually transmitted infections in adults, adolescents, and children. *Clin Infect Dis.* 2015;61(suppl 8):S856-S864.

11. Centers for Disease Control and Prevention. Syphilis - CDC fact sheet (detailed). Centers for Disease Control and Prevention Web site. http://www.cdc.gov/std/syphilis/stdfact-syphilis-detailed.htm. Accessed March 29, 2017.

12. Centers for Disease Control and Prevention. Trichomonas - CDC fact sheet. Centers for Disease Control and Prevention Web site. https://www.cdc.gov/std/trichomonas/stdfact-trichomoniasis.htm. Accessed March 29, 2017.

13. American Academy of Pediatrics. Sexually transmitted infections in adolescents and children. In: Pickering LK, ed. *Red Book: 2006 Report of the Committee on Infectious Diseases*. 27th ed. Elk Grove, IL: American Academy of Pediatrics; 2006:166.

14. Povlsen K, Bjørnelius E, Lidbrink P, Lind I. Relationship of Ureaplasma urealyticum biovar 2 to nongonococcal urethritis. *Eur J Clin Microbiol Infect Dis*. 2002;21(2):97-101.

15. Kouegnigan Rerambiah L, Ndong JC, Medzegue S, Elisee-Ndam M, Dijoba Siawaya JF. Genital Mycoplasma infections and their resistance phenotypes in an African setting. *Eur J Clin Microbiol Infect Dis*. 2015;34(6):1087-1090.

16. Morse SA, Trees DL, Htun Y, et al. Comparison of clinical diagnosis and standard laboratory and molecular methods for the diagnosis of genital ulcer disease in Lesotho: association with human immunodeficiency virus infection. *J Infect Dis*. 1997;175(3):583-589.

17. Panel on Antiretroviral Therapy and Medical Management of HIV-Infected Children. Guidelines for the use of antiretroviral agents in pediatric HIV infection. AIDSinfo Web site. https://aidsinfo.nih.gov/contentfiles/lvguidelines/pediatricguidelines.pdf. Accessed April 20, 2017.

18. World Health Organization. *HIV/AIDs Programme: Strengthening Health Services to Fight HIV/AIDS*. Geneva, Switzerland: World Health Organization; 2007. World Health Organization Web site. http://www.who.int/hiv/pub/guidelines/HIVstaging150307.pdf. Accessed March 30, 2017.

19. Centers for Disease Control and Prevention. Appendix A: AIDS-defining conditions. MMWR Recomm Rep. 2008;57(RR10):9. Centers for Disease Control and Prevention Web site. http://www.cdc.gov/mmwr/preview/mmwrhtml/rr5710a2.htm. Accessed March 30, 2017.

20. Sirotnak AP. Testing sexually abused children for sexually transmitted diseases: who to test, when to test and why. *Pediatr Ann*. 1994;23:370-374.

21. US Dept of Health and Human Services. Guidelines for the use of antiretroviral agents in pediatric HIV infections. AIDSinfo Web site. http://aidsinfo.nih.gov/guidelines/pediatric/PED-112603.pdf. Accessed December 9, 2005.

22. Bamberger JD, Waldo CR, Gerberding JL, Katz MH. Postexposure prophylaxis for human immunodeficiency virus (HIV) infection following sexual assault. *Am J Med*. 1999;106(3):323-326.

23. Babl FE, Cooper ER, Damon B, Louie T, Kharasch S, Harris JA. HIV postexposure prophylaxis for children and adolescents. *Am J Emerg Med*. 2000;18(3):282-287.

24. Caviness AC, Demmler GJ, Selwyn BJ. Clinical and laboratory features of neonatal herpes simplex virus infection: a case-control study. *Pediatr Infect Dis J*. 2008;27(5):425-430.

25. Kimberlin DW. Herpes simplex virus infections of the newborn. *Semin Perinatol*. 2007;31(1):19-25.

26. American College of Nurse-Midwives. Genital herpes. *J Midwifery Womens Health*. 2013;58(5):597-598.

27. Hammerschlag MR. Sexually transmitted diseases in sexually abused children: medical and legal implications. *Sex Transm Infect*. 1998;74(3):167-174.

28. Strick LB, Wald A. Diagnostics for herpes simplex virus: is PCR the new gold standard? *Mol Diagn Ther*. 2006;10(1):17-28.

29. Muram D, Stewart DC. Sexually transmitted diseases. In: Heger A, Emans SJ, Muram D, eds. *Evaluation of the Sexually Abused Child: A Medical Textbook and Photographic Atlas*. 2nd ed. New York, NY: Oxford University Press; 2000:187-224.

30. Centers for Disease Control and Prevention. Sexually transmitted diseases treatment guidelines, 2006. *MMWR Recomm Rep.* 2006;55(RR11):1-94. Centers for Disease Control and Prevention Web site. https://www.cdc.gov/mmwr/preview/mmwrhtml/rr5511a1.htm. Accessed March 30, 2017.

Chapter 13

Pregnancy

Donna Dunn, PhD, CNM, FNP-BC
Annie McCartney, MSN, CRNP, WHNP
Mary Katherine Dunne, MSN, AGPCNP-C, WHNP-BC
Patricia M. Speck, DNSc, ARNP, APN, FNP-BC, DF-IAFN, FAAFS, FAAN

Childhood sexual abuse strongly affects child victims, their parents, and their families. When sexual abuse results in pregnancy, the negative effects are compounded. Sexual abuse alone negatively impacts matriculation at school and participation in social activities. When a pregnancy occurs, risk for adverse outcomes for both the pregnant child and the fetus increase exponentially.

- Children who are victims of incest (ie, the crime of having sexual intercourse with a parent, child, sibling, or grandchild) experience the additional burden of family chaos as family members choose whether or not to believe the child's experiential history.
- When there is a lack of services for early identification, the discovery of pregnancy usually occurs in the second or third trimester.
- Discovery of pregnancy may depend on the presence of menses. For victims who have not begun menstruating at the time of the encounter, there is a unique risk that the pregnancy will be discovered later than the child/adolescent who *has* begun menstruating.
  - Younger children may not understand the resultant changes occurring in their bodies.
- The menstruating female may be in a state of denial, until it becomes physically obvious.

— Chronic stress of sexual abuse is associated with weight gain. Family members may perceive the weight gain as being related to dietary intake until the gravid uterus becomes obvious.

— Dating violence that occurs during a pregnancy is most likely the result of an acquaintance rape.[1]

— The definition of statutory rape varies from state to state; however, statutory rape is always predicated on 2 factors:

1. Differences in ages
2. The relationship between the child and the accused

— In all cases, families are challenged to address the pregnancy while creating an encouraging, supportive network.

— It is imperative that caretakers understand the differences between statutory rape, incest, and rape of a child.

— Support services (eg, social services, community support) facilitate reports mandated by law.

Abuse, Assault, and Adolescent Pregnancy

— Adolescents are overrepresented among abused pregnant women, with as many as 29% of pregnant adolescents experiencing abuse, including sexual abuse and assault. Pregnant teens, compared to those who are not pregnant, are much more likely to have a history of childhood sexual abuse.[2]

— Teen pregnancy and parenthood are associated with adverse outcomes for both mothers and their babies[2]:

  — Abused teens are more likely to smoke cigarettes and abuse drugs and alcohol during pregnancy.

  — Abused pregnant teens tend to enter prenatal care much later than nonabused mothers.

  — Teen mothers display more aggressive, inappropriate, and abusive behavior toward their babies.

  - School-aged children of adolescent mothers have more cognitive and behavioral problems than children of adult mothers.
  - Maternal age under 15 years and short interpregnancy intervals in cases where the maternal age is under 17 years are risk factors for infanticide.
- Abused teens are less likely than adult women to have long-term emotional, financial, and familial attachments to their partners. Abused teens may feel compelled or threatened to remain in abusive relationships.[2]

Role of the Caretaker

- Parents may strongly desire an abortion; however, if the pregnant child/adolescent is opposed to aborting the fetus, the health care provider must respect and advocate for the desires of the child or adolescent.
- Pertaining to care of the pregnancy, the pregnant child or adolescent is considered emancipated with the discovery of the pregnancy.[2]
  - Any other medical issue related to the child, excluding the pregnancy, requires guardian or parent permission to treat.
  - Once the fetus is born, the mother is responsible for the care of her child, regardless of age.
  - Methods to transfer temporary guardian rights vary from state to state.
  - It is incumbent upon the health care provider to understand local state laws regarding child and adolescent pregnancy and guardianship.
- When the offender lives in the victim's household, the support of the victim's mother is critical.
  - The nonoffending mother who is supportive of the child will address the child's needs and seek assistance for desired goals.
  - Mothers that align with offenders are considered secondary offenders, and children may be removed from their custody. Removed children often retract statements made about sexual abuse.
- When the offender lives outside the victim's home and is not related to the victim, families typically rally around the child, and as a result, the victim's psychological outcomes improve.

Pregnant Adolescents With a History of Child Abuse

Child abuse and maternal abuse are inextricably linked. Nearly 60% of abused children have mothers who are also abused.[3]

- Women who were abused as children have earlier first pregnancies than women without a history of childhood abuse; therefore, when a child presents with a pregnancy, medical professionals must explore the possibility of abuse.[4]
- Women who were sexually abused as children are almost 5 times as likely to be sexually abused/assaulted as adults.[4]
- Because abused women may not be able to negotiate sexual activity or contraceptive use, unintended pregnancy is a common outcome in abusive relationships.
- (**Table 13-1** outlines barriers to addressing pregnancy in adolescents.)

Injury and Clinical Manifestations of Abuse in the Pregnant Adolescent

- Due to increased vascularity of the vulva and external structures, blunt trauma to the external genitals in the second and third trimester may be much more severe for the pregnant adolescent than in a nonpregnant adolescent.[5]

Table 13-1. Barriers to Addressing Pregnancy in Adolescents*
1. Caregiver stresses influence the child's pregnancy trajectory.
2. Emancipation is particularly difficult for family members to understand.
3. Pseudo-maturity in the adolescent (empowered by the emancipation) may hinder addressing pregnancy.
**It is incumbent upon the health care provider to inform the pregnant adolescent of her options, to ensure that she understands those options, and to ensure that she makes informed decisions*

— Hematomas are commonly seen in the labia of pregnant adolescents following blunt trauma.

— Vulvar, hymenal, and vaginal tearing are rarely seen due to increased estrogen levels throughout pregnancy. When injury is seen, especially in the second and third trimester, suspect instrumentation.

— Due to increased vascularity during pregnancy, cervical bruising is common.

  — Sexual assault of the pregnant child and adolescent who has a placenta previa places the pregnant child and the fetus at risk for potentially fatal hemorrhage.

  — Sexual assault carries an overall increased risk of miscarriage, rupture of membranes, fetal injury, and fetal death.[5]

— Clinical manifestations include[6]:

  — Inadequate prenatal care

  — Abdominal and genital trauma

  — Signs of physical trauma (eg, bruising, lacerations)

  — Adverse outcomes for the pregnancy

  — Unintended pregnancy and sexually transmitted infections (STIs)

  — Depression

  — Drug and alcohol abuse

  — Pregnancy termination

— Red flags in identifying abuse and assault include[7]:

  — Inability to speak about the father

  — Pregnancy in a young child or adolescent

  — History of abuse in the 12 months prior to pregnancy

  — Unintended pregnancy

  — Late entry into prenatal care (which has been shown to increase negative impact on the mother and fetus)

  — Poor compliance with appointments, medical recommendations

- — Maternal trauma, particularly of the breast, abdomen, or genitals
- — Fetal trauma, particularly fractures
- — Poor or excess weight gain
- — STIs [eg, syphilis, human papillomavirus (HPV), human immunodeficiency virus (HIV), trichomoniasis, gonorrhea, chlamydia], particularly in a child
- — Depression
- — Chronic pelvic pain, dysmenorrhea, sexual dysfunction
- — Generalized pain, eating/sleeping disturbances, strong emotional reactions (eg, anxiety, fear, guilt, anger)
- — Substance abuse
- — Partner refuses to leave or answers questions for the pregnant woman

Pregnancy as a Window of Opportunity for Intervention

— The numerous clinical visits during pregnancy and the common goal of delivering a healthy baby provide the opportunity to develop a trusting relationship between patient and provider.

— Comprehensive social, economic, and community support systems are necessary for the child during pregnancy, and referrals should be provided appropriately by clinicians.

Clinician Response to Pregnancy Resulting From Abuse or Assault

— Identifying abuse through assessment is a powerful form of intervention.

— Pregnant children and adolescents should be periodically screened for sexual abuse during prenatal care.

- — The American Congress of Obstetricians and Gynecologists (ACOG) suggests screening at the initial prenatal visit, once per trimester thereafter, and at the postpartum visit.[8] This is the recommended minimum for screening; screening should occur at any time abuse is suspected.

- If abuse is suspected, take a history of the nature and severity of the abuse to adequately assess danger and potential lethality.
- If a patient calls or presents after an attack, she should be encouraged to go to a local medical facility immediately and to forgo:
  - Bathing
  - Douching
  - Urinating/defecating
  - Brushing teeth
  - Cleaning under fingernails
  - Smoking
  - Eating or drinking
- Ideally, the patient should be taken immediately to a medical facility for assessment by a medical provider specialized in sexual abuse examinations. In areas where this is not possible, the health care provider can perform the interview and assessment but must remain sensitive to the patient's emotional status and document findings in detail, without using incriminating language (eg, "rape," "sexual abuse").
  - Be aware that the pelvic examination and the experience of labor may be particularly traumatic for women who have been sexually abused/assaulted.
  - In many cases, victims of male perpetrators are more comfortable with female examiners.
  - When a woman seems especially frightened during examination, ensure that the examination is as patient-driven as possible.
- As with all victims of abuse, it is vital to assist the pregnant patient in taking necessary steps to ensure her own safety and her baby's safety.
  - Offer assistance at each prenatal appointment.
  - Make safety assessment and safety planning a part of every prenatal visit for all women, not just for those who are being abused.

- Provide safety information and lists of local resources, hotlines, and shelters. Because women may not feel safe taking such information or may deny needing it, place it in all restrooms and exam rooms, where it can be read in private.
- Document the patient's statements concerning abuse, including the perpetrator's name and weapons used.
- If the patient consents, or if required by state/local statues, notify the police.
- Document physical findings associated with battering and sexual assault, ideally using photographs.

Role of Pediatricians in Preventing Both Child Abuse and Domestic Violence

(See Chapter 18, "Prevention.")

Prophylaxis and Treatment of STIs in Pregnancy

Because of the effects of certain antibiotics and other medications on the fetus, treatment for pregnant women with STIs may differ from that of nonpregnant women. Recommended treatment regimens follow[9]:

- ***Genital herpes (herpes simplex virus [HSV] type II)***: Acyclovir may be used for a primary outbreak, for any outbreak at term, or for recurrent herpes. Herpes prophylaxis should begin at 36 weeks in pregnancy.
- ***HPV, condyloma acuminata, or genital warts***: Podophyllin is contraindicated in pregnancy, but cryotherapy and acid preparations can be safely used.
- ***Trichomonas***: Pregnant women may be treated with a 2g single-dose regimen of metronidazole.
- ***Chlamydia***: Azithromycin 1g single dose oral regimen is safe and linked with markedly improved compliance. Amoxicillin 500mg orally 3 times a day for 7 days is also a recommended regimen if azithromycin is unavailable. Erythromycin 500mg orally 4 times a day for 7 days is an alternative treatment option. Doxycycline and all other tetracyclines are contraindicated in pregnancy because they damage fetal bones and teeth.

— ***Gonorrhea***: Treat with ceftriaxone 250mg IM, unless the woman cannot take cephalosporins. Azithromycin 2g orally should be used if the patient is unable to take cephalosporins. Quinolones are contraindicated.

— ***Syphilis***: Penicillin is the drug of choice, but pregnant women who are allergic to penicillin cannot take tetracycline (the alternative given to nonpregnant women who are allergic to penicillin). Erythromycin cannot be used because it does not adequately treat fetal syphilis, which can cause fetal and neonatal death, along with other potentially devastating complications. Penicillin-allergic pregnant women should undergo penicillin desensitization in a hospital setting and receive a therapeutic course of penicillin. Jarisch-Herxheimer reaction occurs rarely in pregnant women, causing uterine contractions. Thus patients receiving penicillin should remain in the clinic or physician's office when they receive their first dose of penicillin.

— ***Hepatitis B***: Use of hepatitis B and hepatitis B immunoglobulin vaccines is not contraindicated in pregnancy.

— ***HIV infection***: HIV-positive women should be offered treatment to reduce the risk of HIV transmission to the fetus. HIV-positive mothers should not breastfeed because HIV crosses into breast milk.

References

1. McCauley HL, Silverman JG, Decker MR, et al. Sexual and reproductive health indicators and intimate partner violence victimization among female family planning clinic patients who have sex with women and men. *J Womens Health (Larchmt)*. 2015;24(8):621-628.

2. Asher J, Berlin M, Petty V. Abuse of pregnant adolescents: what have we learned? *Obstet Gynecol.* 2000;95(4 suppl 1):41S.

3. Kerker BD, Zhang J, Nadeem E, et al. Adverse childhood experiences and mental health, chronic medical conditions, and development in young children. *Acad Pediatr*. 2015;15(5):510-517.

4. Boyer D, Fine D. Sexual abuse as a factor in adolescent pregnancy and child maltreatment. *Fam Plann Perspect.* 1992;24(1):4-11,19.

5. Wright RJ, Wright RO, Isaac NE. Response to battered mothers in the pediatric emergency department: a call for an interdisciplinary approach to family violence. *Pediatrics*. 1997;99(2):186-192.

6. Martin SL, Mackie L, Kupper LL, Buescher PA, Moracco KE. Physical abuse of women before, during, and after pregnancy. *JAMA*. 2001;285(12):1581-1584.

7. American Academy of Pediatrics, Committee on Child Abuse and Neglect. The role of the pediatrician in recognizing and intervening on behalf of abused women. *Pediatrics*. 1998;101(6):1091-1092.

8. American College of Obstetricians and Gynecologists. ACOG committee opinion no. 518: intimate partner violence. *Obstet Gynecol*. 2012;119(2 pt 1):412-417.

9. Centers for Disease Control and Prevention. Sexually transmitted diseases treatment guidelines, 2010. *MMWR Morb Mortal Wkly Rep*. 2010;59(RR-12):1-110. Centers for Disease Control and Prevention Web site. http://www.cdc.gov/std/treatment/2010/default.htm. Updated March 3, 2015. Accessed May 4, 2017.

Additional Reading/Resources

Alhusen JL, Ray E, Sharps P, Bullock L. Intimate partner violence during pregnancy: maternal and neonatal outcomes. *J Womens Health (Larchmt)*. 2015;24(1):100-106.

American College of Obstetricians and Gynecologists, Committee on Health Care for Underserved Women. ACOG committee opinion no. 592: sexual assault. *Obstet Gynecol*. 2014;123(4):905-909.

Berenson A, San Miguel VV, Wilkinson GS. Prevalence of physical and sexual assault in pregnant adolescents. *J Adolesc Health*. 1992;13(6):466-469.

Campbell JC, Alford P. The dark consequences of marital rape. *Am J Nurs*. 1989;89(7):946-949.

Campbell JC, Oliver C, Bullock L. Why battering during pregnancy? *AWHONNS Clin Issues Perinat Womens Health Nurs*. 1993;4(3):343-349.

Christiaens I, Hegadoren K, Olson DM. Adverse childhood experiences are associated with spontaneous preterm birth: a case-control study. *BMC Medicine*. 2015;13(1):124.

Dietz PM, Spitz AM, Anda RF, et al. Unintended pregnancy among adult women exposed to abuse or household dysfunction during their childhood. *JAMA*. 1999;282(14):1359-1364.

Duffy SJ, McGrath ME, Becker BM, Linakis JG. Mothers with histories of domestic violence in a pediatric emergency department. *Pediatrics*. 1999;103(5 pt 1):1007-1013.

Dunn D, McCartney A. Asking the tough questions: obstetrical screening for depression and intimate partner violence. *J Health Care Poor Underserved*. 2014;25(4):1496-1506.

Elster AB, Ketterlinus R, Lamb ME. Association between parenthood and problem behavior in a national sample of adolescents. *Pediatrics*. 1990;85(6):1044-1050.

Fildes J, Reed L, Jones N, Martin M, Barrett J. Trauma: the leading cause of maternal death. *J Trauma*. 1992;32(5):643-645.

Fiscella K, Kitzman HJ, Cole RE, Sidora KJ, Olds D. Does child abuse predict adolescent pregnancy? *Pediatrics*. 1998;101(4 pt 1):620-624.

Flanagan P, Coll CG, Adreozzi L, Riggs S. Predicting maltreatment of children of teenage mothers. *Arch Pediatr Adolesc Med*. 1995;149(4):451-455.

Gazmararian JA, Adams MM, Saltzman LE, et al. The relationship between pregnancy intendedness and physical violence in mothers of newborns. the PRAMS Working Group. *Obstet Gynecol*. 1995;85(6):1031-1038.

Gazmararian JA, Lazorick S, Spitz AM, Ballard TJ, Saltzman LE, Marks JS. Prevalence of violence against pregnant women. *JAMA*. 1996;275(24):1915-1920.

Grant LJ. Effects of childhood sexual abuse: issues for obstetric caregivers. *Birth*. 1992;19(4):220-221.

Holmes MM, Resnick HS, Kilpatrick DG, Best CL. Rape-related pregnancy: estimates and descriptive characteristics from a national sample of women. *Am J Obstet Gynecol*. 1996;175(2):320-324; discussion 324-325.

Horon IL, Cheng D. Enhanced surveillance for pregnancy-associated mortality--Maryland, 1993-1998. *JAMA*. 2001;285(11):1455-1459.

Mayer L. The severely abused women in obstetric and gynecologic care. Guidelines for recognition and management. *J Reprod Med.* 1995;40(1):13-18.

Mayer L, Liebschutz J. Domestic violence in the pregnant patient: obstetric and behavioral interventions. *Obstet Gynecol Surv.* 1998;53(10):627-635.

McCauley J, Kern DE, Kolodner K, et al. Clinical characteristics of women with a history of childhood abuse: unhealed wounds. *JAMA.* 1997;277(17):1362-1368.

McFarlane J. Abuse during pregnancy: the horror and the hope. *AWHONNS Clin Issues Perinat Womens Health Nurs.* 1993;4(3):350-362.

McFarlane J, Parker B. Preventing abuse during pregnancy: an assessment and intervention protocol. *MCN Am J Matern Child Nurs.* 1994;19(4):321-324.

McKibben L, De Vos E, Newberger EH. Victimization of mothers of abused children: a controlled study. *Pediatrics.* 1989;84(3):531-535.

Overpeck MD, Brenner RA, Trumble AC, Trifiletti LB, Berendes HW. Risk factors for infant homicide in the United States. *N Engl J Med.* 1998;339(17):1211-1216.

Raj A, Silverman JG, Amaro H. The relationship between sexual abuse and sexual risk among high school students: findings from the 1997 Massachusetts Youth Risk Behavior Survey. *Matern Child Health J.* 2000;4(2):125-134.

Rhodes H, Hutchinson S. Labor experiences of childhood sexual abuse survivors. *Birth.* 1994;21(4):213-220.

Romero R, Nygaard I. CDC updates guidelines for treating sexually transmitted diseases. *Am J Obstet Gynecol.* 2015;213(2):117-118.

Schechter S, Gary LT. *Health Care Services for Battered Women and Their Abused Children: A Manual About Advocacy for Women and Kids in Emergencies (AWAKE).* Boston, MA: Children's Hospital; 1992.

Spyridou A, Schauer M, Ruf-Leuschner M. Prenatal screening for psychosocial risks in a high risk-population in Peru using the KINDEX interview. *BMC Pregnancy Childbirth.* 2016;16:13.

Stevens-Simon C, McAnarney ER. Childhood victimization: relationship to adolescent pregnancy outcome. *Child Abuse Negl.* 1994:18(7):569-575.

Stewart DE. Incidence of postpartum abuse in women with a history of abuse during pregnancy. *Can Med Assoc J.* 1994;151(11):1601-1604.

Stier DM, Leventhal JM, Berg AT, Johnson L, Mezger J. Are children born to young mothers at increased risk of maltreatment? *Pediatrics.* 1993;91(3):642-648.

Thompson RS, Krugman R. Screening mothers for intimate partner abuse at well-baby care visits: the right thing to do. *JAMA.* 2001;285(12):1628-1630.

Sinozich S, Langton L. *Rape and Sexual Assault Victimization Among College-Age Females, 1995-2013.* Washington, DC: US Department of Justice, Office of Justice Programs, Bureau of Justice Statistics; 2014.

Uppal A, Chou KJ. Screening adolescents for sexually transmitted infections in the pediatric emergency department. *Pediatr Emerg Care.* 2015;31(1):20-24.

Wright RJ. Identification of domestic violence in the community pediatric setting: need to protect mothers and children. *Arch Pediatr Adolesc Med.* 2000;154(5):431-433.

Chapter 14

Medical Child Abuse/ Munchausen Syndrome by Proxy

Stacey A. Mitchell, DNP, MBA, RN, SANE-A, SANE-P
Lisa Creamer, MSHS, BSN, RN
Mary J. Spencer, BA, MD, FAAP

Abuse by pediatric condition falsification/medical child abuse/caregiver-fabricated illness in a child (APCF/MCA/CFIC) is a form of child abuse in which a caregiver, usually a biological mother, has a psychological need for her/his child to appear to be ill or to actually be ill.[1-4] To fulfill this need, the caregiver creates illness, or the appearance of illness, by giving a false, exaggerated, or distorted history; altering laboratory reports; or inducing genuine illness. Note that the differences in terminology reflect formal naming by the American Professional Society on the Abuse of Children (abuse by pediatric condition falsification) and the American Academy of Pediatrics (caregiver-fabricated illness in a child), the informal name medical child abuse, and a related DSM diagnosis, factitious disorder imposed on another. However, Munchausen syndrome by proxy is the most widely known name. For practical purposes, the names are roughly interchangeable. This chapter will refer this form of abuse as medical child abuse (MCA).

— MCA involves physical and emotional abuse, health care and educational neglect, sexual abuse, or any combination thereof.

— It is essential that health care workers be trained to suspect the diagnosis of MCA. Failure to diagnose may cause severe irreparable harm or even death to the child.

— A multidisciplinary approach is important in the diagnosis and treatment of the perpetrator and ensures safety of the child.[5]

Characteristics of the Child Victim

— Child victims of MCA are usually young children, 2 years of age or younger; however, there have been cases identified in the literature with child victims up to the age of 16.[6]

— When older children have been diagnosed with MCA, they tend to be involved in the act.[6] They may participate out of fear of the caretaker, as a way of receiving acceptance, or their participation may be induced through bribery.[6]

— **Table 14-1** lists common characteristics of child victims.

Table 14-1. Common Characteristics of Child Victims of MCA
— May be male or female — Usually younger than 2 years but may be older — Often have a long history of recurrent symptoms — Often present with multiple, unusual symptoms involving multiple organ systems — Often have a history of multiple hospitalizations

Symptoms and Warning Signs of MCA

— There are more than 100 described presenting symptoms of MCA (**Table 14-2**).

— A thorough physical and neurological examination and a mental health evaluation of the child should be completed to exclude illness. These examinations help determine if the presenting symptoms are consistent with the physical examination.

— It is important for the child's medical team to witness symptoms and record them in the health record.[2,12]

— **Table 14-3** lists warning signs of MCA.

Investigation and Diagnostic Studies in Case of Warning Signs

— When any warning signs are identified, the health care provider must add MCA to the differential diagnosis list.

— An investigation should be undertaken to determine whether MCA is or has been occurring. A multidisciplinary investigation team should be assembled to ensure all potential diagnoses are considered.

— Laboratory and other diagnostic studies should be considered, dependent on the presenting history (**Table 14-4**).

Table 14-2. Common Presenting Symptoms of MCA

- History is often inconsistent with physical findings.
- Consider the diagnosis when the patient history includes any of the following:
  - Chronic recurrent diarrhea, vomiting, or nutritional concerns[7]
  - Fever with multiple bacteria in the blood cultures
  - Chronic recurrent urinary tract infections with multiple organisms[8]
  - Unexplained seizure activity that is unresponsive to treatment
  - Poisonings[9,10]
  - Family history of sudden unexplained infant death(s)[11]
  - Unexplained recurrent bleeding episodes (especially gastrointestinal or urinary tract)
  - Apneic episodes
  - Central nervous system depression
  - Low or high blood glucose levels[12]
  - Recurrent, unexplained fevers or illness
  - Appearance of multiple surgical scars
- Symptoms usually occur in the presence of a caretaker and subside when the caretaker leaves.[13]

Table 14-3. Warning Signs of MCA

- Unexplained or recurrent illness with normal laboratory tests.
- No response to treatment or new symptoms with treatment.
- Unresponsive seizure disorder (especially seizures where the caretaker is the only witness).

(continued)

Table 14-3. Warning Signs of MCA *(continued)*

— Occurrence of new symptoms after negative tests.

— Symptoms become more severe with treatment.

— Multiple hospital visits to several hospitals in search of a diagnosis (ie, "hospital shopping").

— A willingness to obtain more tests, procedures, or surgeries.

— Caretaker expresses desire to be transferred to another hospital or seeks a second opinion when confronted with a negative workup.

— Caretaker suggests rare disorders as the cause of the illness.

— Unexplained illness or death in one or more siblings.[12]

Table 14-4. Diagnostic Studies to Consider in Cases of Suspected MCA[14]

LABORATORY STUDIES

— Complete blood count (CBC)

— Urinalysis and urine toxicology screen

— Screens for poisons, when appropriate; drug levels for suspected over- or under-dosing of medications

— Blood and/or urine cultures

— Coagulation tests when bleeding is present

— DNA and blood group typing[15]

RADIOGRAPHIC STUDIES

— Computed tomography (CT) scan, as needed, to rule out intracranial or other pathology

— Magnetic resonance imaging (MRI), as needed, to rule out intracranial pathology

OTHER STUDIES

— Electroencephalography (EEG) to rule out seizure disorder

— Electrocardiogram (EKG) to rule out arrhythmias

Perpetrators of MCA

— Suspected and confirmed perpetrators do not usually acknowledge what they have done[16]; therefore, confronting the perpetrator without law enforcement or Child Protective Services (CPS) present may be dangerous.

— **Table 14-5** includes common characteristics of the MCA perpetrator.

Table 14-5. Perpetrator Characteristics[6]
— Most are female (90% to 98%): — Mothers (85%) — Female guardians — Fathers account for 10% of all perpetrators. — May be highly educated. — May have a background in health-related fields. — May have concurrent psychiatric illness. — Found to lie often and may be histrionic. — May appear as the concerned parent or caregiver. — May become very friendly with health care personnel: — Very comfortable in the health care setting — Rarely leave the bedside — Appear to be devoted and selfless — Eager to order more tests or surgeries for the child to make the diagnosis. — Thrives on sympathy, recognition, and attention. — May become "giddy" when describing near-death situations from which she/he rescued the child. — May have a related Internet presence (eg, blogs of child's illness inconsistent with medical condition or reports from physicians, seeking online donations and/or contacting charitable organizations like the Make-A-Wish Foundation).[17]

The Nonperpetrating Spouse

Little is known about nonperpetrating spouses in cases of MCA, and the literature rarely discusses them. Identified characteristics include:

— Usually married to the perpetrator.

— Tend to assume a passive role in the family.

— May be distant and uninvolved in caring for the child.

— May be intense and overbearing.

— Seldom visits the child during hospitalization (possibly citing conflicts with work schedule).

Approach to the Diagnosis of Medical Child Abuse

When determining the diagnosis of MCA, employ a multidisciplinary approach with medical, psychological, and social services.

— MCA is a medical diagnosis. The medical team may suspect the diagnosis from the history.

  — Diagnosis should be based upon a multidisciplinary team investigation. The team lead should have experience with MCA.

  — This approach provides for division of labor and mutual support, encourages multiple points of view (thus promoting objectivity), and potentially makes the diagnosis more valid.

— Admit the child to the hospital for physical examination and observation, including careful neurological and mental health assessments and appropriate diagnostic testing.

— Conduct a thorough review of all medical records, *especially other hospitalizations.*

— Interview the child, caretaker, and other family members.

— Observe child-caretaker interactions. (This is paramount.)

— Conduct a separation test. (This is vitally important in the diagnosis. In cases of MCA, symptoms disappear in the absence of a perpetrator. The separation test may require the intervention of CPS if the caretaker is unwilling to agree.)

— Document any improvement in symptoms if the caretaker leaves.

— Conduct covert video surveillance, if deemed helpful.[18]

— Notify CPS and law enforcement of the diagnosis. In some jurisdictions, CPS must notify the parents that they are the subject of an investigation, so work with CPS regarding this issue.

— Work with CPS to take the child victim into protective custody for placement in an alternative care situation. It is rarely advisable that relatives or family friends serve as alternate caregivers.

  — Court adjudication is needed for most MCA cases in order for CPS to obtain temporary or permanent custody of the victim.

— Take into consideration that siblings are likely to be past, present, or future victims.

— Refer the perpetrator for psychotherapy with a therapist who is experienced in MCA.

Treatment Plan

The treatment plan for MCA victims includes:

— Re-evaluate all diagnoses that are now suspect.

— Consider an appropriate setting for evaluation (eg, for the child victim who presents as unable to tolerate feedings, begin feeding under observation in the hospital). Determine and plan for appropriate follow-up medical care.

— Offer victims counseling, if they are of appropriate age.

References

1. Roesler TA, Jenny C. *Medical Child Abuse: Beyond Munchausen Syndrome by Proxy*. Elk Grove, IL: American Academy of Pediatrics; 2009.

2. Flaherty EG, MacMillan HL. Caregiver-fabricated illness in a child: a manifestation of child maltreatment. *Pediatrics*. 2013;132(3):590-597.

3. Donaruma-Kwoh MM, Creamer LC, Giardino EI, Giardino AP, Pape J. When the medical system is misused: the condition formerly known as Munchausen syndrome by proxy. In: Clements PT, Burgess AW, Fay-Hillier TM, Giardino EI, Giardino AP, eds. *Nursing Approach to*

the Evaluation of Child Maltreatment. 2nd ed. Saint Louis, MO: STM Learning, Inc; 2015:353-368.

4. American Psychiatric Association. *Diagnostic and Statistical Manual of Mental Disorders*. 5th ed. Arlington, VA: American Psychiatric Association; 2013.

5. von Hahn L, Harper G, McDaniel SH, Siegel DM, Feldman MD, Libow JA. A case of factitious disorder by proxy: the role of the health-care system, diagnostic dilemmas, and family dynamics. *Harv Rev Psychiatry*. 2001;9(3):124-135.

6. Morrell B, Tilley DS. The role of nonperpetrating fathers in Munchausen syndrome by proxy: a review of the literature. *J Pediatr Nurs*. 2012;27(4):328-335.

7. Squires JE, Squires RH Jr. Munchausen syndrome by proxy: ongoing clinical challenges. *J Pediatr Gastroenterol Nutr*. 2010;51(3):248-253.

8. Feldman KW, Feldman MD, Grady R, Burns MW, McDonald R. Renal and urologic manifestations of pediatric condition falsification/ Munchausen by proxy. *Pediatr Nephrol*. 2007;22(6):849-856.

9. Carter KE, Izsak E, Marlow J. Munchausen syndrome by proxy caused by ipecac poisoning. *Pediatr Emerg Care*. 2006;22(9):655-656.

10. Eldridge DL, Van Eyk J, Kornegay C. Pediatric toxicology. *Emerg Med Clin North Am*. 2007;25(2):283-308.

11. Craft AW, Hall DMB. Munchausen syndrome by proxy and sudden infant death. *BMJ*. 2004;328(7451):1309-1312.

12. Kucuker H, Demir T, Oral R. Pediatric condition falsification (Munchausen syndrome by proxy) as a continuum of maternal factitious disorder (Munchausen syndrome). *Pediatr Diabetes*. 2010;11(8):572-578.

13. Brannon GE, Abdulhamid I, Poirier MP. Factitious disorder imposed on another. Medscape Web site. http://misc.medscape.com/pi/iphone/medscapeapp/html/A295258-business.html. Accessed March 29, 2017.

14. Kenedi CA, Shirey KG, Hoffa M, et al. Laboratory diagnosis of factitious disorder: a systemic review of tools useful in the diagnosis of Munchausen's syndrome. *NZ Med J*. 2011;124(1342):66-81.

15. Sahin F, Kuruoglu A, Isik AF, Karacan E, Beyazova U. Munchausen syndrome by proxy: a case report. *Turk J Pediatr*. 2002;44(4):334-338.

16. Bass C, Jones D. Psychopathology of perpetrators of fabricated or induced illness in children: case series. *Br J Psychiatry*. 2011;199(2):113-118.

17. Brown AN, Gonzalez GR, Wiester RT, Kelley MC, Feldman KW. Care taker blogs in caregiver fabricated illness in a child: a window on the caretakers's thinking? *Child Abuse Negl*. 2014;38(3):488-497.

18. Hall DE, Eubanks L, Meyyazhagan LS, Kenney RD, Johnson SC. Evaluation of covert video surveillance in the diagnosis of Munchausen syndrome by proxy: lessons from 41 cases. *Pediatrics*. 2000;105(6):1305-1312.

Chapter 15

Role of Law Enforcement

Jeff Rich, Detective
Janetta Michaels, BSW, MPA
Angelo P. Giardino, MD, PhD
Gus H. Kolilis, BS Ed

Definition

Law enforcement, in cooperation with the multidisciplinary team (MDT), is responsible for handling criminal aspects of child maltreatment investigations,[1] with a particular focus on the safety of children and their families. Law enforcement officers conduct interviews with those involved in a case, preserve and collect evidence for use in criminal prosecution, and engage appropriate actions in the arrest of alleged perpetrators.[2,3] Law enforcement's role in child and adolescent abuse cases spans the entire criminal justice process—from initial report through civil and criminal prosecution. Law enforcement's actions in investigation, or lack thereof, may determine whether or not an offender is held accountable; therefore, specialized training in child abuse investigations is required.

Specific Responsibilities of Law Enforcement

— Ensure the safety of the child victim and other witnesses.

— Preserve the crime scene(s) and prevent destruction of evidence.

— Identify the outcry witness (ie, the person who first heard the victim's allegation of abuse); refer to individual state statutes to determine required age of child victim and outcry witness.

— Interview witnesses and gather statements; include contact information for all witnesses.

— Identify, photograph, and collect evidence.

— Photograph the location where the abuse took place; photograph the victim.

— Determine, with the MDT, whether or not the victim and other children remain at risk of abuse, and if necessary, take appropriate action to place the child in substitute care for safety.

— Interview the alleged offender in compliance with state and federal law.

— Determine if there is probable cause to arrest the offender.

— (See **Table 15-1** for a list of law enforcement roles.)

Table 15-1. Roles of Law Enforcement in Child Maltreatment

Deterrence	Enforce the message that child maltreatment is unacceptable behavior punishable by state and federal law.
Prevention and Advocacy	Reduce risk of child maltreatment by being a community leader in prevention and in advocacy for the MDT approach.[4]
Reporting	Law enforcement personnel are mandated reporters (see Chapter 1, "Introduction to Child Maltreatment"). They often encounter suspected abuse while on other assignments (eg, narcotics or family violence calls).
Immediate Response	Respond rapidly to emergency situations 24 hours a day, 7 days a week. Many states grant law enforcement personnel the authority to remove children from parents or guardians in emergency situations.
Criminal Investigation	Conduct criminal investigations; collaborate with the MDT; interview witnesses, preserve all crime scenes, and determine if probable cause for arrest exists.
Support Child Protective Services (CPS)	Accompany CPS workers as they conduct visits to potentially dangerous locations. Provide enforcement of standing court orders if authorized, and in some states, assist in removing children from the home.
Victim Support	Engage victim advocates to provide services if available; help prepare and support the child victim and the nonoffending parent through the entire case.

Adapted from Pence D, Wilson C.[5]

Recommendations for Improved Law Enforcement Response[6]

— Investigators should have specialized training in recognizing and responding to children who are abused, neglected, or exposed to violence.

— Investigators should be familiar with the child and adolescent forensic interview process, injury identification, child development and linguistics, and the impact of victimization and witnessing violence on children.

— Law enforcement agencies should supply written child abuse protocols to guide important decisions. It is common for these protocols to be part of MDT collaboration.

— Investigators should work collaboratively with members of the MDT (eg, medical and mental health care providers, CPS professionals, victim assistance providers).

— Investigators must rely on admissible evidence rather than the mere belief that something happened.[7]

Preliminary Investigative Actions

Child Protective Services

Joint investigations are often conducted between CPS and law enforcement. (See **Table 15-2** for the CPS process and **Figure 15-1** for a flowchart of a joint investigation.)

Table 15-2. Stages of CPS Service[8]

Phase	Description
Intake	— Receive report. — Determine if report meets the criteria for abuse or neglect. — Determine urgency of response. — Notify law enforcement. — Document receipt of report, case assignment, and law enforcement notification.

(continued)

Table 15-2. Stages of CPS Service[8] *(continued)*

Phase	Description
Investigation	— Asses risk to child/children. — Perform background checks on alleged offender. — Provide services to ensure child safety. — Observe forensic interview of child or adolescent victim. — Interview family members, alleged perpetrators, and other witnesses. — Collaborate with MDT. — Assign disposition for each allegation. — Provide further services or close case.
Family preservation (to prevent removal of child from the home)	— Assess family for strengths and weaknesses (ie, risk and protective factors). — Develop family plan to address needs. — Complete action items (ie, referral to parenting class and counselling). — Review and revise plan as needed. — Maintain regular contact with child and family. — Either seek removal of child or close case.
Substitute care (when a child is removed from the home)	— Select appropriate care provider(s). — Develop permanency goal (ie, permanent placement or return to parent/guardian). — Work with care provider to meet the needs of the child. — Provide information to the court. — Recommend reunification with parents or termination of parental rights.
Family reunification	— Assist risk reduction. — Close case or seek subsequent removal of the child.
Adoption	— Place child with adoptive family. — Develop a service plan. — Provide post-adoption supervision. — Assist during consummation phase [ie, final adoption and integration with adoptive parent(s)].

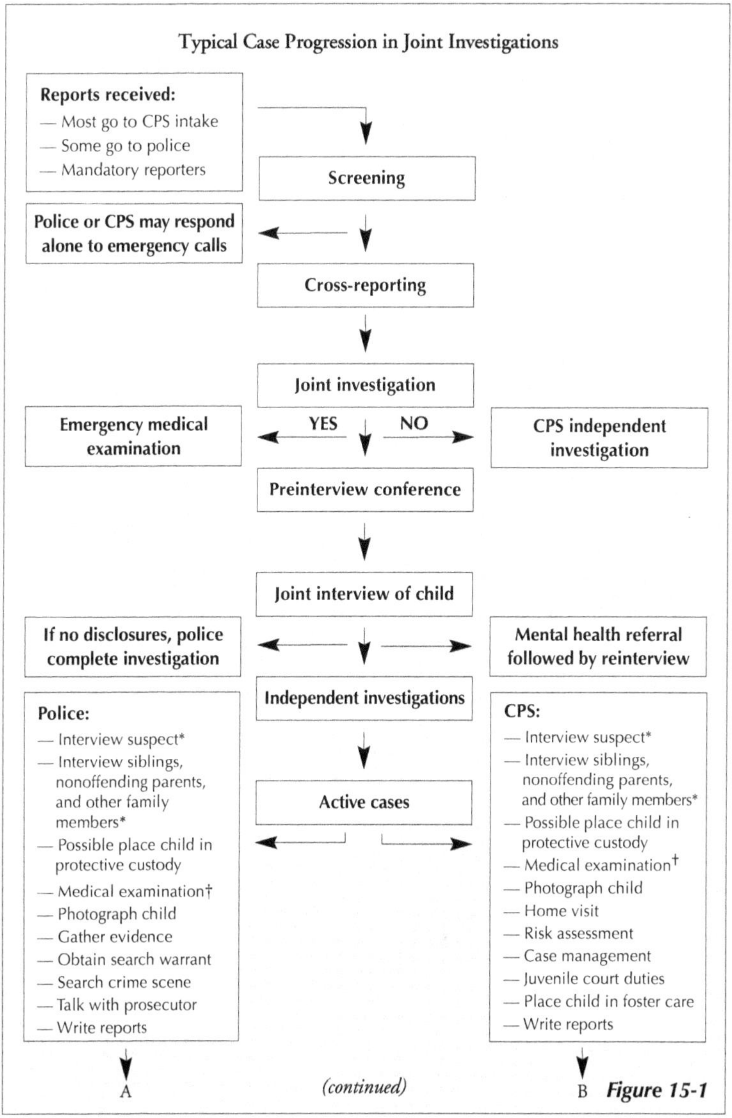

Figure 15-1. *Joint investigations of police and CPS in cases of child sexual abuse. Adapted from Sheppard DI, Zangrillo PS.*[9]

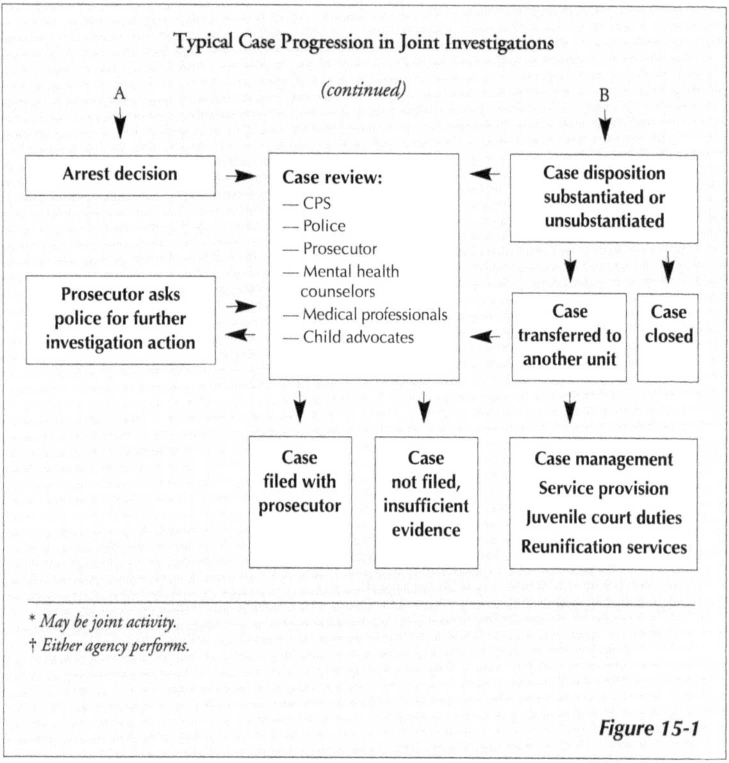

Figure 15-1. *Joint investigations of police and CPS in cases of child sexual abuse. Adapted from Sheppard DI, Zangrillo PS.*[9]

Multidisciplinary Teams (MDTs)

Individually, no single discipline or agency has the ability or resources to successfully respond to allegations of child abuse. It takes a team of professionals working together to hold offenders accountable and promote safety and healing for victims. The MDT consists of members from law enforcement, prosecution, CPS, medicine and mental health services, and victim advocacy. Many MDTs operate within the context of a Children's Advocacy Center (CAC). Teams are formed at the local level to evaluate the scope of the problem within their community, assess resources available for response, and determine the most efficient way to collaborate.[10]

Organization

— The team's ultimate goal is to meet the child's immediate and long-term needs for safe and nurturing care.

— Clarify the roles and responsibilities of each agency involved, and delineate steps to accomplish at each stage of the process or intervention.

  — Set specific time frames for completing each step.

  — Assign responsibility for carrying out each step.

— Provide practical advice for handling both routine and special circumstances.

Dealing With Conflict Constructively[11]

When conducting joint investigations, differences of opinion will inevitably arise. Investigators must deal with conflict appropriately in order to ensure that the investigation, as well as the protection of the child, goes uncompromised.

— Be respectful of all viewpoints, emphasize listening, and clarify positions.

— Consider positive attributes of opposing viewpoints before defending your own.

— State positions clearly, firmly, and without excessive emotion.

— Avoid personalizing your position; rather, focus on the safety and well-being of the child.

— Offer suggestions, not criticism.

— Accept conflict as a natural process and work toward a mutually satisfying resolution.

— Base resolutions on consensus rather than abdication of responsibility or integrity.

— Focus on the purposes stated and refer to the protocol for guidance.

— Recognize that agency policies and procedures influence specific practices.

The Investigation

— Respond according to the urgency of the situation, securing the crime scene and taking initial statements.[12]

— Collect and preserve physical evidence at the scene.

— Interview witnesses.

— Interview child witnesses; utilize a trained forensic interviewer if accessible.

— Facilitate use of special investigative tools.

— Conduct criminal history record checks of alleged perpetrators.

— Interview alleged perpetrators.

— Arrest suspects as indicated.

— Present evidence in criminal cases.

— Testify in court.

— Take children into protective custody if their safety is at risk.

Interview Guidelines

— Understand the process of disclosure (**Table 15-3**).

— Gather all available background and case information pertinent to the interview.

— Never assume guilt or innocence.

— Revisit the crime scene and review photographs if needed.

Table 15-3. Process of Disclosure
— ***Denial***: Denies that abuse occurred
— ***Tentative disclosure***: States that something happened but lacks details
— ***Active disclosure***: Gives detailed information regarding abuse
— ***Recantation***: Retracts previous statement of abuse
— ***Reaffirmation***: States that the abuse occurred and retracts the recantation

Adapted from Sorenson T, Snow B.[13]
**Disclosure is a process, not an event. A child's disclosure of abuse may include one or all of these stages.*

— Identify all persons carefully.

1. Verify that names are spelled correctly.
2. Obtain date of birth, Social Security number, and other identifiers.
3. Obtain home address, including apartment number, floor, and location (front or rear).
4. Note telephone numbers (home, work, mobile).
5. List a secondary contact, including the contact's name, address, and telephone numbers. Parents and grandparents are often less transient and, therefore, may be good contacts.

— Interview each individual away from other persons involved.

— Keep questions clear and concise.

— Confine questions to one topic at a time.

— Avoid questions with yes-or-no answers and leading questions that begin with "did" or "does."

— Use free narrative probes, such as "Tell me more about that." or "Tell me what happened next."

— Use comparison questions to clarify details.

— Follow specific steps to conduct an interview:

1. Develop interview objectives to clarify what needs to be known.
2. Use an introduction and warm-up.
3. Use the opening statement to set the tone of the interview.
4. Ask what happened and then listen.
5. Start over and obtain specific details, including what happened before, during, and after the event.
6. Obtain any other information needed.
7. Bring the interview to a conclusion.

The Victim Interview

(See Chapter 11, "The Sexual Abuse Interview.")

The Witness Interview

— First, allow witnesses to state what happened or what they observed in a narrative style.

— Ask open-ended questions and follow up with direct or specific questions to elicit detail and to access memories.

— Ask for correct spelling of names and for addresses and telephone numbers of persons involved.

— Ask if the victim disclosed the incident to the witness.

— Ask if there is anything you have failed to ask.

— Ask if there is anything else they want to discuss.

— Obtain a written statement if possible.

— At the conclusion of the interview, inform witnesses that there are no further questions at this time but that they may be needed at a later time to discuss new information or to clarify what has been revealed.

— Encourage witnesses to contact authorities if any additional information becomes available.

— Do not promise witnesses that by talking to you now they will not have to appear in court.

Interrogation of the Suspected Perpetrator

The suspect interview is an opportunity for the investigator to gather facts and collect evidence from a suspected offender. Typically, suspect interviews are most successful when conducted in a timely manner, after the interviewer has thoroughly reviewed all available facts about the case. The interviewer has a finite window of time (determined by his/her experience and training) in which to accomplish a successful interview. Law enforcement should conduct the initial interview after Miranda statues are met. For persons in custody, begin the interview by reading the Miranda warning and having the suspect sign and date waivers according to agency policy.

— Before interviewing the suspected perpetrator, gather as much background information as possible, including:

1. Criminal history
2. Social history
3. Medical history
4. Driving record
5. Credit history
6. Social media history and online presence
7. Personal history, such as family, friends, hobbies, likes and dislikes
8. Evidence or previous reports of domestic violence in other relationships

— Read original reports and check with other professionals.

— Build rapport and avoid being judgmental.

— Observe verbal and nonverbal cues.

— Permit suspected perpetrators to talk about themselves; pay attention to their interests and fantasies and appeal to their emotions.

— Seek to obtain information concerning who, what, when, where, why, and how the abuse occurred.

— Do not initially challenge suspects' statements; rather, permit them to freely describe events and circumstances. Evidence can be obtained to support or refute the statements later.

Special Investigative Techniques

(See **Table 15-4**.)

Crime Scene Search

— Obtain legal authority to search the crime scene and preserve the evidence in a way that will be admissible in court.

— Identify, photograph, seize, and process physical evidence.

Table 15-4. Special Investigative Techniques

Monitored pretext telephone or personal conversations

— Two types: telephone and personal conversation

— Issues to consider: authorization, timing, victim maturity/stability, victim preparation, equipment, staffing, perpetrator background

Audio and video recordings of interviews

— Advantages:

 — Provides accurate record of what was said.

 — Actual interview can be reviewed.

 — Does not depend on interviewer's notes or memory.

— Disadvantages:

 — Can be distracting.

 — Small or trivial issues can become major focus that weakens the case and obscures more important issues.

— Images and videos, including deleted data, should be reviewed for forensic artifacts that may provide assistance in the case. Embedded data and other information can be reviewed by technically trained investigators to provide potential evidence in the investigation.

Use of anatomically correct dolls

— Requires specialized training

Polygraphs

Adapted from Pence D, Wilson C.[12]

— Determine if biological evidence exists; document and collect evidence.

— Explore the possibility of electronic and photographic evidence. Today, most people have access to mobile telephones and use them to communicate with others. Records of these communications, including when and where they took place, may be important evidence.

Terms to Know

— ***Probable cause***: Facts that would lead a reasonable person to believe that a crime has been, is being, or is about to be committed and that specific evidence of such exists in a specified location.

— ***Witness***: Someone who has information related to an event and can attest to the facts as observed.

— ***Physical evidence***: Anything that corroborates the victim's account of what happened and where it occurred (eg, body fluids on clothing, carpet, tissue paper; weapons; hair; fabric fibers).

— ***Descriptive recollection***: Describes where events occurred and/or objects used.

— ***Technical evidence***: Technical devices/data related to the suspect (eg, mobile phones, mobile phone records, global positioning systems (GPS), embedded data, Internet history, email and short message service (SMS) communications, recorded media, pornography).

— ***Biological evidence***: Bodily fluids, tissues, and organic materials collected from a crime scene (eg, saliva, blood, sperm, hair, tissue, bones, other bodily fluids).

— ***Search warrant***: A legal document, typically issued by a judge or magistrate, authorizing law enforcement or other officials to enter a location or access a device to search for and seize evidence of an offense. (May also authorize collection of biological evidence.)

— ***Warrant affidavit***: A statement of probable cause by a reasonable and responsible person that serves as the impetus to obtain a warrant.

Evidence to Obtain

Investigators collect evidence to prove or disprove an allegation in a court of law. To be admissible in court, evidence must be relevant, material, and competent; therefore, it is important to maintain a documented chain of custody for all collected evidence. Relevant evidence includes:

— Items that corroborate the alleged offence [ie, biological, physical, and technical evidence (refer to previous section)].

— Items that corroborate surrounding details provided by the victim (eg, substance abuse, location information, other circumstances described by the victim).

— Items that indicate the offender's motivation (eg, pornography, restraints, sexual devices).

Child Death Investigations

It is important to recognize that child fatalities are often the unintended outcome of an abusive incident. It is important that trained child abuse investigators participate in these investigations.

— Use all available resources to determine if the death was caused by an intentional or unintentional act or omission.

— Obtain the child's complete medical history.

— Obtain information on medical services provided to the victim by first responders or other medical personnel.

— Determine through medical personnel if the findings at autopsy are consistent with past and recent medical history.

— Obtain a timeline for the 24 hours preceding death.

— For infant and child fatalities, document according to protocol the circumstances and evidence at the point of death (in addition to preliminary investigative information).

1. Use a death investigation checklist specific to children.
2. Include as much information about the recent history as possible, including the time of death.
3. Be aware of the specific causes of childhood fatalities, including abusive head trauma (see Chapter 3, "Head Trauma") and sudden infant death syndrome.

— Form trusting partnerships with other child protection professionals to more accurately identify cause and manner of death, which can help determine if an event was natural, accidental, intentional, or unintentional.

The Report

— Assemble all of the information in a chronological sequence of events, accurately reflecting the results of the entire investigation.

— Clearly portray all of the known facts of the case.

— If new or additional information becomes available, prepare a supplemental report and distribute as appropriate.

— Record all investigative results according to the policy and procedures of the investigative agency.

References

1. Hammond CB, Lanning KV, Promisel W, Shepherd JR, Walsh B. *Law Enforcement Response to Child Abuse: Portable Guide to Investigating Child Abuse*. Washington, DC: US Department of Justice; 1997.

2. Bittner E. The quasi-military organization of the police. In: Kappeler VE. *The Police and Society: Touchstone Readings*. Prospect Heights, IL: Waveland Press; 1995:173-183.

3. Brooks L. Police discretionary behavior: a study of style. In: Dunham RG, Alpert GP, eds. *Critical Issues in Policing: Contemporary Readings*. Prospect Heights, IL: Waveland Press; 1989:146-161.

4. Vieth VI. Unto the third generation: a call to end child abuse in the United States within 120 years. *J Aggress Maltreat Trauma*. 2006;12:5-54.

5. Pence D, Wilson C. *The Role of Law Enforcement in the Response to Child Abuse and Neglect*. Washington, DC: US Department of Health and Human Services, National Center of Child Abuse and Neglect; 1992.

6. Office for Victims of Crime. *Breaking the Cycle of Violence: Recommendations to Improve the Criminal Justice Response to Child Victims and Witnesses*. Washington, DC: US Department of Justice, OVC Monograph; 1999.

7. Lanning KV. Criminal investigation of sexual victimization of children. In: Berliner L, Briere J, Carloe J, Hendrix T, Myers J, Reid TA, eds. *The APSAC Handbook on Child Maltreatment*. 2nd ed. Thousand Oaks, CA: Sage Publications; 2002:329-347.

8. Cheung M, Ford AF, Sallee AL. Role of the social worker. In: Chadwick DL, Alexander R, Giardino AP, Esernio-Jensen D, Thackeray JD. *Cultures at Risk and Role of Professionals*. 4th ed. Saint. Louis, MO: STM Learning, Inc; 2014:485-524. *Chadwick's Child Maltreatment*; vol 3.

9. Sheppard DI, Zangrillo PS. Coordinating investigations of child abuse. *Public Welfare*. 1996;54:21-31.

10. Rich J, Michaels J. The role of law enforcement in child abuse cases. In: Chadwick DL, Alexander R, Giardino AP, Esernio-Jensen D, Thackeray JD, eds. *Cultures at Risk and Role of Professionals*. 4th ed. Saint Louis, MO: STM Learning, Inc; 2014:161-178. *Chadwick's Child Maltreatment*; vol 3.

11. Ells M. *Forming a Multidisciplinary Team to Investigate Child Abuse*. Washington, DC: Office of Juvenile Justice and Delinquency Prevention, US Department of Justice; 1998.

12. Pence D, Wilson C. *Team Investigation of Child Sexual Abuse: The Uneasy Alliance*. Thousand Oaks, CA: Sage Publications; 1994.

13. Sorenson T, Snow B. How children tell: the process of disclosure in child sexual abuse. *Child Welfare*. 1991;70(1):3-15.

Chapter 16

INTERDISCIPLINARY DEATH INVESTIGATION

Susan B. Patton, DNSc, PPCNP-BC, AFN-BC, FAANP, FAAN
Joyce P. Williams, DNP, AFN-BC, FAAFS, FAAN
Stacey A. Mitchell, DNP, MBA, RN, SANE-A, SANE-P
Tracey S. Corey, MD
Michael Graham, MD

— In the United States, the medicolegal investigation of unusual, suspicious, sudden, and unexplained violent and non-natural deaths, including those deemed a possible threat to the public health, is usually performed by a coroner system or a medical examiner (ME) system. Depending upon regional laws, such systems may be organized at a county, regional, or state level.[1]

— Generally, the agency responsible for death investigation is determined by the geographic location where the body was found or where the individual was officially pronounced dead.

— A substantial number of US states have combination coroner–medical examiner systems. For example, in some states, medical examiner offices may only be located in metropolitan areas, with coroner (or similar) offices in rural counties. In other states, each county may be served by a coroner, with one or more medical examiner offices staffed by forensic pathologists who undertake autopsies for the coroners.[2]

— Notification of that system activates a team of individuals who, depending on their qualifications and profession, collaborate on the autopsy, the nonautopsy aspects including an investigation, and the subsequent follow-up (**Table 16-1**).[3,4]

Table 16-1. The Death Investigation Team: Members and Their Roles

FORENSIC PATHOLOGISTS

Physicians who apply the principles of pathology and medicine in general to legal issues to perform autopsies and participate in the investigation of cause and manner of death.

FORENSIC DEATH INVESTIGATORS

Professionals with education in the medical as well as legal system who directs (as coroner) or assists a medical examiner in the conduct of death investigation.

FORENSIC NURSES

Work in the crime scene investigation of injury, such as in cases of sexual assault and death. Forensic nurses may serve as coroners.

FORENSIC ODONATOLOGISTS

Participate in the collection, evaluation, and proper handling of dental evidence to assist in civil and criminal proceedings.

FORENSIC ANTHROPOLOGISTS

Practice a subfield of physical anthropology (the study of human remains) that involves applying skeletal analysis and techniques in archaeology to solving criminal cases.

FORENSIC SCIENTISTS (CRIMINALISTS)

May work in the following areas:

- Computer and digital image enhancement
- Crime scene reconstruction
- DNA
- Documents
- Drugs
- Entomology
- Fingerprints
- Firearms-ballistics
- Footwear and shoeprints
- Hair and fibers
- Handwriting analysis
- Linguistics
- Paint
- Photography
- Poisons and other toxins
- Polygraphs
- Sculpting
- Tire tracks and skid marks
- Tool marks
- Voice and speech analysis

(continued)

Table 16-1. The Death Investigation Team: Members and Their Roles *(continued)*
FORENSIC PSYCHOLOGISTS/PSYCHIATRISTS
Apply the principles of psychology and psychiatry to legal concerns, such as profiling suspects, determining if suspects are competent to stand trial, or determining if a suspect knew the difference between right and wrong when committing a crime.
FORENSIC RADIOLOGISTS
Interpret radiological examinations and procedures for court proceedings and/or law enforcement. Radiological methods are widely used in identification, age estimation, and establishing cause of death.
LAW ENFORCEMENT
(See Chapter 15, "Role of Law Enforcement")

— In deaths in which abuse or neglect may have played a part, the objectives of the interdisciplinary investigation are to:

- — Investigate the scene(s) of injury and death
- — Interview significant others
- — Review records
- — Collect and preserve evidence
- — Correlate clinical and pathological findings
- — Present expert opinions in proper forums
- — Serve as a member of multidisciplinary death review committees
- — Evaluate surviving children when abuse is suspected

CAUSE OF DEATH

— ***Cause of death***: The disease, injury, or combination of the two that initiates the continuous series of events, whether brief or prolonged, that culminates in death.[5]

— *Immediate cause of death*: Differentiated from remote or underlying cause of death.

— Failure to recognize the relationship between the immediate cause of death and prior initiating events may hinder an adequate death investigation because the medical examiner (coroner) system may not be notified.

Mechanism of Death

— *Mechanism of death*: Lethal physiological derangement through which a cause of death acts.[5]

— Multiple mechanisms can be operative, especially when children survive an initial injury but die of multisystem failure after extensive therapeutic interventions.

Recognizing the Mechanism of Death

— Helps to establish causal relationships and evaluate the clinical course of a process, but should not be substituted for determining the cause of death.

— Helps identify the cause of death when multiple potential causes are present.

— Aids understanding of the physiologic processes that occur in injury and disease and may lead to improved patient care.

Manner of Death

— *Manner of death*: The fashion in which the cause of death arises or the milieu in which the death or lethal injury occurred.[5] It is an opinion separate from cause of death.

— Generally, there are only 5 or 6 categories of manner of death, including natural, homicide, suicide, accident, undetermined, or pending.

1. *Natural*: Due to disease or aging process.
2. *Accident*: The result of an event that is unanticipated and unforeseen by everyone involved (ie, unintentional).[6]
3. *Homicide*: Killing of one person by another through a volitional act (does not reflect the level or presence of criminal culpability). Death certification of homicide does not equal murder.

4. ***Suicide***: The taking of one's own life.
5. ***Undetermined***: Not enough information is available for manner to be determined.
6. ***Pending***: Additional information is needed to determine manner of death (eg, toxicology, other laboratory studies).[7]

— Certification of a manner of death does not preclude or force action by the criminal justice system.

1. Whether or not a criminal investigation should be conducted or continued and whether or not charges should be filed in relation to a death are not matters under the medical examiner's purview; rather, they are legal opinions undertaken by the criminal justice system.
2. The input of the medical examiner plays an important role in these opinions.

— Even if the cause of death is not known, the circumstances surrounding the death can help to identify the manner of death.

Medicolegal Evaluation of Death

Investigation Process

History

— Note the chief complaint and the circumstances before, during, and after death, relying on others to provide these data. Be aware that the history provided in a suspected abuse case is often altered to shift responsibility from the perpetrator and often inconsistent with the observed injuries; it may change as the investigation proceeds.

— Review the complete medical records to document prior injuries and diseases and to assess the child's health and development.

1. Note any episodes in which a child was examined for medical treatment that may, in hindsight, be suggestive of abuse.
2. Identify possible nutritional neglect by carefully assessing the child's growth charts for indications of when chronic problems began.
3. Study previous radiographs to assess the age of healing fractures at postmortem examination.
4. Note well-child visits and screening test results.

— Assess the alleged scene of injury or death. Generally, a law enforcement officer or a medicolegal death investigator conducts the scene investigation.

1. Seek information to corroborate or refute the accuracy of the history of the child's condition.
2. Measure the heights of surfaces, note characteristics of impacting surfaces, assess the possibility of accidental suffocation, and observe for instruments that may have been used to inflict injuries.
3. Use a checklist to standardize investigations (**Table 16-2**).

Table 16-2. Scene Investigation Checklist

Social and Environmental Conditions	
NOTE:	1. Who resides at the residence
	2. Past abuse or neglect
	3. Alcohol or drug involvement
	4. Unattended siblings watching the child
	5. Cultural practices that may influence the death
	6. Social media resources
Family history	
NOTE:	1. Previous child deaths
	2. Age and health of parents and other siblings
Law Enforcement	
NOTE:	1. Caregiver's relationship to the child
	2. Circumstances surrounding the terminal event
	3. Previous deaths in caregiver's custody (if any), including circumstances and disposition of those cases
	4. Medical and social history of caregiver and/or the last person to be with the child when he/she was alive[3]

Physical Examination

— Interpret findings from the postmortem examination.

1. Include a complete autopsy with a thorough gross examination. Pair it with microscopic evaluation as appropriate.
2. Use photographic documentation to permit future review of the case and for legal proceedings. Obtain both scanning and close views, including a scale and case identifier in each photograph. Make sure injuries are the focus of photographs. (See also Chapter 5, "Bruises and Burns.")
3. Perform a complete forensic postmortem examination when any child dies suddenly and unexpectedly or when the circumstances do not reasonably exclude an element of abuse. Consulting a forensic anthropologist may be useful, especially if there are signs of old and healing skeletal injuries.
4. Include a gross external observation when trace evidence can be collected, properly packaged, and handled according to chain-of-custody protocols.
5. Document the body's general features and overall condition, examining the body from head to toe 3 separate times (**Table 16-3**).

— Examine soft tissues and visceral organs.

Table 16-3. Head-to-Toe Examination

First Pass	Emphasize general characteristics (ie, clothing, measurements, hair color and length, general condition and appearance, degree and pattern of rigor mortis, lividity).
Second Pass	Concentrate on physical evidence of medical treatment and/or therapeutic interventions.
Third Pass	Catalog injuries and other lesions specifically and in detail, noting the nature of the injury, location on the body, size, shape, and color. Include a diagrammatical record of injuries.

Ancillary Tests

— Obtain radiological images as indicated (see Chapter 2, "Radiology").

— Send samples of blood, urine, vitreous fluid, and other appropriate tissues for indicated toxicological, chemical, and microbiological analyses. Genetic testing may be useful in some situations. Follow the protocols set for handling these samples [see Chapter 8, "The Chemically Abused Child (Poisoning)" and Chapter 17, "DNA and Evidence Collection"].

Data Interpretation

— Assess the data obtained to develop an opinion that is plausible, scientifically supportable, and admissible as testimony with a reasonable degree of medical certainty.

— State what happened to the child and what did not happen to the child.

— When available, incorporate computer simulation models to demonstrate the biomechanics of injuries and validate or refute various historical scenarios.[8]

— Document the scene by photography or video. Scene re-creation may have value when parents or caregivers may not be able to accurately describe how the child was found. Goals in scene documentation include documenting:

1. Body position (when placed and when found)
2. Head and neck position
3. Materials next to or near the body
4. Any airway obstruction

— Special training is required so the investigator is able to explain the goals and the importance of the scene recreation to the parents or caregivers.[9]

Interpretation of Injuries

— Categorize injuries and determine whether they are major or trivial. Medically trivial injuries can reveal more forensically than injuries with greater physiologic impact.

— Retain the body of the allegedly abused child in the cooler and reexamine 24 hours after the original autopsy to check for further delineation of external injuries and the appearance of other surface injuries not previously noted. The passive drainage of blood from the vasculature, which autopsy augments, clears uninjured areas so that injured areas are more distinct.

— Determine the age of injuries.

1. Injury healing is progressive, so gross and microscopic appearance reflects age to some extent.

2. Factors that influence the appearance and time course of injuries include victim's age and state of health; injury site, depth, and size; overlying skin tone; environmental lighting; specific tissue injured; individual variations; effects of therapy; and development of complications (infection).

3. Evidence of healing indicates post-injury survival and offers some insight into length of survival, with the narrowness of the range inversely proportional to the length of survival.

4. The aging process of injuries helps to determine who did and did not have access to the child when the injury occurred, the child's antemortem behavior, when complications occurred after the initial injury, and when certain injuries occurred in relation to others.

— Note patterned injuries and injury patterns (see also Chapter 5, "Bruises and Burns.")

1. Patterned injuries may have a configuration that indicates the instrument used to inflict the injury.

2. Bite marks are particularly important patterned injuries and may be used to determine the serological and DNA characteristics of the biter, to match the bite of a particular person, and to note whether the source of the bite was human or animal, child or adult, self-inflicted or not (see Chapter 6, "Ophthalmic Manifestations and Oral Injuries").

3. Alternative light sources may yield further delineation of some injuries, as may computer enhancement of photographs.

4. Blunt injuries are usually nonspecific when considered alone, but assessing overall number, location, and age may yield a revealing pattern. A single episode of injury can be differentiated from repeated child battering, and accidental and intentional injuries may be revealed.

— Lethal injury patterns can be evident in abused children.

1. Blunt head trauma, skull fracture, and intracranial hemorrhage (see Chapter 3, "Head Trauma")
2. Shaking (see Chapter 3, "Head Trauma" and Chapter 6, "Ophthalmic Manifestations and Oral Injuries")
3. Intrathoracic, intra-abdominal, other blunt force injuries, mechanical asphyxia, strangulation, smothering, overlying, and choking (see Chapter 5, "Bruises and Burns"; Chapter 6, "Ophthalmic Manifestations and Oral Injuries"; Chapter 7, "Thoracoabdominal Injuries"; and Chapter 10, "Sexual Abuse")
4. Poisoning [see Chapter 8, "The Chemically Abused Child (Poisoning)"]
5. Burns (see Chapter 5, "Bruises and Burns")
6. Neglect (see Chapter 9, "Neglect, Abandonment, and Failure to Thrive")
7. Medical abuse (see Chapter 14, "Medical Child Abuse/Munchausen Syndrome by Proxy")
8. Sexual abuse (see Chapter 10, "Sexual Abuse" and Chapter 12, "Sexually Transmitted Diseases")

Conditions That Are Not Abuse

— Sudden infant death syndrome (SIDS/SUID):

1. SIDS is the most common cause of death among children aged 1 month to 1 year.
2. Mechanical asphyxia is the major abuse/neglect category most likely to be confused with SIDS/SUID.
3. Usually, a thorough death investigation reveals the true nature of a death, but it can be impossible to ascribe some deaths to abuse or SIDS/SUID.
4. When reasonable suspicion exists that a death is not innocuous, certify the cause and manner of death as undetermined rather than SIDS/SUID.[10,11]

— Metabolic and other disorders:

1. Various conditions predispose the child to skeletal, cutaneous, visceral, or soft-tissue damage or manifest as "pseudo injuries" that must be differentiated from actual physical assaults.
2. Included in these disorders are osteogenesis imperfecta, some neoplasms, infantile cortical hyperostosis, congenital syphilis, Menkes syndrome, coagulopathies, metabolic disorders, some connective tissue diseases, inborn errors of metabolism, hematologic disease processes, hemophagocytic lymphohistiocytosis, and occult lymphoblastic leukemia.[12]

— Injuries related to therapeutic intervention

— Folk medicine (see Chapter 5, "Bruises and Burns")

— Postmortem changes

Organ and Tissue Transplantation Issues

— Deaths coming under the jurisdiction of the medical examiner are a major potential source for suitable donor organs and tissues.

— Balancing the need for these organs and tissues with the requirements for potential legal actions related to abuse and neglect causing the child's death requires close cooperation between all medical, medicolegal, and legal personnel and family members. **Table 16-4** outlines a proposed protocol.

Table 16-4. Proposed Protocol for Retrieving Organs and Tissues
1. Attending physician notifies the medical examiner of the impending death.
2. Medical examiner collects investigational information from other agencies to make an informed evaluation about which organs or tissues may potentially be retrieved and what further studies are needed before retrieval.
3. Family is approached for permission to retrieve those organs or tissues approved by the medical examiner.
4. If the medical examiner does not attend the retrieval procedure and the operating surgeon finds an occult injury, the procedure is halted, pending further consultation with the medical examiner.

— No procedure can be carried out on the body of an individual whose death falls under medicolegal jurisdiction without the permission of the medical examiner or coroner.

— Unless otherwise specified by local statute or regulation, the next of kin or legal guardian must give permission for organ and tissue retrieval.

— Organ or tissue retrieval cannot interfere with the fulfillment of statutory and professional responsibilities.

— Consult with transplantation personnel to determine the guidelines for organ/tissue recovery and to optimize the medicolegal examination in difficult cases.[13]

Mass Fatalities

— Follow scientific methods

— Disaster Mortuary Operational Response Team (DMORT) may be activated when resources are strained

1. Part of the National Disaster Medical System (NDMS) [as part of the Department of Health and Human Services (DHHS)]
2. Falls under Emergency Support Function #8 (ESF #8)
3. Provides victim identification and mortuary services [eg, temporary morgue facilities, forensic dental pathology, forensic anthropology, processing, preparation (disposition of remains)[14]]

— DMORT supports the medical examiner/coroner and local authorities

— The Family Assistance Center Team (FACT)

1. Obtain antemortem data and medical/dental records of victims
2. Reunite displaced families
3. Liaise with government and nongovernment agencies

References

1. Davis GJ, Hanzlick RL. The medical examiner and coroner systems. Medscape Web site. http://emedicine.medscape.com/article/1785357-overview. Updated December 4, 2015. Accessed April 5, 2017.

2. Hanzlick RL. Medical examiners, coroners, and public health: a review and update. *Arch Pathol Lab Med.* 2006;130(9):1274-1282.

3. Lynch VA, Koehler SA. Forensic investigation of death. In: Lynch VA, Duval JB, eds. *Forensic Nursing Science.* 2nd ed. Saint Louis, MO: Mosby, Inc; 2011:179-194.

4. Prahlow JA, Byard RW. Death investigation. In: Prahlow JA, Byard RW, eds. *Atlas of Forensic Pathology.* New York, NY: Humana Press; 2012.

5. Centers for Disease Control and Prevention. *Medical Examiners' and Coroners' Handbook on Death Registration and Fetal Death Reporting: 2003 Revision.* Hyattsville, Md: National Center for Health and Human Services, Centers for Disease Control and Prevention, National Center for Health Statistics; 2003.

6. USLegal. Accidental death law and legal definition. USLegal Web site. http://definitions.uslegal.com/a/accidental-death/. Accessed April 5, 2017.

7. Hazlick RL, Hansaker JH, Davis GJ. *A Guide for Manner of Death Classification.* Saint Louis, MO: National Association of Medical Examiners; 2002. Charly D. Miller Web site. http://www.charlydmiller.com/LIB03/2002NAMEmannerofdeath.pdf. Accessed April 5, 2017.

8. Pierce MC, Bertocci G. Injury biomechanics and child abuse. *Annu Rev Biomed Eng.* 2008;10:85-106.

9. Diebold K. Conducting the doll reenactment. In: Centers for Disease Control and Prevention, ed. *Sudden, Unexpected Infant Death Investigation.* Atlanta, GA: Centers for Disease Control and Prevention; 2006:170-185.

10. Centers for Disease Control and Prevention. *Sudden, Unexplained Infant Death Investigation.* Atlanta, GA: Centers for Disease Control and Prevention; 2006.

11. Centers for Disease Control and Prevention. Sudden unexpected infant death and sudden infant death syndrome. Centers for Disease Control and Prevention Web site. http://www.cdc.gov/sids/index.htm. Updated October 3, 2016. Accessed April 5, 2017.

12. Krous H. Sudden infant death syndrome (SIDS), sudden unexpected death in infancy (SUDI), and sudden unexpected death in childhood (SUDC). In: Collins KA, Byard RW, eds. *Forensic Pathology of Infancy and Childhood*. New York, NY: Springer; 2014:193-206.

13. Shafer TJ. Organ donation and tissue transplantation. In: Lynch VA, Duval JB, eds. *Forensic Nursing Science*. 2nd ed. Saint Louis, MO: Mosby, Inc; 2011:581-597.

14. Public Health Emergency. Disaster mortuary operational response teams. Public Health Emergency Web site. http://www.phe.gov/preparedness/responders/ndms/teams/pages/dmort.aspx. Accessed April 5, 2017.

Chapter 17

DNA and Evidence Collection

Patricia A. Melton, PhD
Jack Ballantyne, PhD
Diana K. Faugno, MSN, RN, CPN, SANE-A, SANE-P, FAAFS, DF-IAFN
Sergeant Joanne Archambault (Ret.)
Kathy L. Bell, MS, RN
Jane M. Lavelle, MD
Patricia M. Speck, DNSc, ARNP, APN, FNP-BC, DF-IAFN, FAAFS, FAAN

DNA

Forensic DNA analysis develops a DNA profile from an evidence sample. This process is often referred to as DNA typing of biological evidence.[1-3] The goal of DNA analysis with respect to child abuse and neglect is to determine the individuals who contributed the biological evidence found.

Types of DNA Tests

Short Tandem Repeats (STRs)

— STRs are genetic markers that vary in the population due to differing numbers of repeats of a simple DNA base sequence at a particular location on a particular chromosome (ie, locus/loci).

— For example, the STR on chromosome 8 (D8S1179) has a TATA base repeat sequence, and an individual may have a D8S1179 type of 12, 15 (ie, his/her chromosome 8s have twelve and fifteen repeats of TATA respectively). Another individual may have a 9, 10 type and is, therefore, distinguishable on the basis of this single genetic test from the first individual.

— A standard DNA profile will comprise multiple genetic tests of different STRs on a number of chromosomes.

- The DNA test is carried out by amplifying (ie, making many copies of) the sample DNA by the polymerase chain reaction (PCR) technique.
    - The above refers to standard DNA profiling that tests STRs on the autosomes, comprising 22 pairs of the human complement of 23 pairs chromosomes; however, STRs also exist on the sex chromosomes [eg, the male-specific Y chromosome (Y-STRs)].
- Y-STRs can be useful when standard autosomal DNA profiling fails due to the presence of overwhelming quantities of a female victim's DNA.
- Due to the biology of the Y chromosome, Y-STRs are not as discriminating as autosomal STRs, but the recovery of Y chromosome genetic information from the male donor can be very important in individual cases.

Polymerase Chain Reaction (PCR) Analysis

- PCR analysis allows the analysis of small quantities of DNA because the scientist can, within hours, create millions of copies of a specific DNA sequence that can be isolated and assessed.
- Because millions of copies of a specific DNA sequence are created in the analytical process, PCR analysis allows for typing of small quantities of DNA. These newly generated sequences can be isolated and assessed.
- Primers (short, chemically synthesized segments of DNA typically 15 to 40 nucleotides long) are designed. They often correspond to unique DNA sequences in the human genome. A pair of primers flanks the region of interest.
- An enzyme is used to replicate the DNA sequence of interest. This polymerase enzyme is isolated from bacteria and functions at elevated temperatures.
- The PCR process is conducted within a thermal cycler (a device that cyclically alters the temperature of a DNA reaction mix, creating denaturation, annealing, and elongation phases for PCR) to replicate a specific DNA sequence.[4-6]

— The ability to alter temperatures and, therefore, generate the 3 phases of PCR is key to controlling the functionality of the polymerase and exponentially copy the DNA of interest.

— The PCR process produces millions of copies of a specified sequence of DNA from a single DNA molecule. This level of sensitivity allows accurate DNA typing from a significantly smaller biological sample than the historical RFLP DNA process.[6,7]

— PCR testing is extremely sensitive and allows analysis of DNA from trace samples (eg, "touch DNA") and degraded samples.

— Biological samples that can be tested include deposited body fluid samples with a source of cellular material (eg, sperm cells from semen, blood cells, epithelial cells from saliva) or via significant skin contact (ie, touch DNA).

— Before the sample is subjected to analysis in the laboratory, it is often impossible to predict the amount of DNA present on an evidence sample. As the technological sensitivity for detection and typing of DNA continues to advance, it is encouraged to obtain biological samples that have the potential to provide a DNA result.[6,7]

— Forensic test kits based on STRs exploit multiplexing, wherein as many as 20 or more genetic markers can be analyzed in a single reaction using a common analytical platform known as capillary electrophoresis.

— Laboratories in the United States have established a standard panel consisting of the 13 core STR loci that permits comparison of DNA profiles. As of January 2017, there are 20 recognized STR loci. This expansion permits more individual discrimination and helps resolve missing persons investigations and international investigations.

— Capillary electrophoresis is the current standard mode of technology; however, advances in sequencing technology using massively parallel sequencing (MPS) will allow increased sensitivity and the ability to observe additional genetic markers.

Convicted Offender Databases

— All 50 states have authorized legislation requiring certain convicted offenders to provide biological samples for analysis and entry into the Combined DNA Index System (CODIS) database.[8]

— CODIS has 3 hierarchical levels: local, state, and national.

— The tiered approach permits exchange and comparison of DNA profiles between states, within a state, and locally.

— CODIS is composed of multiple indices that can be searched against each other based on specific circumstances. The indices are:

  — Convicted Offender

  — Forensic

  — Missing Persons

  — Unidentified Human Remains

  — Biological Relatives of Missing Persons

— Some states also permit an Arrestee Index within CODIS.

— The Forensic Index, Convicted Offender Index, and Arrestee Index are the most commonly searched for criminal casework.

— More information can be found at https://www.fbi.gov/about-us/lab/biometric-analysis/codis and https://www.fbi.gov/about-us/lab/biometric-analysis/codis/codis_brochure

— CODIS has several indices in which DNA profiles are stored and searched[8]:

1. ***Forensic Index***: Contains DNA profiles from crime scene evidence, referred to as forensic unknowns.
2. ***Offender Index***: Contains DNA profiles of individuals convicted of crimes that require a biological sample to be provided to law enforcement for DNA profiling.
3. ***Arrestee Index***: Contains DNA profiles of arrested persons (if State law permits the collection of arrestee samples).

4. ***Missing Persons, Unidentified Human Remains, Biological Relatives of Missing Persons, Pedigree Tree Indices*:** Contains DNA profiles from missing persons and unidentified human remains and appropriate reference samples for the identification of missing persons.

— When an offender is identified, an additional reference sample is obtained and the evidence examined to confirm the match.

Consent Issues

— Suspected sexual contact with a child under age 18 years is a mandatory child abuse reporting offense in most states, except when Title X guarantees reproductive health care for consensual sexual activity, birth control, and pregnancy care. Some adolescent victims may consent to intercourse but may not be able to give consent legally because of relevant state statutes (eg, statutory rape).

— Know the statutes that differentiate between child molestation and statutory rape, as well as the applicable reporting laws.

— Some community protocols encourage and provide a forensic examination in addition to the medical examination, even if the victim refuses to report to the police.

Collecting Evidence in Sexual Assault Cases

— The frequent lack of physical injury to corroborate a child's disclosure of assault makes properly identifying, collecting, and preserving DNA evidence extremely important (based on the time line of the occurrence).

— Specific material needed for evidence collection is listed in **Table 17-1**. The examiner must wear gloves throughout the procedure, taking care to discard gloves frequently between procedures.

— In sexual assault cases the entire range of possible biological evidence may prove useful in linking the victim to the suspect, the victim to the crime scene, and the suspect to the crime scene.

1. Law enforcement personnel typically collect evidence from the location where the incident occurred.

2. Medical professionals typically collect evidence from the human body and from clothing.

Table 17-1. Materials for Evidence Collection
— Paper bags
— Letter-sized envelopes
— Labels (patient name, medical record number, date, examiner initials)
— Seals (to secure envelops)
— Specimen checklist with space for additional evidence documentation
— Chain of evidence form
— Cotton-tipped swabs
— Gauze (2 x 2)
— Wooden sticks
— Sterile urine cups for liquid evidence (usually requires freezing)
— Sterile urine cups for debris or other biological dry evidence
— Clean glass slides
— Disposable sterile eyedropper
— Comb
— Wood's lamp
— Other alternate light source
— Sterile saline solution
— Sterile distilled water

Medical Guidelines

— The details of the assault will guide the examiner in what evidence to collect and how to collect it. This information is obtained through a forensic medical interview of the victim and discussion with law enforcement and sometimes caregivers.

— It is best to collect a complete sexual assault kit (SAK), with the patient's permission. In patient-centered care, the patient may decline any collection.

1. Include swabbings of possible bite marks; breast, areola, and nipple swabs when indicated; skin swabs when kissing, licking, or sucking is reported; and fingernail scrapings and swabbings.
2. Collect clothing worn directly after the assault and clothing worn to the examination, particularly underwear. Lay a large sheet of paper on the floor and cover it with a second sheet. Have the child stand on the sheet so that anything that drops as the child undresses falls onto the paper. Place each article of clothing and then the sheets of paper in separate paper bags. Label, seal, and initial the bags to preserve the evidence.
3. With continued improvements in DNA detection, it is currently recommended to collect up to ten days after the incident. Collect 1 or 2 cervical and vaginal swabs, and sweep the swabs in the posterior fornix in menstruating postpubescent victims. Carefully preserve any loose hairs found on the victim or the victim's clothing.
4. Be aware that DNA evidence can be found in areas other than the genitalia, such as the hair, navel, abdomen, and gluteal clefts.
5. It is common for penile penetration of the vagina to be absent in the prepubescent assault, but there may have been penile/abdominal touching, labial penetration, or rubbing of the penis between the buttocks.

— Samples from suspects may require a search warrant or court order. Include:

1. Penile swabs can be recovered from male suspects who are taken into custody within a day of the assault and who have not bathed in the interim. Consider seeing the suspect within 72 hours. Include the glans, shaft, and scrotum area, particularly at the penile scrotal junction.
2. Fingernail scrapings or swabbings, especially if digital penetration is alleged.
3. Clothing. Look for bodily fluids from the victim. If the suspect is not apprehended wearing the clothing believed to be worn at the time of the assault, law enforcement should obtain a warrant or consent to search any premises where the clothing may be found.

4. Notation of any genital abnormalities, tattoos, jewelry, venereal warts, and evidence of scratches, bites, and abrasions.

— Law enforcement should take samples from the environment where the sexual assault took place.

1. Vehicles, apartments, and houses are examined with an alternate light source to detect possible biologic fluids.
2. Obtain condoms, tissues, or hairs from the scene.
3. Substances may not be visible to the naked eye, so a Wood's lamp or alternate light source may be used. In the presence of the 320 to 400 nm wavelength light emitted, certain substances become fluorescent.[9] If this occurs, moisten a sterile cotton swab with 1 drop of nuclease-free sterile water, roll the swab over the area in question, place the swab in a labeled holder, and let it air-dry before packaging it for later evaluation. Repeat the procedure with a second sterile swab.
4. Collect saliva evidence by placing 1 drop of sterile, nuclease-free water on a swab, rolling it over the area, and then taking a dry swab and rolling it over the same area; this 2-step process collects more DNA.

— When dictated by standards of care in your community, collect reference standards from the skin or buccal areas of the victim, suspect, and all consensual partners for comparison.

1. These can be as simple as a buccal swab from inside the individual's cheek, which is the preferred method, or as invasive as drawing a tube of blood.
2. Try to obtain these with as little trauma as possible to the victim.

— Document:

1. Consent for the examination.
2. The history of the assault.
3. Medical information and findings.

4. Postassault hygiene activities (less influential as DNA detection methods develop).
5. The process of evidence collection during the examination.

— Nursing Guidelines:

1. The American Nurses Association's *Forensic Nursing: Scope and Standards of Practice* is the standard for care for all forensic nursing patients of all ages and stages of development.[10]
2. The International Association of Forensic Nurses offers educational guidelines for the forensic nurse in pediatric sexual abuse care.[11]
3. These documents outline the minimum standards of nursing practice, the minimal level of instruction for the sexual assault nurse examiner, and additional minimum educational recommendations for individuals examining children.

Specifics With Respect to the Child Victim

— See Chapters 10, "Sexual Abuse," and 11, "The Sexual Abuse Interview," for a discussion of the examination of a child victim.

— Use a team approach to evidence collection to ensure contamination control and accurately document, prioritize, collect, package, transport, and submit the evidence according to established protocols.

— Guidelines are listed in **Table 17-2**.

Use of DNA Evidence as a Prosecutorial Tool

— The forensic medical examination follows the circumstances of the assault and the victim's experiential history.

— DNA detection diminishes over time when collected from both the cervix and posterior fornix. In a 2015 prospective study, DNA detection occurred in 65% of women after 10 days; therefore, as detection methods improve, it is possible the time frame for collection of swabs will expand.[12]

— Typically, a standard DNA profile (autosomal STRs using the CODIS loci with the DNA profile being more rare than 1 in 1 billion) is only readily recoverable up to 3 to 4 days after ejaculation. Y-STRs can be recovered up to 9 days after ejaculation.

Table 17-2. Guidelines for Collecting Evidence

— Do not force children to cooperate. If the child is old enough, allow him/her to hold your hand while you collect so he/she can stop you if collection is uncomfortable.

— Use only paper to package evidence.

— Package clothing items separately. If the child undressed on a paper sheet (as described above) pick up the clothing separately, place a paper on top of the clothing, and fold the clothing with the paper, protecting the surfaces from cross-contamination. Fold the top paper drape and place in a separate bag. Discard the bottom paper/cloth drape.

— Air-dry all evidence at least 30 to 60 minutes before packaging. Using air-drying and paper packaging avoids encouraging mold and bacteria growth. Do not use heat to dry samples.

— Use only 1 drop of sterile nuclease-free water to moisten swabs. Note that tap water contains various metals and salts, so do not use tap water. Use saline solution only when there is an open wound.

— Use only cotton-tipped swabs. Consult with the forensic laboratory before using other materials. Cotton has suitable absorption properties and does not contain material that destroys DNA material.

— Do not lick any seals on evidence envelopes. Licking can contaminate the evidence and expose the examiner to potentially infectious agents.

— Maintain chain of custody at all times. Document who collected the evidence, from whom the evidence was collected, who transferred and picked up the evidence, what was done to it, and where and when it goes every time it is handled.

— The probative information recovered from Y-STRs is not as statistically significant as autosomal STRs and cannot be loaded into CODIS. It is not uncommon to eliminate 99.9% of falsely accused suspects by this method, with the DNA profile being present in 1 in 100 individuals or as rare as 1 in 10 000 individuals.

— Law enforcement officers are instructed to collect and impound evidence for later analysis by criminalists who have the proper equipment and training to identify and extract biological evidence.

— When evidence cannot be moved, a criminalist, crime scene specialist, or patrol officer trained in forensic evidence collection procedures should collect the samples.

— The National Institute of Justice (NIJ) provides resources for the identification, preservation, and collection of DNA evidence at crime scenes, including the *Biological Evidence Preservation Handbook*, a collaboration of the National Institute of Standards and Technology (NIST) and the NIJ (http://nvlpubs.nist.gov/nistpubs/ir/2013/NIST.IR.7928.pdf).[13]

Specimens for Seminal Products

— Use cotton-tipped swabs to obtain 2 specimens from each site, collected at the same time. A 2-step method and Dacron swabs may be used, but consultation with the forensic laboratory is suggested.

1. Avoiding the parotid and sublingual salivary glands, swab the mouth along the buccal mucosa pockets, the gum line, between the teeth, in cavities, and where food and fluid has pooled. Swab nasal orifices, and have the patient blow his/her nose in a 4x4 sterile gauze, particularly if he/she complained of reflux or vomiting of ejaculate.
2. Evaluate the estrogen effect of the hymen and surrounding tissue (**Table 17-3**).
3. If a microscope is immediately available and the health care provider and institution is CLIA cleared, perform a wet mount to look for motile sperm. Place a drop of saline solution on a glass slide, mix the saline solution with one of the specimen swabs, and place a coverslip over the sample. For best results, use a magnification of 400 and lower the light source.[14] Send this slide to the laboratory, maintaining chain of custody.
4. To collect an anal swab, place the cotton swab on the anus, and swab the separated folds. Collect the feces in the area on 1 or 2 swabs.
5. After collection of the anal swabs and evaluation of the tissue with Toluidine blue (including photodocumentation), collect rectal swabs. To collect a rectal specimen, place an anoscope in the rectum, thread the cotton swab into the proximal rectum, pick up debris, swab the mucosa gently, remove it, and dry it. (Note that seminal contents that drained from the vagina may be found in anal folds.)

Table 17-3. Evaluation of Estrogen Effect of the Hymen

- Estrogen effect allows the health care provider to examine the vestibule, hymen, and vagina without eliciting pain.
  - The child's first examination should proceed with caution, paying close attention to the child's reaction to the methods used in evaluation. Any resistance from the child should stop the examination until additional trust-building occurs between health care provider and patient.
  - If the child presents with evidence of sexual penetration or is menstruating regularly, a speculum examination is recommended, as objects (including condoms) may be found in the posterior fornix and collected as evidence of penetration.
  - The child has full control over cooperation. No child should be made to participate in an evaluation.
  - If the forensic medical examination is medically necessary, conscious sedation is recommended.
  - Delaying examination may result in cooperation on the second meeting.
- When there is evidence of hymenal estrogen effect, collect vaginal secretions by placing a swab through the hymen, holding the labia together, and waiting for the swab to absorb the moisture.
- If the child's hymen has no estrogen effect, do not penetrate the thin hymenal tissue with a swab when the child is conscious. If the child is cooperative, drip 2 to 3 drops of warm normal saline solution into the vagina through the hymenal orifice. Collect the moisture from the vaginal area as it settles in the posterior vestibular area.
  - If moisture is trapped in the vaginal tube, encourage the child to cough. Fluid will escape the area into the posterior vestibular structures where the cotton tipped swab will absorb cellular materials.
  - Using the same moist swab, swab the structures of the vestibule, applying light pressure. Dry the swab.

6. Inspect and photograph the vestibular area. Using 2 swabs slightly moistened with sterile nuclease-free water, gently swab the vestibular area, swabbing folds and the hymenal sulcus. Apply Toluidine blue and remove. Note any iatrogenic injuries created in the process of inspection and collection.
7. Note and swab any areas of dried secretion on the body. Use a Wood's lamp or an alternate light source to identify areas for swabbing. Consider swabbing the genital area and inner thighs, even if the Wood's lamp reveals no fluorescence.[9,15,16]
8. Air-dry all swabs for at least 1 hour; store them in envelopes or drying boxes, or use protective tips; and label them for processing by the crime laboratory.

Hair Specimens

— Collect any extraneous hairs found on the victim's body as trace evidence and package accordingly.

— If the individual has pubic hair, comb it and collect debris in a paper towel. Place debris in an envelope along with the comb.

— If the hair is matted with secretions, cut it, place it in a separate envelope, and store it in a paper envelope.

Foreign Debris

— Fibers, dirt, or other foreign material can help identify where events took place.

— If there was a history of a struggle, scrape under the child's fingernails with a wooden stick. Swabbing with a moistened swab is also acceptable.

— Place the scrapings and wooden stick in a paper envelope.

— Collect debris, such as dirt or threads, in paper envelopes. Using a scotch tape lift may secure this evidence for crime lab analysis.

Blood Specimens

— On rare occasion, a specimen may be requested to document a child's blood type or to obtain a DNA profile. Trained personnel collect blood with appropriate collection vessels, often with different preservatives, depending on subsequent testing.

Chain of Evidence

Collection Guidelines

— Label every specimen with the child's name, record number, date and time, the specimen's collection site, and name and initials of the collector.

— Place all dried specimens in separate envelopes or paper bags and seal with evidence tape.

— Document the transfer of evidence with the date, time, and name of both the person giving and the person receiving the evidence.

— Transfer evidence to the appropriate officials immediately, recording the officer's name, identification number, agency, and the date.

— Ensure that all individuals handling evidence sign for it. This procedure must be strictly observed to make the evidence admissible in a court proceeding.[17-24]

Proper Transportation and Storage of DNA Evidence

— Deliver the dried biological samples to the laboratory as soon as possible but preferably within 12 hours of collection.

— In the event of immediate transfer to the laboratory, laboratory personnel will follow their protocol for handling wet biological evidence.

— Keep other evidence dry and at room temperature in paper bags or envelopes.

— Direct sunlight and warm conditions may be harmful to DNA, so do not place evidence where it may become hot.

— For longer storage (ie, > 1 day), refrigeration (or at a minimum, dry, cool storage) is recommended. Most jurisdictions have temperature- and moisture-controlled environments for stored evidence.

— Law enforcement personnel who maintain the chain of custody transport evidence to the police property room or forensic laboratory. Some programs have temporary storage facilities at the examination site, permitting the victim to leave as soon as the examination is over while the examiner completes drying, packaging, and documenting the evidence.

— The SAFER legislation is a resource for sexual assault response team (SART) members addressing the issue of rape kit backlogs.

Testing Specimens

Semen Products

— Semen ejaculate comprises a cellular component (ie, spermatozoa from the testes and leukocytes) and noncellular secretions (ie, seminal fluid from accessory organs, including the prostate, seminal vesicles, and Cowper's glands).

— Sperm cells are the primary source of DNA in semen from nonvasectomized individuals. Seminal fluids carry DNA from epithelial cells.

— Even with properly collected specimens, all of the tests for semen products may be negative. Assault cannot be dated or proved using forensic evidence alone.

— Successful detection of semen depends on using correct swabbing methods.

  — Use 2 swabs in the vagina (first in the cervix, followed by sweeping the posterior fornix).

  — Swabs should be fully air-dried and stored in temperature-controlled environments in separate envelopes or bags.

  — Store specimens correctly and transfer them to the laboratory as soon as possible or practicable.

Sperm

— If a microscope is available, look for motile and nonmotile sperm. If not, use rapid detection kits. The microscopic presence of sperm cells is confirmation of the presence of semen.

— In the postpubertal girl, DNA from sperm remain in the vaginal tube for 10 days in 65% of females.[12] Menses and oral hormones reduce but do not eliminate DNA detection using the most sensitive Y-STR testing methods.[12]

1. Early research determined that sperm are rarely present in oral specimens after 6 hours and in rectal specimens after 24 hours.[25] Research about more recent methods for testing DNA is sparse but

developing. Work with the forensic laboratory for guidance on the timing of collection in cases of oral assault.

2. Urination, defecation, douching, and bathing do not alter findings.

— Survival time in prepubertal girls is shorter because cervical mucus is absent.[18] Recent research suggests that morphological appearance and pH change due to estrogen levels is the reason for a lack of detection in prepubertal girls and menopausal women.[12]

— Dried secretions on clothing are stable, permitting detection of sperm for more than 1 year, and may still persist on clothing after laundering.[19-21,26,27]

Acid Phosphatase

— Elevated levels of acid phosphatase (AP) are a general indicator of recent sexual intercourse and ejaculation. However, because acid phosphatase is also present in vaginal secretions, such tests are regarded as presumptive in nature and cannot be used to confirm the presence of semen. Thus, AP is used primarily as a screening test for semen.

— Very high concentrations are seen in semen for approximately 8 hours post coitus. Low levels occur within 72 hours.

— Elevated levels persist for a much shorter time in the mouth and rectum.

— Clothing specimens, depending upon the storage environment and the extent of laundering, may contain traces for up to 3 years.[19-22,26,27]

Prostate-Specific Antigen (PSA, p30, KLK3) and Seminal Vesicle-Specific Antigen Semenogelin (Sg, SVSA, SEMG1 or 2)

— Perform immunochromatographic or enzyme-linked immunosorbent assay on vaginal fluid to detect p30 or Sg.

— If p30 or Sg is present in vaginal fluid, semen is confirmed.

— Postcoital samples show a decline in p30/Sg to undetectable levels in 48-72 hours.

— p30 (and probably Sg too) is detectable in dried specimens for up to 12 years.[28,29]

— This specific test is being eliminated in favor of first testing for DNA. There are some office (point-of-use) tests for p30, performed by providers and law enforcement.

DNA Markers

— DNA markers can identify the likelihood that a body fluid came from an alleged perpetrator.

— For evidence collection and proper analysis of the results, specimens are compared with samples taken from the victim and any potential suspects.

Hair Specimens

— Microscopic analysis of hair is considerably less specific than seminal fluid analysis for identifying a perpetrator. The microscopic comparison of hair samples to match the hair with a specific individual or exclude potential donors is no longer routinely performed.

Photodocumentation

(See **Table 17-4** and Chapter 6, "Ophthalmic Manifestations and Oral Injuries.")

Table 17-4. Documentation Systems

— Digital camera with a tripod or colposcope with attached camera
  — A/C power adapter
  — Photo relay lens
  — Compact flash card (minimum of 64 megabytes)
  — Compact flash reader
  — Standard RCA cables
— Video monitor to view examinations
— Computer: The images captured on the compact flash card should be transferred to a computer after each examination. Store downloaded images in a protected network drive or transfer them to a CD-ROM or DVD.

Other Investigational Tools

— Use measurements to ascertain whether the proposed mechanism of injury is possible. Create comprehensive and detailed documentation of the examination of the child.

  — A straight ruler helps in setting up a photograph.

  — In addition, a familiar object, such as a coin, can be placed in the frame to establish a relative scale for comparing injuries.

  — To avoid distortion, use an L-shaped ruler (square). Keep several of these rulers on hand.

— Use a tape measure to measure objects and surfaces, particularly when falls are reported.

References

1. Gaensslen RE. *Sourcebook in Forensic Serology, Immunology, and Biochemistry*. Washington, DC: National Institute of Justice; 1983.
2. Saferstein R, ed. *Forensic Science Handbook*. Englewood Cliffs, NJ: Prentice-Hall; 1982.
3. Saferstein R, ed. *Forensic Science Handbook*. Vol 2. Englewood, NJ: Prentice-Hall; 1988.
4. National Research Council. *The Evaluation of Forensic DNA Evidence*. Washington, DC: National Academy Press; 1996.
5. Inman K, Rudin N. *An Introduction to Forensic DNA Analysis*. New York, NY: CRC Press; 1997.
6. Butler JM. *Forensic DNA Typing*. Burlington, MA: Elsevier Academic Press; 2005.
7. Butler JM. *Advanced Topics in Forensic DNA Typing: Methodology*. Waltham, MA: Elsevier Academic Press; 2011.
8. Federal Bureau of Investigation. *The FBI's Combined DNA Index System (CODIS) Program Brochure*. Washington, DC: US Department of Justice; 2000.

9. Santucci KA, Nelson DG, McQuillen KK, Duffy SJ, Linakis JG. Wood's lamp utility in the identification of semen. *Pediatrics*. 1999;104(6):1342-1344.

10. American Nurses Association, International Association of Forensic Nurse. *Forensic Nursing: Scope and Standards of Practice*. Silver Spring, MD: American Nurses Association, International Association of Forensic Nurses; 2015.

11. International Association of Forensic Nurses. *Sexual Assault Nurse Examiner (SANE) Education Guidelines*. Elkridge, MD: International Association of Forensic Nurses; 2015.

12. Speck P, Ballantyne J. *Post-Coital DNA Recovery Study*. Washington, DC: National Criminal Justice Reference Service; 2014.

13. National Commission on the Future of DNA Evidence. National Institute of Justice Web site. https://www.nij.gov/topics/forensics/evidence/dna/commission/pages/welcome.aspx. Accessed April 13, 2017.

14. Collins KA. The laboratory's role in detecting sexual assault. *Lab Med*. 1998;28:361-365.

15. Gabby T, Winkelby MA, Boyce T, Fisher DL, Lancaster A, Sensabaugh GF. Sexual abuse of children: the detection of semen on skin. *Am J Dis Child*. 1992;146(6):700-703.

16. Atabaki S, Paradise JE. The medical evaluation of the sexually abused child: lessons from a decade of research. *Pediatrics*. 1999;104(1 pt 2):178-186.

17. US Department of Justice, Office of Justice Programs, Office for Victims of Crimes. *Sexual Assault Nurse Examiner: Development and Operation Guide*. Washington, DC: US Department of Justice, Office of Justice Programs, Office for Victims of Crimes; 1999.

18. Paradise JE. The medical evaluation of the sexually abused child. *Pediatr Clin North Am*. 1990;37(4):839-862.

19. Reece RM, Ludwig S, eds. *Child Abuse: Medical Diagnosis and Management*. 2nd ed. Philadelphia, PA: Lippincott Williams & Wilkins; 2000.

20. Giardino AP, Christian CW, Giardino ER. *A Practical Guide to the Evaluation of Child Physical Abuse and Neglect*. Thousand Oaks, CA: Sage Publications; 1997.

21. Bays J, Chadwick D. Medical diagnosis of the sexually abused child. *Child Abuse Negl.* 1993;17(1):91-110.

22. DeJong AR, Finkel MA. Sexual abuse of children. *Curr Probl Pediatr.* 1990;20(9):489-567.

23. Muram D. Child sexual abuse. *Obstet Gynecol Clin North Am.* 1992;19:193-207.

24. American College of Emergency Physicians. *Evaluation and Management of the Sexually Assaulted or Sexually Abused Patient.* Dallas, TX: American College of Emergency Physicians; 1999.

25. Willott GM, Allard AE. Spermatozoa—their persistence after sexual intercourse. *Forensic Sci Intl.* 1982;19(2):135-154.

26. Silverman EM, Silverman AG. Persistence of spermatozoa in the lower genital tracts of women. *J Am Med Assoc.* 1978;240(17):1875-1877.

27. Ricci LR, Hoffman SA. Prostatic acid phosphatase and sperm in the postcoital vagina. *Ann Emerg Med.* 1982;11(10):530-534.

28. Graves HC, Sensabaugh GF, Blake ET. Postcoital detection of a male-specific semen protein. Application to the investigation of rape. *New Engl J Med.* 1985;312(6):338-343.

29. Kamenev L, Leclercq M, Francois-Gerard C. Detection of p30 antigen in sexual assault case material. *J Forensic Sci Soc.* 1990;30(4):193-200.

Chapter 18

Prevention

Christopher Spencer Greeley, MD, FAAP

Importance of Prevention

- Early efforts to support a family with a new baby in order to strengthen their parenting abilities may set in motion a positive parent-child relational trajectory. Years later, this may not be possible if problematic parenting behaviors have become entrenched and difficult to change.[1-3]
- Research has demonstrated the importance of supporting parent-infant attachment and its significance for later life social competencies,[4] and recent brain research has underscored the importance of the early years of development for later functioning.[5,6]
- If prevention is effective, there is the potential to save substantial costs related to the medical and mental health sequelae of maltreatment, educational problems, and costs associated with involvement of the judicial system.[7]
- As adults, children who were victims of maltreatment have both an increased utilization of medical resources, particularly mental health services,[8] as well as a greater likelihood of unemployment and poverty.[9] Other potential problems include brain damage, learning problems, aggression, juvenile delinquency, adult criminal behavior, and depression.

Types of Prevention

- Prevention is often categorized as ***universal*** (or primary), ***selected*** (or secondary), or ***indicated*** (or tertiary). In practice, there is often considerable overlap and one intervention, eg, home visiting, might apply to all 3 categories, albeit in varying circumstances.

1. Universal efforts target an entire population such as all children receiving pediatric primary care.
2. Selected interventions focus on high-risk groups such as low-income teenage mothers.
3. Indicated interventions are synonymous with treatment, aiming to prevent recurrences and potential sequelae.

— Alternatively, prevention may be described in terms of its intended target and timing and might be described as "proactive" or "reactive" to abuse and targeted at the "individual" or "community."[10] This removes some potential boundaries in the primary, secondary, and tertiary construct.

1. ***Proactive and community prevention strategies*** (previously known as universal prevention) are based on an understanding that a problem is prevalent in the population, and a strategy is known or thought to be effective in mitigating the likelihood of the problem, eg, child neglect, occurring.
2. ***Proactive and individual prevention strategies*** (previously known as selected prevention) use research, theory, and experience to identify high-risk groups for targeted interventions, such as single teenage mothers having their first baby. Available strategies are often based on the identification of high-risk status or risk factors and conditions that may lead to maltreatment and must be addressed.
3. An example of a ***reactive and community effort*** would be a bullying program rolled out in a school in response to high rates of peer-on-peer violence.
4. Examples of ***reactive and individual strategy*** might include prison terms for perpetrators of abuse or mandatory parenting classes for offenders.

Etiology of Child Abuse and Neglect: Risk and Protective Factors

— Research has identified a wide array of risk factors for physical child abuse and neglect. These can be organized in a multilevel fashion, often using an ecological, or ecological-developmental, framework.[11-13] This framework highlights that physically abusive and/or neglectful behavior derives from the complex set of transactions within and between:

1. The parent and child and their interactions (***microsystem***)
2. The familial and community contexts within which the parent-child dyad are embedded (***exosystem***)
3. Societal contexts comprising overarching cultural and social structural elements within which the parent, child, family, and community settings are themselves lodged (***macrosystem***)[11,12,14,15]

— These spheres of influence are not static. Bronfenbernner[16] includes the chronosystem to account for changes in these various domains over time. Throughout the life of a child, the relative influence of these spheres may change.[16]

Parent-Child Dyad

— The quality of the primary attachments that parents formed in childhood with their own parental figures has been identified as an important element shaping maltreatment risk, especially when parents themselves have experienced abuse or neglect in childhood.[17-19]

— Parents at risk of physical child abuse have often been observed to exhibit a hyper-responsivity to child-related stimuli.[20,21]

— Some studies have found that parents at high risk for physical abuse tend to exhibit cognitive deficits,[22] particularly in the way they interpret and respond to social cues from their children and others.[23]

— Only a small proportion of parents who physically abuse or neglect their children may hold a diagnosable mental illness,[24] but parents at risk of physical abuse and neglect often suffer from depression,[25-28] low self-esteem,[29,30] and alcohol or substance abuse problems.[27,31]

— Studies considering the dyadic relationship between parent and child have noted that in abusive and neglectful families, parental discipline is often harsh, inattentive, and inconsistent.[32-33] Maltreating parents, particularly physically abusive ones, have often reported feeling out of control as parents and often hold an external locus of control orientation.[33-36]

— Very early childhood appears to hold comparatively higher risk for both physical abuse and neglect.[37-39] Families face tough challenges during this phase, including biological, psychological, familial, and economic adjustments associated with caring for a new child.

Family and Community Context

— Studies across age-groups have documented that family stressors such as material deprivation, unemployment, negative life events, or geographical moves are associated with heightened risk for child maltreatment.[40-43]

— Studies of children suspected of being abused have reported that between 45% and 59% of their mothers showed evidence of being battered by their partners.[44,45] Other estimates of the co-occurrence of domestic violence with child abuse range from 30%[46] to 77%.[47] Eighty percent of children of abused mothers witness their mother's victimization.[48]

— One of the central stressors identified in maltreatment risk is that of family poverty. Studies have found that families reported to child protective services (CPS) are more likely to be single mothers, have unemployed fathers, receive public assistance, and/or live in poor neighborhoods.[49-54]

Maltreating families may have smaller, less dense social networks with which they have less contact and fewer reciprocal exchanges.[55-59] When neighborhood life is characterized by fewer community resources, and neighbors feel less connectedness and identification with one another, parents may lack important protective resources and a sense of parenting norms, which can heighten maltreatment.[15,50,60,61]

— (See **Table 18-1** for examples of risk factors for child neglect and physical abuse.)

Societal Contexts

Wide variation has been noted across cultural contexts regarding normative supervisory arrangements, the number and nature of caregivers, and disciplinary practices employed with children.[62-64] Corporal punishment that may appear to be physical abuse within some cultural contexts may be wholly acceptable and defined as normative within other contexts,[65] and what may be accepted as normative childrearing patterns within a specific cultural context can be misconstrued across cultural boundaries as child maltreatment, especially in situations in which mandated professionals must enact child protection laws and policies derived from a majority cultural value system.[66] Pediatricians must take precautions against culturally biased labeling of child maltreatment risk.

Table 18-1. Examples of Risk Factors for Child Neglect and Physical Abuse

Child:	Family:	Society:
— Disability — Prematurity — Difficult temperament (infant colic)	— Intimate partner violence — Uninvolved father — Multiple children	— Poverty — Lack of health insurance — Cultural values condoning violence
Parent:	**Community:**	
— Depression — Substance abuse — Cognitive deficits — Harsh, inconsistent discipline	— Social isolation — Violence — Few resources	

Screening

— Comparatively speaking, high-risk families underutilize professional assistance systems[67,68]; however, most high-risk families will seek out medical care for their children. Given this, health care services provide a critical access point from which at-risk families can be screened and identified.

— Screening involves efforts to determine whether there is a high risk of a problem occurring, ie, prevention opportunity, or whether a problem already exists, ie, detection. Individual/target ("selected") interventions require identification of those at risk. [Note: proactive, community ("universal") efforts are offered to an entire population, obviating the need to screen.]

— Some risk factors are unlikely to be detected unless specific screening efforts are made. For example, parental depression is often not obvious and is frequently not recognized by pediatricians.[69] Intimate partner violence is often a well-kept family secret. Food shortages and hunger are seldom part of the medical history; impaired growth is a relatively late development. Parents' ability to obtain a medication may not be known.

Introducing Sensitive Questions

— Some of the information sought is sensitive, and parents may be uncomfortable divulging it, especially if pediatricians are uncomfortable asking. It is essential to carefully introduce such questions. For example: "We want to make sure every kid is in a safe environment. There are some problems lots of families have, so I'm asking everyone these questions. If there's a problem, I'll try to help. Also, it's OK if you prefer not to answer some questions."

— It is useful to begin with some well-accepted issues such as bike helmets, smoke alarms, and guns at home. Building on pediatricians' long-standing interest in child safety, there is a helpful and logical transition to areas such as corporal punishment, parental depression, substance abuse, and domestic violence. Each of these issues can be construed in terms of home safety.

Gathering the Information

— Pediatric practices can tailor screening tools for the perceived problems applicable to their population. Relevant items could be incorporated into an existing questionnaire, or a new one may be developed. (**Appendix 18-1** shows an example of a questionnaire that has been developed.)

— Questionnaires can be completed by parents before the visit and then handed to the pediatrician or read to the parent by the pediatrician as part of the history taking.

— Another strategy is to have a "child development specialist" in the clinic as part of the primary care team. This person focuses on psychosocial screening, with questions pertaining to children's development, behavior, and school performance, alleviating the demand for physician time.

— Valuable information can be obtained directly from children and teenagers. It is now customary to spend some time alone with adolescents and to obtain a history independently[70]; this can be extended to younger children. Some suggested questions appear in **Appendix 18-2**.

Assessment

— Pediatricians, or qualified ancillary staff, can conduct brief assessments to guide the initial management (see **Appendix 18-2** for examples).

— It is important to know what interventions have been tried and with what results.

— There is a need to estimate the risks and the prospects for intervening successfully.

— Determining a parent's insight into the problem and willingness to accept services helps determine readiness to change.[71]

— It is important to assess for potential protective factors that can buffer the impact of risk factors (see **Table 18-2**). These are crucial in considering the overall situation and for effective intervention.

Management

— In some instances, pediatricians can provide education and guidance, such as helping a parent manage challenging child behavior or supporting a parent suffering an emotional loss.

— In other instances, such as domestic violence or substance abuse, pediatricians serve primarily as gatekeepers, facilitating referrals.

Table 18-2. Examples of Protective Factors Against Child Neglect and Physical Abuse

Child: — Intelligence — Good social skills **Parent:** — Motivation to provide good care — Intelligence — Good coping skills	**Family:** — Supportive — Father involved **Community:** — Food programs — Mental health programs — Safe neighborhoods	**Society:** — Health insurance — Cultural values that support child development — Social policies and programs that support families and children

— The following are general principles concerning preventive efforts:

1. Effective programs focus on basic problem-solving skills and concrete family needs,[72] provide behavior management strategies, and address environmental factors.
2. Goals expressed by children and parents should be incorporated into the plan.
3. Identification of a family's strengths and resources, eg, familial support, available communal resources, constructive coping skills, is key to effective intervention
4. Encourage the use of informal support, eg, by family, friends, qualified professionals.
5. Support via religious affiliation can be valuable; however, some religious movements may encourage corporal punishment and may thus exacerbate the risk for physical abuse.
6. Consider the need for concrete services, eg, medical assistance; Temporary Assistance to Needy Families [TANF]; food stamps; Women, Infants, and Children[WIC].
7. Risk factors for maltreatment must be identified and addressed (see **Appendix 18-2**).
8. Offer anticipatory guidance in routine pediatric care to avoid accidental injuries in the home due to poor supervision and to ensure ongoing care for children with health conditions.
9. Provide support, follow-up, review of progress, and adjust plan if needed. Pediatricians can help by scheduling more frequent visits to provide counseling, support, and monitoring.
10. Be knowledgeable about community resources and facilitate referrals.

Community Resources

Communities are increasingly mounting home visitation programs that either explicitly or implicitly aim to prevent physical abuse and neglect.[3] Strong evidence now exists supporting the effectiveness of early home visitation services in preventing child abuse and neglect.[73]

- — Home visitation services typically engage families during prenatal clinical visits or in the hospital at the point of birth or shortly afterward. They then assign a home visitor to deliver parenting education and case management assistance in the homes of families at risk. Detailed reports on home visiting effectiveness are available in full at http://homvee.acf.hhs.gov/EvidenceOverview.aspx#go1.

— The Positive Parenting Program ("Triple P") is a community-based, 5-tiered program which escalates in intensity from public awareness campaigns (Tier 1) to intensive home visitation (Tier 5).[74]

- — A large, 18-county randomized controlled trial in South Carolina demonstrated favorable outcomes in child maltreatment rates in counties allocated to Triple P, as compared with those allocated to routine practice.[75]

- — The cost profile of Triple P is very favorable, with the first tier costing approximately $1 per child in the population and the most intensive fifth tier costing under $12 per child in the population.[76]

— Center-based family support programs may provide a variety of supports and activities, some emphasizing early cognitive development in the infant, others providing parenting education and training, as well as mutual aid activities where parents can learn to overcome isolation and assist one another.[77,78]

— With an increase in public support, childcare centers will increasingly become a venue through which to support maltreatment prevention. Initial evidence from early childhood centers is beginning to point out the potential for such centers to avert physical child abuse and neglect effectively before it occurs.[79,80]

Challenges

— *"There's not enough time to delve into these problems."*: Serious and prevalent problems affecting children deserve attention. It does take time, but there are ways to briefly assess and manage them. Strategies such as having parents complete a questionnaire while waiting helps save time.

— *"I'm not sure how to handle these problems."*: It is clear that most pediatricians have had little training in some of these issues, eg, domestic violence. There is a need to obtain such training and to identify local resources for consultation and referral.

— *"These problems are very sensitive. I don't feel comfortable addressing them."*: If framed carefully, most families will not be offended, and some will be grateful. Discomfort is also related to not knowing what to do; knowledge and skill help overcome this discomfort.

— *"What if the screen is incorrect? There's the problem of false positives and false negatives."*: Risk screening protocols specifically designed for identifying future physical child abuse and neglect have variously reported false negative rates ranging from 1% to 3% and false positive rates ranging from 48% to 90%.[81-83] Only after further in-depth assessment should a strategy to address presenting needs be enacted.

Appendix 18-1: Seeking a Safe Environment for Every Child Screening Questions

Appendix 18-1. Seeking a Safe Environment for Every Child

Dear parent or caregiver: We want to help families have a safe environment for kids. Being a parent is not easy. The questions below are about issues that affect many families, so we're asking everyone these questions. If there is a problem, we will try to help. If you prefer, you can choose not to answer a question.

Today's Date: / /

Age of Child: ________

Sex of Child: __ M __ F

1. Are any medications, household cleaners, or other dangerous things kept where your child could reach them? __ Y __ N
2. Does your child ever ride a bike without a helmet? __ Y __ N

(continued)

Appendix 18-1. Seeking a Safe Environment for Every Child *(continued)*

3. Does your home have a working smoke alarm? __ Y __ N
4. Do you feel that teaching kids about sexual abuse is necessary? __ Y __ N
5. Is there a gun in your home? __ Y __ N
6. Does anyone smoke at home? __ Y __ N
7. Do you have trouble getting medical care or medicines for your child? __ Y __ N
8. Do you sometimes have trouble getting enough food for your family? __ Y __ N
9. Do you sometimes think you need to hit/spank your child? __ Y __ N
10. Do you worry that your child may have been abused? __ Y __ N
11. Is anyone harassing you, making you afraid, or physically hurting you? __ Y __ N
12. Does anyone at home use drugs? __ Y __ N
13. Has anyone ever said you or your partner drink too much? __ Y __ N
14. Have you been feeling down, depressed, or hopeless? __ Y __ N
15. Were you abused as a child? __ Y __ N
16. Have you ever thought of getting a restraining order? __ Y __ N
17. Do you often feel your child is difficult to take care of? __ Y __ N
18. Do you often feel lonely and wish you had more help? __ Y __ N
19. Has your child ever seriously hurt or been hurt by another child at home? __ Y __ N
20. Are there any problems you would like help with today? __ Y __ N

Appendix 18-2: Screening Questions for Pediatrician Assessment

Appendix 18-2. Screening Questions for Assessment

The following are examples of specific ways pediatricians can play a limited but important role in helping address common risk factors for abuse and neglect. The approach should fit the specific circumstances. A computerized listing of community resources was developed as well as user-friendly leaflets for parents.

Depression

Screening question: "Do you often feel down, depressed, or hopeless?"

Brief assessment: "You said that you sometimes feel sad. I am sorry you feel this way. Maybe I can help."

—"How long have you felt this way?"

—"Has anything happened to make you feel this way?"

—"Have there been any changes in the way you eat or sleep?"

—"Have you seen a counselor or taken medications for depression? How did that work?"

—"Do you sometimes wake up in the morning and wish that you were dead?"

—"Do you think about killing yourself? What do you do when you feel this way?"

—"Many people who feel down make a plan to kill themselves. Do you have a plan to kill yourself?"

Factors increasing the risk of suicide:

—Previous suicide attempts

—Untreated mental illness

—Current plan of suicide, eg, set date or timeframe for suicide attempt, chosen method

—Means to carry out suicide attempt, eg, access to a weapon, collection of medication

(continued)

Appendix 18-2. Screening Questions for Assessment *(continued)*

—Active substance abuse

—Unwillingness to access mental health services

Initial management: "No one deserves to feel down and alone. This must really be hard on you and your family. You do not have to go through this by yourself. There are people who can help. I really recommend calling this number to get help."

Consider giving parent handout: Depression

Referral information: Develop/use directory of local resources

SUBSTANCE ABUSE

Screening questions:

—"Does anyone at home use drugs or gone to drug rehab?"

—"Has anyone said that your drink too much?"

Brief assessment: "You said that someone at home is abusing drugs/alcohol. This must be really tough on you and your family. I need to ask you a few questions to see if I can help."

—"Who is using?"

—"What is [person] using? How often? How much?"

—"Is he/she getting help?"

—"How has the alcohol/drug use changed things at home?"

—"How has the alcohol/drug use affected the kids?"

—"What worries you the most about the drug/alcohol abuse?"

If it is suspected that the parent has an alcohol or substance abuse problem, the CAGE screening tool may be used. A substance abuse evaluation should be recommended if a parent appears to be under the influence or there is a "yes" to any of the CAGE questions:

(continued)

Appendix 18-2. Screening Questions for Assessment *(continued)*

C Have you ever felt that you needed to **C**ut down on your drinking or drug use?

Alcohol: __ Y __ N Other drugs: __ Y __ N

A Have people **A**nnoyed you by criticizing your drinking or other drug use?

Alcohol: __ Y __ N Other drugs: __ Y __ N

G Have you ever felt bad or **G**uilty about your drinking or drug use?

Alcohol: __ Y __ N Other drugs: __ Y __ N

E Have you ever used alcohol or other drugs first thing in the morning (as an **E**ye opener) to get going, steady your nerves, or get rid of a hangover or withdrawal?

Alcohol: __ Y __ N Other Drugs: __ Y __ N

Initial management:

I. If the parent answers "Yes" to any of the CAGE questions:

— Offer support.

— "You must be hurting badly to use drugs/alcohol so much. No one should have to hurt that much. It is time for a change, for you, and for your kids. You will feel better."

— "You have figured out that using drugs/alcohol helps you forget your problems for a while, but the problems always come back. This must be really hard on you. It is also hard on the kids. It is possible to deal with the problem differently. There are good people who can help."

— Refer to a social worker or other community resource.

— If the parent denies drug/alcohol abuse and refuses a referral, assess who cares for the child. Consider a CPS report if you think the child's welfare is at risk.

(continued)

Appendix 18-2. Screening Questions for Assessment *(continued)*

II. If someone other than the parent is suspected of using drugs/alcohol:

— Encourage parent to get support for him/herself. They may not "fix" another's problem, but they can benefit from talking with others.

— Advise parent to never leave the person using alcohol/drugs in charge of the children.

— Refer to a social worker or other community resources.

Consider giving parent handout: Drugs and Alcohol

Referral information: Develop/use directory of local resources.

Domestic Violence

Screening question: "Is anyone harassing you, making you afraid, or physically hurting you?"

Brief assessment: When assessing for domestic violence, it is important that interviews be private (in the absence of a partner, family members, or a friend). Any questions about violence in the home with others present may endanger the adult victim after she/he leaves the office. Try to meet with the parent separately from the child(ren) as well.

I. Questions for the parent:

— "Is the person making you afraid in the clinic today? Who is it?"

— "What has he/she done? How long has this been happening?"

— "When was the last time he/she hurt or harassed you?"

— "Has he/she used a weapon against you?
Do you think he/she still has the weapon(s)?"

— "Has he/she ever threatened to kill you?"

— "Has he/she ever threatened to hurt or take the kids?
Has he/she ever carried out the threat(s)?"

(continued)

Appendix 18-2. Screening Questions for Assessment *(continued)*

—"How do you usually protect yourself and the kids?"

—"What choices do you have? What have you tried?"

—"What would you like to see happen?"

—"Who helps you? How?"

—"How safe is it for you and the kids to go home today?"

II. Questions for the child:

— "Sometimes grown-ups get mad at each other and fight. What happens in your house when grown-ups get mad?"

— "Does anyone get hurt?"

— "How does it make you feel when they fight? Are you ever afraid you will get hurt?"

— "What do you do when they fight? Do you ever see them fighting?"

— "Do you get in trouble when they fight? If so, what happens?"

— "Do you ever feel like hurting yourself? If so, what have you done?"

Initial management: "Domestic violence is a problem for lots of families. No one deserves to be treated this way. I am concerned about you and the kids. I understand there may not be an easy way to fix things, but there are good people who can help you."

I. Offer support:

—"The violence is not your fault."

—"The violence is a crime."

—"You do not deserve to be hurt this way."

—"You are not alone."

—"Help is available for you and your children."

(continued)

Appendix 18-2. Screening Questions for Assessment ***(continued)***

II. Offer information on the dynamics and effects of domestic violence:

—Most violence continues and gets worse.

—Domestic violence is a crime.

—Kids are hurt badly by domestic violence. Kids usually know what is going on. When adults fight, kids feel scared, confused, and alone. This can lead to serious mental health and behavior problems. Kids can also get injured.

III. Advise the parent to develop a safety plan. This is important whether or not the parent plans to leave the violent relationship. A social worker or a hotline counselor can help. The following are sample questions for developing a safety plan:

— "Where can the kids go if there is fighting so they can be safe?" (eg, a neighbor's house, another room, the backyard)

— "Where could you and the kids go if you have to escape?"

— "Would [your partner] know how to find you?"

— "There are things you need to take with you: birth certificates, Social Security and insurance cards, medicines, money, a change of clothes, and a few toys. Many parents put together an emergency bag with these things."

— "Where could you hide an emergency bag so that he/she could not find it?"

— "When would be the best time to leave?"

— "Who could help you? How?"

— "What should the kids know about your safety plan?"

IV. Refer for supportive services.

Give parent handout: Are You Scared of Someone?

(continued)

Appendix 18-2. Screening Questions for Assessment *(continued)*

Special considerations:

I. Parent declines referrals, no immediate safety concerns:

- —Encourage meeting with a social worker or a community resource.
- —Encourage developing a safety plan.
- —Offer a private clinic phone to call a hotline.
- —Follow-up at next visit, sooner than regular appointment.

II. Parent declines referral, child(ren) clearly affected:

- —Inform parent that most children know when domestic violence occurs, even when adults try to hide it from them.
- —Tell parent that domestic violence can really harm children, eg, learning problems, psychosomatic complaints, behavior problems, high anxiety, depression, sleep and eating disturbances.
- —Clearly state how the child's presenting problem(s) may be caused by the domestic violence and that counseling should help.
- —If the child exhibits suicidal ideation/gestures or self-injurious behavior, inform parent of the limits of confidentiality, eg, "This is serious. We need to make sure that _____ gets help so he/she does not hurt himself/herself. This information cannot be kept private. We have to make a referral so that _____ gets the help he/she needs." Refer child for an immediate mental health evaluation.

III. Child maltreatment is a significant concern:

- —Refer to a social worker or other resource for further assessment and services.
- —Refer to CPS if child abuse or neglect is suspected (eg, "The law requires me to make a referral to CPS when a child may have been abused or neglected.").
- —Plan a follow-up visit, reassess.

(continued)

Appendix 18-2. Screening Questions for Assessment *(continued)*

IV. If the parent is afraid to return home:

— Refer to a social worker or a hotline before leaving the office to consider options, including emergency shelter.

— Discuss a safety plan for parent and child(ren).

— Clearly document suspected child abuse or neglect.

— If a CPS referral is made, document the name and phone number of the CPS screener and the date and time of the referral.

— Any notation of suspected domestic violence and related referrals must be nonspecific (eg, family discord, social stressors). Such notation should also be a provider's assessment, rather than a disclosure by an adult victim.

— If possible, document domestic violence in a separate section of the main medical section, or in a file kept by in-house social work.

DISCIPLINE

Screening question: "Do you sometimes think you need to hit/spank your child?"

Brief assessment: "You said you sometimes need to spank __________. Can we talk a bit about that?"

I. Questions for the parent:

— "What kinds of things does __________ do to make you hit him/her?"

— "How often do you hit __________?"

— "What do you use to hit __________?
Are __________'s clothes on or off?"

— "Have there ever been red marks or bruises from hitting?"

— "Does hitting __________ seem to help? What else have you tried?"

— "How do you feel after hitting __________?"

(continued)

Appendix 18-2. Screening Questions for Assessment *(continued)*

II. Questions for the child:

- —"Lots of kids get in trouble. What happens to you when you get in trouble?"
- —If __________ gets spanked: "Who spanks/beats you? How does [that person] spank/beat you?"

Initial management:

I. Parent says hitting works.

"It seems like hitting __________ works for you now, but there are a few reasons lots of people prefer other ways. Can I tell you about them? We recommend not hitting kids because":

- —Hitting teaches kids it is okay to hit others when you're angry.
- —Hitting teaches kids it is okay to hit people you love.
- —Hitting does not teach kids to respect you; it makes them afraid of you.
- —An adult can injure a child, especially if you are really angry.

"Changing behavior is difficult. Change will not happen overnight, but if you use these recommendations you should see a difference in a few weeks."

(Go to recommendations in section II.)

Documentation: Documentation of domestic violence in a child's chart must be handled with care. An adult offender may have access to the chart if this person is a biological parent or a legal guardian. Information on the violence and referrals made may place the adult victim at risk of retaliation. The following is recommended:

II. Parent says hitting does not really work or that it leaves him/her feeling bad:

"Many parents feel bad after they hit their kids. They also feel stuck because they do not know what else to do. Changing behavior is hard; it does not happen overnight. I have some questions. If you stick to these suggestions, you should see a difference in a few weeks, and you will feel a lot better."

(continued)

Appendix 18-2. Screening Questions for Assessment *(continued)*

—Pick battles, prioritize; ignore little things.

—Praise child for good behavior.

—Remember, "bad" behavior may really be normal (eg, young child does not understand your expectations).

—Remind __________ of rules, often. Explain what is expected and what exactly will happen if a rule is broken.

—Be consistent with follow-through.

—Make sure everyone who cares for the child agrees on consistent rules and consequences.

—Use "time out" for children 2 to 8 years old (eg, 1 minute per year of child's age). Time out is to stop the child's behavior and to help the child control his/her feelings before joining the family again. It also helps the parent to control his/her feelings.

—Withhold privileges from older children, such as TV, a bike ride, or playing with friends.

—Withholding food should never be a form of punishment.

—Discuss bad behavior with the child, without telling the child that he/she is a bad person. Instead say, "I am disappointed in what you did."

Give parent handout: Discipline: Tips for Parents

Referral information: Consider referral to parenting group or class.

References

1. Dubowitz H. Prevention of child maltreatment: what is known. *Pediatrics.* 1989;83(4):570-577.

2. Larson CP. Efficacy of prenatal and postpartum home visits on child health and development. *Pediatrics.* 1980;66(2):191-197.

3. Guterman NB. *Stopping Child Maltreatment Before It Starts: Emerging Horizons in Early Home Visitation Services.* Thousand Oaks, CA: Sage Publications; 2001.

4. Kobak RR, Sceery A. Attachment in late adolescence: working models, affect regulation, and representations of self and others. *Child Dev.* 1988;59(1):135-146.

5. Greenough WT, Wallace CS, Alcantara AA, et al. Development of the brain: experience affects the structure of neurons, glia, and blood vessels. In: Anastasiow NJ, Harel S, eds. *At-Risk Infants: Interventions, Families, and Research.* Baltimore, MD: Paul H. Brookes; 1993:173-185.

6. Dawson G, Hessl D, Frey K. Social influences on early developing biological and behavioral systems related to risk for affective disorder. *Dev Psychopathol.* 1994;6(4):759-779.

7. Dubowitz H. Costs and effectiveness of interventions in child maltreatment. *Child Abuse Negl.* 1990;14(2):177-186.

8. Bonomi AE, Anderson ML, Rivara FP, et al. Health care utilization and costs associated with childhood abuse. *J Gen Intern Med.* 2008;23(3):294-299.

9. Zielinski DS. Child maltreatment and adult socioeconomic well-being. *Child Abuse Negl.* 2009;33(10):666-678.

10. Prilleltensky I. Promoting well-being: time for a paradigm shift in health and human services. *Scand J Public Health.* 2005;33(suppl 66):53-60.

11. Garbarino J. The human ecology of child maltreatment: a conceptual model for research. *J Marriage Fam.* 1977;39(4):721-731.

12. Belsky J. Child maltreatment: an ecological integration. *Am Psychol.* 1980;35(4):320-335.

13. Cicchetti D, Lynch M. Toward an ecological/transactional model of community violence and child maltreatment: consequences for children's development. *Psychiatry.* 1993;56(1):96-118.

14. Bronfenbrenner U. Contexts of child rearing: problems and prospects. *Am Psychologist.* 1979;34(10):844-850.

15. Garbarino J, Sherman D. High-risk neighborhoods and high-risk families: the human ecology of child maltreatment. *Child Dev.* 1980;51(1):188-198.

16. Bronfenbrenner U. *The Ecology of Human Development.* Cambridge, MA: Harvard University Press; 1979.

17. Widom CS. Child abuse, neglect, and adult behavior: research design and findings on criminality, violence, and child abuse. *Am J Orthopsychiatry.* 1989;59(3):355-367.

18. Egeland B, Jacobvitz D, Sroufe LA. Breaking the cycle of abuse. *Child Dev.* 1988;59(4):1080-1088.

19. George C. A representational perspective of child abuse and prevention: internal working models of attachment and caregiving. *Child Abuse Negl.* 1996;20(5):411-424.

20. Crowe HP, Zeskind PS. Psychophysiological and perceptual responses to infant cries varying in pitch: comparisons of adults with low and high scores on the Child Abuse Potential Inventory. *Child Abuse Negl.* 1992;16(1):19-29.

21. Pruitt DL, Erickson MR. The Child Abuse Potential Inventory: a study of concurrent validity. *J Clin Psychol.* 1985;41(1):104-111.

22. Budd KS, Heilman NE, Kane D. Psychosocial correlates of child abuse potential in multiply disadvantaged adolescent mothers. *Child Abuse Negl.* 2000;24(5):611-625.

23. Milner JS, Crouch JL. Child physical abuse: theory and research. In: Hampton R, ed. *Family Violence Prevention and Treatment.* 2nd ed. Newbury Park, CA: Sage Publications; 1999:33-65.

24. Milner JS. Individual and family characteristics associated with intrafamilial physical and sexual abuse. In: Trickett PK, Schellenbach CJ, eds. *Violence Against Children in the Family and the Community.* Washington, DC: American Psychological Association; 1998:141-170.

25. Ethier LS, Lacharite C, Couture G. Childhood adversity, parental stress, and depression of negligent mothers. *Child Abuse Negl.* 1995;19(5):619-632.

26. Kotch JB, Browne DC, Ringwalt CL, et al. Risk of child abuse or neglect in a cohort of low-income children. *Child Abuse Negl.* 1995;19(9):1115-1130.

27. Chaffin M, Kelleher K, Hollenberg J. Onset of physical abuse and neglect: psychiatric, substance abuse, and social risk factors from prospective community data. *Child Abuse Negl.* 1996;20(3):191-203.

28. Nair P, Black MM, Schuler M, et al. Risk factors for disruption in primary caregiving among infants of substance abusing women. *Child Abuse Negl.* 1997;21(11):1039-1051.

29. Christensen MJ, Brayden RM, Dietrich MS, McLaughlin F. The prospective assessment of self-concept in neglectful and physically abusive low income mothers. *Child Abuse Negl.* 1994;18(3):225-232.

30. Culp RE, Culp AM, Soulis J, Letts D. Self-esteem and depression in abusive, neglecting, and nonmaltreating mothers. *Infant Ment Health J.* 1989;10(4):243-251.

31. US Department of Health and Human Services. *Blending Perspectives and Building Common Ground: A Report to Congress on Substance Abuse and Child Protection.* Washington, DC: US Government Printing Office; 1999.

32. Crittenden PM. Abusing, neglecting, problematic, and adequate dyads: differentiating by patterns of interaction. *Merrill-Palmer Q.* 1981;27(3):201-218.

33. Stringer SA, LaGreca AM. Correlates of child abuse potential. *J Abnorm Child Psychol.* 1985;13(2):217-226.

34. Ellis RH, Milner JS. Child abuse and locus of control. *Psychol Rep.* 1981;48(2):507-510.

35. Gunn-Orenstein JS. The relationship between moral reasoning, locus of control, emotional empathy, and parenting profile in physically abusing mothers. *Diss Abstr Int.* 1981;42:2056-2057.

36. Nurius PS, Lovell M, Maggie E. Self-appraisals of abusive parents: a contextual approach to study and treatment. *J Interpers Violence.* 1988;3(4):458-467.

37. Sedlak AJ, Mettenburg J, Basena M, et al. *Fourth National Incidence Study of Child Abuse and Neglect (NIS–4): Report to Congress.* Washington, DC: US Department of Health and Human Services, Administration for Children and Families; 2010.

38. Sedlak AJ, Broadhurst DD. *Third National Incidence Study of Child Abuse and Neglect: Final Report.* Washington, DC: US Department of Health and Human Services; 1996.

39. US Department of Health and Human Services, Administration on Children, Youth and Families. *Child Maltreatment 1998: Reports From the States to the National Child Abuse and Neglect Data System.* Washington, DC: US Government Printing Office; 2000.

40. Crittenden PM. Child neglect: causes and contributors. In: Dubowitz H, ed. *Neglected Children: Research, Practice, and Policy.* Thousand Oaks, CA: Sage Publications; 1999:47.

41. Egeland B, Breitenbucher M, Rosenberg D. Prospective study of the significance of life stress in the etiology of child abuse. *J Consult Clin Psychol.* 1980;48(2):195-205.

42. Chan YC. Parenting stress and social support of mothers who physically abuse their children in Hong Kong. *Child Abuse Negl.* 1994;18(3):261-269.

43. Justice B, Calvert A, Justice R. Factors mediating child abuse as a response to stress. *Child Abuse Negl.* 1985;9(3):359-363.

44. McKibben L, De Vos E, Newberger EH. Victimization of mothers of abused children: a controlled study. In: Hampton RL, ed. *Black Family Violence.* Lexington, MA: Lexington Books; 1991:75-83.

45. Stark E, Flitcraft AH. Women and children at risk: a feminist perspective on child abuse. *Int J Health Services.* 1988;18(1):97-118.

46. Edleson JL. The overlap between child maltreatment and woman battering. *Violence Against Women*. 1999;5(2):134-154.

47. American Academy of Pediatrics Policy Statement. The role of the pediatrician in recognizing and intervening on behalf of abused women. *Pediatrics*. 1998;101(6):1091-1092.

48. Shipman KL, Zeman J. Emotional understanding: a comparison of physically maltreating and nonmaltreating mother-child dyads. *J Clin Child Psychol*. 1999;28(3):407-17.

49. Hampton RL, Newberger EH. Child abuse incidence and reporting by hospitals: significance of severity, class, and race. *Am J Public Health*. 1985;75(1):56-60.

50. Coulton CJ, Korbin JE, Su M, Chow J. Community level factors and child maltreatment rates. *Child Dev*. 1995;66(5):1262-1276.

51. Drake B, Pandey S. Understanding the relationship between neighborhood poverty and specific types of child maltreatment. *Child Abuse Negl*. 1996;20(11):1003-1018.

52. Lindsey D. *The Welfare of Children*. New York, NY: Oxford University Press; 1994.

53. Zuravin SJ. The ecology of child abuse and neglect: review of the literature and presentation of data. *Violence Vict*. 1989;4(2):101-20.

54. Ards S. Estimating local child abuse. *Eval Rev*. 1989;13(5):484-515.

55. Elmer E. *Children in Jeopardy*. Pittsburgh, PA: University of Pittsburgh Press; 1967.

56. Salzinger S, Kaplan S, Artemyeff C. Mothers' personal social networks and child maltreatment. *J Abnorm Psychol*. 1983;92(1):68-76.

57. Corse SJ, Schmid K, Trickett PK. Social network characteristics of mothers in abusing and nonabusing families and their relationships to parenting beliefs. *J Community Psychol*. 1990;18(1):44-59.

58. Kotelchuck M. Child abuse and neglect: prediction and misclassification. In: Starr R, ed. *Child Abuse Prediction: Policy Implications*. Cambridge, MA: Ballinger; 1982:67-104.

59. Crittenden PM. Social networks, quality of child rearing, and child development. *Child Dev.* 1985;56(5):1299-1313.

60. Furstenberg FF. How families manage risk and opportunity in dangerous neighborhoods. In: Wilson WJ, ed. *Sociology and the Public Agenda.* Newbury Park, CA: Sage Publications; 1993:231-258.

61. Sampson RJ, Raudenbush SW, Earls F. Neighborhoods and violent crime: a multilevel study of collective efficacy. *Science.* 1997;277(5328):918-924.

62. Korbin J. Sociocultural factors in child maltreatment. In: Melton GB, Barry FD, eds. *Protecting Children From Abuse and Neglect: Foundations for a New National Strategy.* New York, NY: Guilford; 1994:182-223.

63. Fischler RS. Child abuse and neglect in American Indian communities. *Child Abuse Negl.* 1985;9(1):95-106.

64. Ritchie J. Child rearing and child abuse: the Polynesian context. In: Korbin J, ed. *Child Abuse and Neglect: Cross-Cultural Perspectives.* Berkeley, CA: University of California Press; 1981:186-294.

65. Solheim JS. A cross-cultural examination of use of corporal punishment on children: a focus on Sweden and the United States. *Child Abuse Negl.* 1982;6(2):147-154.

66. Gray E, Cosgrove J. Ethnocentric perception of childrearing practices in protective services. *Child Abuse Negl.* 1985;9(3):389-396.

67. Burns BJ, Costello EJ, Angold A, et al. Children's mental health service use across service sectors. *Health Affairs.* 1995;14(3):147-159.

68. Offord DR, Boyle MH, Szatmari P, et al. Ontario Child Health Study. II. Six-month prevalence of disorder and rates of service utilization. *Arch Gen Psychiatry.* 1987;44(9):832-836.

69. Zuckerman BS, Beardslee WR. Maternal depression: a concern for pediatricians. *Pediatrics.* 1987;79(1):110-117.

70. Marks A, Fisher M. Health assessment and screening during adolescence. *Pediatrics.* 1987;80(1 pt 2):131-158.

71. Prochaska JO, Johnson S, Lee P. The transtheoretical model of behavior change. In: Shumaker SA, Schron EB, eds. *The Handbook of Health Behavior Change.* 2nd ed. New York, NY: Springer; 1998:59-84.

72. Daro D. *Confronting Child Abuse: Theory, Policy and Practice*. New York, NY: Free Press; 1989.

73. Hahn RA, Bilukha OO, Crosby A, et al. First report evaluating the effectiveness of strategies for preventing violence: early childhood home visitation. *MMWR Morbid Mortal Wkly Rep*. 2003;52:1-20.

74. Sanders M, Markie-Dadds C, Turner K. *Theoretical, Scientific and Clinical Foundations of the Triple P-Positive Parenting Program: A Population Approach to the Promotion of Parenting Competence*. Brisbane, Queensland, Australia: Parenting and Family Support Centre; 2003.

75. Prinz R, Sanders M, Shapiro C, et al. Population-based prevention of child maltreatment: the U.S. Triple P system population trial. *Prev Sci*. 2009;10(1):1-12.

76. Foster EM, Prinz RJ, Sanders MR, et al. The costs of a public health infrastructure for delivering parenting and family support. *Child Youth Serv Rev*. 2008;30(5):493-501.

77. Andrews SR, Blumenthal JB, Johnson DL, et al. The skills of mothering: a study of parent child development centers. *Monogr Soc Res Child Dev*. 1982;47:1-83.

78. Affholter DP, Connell D, Nauta MJ. Evaluation of the child and family resource program. *Eval Rev*. 1983;7(1):65-79.

79. Reynolds AJ, Robertson DL. School-based early intervention and later child maltreatment in the Chicago Longitudinal Study. *Child Dev*. 2003;74(1):3-26.

80. Kisker EE, Ross CM. Arranging child care. *Future Child*. 1997;7(1):99-109.

81. Altemeier WA III, Vietze PM, Sherrod KB, Sandler HM, Falsey S, O'Connor S. Prediction of child maltreatment during pregnancy. *J Am Acad Child Adolesc Psychiatry*. 1979;18(2):205-218.

82. Lealman GT, Haigh D, Phillips JM, Stone J, Ord-Smith C. Prediction and prevention of child abuse: an empty hope? *Lancet*. 1983;1(8339):1423-1424.

83. Murphy S, Orkow B, Nicola R. Prenatal prediction of child abuse and neglect: a prospective study. *Child Abuse Negl*. 1985;9(2):225-235.

Index

A

Figures and tables are indicated by f and t respectively.

B

D

G

H

M

N

O

P

R

S

W

Y